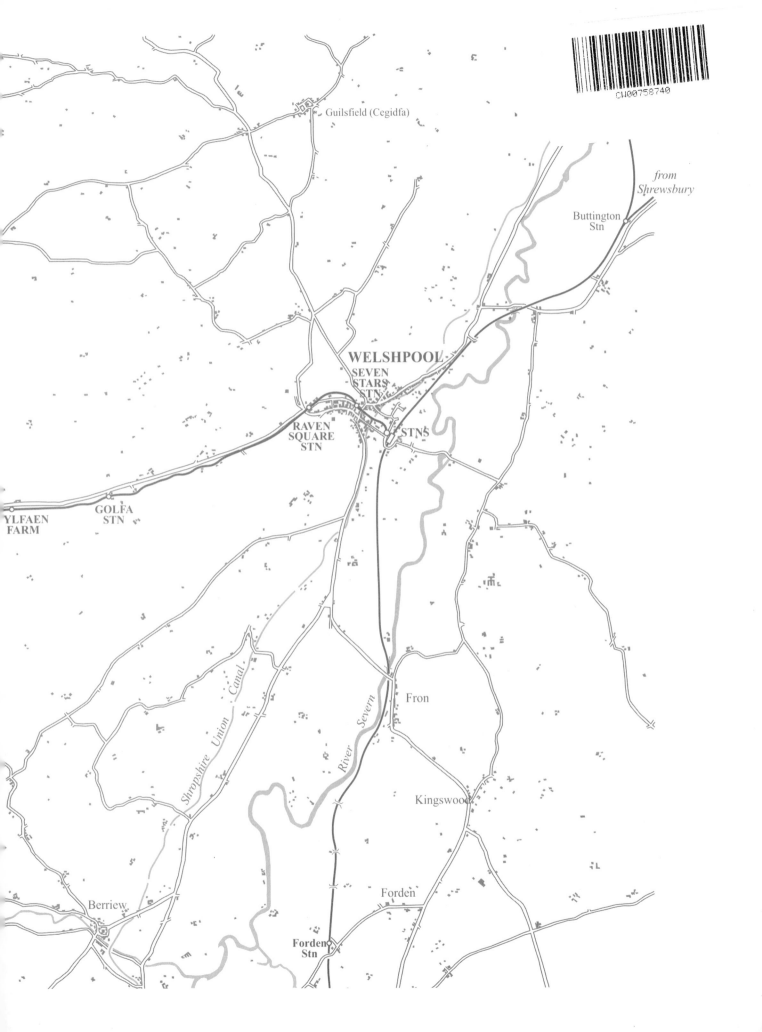

Guilsfield (Cegidfa)

from
Shrewsbury

Buttington
Stn

WELSHPOOL

SEVEN
STARS
STN

RAVEN
SQUARE
STN

STN5

YLFAEN
FARM

GOLFA
STN

Shropshire Union Canal

River Severn

Fron

Kingswood

Berriew

Forden

Forden
Stn

THE
WELSHPOOL & LLANFAIR
LIGHT RAILWAY

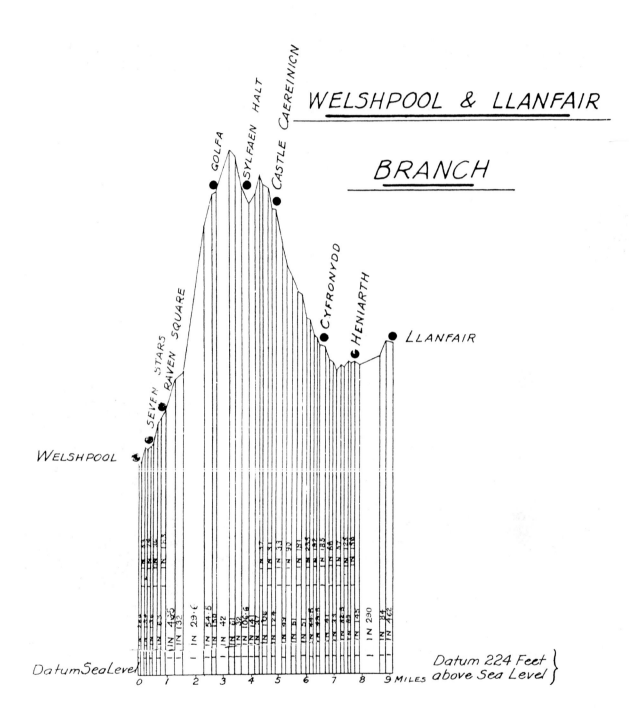

WELSHPOOL & LLANFAIR

BRANCH

Designed by Paul Karau
Printed by Amadeus Press, Cleckheaton

Published by
WILD SWAN PUBLICATIONS LTD.
1-3 Hagbourne Road, Didcot, Oxon, OX11 8DP

THE
WELSHPOOL & LLANFAIR
LIGHT RAILWAY

BY

GLYN WILLIAMS

Welshpool's Smithfield forms the background to this portrait of the railway's two locomotives. Countess had drawn The Earl out of the locomotive shed so that they could be photographed by members of the Birmingham Locomotive Society in July 1949.
W. A. CAMWELL

WILD SWAN PUBLICATIONS LTD.

Llanfair yard as it appeared in the early 1950s. At this time the Montgomeryshire Farmers Association, W. D. Peate and Sons and Morgan Brothers dealt in coal at the station. Loaded wagons are seen on the back and warehouse roads, whilst coal had been stacked between the warehouse road and the loop. The railway served a large agricultural district and animal feeds were stored in the buildings, carriage and van bodies beyond the former platform road. Animal feeds and fertilisers were delivered to local farms by lorry. A Montgomershire Farmers Association lorry can be seen near the goods warehouse.

A train for Welshpool passing Sylfaen.

CONTENTS

A goods train waiting for time in the standard gauge yard at Welshpool.

INTRODUCTION

PASSING Llangyniew church I hear a Swindon whistle sing out across the valley as one of the Llanfair Railway's Peacocks approaches Heniarth crossing. It is a sound that grows fainter as the train passes Cyfronydd, Dirty Lane, Dolarddyn and Castle, becoming barely audible on the approach to Coppice Lane. The sound carries me back nearly sixty years to the last days of the line's existence as a purely commercial undertaking when Church Street seemed to be a magical place where the rumble of road traffic was briefly silenced as a compact black engine with three or four ageing wagons and the odd van made their stately progress over the level crossing.

Sixty years earlier, with public funding available for railways that opened up undeveloped districts, it seemed as if Llanfair might finally obtain a railway after so many previous disappointments. In the mid 1840s a trunk route designed to carry traffic to Ireland was projected through the town, but the Government of the day would not countenance the extension of the broad gauge through mid and north Wales. From the mid 1860s until the late 1880s several proposals were made to join the town to the railway network. These schemes failed because of disagreements as to whether Llanfair should make Welshpool or Oswestry its market town, about the gauge to be adopted, but principally because local landowners would not advance sufficient capital to induce traders in the locality to invest in a railway.

Following the passage of the Light Railway Act in 1896, two proposals were made to bring a railway to the town, which broadly recapitulated earlier plans. Whilst Llanfair folk favoured a standard gauge line through Meifod to a junction with the Cambrian main line at Arddleen that provided direct access to Oswestry, Welshpool people preferred a shorter narrow gauge line, built on the principles advocated by Everard Calthrop, which would ensure that the trade of the Banwy valley continued to pass through their town. When the rival schemes were examined by the Light Railway Commissioners at an Inquiry held in the Board School at Llanfair, the Welshpool proposal won the day, largely because of the support it commanded from the landowners through whose property it passed. It supported the established flow of trade, and had a lower capital base that not only offered the possibility of a better return on investment but also placed fewer demands on the public purse.

Although the Commissioners announced their decision in September 1897, a further two years were to elapse before the Board of Trade issued a Light Railway Order sanctioning the construction of the line. While some of the delay might be attributed to Government officials' inexperience of and hostility to the new legislation, the Cambrian Board, which had favoured the rival proposal, was slow to agree terms to build and work the line. The company's last minute opposition to a siding connecting the light railway to a wharf on the Shropshire Union Canal at Welshpool very nearly killed off the whole scheme.

Once these obstacles had been overcome, it became apparent that the estimated cost of building the line. had risen significantly. Additional funding was secured from the Treasury and local authorities, which, combined with pledges of support received from the public, enabled a contract for the construction of the line to be let in April 1901.

Notices to treat were served on those landowners whose property was required for the railway. Considerable difficulty was encountered with the Rev. Pughe, an absentee Anglican clergyman, who was eventually compelled to part with a narrow strip of land below Golfa Hall.

Construction of the line was underway by June 1901 and there were hopes that the railway would be opened at the beginning of September 1902. Although the contractor's track reached Llanfair by the end of that month, nearly six months were to elapse before the line could be opened for goods traffic and the passenger service did not begin until 6th April 1903. The delay in completing the line increased the cost of construction and more capital had to be raised.

After the railway opened, it soon became apparent that additional facilities were required, particularly at Llanfair, and that more rolling stock was needed. Although six new timber trucks were acquired in 1904, a dispute with the Contractor went to arbitration and, although his inflated claim was greatly reduced, the Llanfair Railway was forced to pay all the costs of the case which were considerable. An application for a Treasury loan to discharge these liabilities was refused and the Cambrian paid most of the Llanfair Railway's legal fees.

The light railway remained indebted to the working company for the rest of its separate existence and was unable to acquire any more rolling stock or to fully develop the facilities that it needed. The company never paid its ordinary shareholders a dividend and when the Great Western absorbed the line they lost three quarters of the nominal value of their shares.

In the railway's heyday before the Great War, one or two carriages generally sufficed for passenger traffic, but on fair and show days the line could not always accommodate the traffic offered, so that prospective passengers were forced to hire traps, cycle or walk to their destination. The more affluent families in Llanfair acquired motor cars from the mid 1900s onwards and after the Great War road transport became a significant competitor. When motor buses were introduced in the mid 1920s, they took much of the passenger traffic on all but Welshpool market days. Motor lorries proved to be faster and more flexible than the railway which lost much of the general merchandise and livestock traffic that it once carried.

A review carried out by the Great Western in 1926 showed that the revenue produced by the branch did not cover its direct operating costs, so with losses mounting, the passenger service was withdrawn in February 1931. Although the railway continued to carry coal, fertilisers and animal feeds, its future was re-examined in the late 1930s. The line's continued existence was almost certainly due to the outbreak of the 1939–1945 war when petrol rationing was introduced and traffic increased significantly. Although the railway's viability in the postwar world seemed doubtful, it passed into state ownership in 1948. In 1950 the British Transport Commission attempted to close the line, arguing that it would be more efficient to deliver merchandise by road. However, it was not until 1956 that the closure of the railway was finally approved after a deal was struck with local road hauliers to limit increases in the rates charged for the carriage of goods between Welshpool station and Llanfair. On 3rd November the Midlands Area of the Stephenson Locomotive Society organised a commemorative last train over the line, the last public goods service having run on the previous day.

In the early 1950s when it became known that the line's future was in doubt, the feasibility of preserving it was considered but the task appeared to be too daunting. Later in the decade, a preservation society was formed to acquire the line and its rolling stock, but Welshpool Borough Council, which had done so much to promote the line sixty years earlier, was determined to acquire the town section while the County Council was unwilling to see trains operated by railway enthusiasts cross public roads. At first the preservation society was unable to convince the various authorities of the railway's potential as a tourist attraction and struggled to attract sufficient members or money to make the project viable. After much hard work, a preservation company was incorporated in 1960 and eventually managed to lease the line from the western side of Llanfair & Guilsfield Road level crossing to Llanfair. The loss of the town section resulted in the preservation company basing its operations at Llanfair. On 6th April 1963, exactly sixty years after the railway had opened for passenger traffic, a special train was run from Welshpool to Llanfair and back to celebrate the reopening of the line. In the first operating season, passenger trains ran between Llanfair and Castle Caereinion and were later extended to Sylfaen. In March 1974 the freehold of the line was acquired but it was not until 18th July 1981 that passenger services were extended to the new terminus at Welshpool Raven Square.

CHAPTER ONE

A RAILWAY FOR LLANFAIR

BEFORE the coming of the railway, Llanfair was the natural and only centre for the trade and business of a large district centred on the valley of the River Banwy. Each year eight livestock markets attracted dealers from Shrewsbury and the Midlands. There were also three hiring fairs every year and a Saturday market.[1] These markets developed informally, primarily to meet local needs, and the town was never granted a charter. By the mid nineteenth century Llanfair had emerged as a small but important service centre for the surrounding parishes and scattered communities in the Banwy valley. By 1841 the population reached a peak of 2,137 of which about one third lived in the town but by 1931 it had fallen to 1,665.[2]

Poor transport links with the outside world made Llanfair a self-contained community that supplied its own needs. Three woollen mills in the town, powered by water, produced cloth, any production that was surplus to local needs being sold at Newtown. Flour mills at Melin-y-ddol, Dolrhyd and Henllan supplied the town, while the larger mills at Dolgoch and Heniarth also sent flour to Dolgellau and Machynlleth. Barley for malting was brought into Llanfair from the surrounding district, there being four malt houses in the town. Beer was brewed for the dozen or so public houses as well as some in the Dolgellau and Machynlleth districts.[3]

By the early 1850s, stage coaches ran between Shrewsbury and Aberystwyth, calling at Llanfair on their way. In summertime the service ran on every weekday, but in the winter it only ran on Fridays. There was also a summer service to Barmouth on Wednesdays. Stage wagons passed through the town carrying goods and merchandise to Machynlleth and Dolgellau. Livestock from Meirionnydd and Ceredigion were driven through Llanfair on their way to Shrewsbury and the Midlands. With the opening of railways through mid Wales in the 1860s much of this traffic ceased to pass through the town.[4]

The development of a regular passenger service to Welshpool was discouraged by the heavy tolls that were levied on four-wheeled vehicles as they passed along the turnpike. In 1851 Thomas Humphreys invented a three-wheeled vehicle, *The Exhibition*, which could pass through tollgates at the same rate as for two-wheelers and it ran for several years.[5] From 10th September 1860 a daily bus service ran between Llanfair and Welshpool in connection with the 11.45am train to, and the 3.45pm train from, Oswestry.[6] Later in the century a daily service of horsedrawn buses was run by three rival firms, one of which was forced out of business while the other two amalgamated. The journey to Welshpool took an hour and a half, with the return journey taking up to twice as long. Gentlemen were expected to walk the mile or so from Raven Square to the top of Spring Bank. For many years there was no protection from the weather but after one man was frozen to death a cover was provided.[7]

Between 1845 and 1895 many proposals were made to build railways through or to Llanfair. Two trunk lines projected through the town came to nothing, while five attempts to build branch lines to Llanfair failed because the capital required for their construction could not be realised. Schemes to put Llanfair on the railway network failed so often that local wits coined the aphorism '*it's as dead as the Llanfair Railway*'.[8] Describing the situation in the mid 1890s at a distance of more than fifty years, Mr Charles Herber Humphreys, a Llanfair shopkeeper, recalled that '*None but old inhabitants can realise the isolation and inconvenience resulting from the absence of a railway. All goods traffic had to be hauled in carts and wagons drawn by horses or donkeys while passenger traffic was by slow horse-drawn conveyance once daily.*'[9]

TRUNK ROUTES TO IRELAND 1835–1846

Holyhead, the nearest Welsh port to Dublin, became the embarkation point for a weekly mail service to Ireland in 1576. The journey from London through the Midlands to Chester, then along the north Wales coast, was slow, tortuous and not without danger. In 1815 work began on Thomas Telford's highway from Shrewsbury to Holyhead and much of the work had been completed by 1819 when steam packets were introduced between Holyhead and Howth. Mail coaches continued to be ferried across the Menai Straits until 10th January 1826 when the Menai suspension bridge was opened. By 1832 the journey from London to Holyhead took over twenty-eight hours while the sea crossing took another six hours in good weather. The rapid growth of the railway network in the late 1830s made further reduction in the journey time possible and for a time most mail for Ireland passed through Liverpool. Several inquiries were commissioned to select the most suitable port for the Irish mails and the best railway line to serve it.[10]

In August 1835 Henry Archer, the Managing Director of the Festiniog Railway, made proposals for a combined rail and steamer route from London to Dublin. The natural harbour at Porthdinllaen on the north western coast of Caernarfonshire would be developed as a packet station and a railway would be built through north Wales to Newtown, from where it would make its way to London through Ludlow, Worcester and Oxford. On St. Patrick's Day 1836, a deputation of Members of Parliament, merchants and bankers met Mr Spring Rice, the Chancellor of the Exchequer, to press for an investigation of the merits of a direct route between the two capital cities. Members of the deputation stated that the journey time could be reduced to twelve hours, emphasised the benefits of improved communication, and extolled the advantages of the natural harbour at Porthdinllaen. A new railway of between 120 and 130 miles would be required, for which government assistance was needed. Mr Rice said that the possibility of securing reduced journey times between

Llanfair, looking east along the Banwy Valley from Cae Boncyn.

London and Dublin was of the greatest national importance. He would normally expect projects of this kind to be financed by private capital but in this case state assistance might be available if the proposal was insufficiently profitable to appeal to private investors. He asked for a statement showing the cost of the proposed line and harbour together with an estimate of the time saved, compared with the routes via Liverpool and Bristol when the railways from London to those places were completed.[11]

During the spring and early summer of 1836 Charles Blacker Vingoles and John Rastrick surveyed several routes between Porthdinllaen and the Grand Junction Railway. Having reached Pwllheli, their preferred route followed the arc of Cardigan Bay to Barmouth, turned inland along the Bala fault to Llangollen, then passed through Shrewsbury to join the Grand Junction near Wolverhampton. Although the engineers attempted to find direct routes from Tremadoc to Bala and from Barmouth to Shrewsbury via Llanfair, the steep gradients and long tunnels that were required led them to believe that a direct line through North Wales was impractical. Subsequently surveys from Chester to Holyhead and Porthdinllaen were made but dismissed on the grounds of engineering difficulties, as was a line based on Henry Archer's proposal.[12]

The incorporation of the Chester and Crewe Railway in 1837 revived interest in a coastal route to Holyhead and lines from Chester were surveyed by Francis Giles and George Stephenson.[13] The Great Western was also keen to capture the Irish traffic, so in 1840 Isambard Kingdom Brunel surveyed a broad gauge line from Didcot through Oxford, Worcester, Ludlow, Newtown, Dinas Mawddwy, Dolgellau, Barmouth and Tremadoc to Porthdinllaen.[14] Brunel estimated that his line would put London and Dublin within 14¾ hours of each other, a journey time that was three hours faster than that planned for the route via Holyhead.[15] Supporters of the broad gauge line suffered a setback when a Government committee set up to report on communication between London and Dublin selected Holyhead as the port for the Irish packets and Stephenson's railway from Chester to Holyhead. A Select Committee report on Post Office communication with Ireland published in 1842 appeared to settle the matter in favour of the Holyhead line.[16]

When the Chester and Holyhead Railway bill received the Royal Assent on 4th July 1844, it seemed as if no more would be heard of a trunk route from Porthdinllaen to London. However, the Great Western was still unwilling to see the Irish traffic pass to a rival. In 1843 Brunel and Thomas Penson began to survey a broad gauge railway from Worcester to Porthdinllaen and on 3rd January 1845 the prospectus for a company formed to build it was published. The estimated cost of the proposed line was £2,750,000 which would be satisfied by the issue of 137,500 shares, each with a nominal value of £20. The Great Western, Oxford Worcester and Wolverhampton, Shrewsbury and Hereford, and Waterford Wexford Wicklow and Dublin railway companies intended to take up three quarters of the share capital.[17] In August Charles Russell, the Great Western Chairman, told his shareholders that the completion of the Oxford Worcester and Wolverhampton Railway would naturally lead to an extension from Worcester to Porthdinllaen and so create the shortest route to Ireland. The shareholders gave their Board the power to assist the Worcester and Porthdynllaen Company as it saw fit.[18]

The Worcester and Porthdynllaen Railway left the Oxford Worcester and Wolverhampton line near Rainbow Hill Worcester, then followed the route of the line proposed in 1840 as far as the Severn valley, east of Newtown. The line crossed the Severn near its confluence with the Rhiw and having skirted Berriew, passed through thinly populated, mountainous country to Tremadoc where the line of 1840 was regained. Between Berriew and Tremadoc the railway was heavily engineered with lengthy tunnels at Llanfair, Dolanog and Garth Bwlch near Llanwddyn. Berwyn tunnel, between Llanwddyn and Llanuwchllyn, was over 2¾ miles in length while another at Cefn Glas, between Llanuwchllyn and Trawsfynydd, was nearly 2½ miles long. The descent from the summit to Tremadoc was on a continuous gradient of 1 in 60 in the course of which the Dwyryd was crossed on a viaduct that was 383 yards long and carried the rails 220ft above the river bed.[19]

Although broad gauge railways were technically superior to standard gauge lines, it was necessary to tranship passengers, luggage and freight wherever the two gauges met, which was expensive and inconvenient. In February 1846 a Royal Commission set up to inquire into the matter recommended that the broad gauge should be abolished and that all new railways in mainland Britain should be built to a gauge of 4ft 8½in.[20] The Commission's recommendations were strenuously opposed by the Great Western and its allies. In May Mr Russell told a special meeting of the Great Western shareholders that the Worcester and Porthdynllaen bill was one of only four schemes that the company intended to bring before Parliament in the current session. He considered the railway to be of immense importance and, if built, it would become the main line of communication between London and Dublin. However, the Great Western Board was only prepared to build a broad gauge railway, for which the Government's agreement was required. Mr Russell believed that the benefits of the proposed line were so overwhelming that the required consent would be secured.[21] Despite Mr Russell's optimism, the passage of the Gauge Act into law on 18th August 1846 prevented the extension of a purely broad gauge railway into north Wales and so the Worcester and Porthdynllaen bill was abandoned.[22]

Another proposal might have put Llanfair on a trunk line. In an attempt to frustrate the Great Western's ambitions in Wales, a standard gauge railway styled the Great Welch Junction Railway was promoted in 1845. Lines from Bangor and Porthdinllaen met near Tremadoc, then ran to Shrewsbury through Barmouth, Dolgellau, Dinas Mawddwy and Welshpool. From Shrewsbury the proposed railway headed south to

Monmouth, then made its way to Pembroke via Merthyr, Swansea and Carmarthen. The project made little progress and failed to deposit plans, sections or a bill to Parliament. No more trunk lines were promoted through Llanfair and all subsequent proposals for railways to the town were purely local affairs.[23/24]

BRANCH LINES TO LLANFAIR 1862–1892
The Llanfair Railway 1862–1866

After the opening of the Oswestry and Newtown Railway as far as Welshpool on 14th August 1860, serious consideration was given to building a branch line to Llanfair.[25] On 27th June 1862 a meeting was held in the town to assess support for a proposal to build a railway from Welshpool. The meeting was chaired by the Vicar, the Rev. Enoch Pughe, who said he had been told that short lines that were inexpensive to build could pay and he was in no doubt that a line to Llanfair would pay well. The road between Welshpool and Llanfair was heavily used and great improvements had been made in recent years.[26] Messrs Piercy the Engineers had surveyed two routes from Welshpool to Llanfair. The first passed through Welshpool, then ran along Glyn Golfa and on to Sylfaen, Castle Caereinion and Llanfair. Although this was the most direct route, some property in Welshpool would have to be demolished and a tunnel was required near the town's parish church. The line was opposed by the Earl of Powis because it would interfere with one of his favourite roads on the Powis Castle estate. The second route left the Oswestry and Newtown railway west of Welshpool station, then passed through Dysserth dingle to approach Castle Caereinion from the south before continuing to Llanfair. However, the engineers considered that this route was impractical. A railway from Llanfair to the Llanfyllin branch that passed through Meifod had also been considered but was dismissed because it was too indirect.

Capt. R.D. Pryce, Cyfronydd, told the meeting that when he had discussed the matter with the Earl he had told his Lordship that the landed gentry would not tolerate the existing road for much longer and required a better road or a railway. However, the Earl's objections would have to be addressed if the line was to succeed. Capt. Pryce hoped that his Lordship would recognise that a railway to Llanfair was in his interest because it would increase the value of his estates at Llangadfan and Garthbeibio. After careful consideration of the matter it was decided to ask the Earl to receive a deputation of those in favour of the line.[27]

When the deputation met the Earl, he agreed to withdraw his objections if a route that avoided Glyn Golfa could be found. The route favoured by the Earl left the Oswestry and Newtown Railway three furlongs west of Welshpool station, crossed the canal and turnpike road between Red Lane and Whitehouse Bridge, then passed through Dysserth dingle to reach Castle Caereinion. It ran around the eastern side of the village then crossed Coppice Lane before making its way to Llanfair through Dolarddyn and Cyfronydd. Its terminus was in a field adjoining the former turnpike gatehouse at the south eastern side of Llanfair Bridge.[28] The estimated cost of construction was £50,000.[29] When the Oswestry and Newtown Directors heard that the construction of a railway between Welshpool and Llanfair was being contemplated, they decided to enter into traffic arrangements that were to their mutual benefit, but not to offer any financial support to the undertaking.[30]

Another meeting was held at *The Goat Inn*, Llanfair on 29th August when Mr Howell, the Solicitor to the Oswestry and Newtown Railway, stated that there was no doubt that a railway would be of considerable benefit to the district. Enquiries had been made about the traffic potential of the line which appeared to be surprisingly good. If made inexpensively there was little doubt that the railway would be a paying concern. He suggested that the line should be paid for by the landowners and inhabitants of the district because the value of their property would be increased. Thus they would see a return on their investment even if the line did not pay a dividend. When the matter was discussed it was agreed that a railway from Welshpool to Llanfair would be a paying proposition, that it would be of great benefit to the district and that a provisional committee should be formed with Mr William Baxter as its Secretary.[31]

The benefits of a building a railway to the town were presented to a public meeting at the end of September 1862. Mr Howell explained that the capital required to build the railway would have to be raised in the district through which it passed. Enquiries had been already been made to see what help the landowners would give them, but the help of local tradesmen and other interested parties was also needed. A proposal to make the line to Newtown was rejected because most Llanfair people traded at Welshpool and a costly bridge over the Severn would be required.[32] Mr E. Hilton said that if the landowners along the line would assist the project by giving their land at a fair price and by taking shares in the railway, it would be a good investment. At the conclusion of the meeting it was agreed that members of the provisional committee would canvas the support of landowners and others who were interested in the undertaking. However, when Mr Howell consulted Mr David Davies, Llandinam, the highly respected railway contractor, he was advised that the line could not pay and so the scheme was abandoned.[33]

In summer 1864 David Davies, Abraham Howell and his brother David walked over the course of the railway proposed in 1862 and concluded that a standard gauge line could not pay.[34] However, events on the narrow gauge Festiniog Railway caused them to reconsider the matter. In 1863 steam locomotives had been introduced on the railway and in June 1864 the company gave the Board of Trade notice of its intention to open the line to passenger traffic. The railway was inspected by Capt. Tyler on behalf of the Board of Trade on 27th October 1864 and, although further work was required before passenger services could be introduced, it was obvious that narrow gauge railways could carry passengers and freight efficiently.[35] Such lines were cheaper to build and operate than standard gauge railways and had the potential to open up undeveloped districts.

A proposal to build a railway from Welshpool to Bala via Llanfair and a tunnel under the Berwyns was published in October 1864. When consulted, Mr David Davies suggested that a gauge of 2ft 3in should be adopted to reduce the costs of building and working the line. Although goods and livestock would have to be transhipped where the line met the standard gauge, this was not considered to be a major inconvenience. It was intended to make the bridges of sufficient width, and to take sufficient land, to convert the line to standard gauge if the traffic justified it. Although a change of gauge would render the rolling stock valueless, it would be relatively inexpensive to buy and if more narrow gauge lines were built in the intervening years there would be a market for it. Mr Russel Aitkin C.E., one of the leading advocates of the scheme, suggested to the Earl of Powis that the line should be built as far as Llanfair and then extended to Bala when funds permitted. However, his Lordship objected to the proposed route between Welshpool and Sylfaen so an alternative scheme to build a railway from Welshpool to Llanfair by way of Dysserth dingle was prepared.[36/37]

Plans, sections and books of reference for the Llanfair Railway were deposited in Parliament and with the Clerk of the Peace for Montgomeryshire on 30th November 1864. The Llanfair Company sought powers to acquire land required for the railway by compulsory purchase; to construct the railway to such a gauge as it considered fit for purpose; to enter into agreements with the Cambrian, Shrewsbury and Welshpool, London and North Western and Great Western railway companies, either individually or jointly, to build and work the line; and to obtain running powers over the Cambrian into Welshpool station.[38]

A public meeting was held at *The Goat Inn*, Llanfair on 31st December 1864 to canvas support for the proposed railway which was ten miles, two furlongs and four chains long. The line was expected to carry 16,800 passengers and 25,000 tons of freight each year producing annual revenues of £3,500. If the line was worked for 50% of the gross receipts, investors would receive a return of £1,570 on capital of £33,000. Half the capital needed to build and equip the railway would be raised by the issue of ordinary shares, while the balance would be satisfied by the issue of preference shares and debentures. Mr Davies was prepared to build and equip the line for £33,000 or he would assist the promoters in finding a suitable contractor. Once again the possibility of lines via Glyn Golfa and Meifod were considered and rejected. After some discussion a resolution in support of the scheme was passed unanimously.[39] However, with little practical support forthcoming, the Llanfair Railway bill was withdrawn in the first quarter of 1865.[40] Although there were hopes that the bill would be reintroduced in the next session of Parliament, a proposal for a standard gauge line from Llanymynech to Llanfair made later that year was preferred by Llanfairians. With little support from Llanfair and none from the railway companies that served Welshpool, the Llanfair Railway withered way.[41]

The Shrewsbury and North Wales Railway's Meifod Valley Extension 1865–66

In 1865 plans were published for a standard gauge railway from Llanymynech to Llanfair. The proposed line left the Shrewsbury and North Wales Railway's Nantmawr branch near Carreghofa, then ran south of the Cambrian Railways' Llanfyllin branch to Llansantffraid, where it crossed the Vyrnwy twice before following the river through Meifod and on to Newbridge. Here the railway entered the Banwy valley and having crossed the river west of Pontsycoed it continued along the south bank of the river to terminate in a field between the Wesleyan chapel and the vicarage.[42] The proposed railway was to be a single line although sufficient land would be acquired to allow it to be doubled and the overbridges would be built to accommodate double track. The cost of the railway was estimated to be £119,730.[43] In the difficult financial climate that followed the collapse of Overend, Gurney & Co. in May 1866, investor confidence evaporated and the proposed line was abandoned without an Act being obtained.[44]

Rival schemes 1872–1873

In October 1872 two schemes were projected from Llanfair that anticipated the proposals made in response to the Light Railways Act of 1896. One line was projected to Welshpool essentially following the route of the Llanfair Railway of 1864, while the other ran along the Banwy and Vyrnwy valleys before turning through Trefnannau and Sarnau to join the Cambrian main line at Four Crosses. Welshpool people, fearing that the town's trade with Llanfair would be lost to Oswestry, supported the route via Castle Caereinion but in Llanfair the line through Meifod was preferred.

At a meeting held in *The Cross Foxes*, Llanfair on 26th October 1872, Capt. R.D. Pryce spoke in favour of the Four Crosses route. The Van Railway had been built from a junction with the Cambrian at Caersws without obtaining an Act of Parliament because it had been supported by all the landowners along its length and he hoped they would be able to do likewise. Capt. Pryce thought that the Cambrian Board, of which he was a member, would provide facilities for through traffic to Llanymynech from where connections for north western England, the Midlands and London would be available. The only disadvantage was that a line to Four Crosses would not serve their market town directly. This difficulty was mitigated to some extent because the existing facilities for going to Welshpool would be retained. Capt. Mytton said he believed that the line to Four Crosses presented few engineering difficulties, could be constructed inexpensively and would be a good paying concern. Supporters of the Welshpool route argued that their line was shorter and more direct. Welshpool with its markets and important junction would serve Llanfair's needs far better than Llanymynech. Four Crosses was just a village with a third class station that had few facilities. Following a discussion of the relative merits of the two routes, there was overwhelming support for a railway to Four Crosses. Capt. Pryce then asked Mr George Owen, the Cambrian Railways' Chief Engineer, to address the meeting. Mr Owen said that based on his knowledge of the Festiniog Railway he was in favour of a narrow gauge line and recommended that a gauge of 2ft 3in or 2ft 6in should be adopted. Not only would it be cheaper to build and work than a standard gauge line, it could carry passengers and goods safely at speeds of up to thirty miles an hour. When Capt. Pryce took the opinion of the meeting it was equally divided between those in favour of the standard and narrow gauges.[45]

Another meeting was held on 30th November at which Capt. Pryce proposed that a standard gauge line should be constructed from Llanfair to Llansantffraid, Llanymynech or Four Crosses at an estimated cost of £60,000. He was in favour of the ordinary gauge because it avoided the difficulties of transhipping goods and livestock. The meeting adopted the proposal and two committees were formed to collect subscriptions to defray the preliminary expenses.[46] Although *The Oswestry Advertiser* reported that landowners pledged exceptional support for the Four Crosses route, no tangible progress was made.[47] An attempt to revive the scheme in May 1873 was unsuccessful.[48]

The Welshpool and Llanfair Railway 1874–1882

The following year Mr George Slater, a gentleman who owned property in Northwich and Llanfair, made proposals for a standard gauge railway to Welshpool via Castle Caereinion and Dysserth. Mr Slater believed that a line to Welshpool was to be preferred to one through Meifod because it provided a more direct route to Manchester, the Midlands and London. Most coal for Llanfair came through Shrewsbury, making Welshpool the more direct route, whilst the cost of transporting lime was thought to be the same whichever route was used. The estimated cost of the railway was £35,000 with a further £5,000 being required for compensation payments.[49/50]

In October and November 1874 meetings were held in Llanfair and Llangadfan to test support for the railway. Those present were told that subscriptions totalling £10,000 had been promised by landowners within and beyond the district.[51/52] By August 1875 the Provisional Committee of twenty-five landowners were sufficiently confident to request a meeting with the Earl of Powis to canvass his support for the line. When the Earl met a deputation on 9th September he agreed to let the railway cross his estate and promised to invest £4,000 in the undertaking.[53] A meeting at Welshpool on 4th October strongly supported the scheme.[54]

Following the meeting in Welshpool it was decided to form a joint stock company to acquire the land needed for the railway, then commence construction making use of powers conferred by the Railways Construction Facilities Act 1864.[55] This approach had been used to build the Van Railway and had the advantage of reducing the Parliamentary and legal costs associated with a private Act of Parliament. However, the consent of all the landowners along the route was required. Mr Abraham Howell, who acted as the legal advisor to the Van Railway and the Welshpool and Llanfair scheme, drafted

articles of association for the joint stock company which allowed the Directors to make calls on shareholders before the share issue was fully subscribed. This enabled the company to acquire land and let a contract to build the line before all the capital required to complete it had been secured.

The approach advocated by Mr Howell was strongly opposed by Mr Slater who argued that without an Act of Parliament the company could not acquire land by compulsory purchase. Without an Act the scheme would fail if any landowner refused to sell land required for the line. He stated that the railway had been promoted on the basis that no attempt would be made to build it until the share issue was fully subscribed. If the share issue was only partially successful, interest payments on loans and preference shares issued to make good the deficiency could extinguish any profits, leaving nothing for the ordinary shareholders. Although Mr Slater's views were opposed by Mr Howell and some influential members of the Provisional Committee, his arguments eventually prevailed and on 28th October 1876 the Committee decided to obtain an Act of Parliament.[56]

In September 1875 Mr Slater approached the Cambrian Board and secured its agreement to co-operate with the Welshpool and Llanfair promoters. Once the plans for the railway were deposited in Parliament, George Owen prepared a report on the proposed undertaking which was discussed by the Cambrian Board on 10th January 1877. The promoters intended to build their own station at Welshpool which would be served by a railway that ran next to the Cambrian main line for three quarters of a mile. This line, referred to as Railway No.2 in the deposited plans, was not acceptable to the Cambrian, so the company lodged an objection to the Welshpool and Llanfair bill. At the January Board meeting the Cambrian Directors decided to invite the Welshpool and Llanfair promoters to a meeting with a view to gaining their agreement to remove Railway No.2 from their bill.[57/58]

When representatives of the promoters and the Cambrian Railways' Directorate met to discuss an outline working agreement the Llanfair Company was offered accommodation at Welshpool station. If the Board of Trade required the Cambrian line to be doubled from Welshpool station to the junction with the proposed railway, the Llanfair Company would be required to fund the work. The Cambrian also intended to levy a toll for the use of its railway from the station to the junction as if the distance was two miles. Heavier rails than those specified by the Llanfair Company's Engineer were required so that the Cambrian's locomotives could work the line, so the company offered to contribute £2,000 towards the additional expenditure. While some of the terms offered by the Cambrian were not accepted by the promoters, it was agreed that the draft working agreement could be used as the basis for further negotiation.[59] However, at the insistence of the larger company, Railway No.2 was withdrawn from the Welshpool and Llanfair bill.[60]

The Welshpool and Llanfair Railway Act received the Royal Assent on 10th August 1877. The company was empowered to build a railway nine miles, five furlongs and two chains long at an estimated cost of £34,976. The line began at a

Broad Street, Welshpool, photographed during the first decade of the twentieth century.
VALENTINES

junction with the Cambrian Railways approximately three quarters of a mile west of Welshpool station and ended in a field south east of the Welshpool to Llanfair road on the outskirts of the town. The company had an authorised share capital of £39,000 which would be raised by the issue of 3,900 shares, each with a nominal value of £10. Once the shares had been allocated, accepted and paid in full, a further £13,000 could be borrowed against the assets of the undertaking. Land required for the railway could be acquired by compulsory purchase up to three years after the passage of the Act and the line had to be completed within five years. The company was also given the power to contribute up to £2,000 towards the cost of making a carriage road from a point near Mathyrafal Castle in the Vyrnwy valley, to Pontsycoed on the Welshpool to Llanfair road, on condition that the Llanfyllin Highway Board would maintain it.[61/62/63]

Although substantial pledges of financial support for the proposed railway were received, it proved impossible to raise sufficient capital to commence construction of the line. Some Llanfair people believed that once the railway was open, their town would be reduced to a country village because farmers and traders would take their custom to Welshpool and their own market would decline. There was also disappointment that the station would be situated on the northern bank of the River Banwy at some distance from the town centre.[64] In June 1879 supporters of the railway met at *The Cross Foxes* to receive a report on the financial position of the company and to see what progress could be made towards letting a contract to build the line. The cost of labour, iron and steel were depressed, affording an ideal opportunity to build the railway. It was estimated that the line would cost £40,000 on which a return of five percent was required. Revenue of £8 per mile per week was needed to produce a five percent return on capital if the line was worked for half the gross receipts. The Llanfyllin line produced £9 per mile per week so that investors had to decide whether the proposed railway was capable of producing a similar amount.

Capt. R.D. Pryce suggested that a syndicate of thirteen individuals should be formed to build the railway. The cost of building and equipping the line would be limited to £40,000 to ensure that it was remunerative and would be shared equally by the members of the syndicate. An alternative option was to build a narrow gauge line at an estimated cost of £30,000. If this course was taken, the benefits of cheaper construction and lower working expenses had to be weighed against the cost of transhipping goods and minerals. A new Act of Parliament would be required to enable a gauge of less than 4ft 8½in to be adopted and a further £10,000 would have to be pledged before construction could begin. When the options were discussed, many of those present recognised that it would be preferable to have a narrow gauge line than no railway at all but a standard gauge line was preferred.[65] At a meeting held during the following month, it was decided that if all the capital required to build a standard gauge railway had not been secured by 1st November the narrow gauge would be adopted.[66]

By November no new subscriptions had been received, so a meeting was held at *The Cross Foxes* to decide whether to build the line as far as Pontsycoed or to apply for an Act of Abandonment. Although the feeling of the meeting was against abandoning the railway, the proposal to build the line as far as Pontsycoed was strongly opposed by two influential landowners who had promised to invest in the line on the understanding that it would be made to Llanfair. After a long debate it was decided to build the line as far as Pontsycoed in the hope that further money would then be found to extend it to Llanfair. However, with opinion divided on the wisdom of building a truncated line, nothing was done to let a contract for its construction.[67]

With no progress in prospect, it appeared that the railway authorised by the 1877 Act would have to be abandoned but in November 1881 Mr Humphreys-Owen of Glansevern Hall attempted to revive it. He proposed that two bills should be laid before Parliament, one for continuing the powers of the existing Act and another to abandon the undertaking. Before the bills were examined in Committee, an attempt would be made to raise £22,500 locally. If they were successful, the abandonment bill would be withdrawn, but if the capital required could not be found, the continuation bill would be dropped and the line abandoned. It was proposed to adopt the narrow gauge because it would reduce the costs of building, equipping and working the line. The returns of the North Wales Narrow Gauge Railway had been examined because it was of similar length to the proposed line. They showed that between 1878 and 1880 the working expenses varied from £1,800 to £2,400 per annum. The line was worked by two engines in steam, its gradients were severe, and its main traffic was slate, so that the track and rolling stock required more maintenance than was anticipated for the proposed line to Llanfair. Mr Humphreys-Owen believed that the annual cost of working the railway to Llanfair would not exceed £2,000, a figure that was comparable to that of the Watlington and Princes Risborough Railway. With respect to the revenue that the line might produce, Cambrian officials had advised that in 1880 the receipts of the Llanfyllin branch amounted to approximately £400 per mile per annum. This sum was comparatively low because trade was badly depressed and traffic for Shrewsbury and beyond was charged as if it passed over the defunct Potteries line, although in practice it was carried via Buttington or Oswestry. Mr John Conacher, the Cambrian Railways' Accountant, believed that the proposed railway to Llanfair should yield £415 per mile per annum. Mr Humphreys-Owen estimated that the railway would produce receipts of between £3,500 and £4,000 per annum because it passed through a more populous district with a higher rateable value than the Llanfyllin branch, so that investors could expect a return of £1,500 on capital of £34,000.[68] Once more it proved impossible to secure sufficient financial support for the proposal, so on 19th June 1882 the Act to abandon the railway authorised in 1877 received the Royal Assent.[69]

Another narrow gauge line: The Welshpool and Llanfair Railway 1886–1892

Four years later, plans for another narrow gauge railway between Welshpool and Llanfair were prepared by Messrs Simpson, Davies and Hurst, Civil Engineers of London. At meetings held in Llanfair to canvass support for the undertaking Mr J.R. Dix, the manager of the Corris Railway, explained that the railway would take the route through Castle Caereinion, with stations at Llanfair, Pontsycoed, Castle Caereinion, Berriew and Welshpool. Although merchandise and minerals would have to be transhipped between the standard and narrow gauge lines at Welshpool, the estimated cost was only 3d per ton. The rolling stock would consist of at least two engines, four composite carriages, five cattle vans and four timber trucks. The cost of building and equipping the line was estimated to be £40,000. If local people subscribed £15,000 towards the undertaking, the promoters undertook to find the balance. No calls would be made on the share-

holders until half the line had been completed when half the nominal value of their allocations would fall due. The call for the balance would be made when the line was ready to be inspected by the Board of Trade. A letter was read from Capt. R.D. Pryce in support of the proposed railway. Whilst he was prepared to allow the proposed line to cross his property, the now elderly landowner did not have the heart to become actively involved in promoting the line after the repeated failures of the past. The proposed railway was generally welcomed by those who attended the meetings, although some concern was expressed about the estimated cost of the line. In reply Mr Dix explained that the estimate was based on the proposal made in 1877. A local committee was formed to liaise with Messrs Dix and Hurst.[70]

A letter written in February 1887 by Mr A.C. Humphreys-Owen to Mr Stuart Rendal, the then Member of Parliament for Montgomeryshire, provides an insight into the reasons why so many schemes were unsuccessful. Mr Humphreys-Owen believed that the landowners would not pledge sufficient capital to induce local traders and others to invest in the undertaking. He thought that the district might pledge between ten and fifteen thousand pounds towards the railway, which would enable the promoters to construct an indifferent line by borrowing money through an issue of debentures and preference shares. The ordinary shares would probably be worthless because interest charges on the borrowings would extinguish the operating profits and only the engineers, contractor and lawyers would make any money out of the railway. In Mr Humphreys-Owen's opinion, the scheme would only be viable if £30,000 was raised by an issue of ordinary shares. If that sum was raised he would be prepared take a seat on the Board and would take shares in exchange for his land. He concluded that a railway to Llanfair could only succeed if it was guaranteed by the local authorities in the district as the law permitted for certain railways in Ireland.[71]

The Welshpool and Llanfair Railway Act received the Royal Assent on 23rd August 1887. The Act gave the company the power to construct a three foot gauge railway, ten miles two furlongs and eight chains in length, from a field on the west side of Severn Road, Welshpool to one on the south-eastern side of the Welshpool to Llanfair road about three hundred and forty yards from the north eastern end of Llanfair bridge. For much of its length the railway followed the route of the line authorised in 1877 quite closely, but at Heniarth it crossed the Banwy and then made its way along the north bank of the river to the terminus. The estimated cost of construction was £31,210. The company had an authorised share capital of £45,000 which would be realised by the issue of nine thousand shares, each with a nominal value of £5. Once the shares were issued, accepted and half paid, a further £15,000 could be raised as a mortgage secured on the assets of the company. Land required for the railway could be acquired by compulsory purchase within three years of the passage of the Act, while five years were allowed for the completion of the line. The company had the power to enter into a working agreement with the Cambrian.[72/73/74] The promoters were unable to raise sufficient support locally to build their railway, so in 1892 an Act to abandon the line was obtained.[75] Llanfair it seemed would never obtain a railway.

Proposals for a Light Railways Act 1895–1896

In 1894 a Board of Trade conference on light railways received reports about how such lines were developed overseas. A Committee was appointed to consider how the Board of Trade's regulations for building and working light railways could be relaxed, especially in the case of lines serving sparsely populated or agricultural areas, and if new legislation was needed to authorise the construction of light railways, tramways and tramroads. In January 1895 the Committee reported that very few light railways had been built under the provisions of the Railways Construction Facilities Act 1864 or Regulation of the Railways Act 1868 because the consent of all the landowners and existing railway companies directly affected by the proposed undertaking was required; the Board of Trade was unwilling to relax regulations that it considered to be in the interest of public safety; and local authorities frequently imposed onerous conditions on tramroads and tramways which discouraged their development.

The Committee found that in the case of short, lightly used lines, regulations introduced to ensure public safety could be relaxed without endangering railwaymen or the public generally. Such regulations discouraged the development of light railways because they materially increased the cost of building and operating them. There appeared to be no good reason why they should not be applied selectively if the nature of the undertaking, the country through which it passed, and the traffic that it was intended to carry were taken into consideration. Significant economies could be achieved in the cost of obtaining permission to build and operate light railways. In particular, applications for railways of limited scope that were approved of by the locality they were intended to serve should not be subjected to Parliamentary inquiry. The Committee believed that County Councils and large municipalities should be allowed to authorise and regulate light railways, tramroads and tramways that served communities within their boundaries. Lines should only be approved when the majority of landowners, in terms of numbers and value, assented to them. The Board of Trade would be given powers to act as an arbitrator when land was acquired by compulsory purchase and when issues concerned with public safety required resolution. The Committee did not express any opinion on whether it was desirable for local authorities to promote, or provide aid to, light railways.

Some members of the Committee believed that no legislation could be effective in securing the development of light railways unless simple procedures were introduced to allow County Councils to examine and approve proposals for such lines. Proposals that were approved should then be sanctioned by the Board of Trade. The opposition of landowners should not prevent the examination of a proposal on its merits and a cheap and simple process was required for the compulsory purchase of land. County Councils should be given powers to construct light railways, or to provide aid for their construction. No deposit should be required until construction was about to commence. These conclusions were annexed to the main report.[76]

The report of the Light Railways Conference Committee was generally welcomed. However, farmers contended that light railways were not a panacea for the depressed state of agriculture while business interests were vociferous in their opposition to the provision of financial support from public funds. The great railway companies recognised the benefits of light railways to agriculture and their value as feeder lines.[77] In April the Government introduced a Light Railways bill into the Commons which allowed Borough and County Councils to examine and approve draft Light Railway Orders. The draft Orders had to be submitted to the Board of Trade to ensure that they complied with the provisions of the law and that public safety was ensured. The Board was given powers to protect the interests of landowners when land was acquired by compulsory purchase. There was no provision for public funding in the bill and amendments to permit such funding were talked out. The bill was seen to be of limited value and failed to pass into law.[78]

Despite the loss of the Light Railways bill, public opinion still favoured the development of light railways in Britain. In November 1895 meetings were held in London at which a Light Railway Association was formed and resolutions were passed urging the Government to introduce new legislation to facilitate the construction of light railways in the next session of Parliament.[79] At Llanfair a Parish Council Committee met on 26th November to pass a resolution asking the Government to proceed with a Light Railways bill that permitted local authorities and the Treasury to contribute towards the capital cost of such lines. A copy of the resolution was sent to Mr A.C. Humphreys-Owen, the Member of Parliament for Montgomeryshire, so that he could present it to a light railway conference that was held two days later. A copy of the resolution was also sent to Montgomery County Council asking its Members to urge the Government to introduce a Light Railways bill at the earliest opportunity.[80]

When the County Council met on 20th December, its Chairman, Mr Humphreys-Owen, reported that he had received a letter from the Light Railways Association of Great Britain seeking his views on the desirability of introducing a simplified regulatory regime for the promotion, construction and operation of light railways. The Association also sought observations on the provision of state funding to such lines. Mr Humphreys-Owen thought that such matters were largely technical and should be left to the Board of Trade, but his view did not prevail. After a short debate it was decided to postpone further consideration of the matter until the following month.[81] When Members reconvened, they decided that light railways should receive financial support from public bodies. Some took the view that if assistance was provided by the County Council, only the locality through which the railway ran should be rated. However, majority opinion was that when aid was provided by the County it should be funded by a general rate. Members of the Council also decided that the gauge of light railways should be determined by local circumstances and attempted to obtain exemption from legislation that required points and signals to be interlocked and passenger trains to be fitted with continuous brakes.[82]

The Light Railways Act received the Royal Assent on 14th August 1896. Its primary objectives were to simplify the procedure for obtaining the power to make light railways so that rural and undeveloped areas could be opened up at minimal cost, and to give the promoters of such railways the power to acquire land required for their schemes by compulsory purchase without recourse to Parliament. Contemporary opinion was that most of the schemes built under the provisions of the Act would run alongside existing roads and would only deviate from them to avoid hills or other natural objects. Some commentators thought that the great railway companies would use the Act to extend their lines into districts that were not served by railways, so providing the means of communication between agricultural communities or fishing harbours and their market towns. It was hoped that railways built under the provisions of the Act would be freed from the Board of Trade's onerous regulations in respect of permanent way, gauge, fencing, level crossings, block signalling, etc.[83] Such expectations were not fully realised because by the time the legislation was enacted, much of the country was already well-served by the existing railway network, while the railway companies and Board of Trade had entrenched ideas about how railways should be built and equipped.[84]

The Act established a Light Railway Commission consisting of three members which received applications and evaluated their viability. Where applications were considered to be worthwhile, the Commissioners could grant a Light Railway Order which required the approval of the Board of Trade on various technical aspects. County, Borough and District Councils could promote light railways, make loans to them and subscribe to their share capital. Where money was advanced by a local authority, a Treasury loan of twenty-five percent of the capital cost was also available. The Treasury could make grants or loans of up to fifty percent of the capital cost if the Board of Agriculture certified that a light railway was necessary to develop the district, provided the co-operation of all the interested parties was assured.[85]

The Llanfair & Meifod Valley Light Railway 1895–1897
The prospect of building a light railway with aid from public funds revived interest in promoting a railway to Llanfair. On 7th December 1895, members of Llanfair Parish Council decided to invite the neighbouring Parishes to help them bring a railway to the town.[86] Nothing more was heard about the matter until 12th May 1896 when a parish meeting was held at the Board School, Llanfair. Addressing those present the Chairman, Dr C.E. Humphreys, said that for more than twenty years many schemes to bring a railway to Llanfair had been proposed but all had failed because the capital required to build them could not be realised. However, the prospect of securing aid from public funds greatly increased the chances

of success. Llanfair was a rich and important agricultural district that had long been in need of a railway. He dismissed the idea of a narrow gauge line and stated that opinion in the locality was strongly in favour of a standard gauge railway. There were two routes that were practical, one to Four Crosses and the other to Welshpool. A third route to Newtown had been suggested but was impractical because of the hilly terrain between the two towns. Dr Humphreys did not believe that they would come to a decision about the route that night but whichever was chosen he hoped that they would all pull together.

Mr R. Humphreys said that a railway was needed so that farmers could get a better price for their produce and procure their coal, lime and manure at less cost, while the townspeople would be able to buy their provisions more cheaply. He thought a railway would attract tourists to the town which might even become a second Llandrindod. The railway would probably cost about £40,000 which could be funded in equal measure by the Government, Montgomery County Council, private capital and an issue of debentures. He asked the meeting to support a resolution that invited the County Council to convene a special meeting to apply to the Light Railway Commissioners for the necessary powers to build a railway to Llanfair, and asked the Parish Council to apply to the Government for financial support for the line.

When Mr Thomas Watkin seconded the resolution, he spoke in favour of the Welshpool route. Private individuals would have to find a quarter of the cost of constructing the line. The distance from Llanfair to Welshpool was about $7\frac{1}{2}$ or 8 miles, while the distance to Four Crosses or Llanymynech was between 13 and 15 miles. He did not think it would be possible to build a line for less than £4,000 per mile so the cost of a railway to Welshpool would be £24,000, while one to Four Crosses would cost £45,000. Private subscribers would have to find £6,000 in the first case and £11,500 in the other. Welshpool, a town with a population of six thousand, was more likely to assist them than a village like Meifod. When a railway between Welshpool and Llanfair had been proposed some years ago, the Earl of Powis offered to subscribe £4,000. They were more likely to get the support of private individuals if they adhered to that route. The Meifod route gave access to one town, Oswestry, while Welshpool gave the option of Shrewsbury, Newtown and Oswestry which were equidistant. Most buyers of eggs and poultry came from Welshpool while tourists were more likely to come from London and the Midlands. He had never seen farmers from the Llanfair district at Oswestry market but saw as many as twenty at Newtown. From all points of view, the route from Welshpool was superior.

Other speakers favoured the Meifod route, maintaining that they could get lime directly from Llanymynech and that butter sellers could get a better price for their produce at Oswestry. This route would put them in direct communication with Ruabon so that coal and building materials could be obtained more cheaply, while timber from the area could be sent to the pits in the Wrexham district. Some present thought that the most sensible plan would be to have two railways with the

The Vyrnwy with Broniarth rising above it. The Llanfair & Meifod Valley Light Railway would have run to the right of the river.
F. FRITH

Welshpool route joining the Meifod line at Cyfronydd. Mr Theodore said that railway companies, local authorities and landowners interested in both routes should be contacted so that an assessment of the support for each of them could be made. Until they knew what assistance was available, they should not bind themselves to either route. Mr Humphrey's resolution was then carried unanimously.[87]

The debate continued in the local press with the advocates of the Meifod route maintaining that their line would open up a larger tract of country than its rival, that it was the most direct route to the coal and lime producing districts, and was the cheapest route to Liverpool and Manchester. They argued that their railway would be easier to construct, served a more populous area and would secure more timber traffic. Welshpool, it was claimed, was making no attempt to promote a line to Llanfair even though its inhabitants must know that a line to Four Crosses would damage their trade. The supporters of the Welshpool route contended that the railway through Meifod was promoted by Llanfair traders who feared that a direct line would divert their trade to the larger town; that the rates charged from Liverpool, Manchester and the coal producing districts would be the same whichever route was chosen; and that their line could be extended to Llangadfan, opening up as much country as the rival route. Most livestock and dairy produce from the Llanfair district was sent to Shrewsbury, Uttoxeter and Leicester and almost all the coal used in Llanfair came from Hanwood. All these places could be reached more easily through Welshpool.[88/89/90/91]

Another meeting was held at Llanfair on 3rd July to consider the best route for the railway to take.[92] Several letters were read from firms offering to survey the proposed routes. Noting that the advocates of a line from Welshpool intended to survey a route from the town to Llanfair, Capt. Luxmore proposed that a survey should be made of the route to Four Crosses. Seconding the motion, the Rev. J. Wilym Jones, the Vicar of

Meifod, stated that one of the objectives of the Light Railways bill was to open up districts without railway accommodation and that the Meifod route was the best one for this purpose. After some debate it was agreed to survey a line from Llanfair to Four Crosses and appoint collectors in each parish to defray the cost of the survey. A resolution calling for the railway to be extended to Llangadfan was adopted unanimously.[93]

On 31st July representatives of the Parish Councils met at the National School, Meifod and invited Mr J.E. Thomas C.E. of Wrexham to make a preliminary survey of the Four Crosses to Llanfair route. He began work on Monday 3rd August and his survey was completed during the month.[94/95] At a public meeting held on 20th August, Mr Thomas said that the proposed line would leave the Cambrian Railways at Arddleen and then pass through Sarnau, Trefnannau and Pwllychwaid to Pant, from where it kept to the south side of the river as far as Llanfair. He had taken the most direct route to keep the cost to a minimum but in doing so the railway cut across several estates so that some opposition from landowners could be expected. Eleven of the fourteen miles were almost as flat as a table so the line would be cheap to build. The sharpest radius was only ten chains while the steepest gradient was 1 in 80. The gauge would be standard, rails weighing 45lbs per yard would be used, and trains could travel over the line at 15 miles an hour. Mr Thomas estimated that the line would cost £36,141 inclusive of land, stations and legal fees. He thought that it could be worked for 50% of the gross receipts. Dr Humphreys told the meeting that the Light Railways bill had passed into law and that the State might contribute as much as half the cost of building the line. Mr Storey, the Promoter's Secretary, said that the Great Western and Cambrian companies had been approached to see if they would be prepared to work the railway and that the Cambrian had offered the more favourable terms. A deputation was then appointed to meet that company's officials.[96]

On 17th September a deputation representing the promoters of the Llanfair & Meifod Valley Light Railway met Mr Denniss, the General Manager of the Cambrian Railways, and Mr George Owen at Oswestry. Dr Humphreys stated that the proposed railway would form a natural outlet for Llanfair and the nearby villages. He believed that about three quarters of all the flour, corn and groceries for Llanfair came to Welshpool by canal. If a railway was built from Arddleen to Llanfair, the Cambrian would get all the traffic and not just a portion of it as at present. The canal company's traffic for Llanfair was worth between £800 and £1,000 per annum. In 1887 it was estimated that 57,000 passengers and 27,000 tons were carried over the road between the two towns each year. In winter large quantities of coal passed along the road, while in the autumn farmers carted a considerable tonnage of lime. It cost eight shillings a ton to haul goods from Welshpool to Llanfair. If the railway was made, the cost of haulage could be reduced significantly. Although the district around Llanfair was rich in timber, it was hardly worth felling because the cost of hauling it to Welshpool was equivalent to half its sales value. A considerable quantity of timber would pass over the proposed line for many years and butter factories could be established in the district. Mr Joseph Richards, who farmed at Lower Hall, Meifod, said that the proposed railway would be of great value to agriculture. There were dairy farms along the route and they all produced butter. Farmers had to travel long distances over bad roads to get their produce to market and would be prepared to travel four or five miles to the nearest station on the line.

Mr Denniss told the deputation that his company could only consider building and working the line if it was supported financially by Sir Watkin Williams Wynn, the Earl of Powis

Carter James and his donkeys outside the New House, Meifod, then a lodging house for drovers. In areas without a railway, general merchandise, coal and lime were carried in carts hauled by donkeys or horses. This view dates from the late nineteenth century.   NLW, JOHN THOMAS COLLECTION

and other large landowners. Dr Humphreys assured him that there would be no difficulty in obtaining the support of the landowners, farmers and traders if the Cambrian would agree to build and work the line. When Mr Denniss replied that the Cambrian was a public company and had to take the interests of Welshpool and Oswestry into account lest they should commit themselves to the interests of one to the detriment of the other, Dr Humphreys reminded him that the Meifod Valley line was the only serious proposal for bringing a railway to Llanfair. Its promoters had surveyed the route and intended sending their application for a Light Railway Order to the Light Railway Commissioners before 1st November. A railway from Llanfair to Welshpool would be opposed by the Earl of Powis because it would pass through Powis Castle Park and required a tunnel near Christ Church. Mr Denniss agreed to lay the information that they had provided before his Directors at the next Board meeting.[97/98]

When the Cambrian Board met on 26th September, Mr Denniss reported that a light railway from Arddleen to Llanfair was being promoted and that a number of meetings had been held in support of the scheme. He then submitted a letter from Mr Marshall Dugdale, a landowner from Llanfyllin, in support of the proposed railway. Mr Denniss recommended that the traffic potential of the proposed line should be assessed before the Board made any commitment to build and work it. In the meantime he suggested that a committee should be appointed to go over the ground and interview those most concerned in the proposed undertaking.[99] Once the matter had been fully considered, the Directors instructed Mr Denniss to inform the L&MVLR promoters that they were unable to express any opinion on the route that had been adopted and that their company had no funds to invest in the undertaking.[100]

Three days later, Mr Denniss wrote to Dr Humphreys stating that as a matter of policy his Directors would encourage the development of light railway schemes that connected with their system, especially where they opened up new districts. In such cases the Board would consider applications from promoters to enter into agreements to build and work their lines once their schemes had been fully developed. In such cases his company would give such assistance as it could by supplying evidence at Inquiries held by the Light Railway Commissioners. The Cambrian Directors were prepared to give very favourable consideration to an application from the Meifod Valley promoters once their scheme was more fully developed and they could see their way to raising the required capital.[101] Following their meeting with Mr Denniss, the promoters attended the meetings of Montgomery County Council and Llanfyllin Rural District Council to obtain their agreement in principle to support their scheme financially.[102/103] When a meeting was held at Meifod in December, sixty percent of those present indicated that they would invest in the scheme.[104]

On 10th December 1896 Mr Woosnam, the promoter's solicitor, sent their application for a Light Railway Order to the Board of Trade. The proposed railway was 13 miles 7 furlongs and $7\frac{1}{2}$ chains long with stations at Arddleen, Sarnau, Trefnannau, Meifod, Newbridge, Pontsycoed and Llanfair. The draft Order gave the light railway company powers to enter into agreements with any existing railway company to build, work or lease it. The cost of construction was estimated to be £41,343 6s 3d, so the draft Order proposed that the company should be given powers to raise capital totalling £41,000 and to borrow up to £10,000. Local authorities in Montgomeryshire and the Cambrian Railways Company were given the power to invest in the line.[105]

Representatives of the L&MVLR promoters met Members of Oswestry Borough Council on 1st February 1897 to canvass their support for the scheme. Dr Humphreys stated that their proposal had been submitted to the Light Railway Commissioners. The line would serve an area of 160 square miles with a population of 10,000 and rateable value of £60,000. It would cost £42,000 to build, half of which sum they hoped to obtain as a Treasury Grant with the balance being raised through the issue of shares to local authorities and the public in equal measure. A map showing the route of the line was shown to members of the Council. The Mayor, Mr T. Edwards, stated that that his Council was disposed to help the scheme in every legal way that it could. That afternoon a public meeting was held in the Guildhall at which the Mayor presided. Addressing the meeting, Mr Edwards said that Oswestry fully recognised the advisability of making the town the terminus for Llanfair. The district that the line would serve was a large and fertile area and its inhabitants were practically unanimous in their wish to make Oswestry their market town. He had no doubt that Oswestrians would take up shares in large numbers in due course, indeed some gentlemen in the town had already promised to invest in the line. A resolution pledging strong support for the line was put and carried with enthusiasm.[106]

Although members of Oswestry Borough Council wished to offer the light railway a loan of £2,500, they were uncertain whether their Council had the necessary powers to do so. When Mr J. Parry-Jones, the Town Clerk, asked the Board of Trade to clarify the matter, officials replied that if the scheme's Light Railway Order gave the Council the necessary powers they would be able to invest in the company. However, when pressed they appeared to be less certain.[107] An outline working agreement with the Cambrian was drafted in February 1897 but then the promoters of the Welshpool and Llanfair Light Railway lodged a notice of objection to the L&MVLR promoter's application for a Light Railway Order.[108/109] Although the Meifod Valley promoters continued to lobby the local authorities and obtained a Board of Agriculture certificate stating that the proposed railway would be of benefit to agriculture in the district through which it was projected, they were unable to make any further progress until the Light Railway Commissioners held their Inquiry into the merits of the rival schemes.[110]

[1] *The Trade and Industries of Llanfair Caereinion a hundred years ago* Charles H Humphreys The Montgomeryshire Collections v.46 pp.103–113

[2] *Llanfair Caereinion in the Mid-Nineteenth Century* WTR Pryce and J A Edwards The Montgomeryshire Collections v.67 pp.45–93

[3] *The Trade and Industries of Llanfair Caereinion a hundred years ago* Charles H Humphreys The Montgomeryshire Collections v.46 pp.103–113

[4] *The Trade and Industries of Llanfair Caereinion a hundred years ago* Charles H Humphreys The Montgomeryshire Collections v.46 pp.103–113

[5] *A Hundred Years of Transport* C Newman Humphreys The Montgomeryshire Collections v.51 pp.127–8

[6] *The Oswestry Advertiser and Montgomeryshire Mercury* 5th October 1860

[7] *A Hundred Years of Transport* C. Newman Humphreys The Montgomeryshire Collections v.51 pp.127–8

[8] *The Oswestry Advertiser and Border Counties Advertiser* 13th May 1896

[9] *The Welshpool & Llanfair Light Railway* Lewis Cozens 1951

[10] *The Chester and Holyhead Railway v.1 The Main Line up to 1880* Peter E. Baughan, David and Charles 1972

[11] *Reports and returns made to Parliament on communication between London and Dublin since the meeting held in Dublin on 22nd January 1836* Gwynedd Archive Service XD2/13330

[12] *Report on the various lines by which a railway could be carried from London to Porth-Dynllaen in north Wales* Charles Vignoles Civil Engineer Gwynedd Archive Service XD2/13330

[13] *The Chester and Holyhead Railway v.1 The Main Line up to 1880* Peter E. Baughan, David and Charles 1972

[14] *History of the Great Western Railway v.1 1833 to 1863* E.T. MacDermot revised by C.R. Clinker, Ian Allan 1982

[15] NLW Brogyntyn 2 PQN 137 *The Worcester Chronicle* c.1840

[16] *The Chester and Holyhead Railway v.1 The Main Line up to 1880* Peter E. Baughan, David and Charles 1972

[17] Worcester & Porthdynllaen Railway prospectus Gwynedd Archive Service XD2/13359

[18] ZPER 2 9 *The Railway Times* 16th August 1845

[19] Plan and section of the Worcester and Porthdinllaen Railway 1845

[20] ZPER 2 10 *The Railway Times* 21st February 1846

[21] ZPER 2 10 *The Railway Times* 30th May 1846

[22] ZPER 2 10 *The Railway Times* 15th August 1846

[23] ZPER 2 9 *The Railway Times* 23rd August 1845

[24] Plan of Great Welch Junction Railway Gwynedd Archive Service XD2/13357

[25] *The Oswestry Advertiser and Montgomeryshire Mercury* 1st October 1862

[26] *The Oswestry Advertiser and Montgomeryshire Mercury* 2nd July 1862

[27] *The Oswestry Advertiser and Montgomeryshire Mercury* 2nd July 1862

[28] *The Oswestry Advertiser and Montgomeryshire Mercury* 3rd September 1862

[29] *The Oswestry Advertiser and Montgomeryshire Mercury* 1st October 1862

[30] Rail 552 3 Oswestry and Newtown Board 27th August 1862

[31] *The Oswestry Advertiser and Montgomeryshire Mercury* 3rd September 1862

[32] *The Oswestry Advertiser and Montgomeryshire Mercury* 1st October 1862

[33] *The Oswestry Advertiser and Montgomeryshire Mercury* 11th January 1865

[34] *The Oswestry Advertiser and Montgomeryshire Mercury* 11th January 1865

[35] *The Festiniog Railway v.1 History and Route 1800–1953* James I.C. Boyd The Oakwood Press 1975

[36] *The story of the Cambrian a biography of a railway* C.P. Gasquoine Woodall, Minshall, Thomas & Co. Ltd 1922

[37] *The Oswestry Advertiser and Montgomeryshire Mercury* 11th January 1865

[38] Llanfair Railway Plans Parliamentary Notice 11th November 1864

[39] *The Oswestry Advertiser and Montgomeryshire Mercury* 11th January 1865

[40] ZPER 2 29 *The Railway Times* 4th March 1865

[41] *The Montgomery County Times and Shropshire and Mid-Wales Advertiser* 16th May 1896

[42] Shrewsbury and North Wales Railway (Meifod Valley Extension etc) Plans and sections 1865–66

[43] Shrewsbury and North Wales Railway (Meifod Valley Extension etc) Estimate

[44] *The Montgomery County Times and Shropshire and Mid-Wales Advertiser* 16th May 1896

[45] *The Oswestry Advertiser and Montgomeryshire Mercury* 30th October 1872

[46] *The Newtown and Welshpool Express* 3rd December 1872

[47] *The Oswestry Advertiser and Montgomeryshire Mercury* 30th October 1872

[48] *The Oswestry Advertiser and Montgomeryshire Mercury* 4th June 1873

[49] *The Oswestry Advertiser and Montgomeryshire Mercury* 4th November 1874

[50] *The Oswestry Advertiser and Montgomeryshire Mercury* 25th November 1874

[51] *The Oswestry Advertiser and Montgomeryshire Mercury* 4th November 1874

[52] *The Oswestry Advertiser and Montgomeryshire Mercury* 25th November 1874

[53] *The Newtown and Welshpool Express* 14th September 1875

[54] *The Oswestry Advertiser and Montgomeryshire Mercury* 6th October 1875

[55] *The Oswestry Advertiser and Montgomeryshire Mercury* 2nd February 1876

[56] *The Newtown and Welshpool Express* 31st October 1876

[57] Rail 92 2 Cambrian Board 29th October 1875

[58] Rail 92 2 Cambrian Board 10th January 1877

[59] *The Oswestry Advertiser and Montgomeryshire Mercury* 31st January 1877

[60] Welshpool and Llanfair Railway Act 1877 Ch. ccxxv

[61] Welshpool and Llanfair Railway Act 1877 Ch. ccxxv

[62] Welshpool and Llanfair Railway Plans and sections 1877

[63] Welshpool and Llanfair Railway Estimate 28th December 1876

[64] *The Oswestry Advertiser and Montgomeryshire Mercury* 6th December 1876

[65] *The Oswestry Advertiser and Montgomeryshire Mercury* 18th June 1879

[66] *The Oswestry Advertiser and Montgomeryshire Mercury* 9th July 1879

[67] *The Oswestry Advertiser and Montgomeryshire Mercury* 12th November 1879

[68] *The Oswestry Advertiser and Montgomeryshire Mercury* 2nd November 1881

[69] Welshpool and Llanfair Railway (Abandonment Act) 1882 Ch. xii

[70] *The Montgomeryshire Express and Radnor Times* 12th October 1886

[71] NLW Glansevern 19462C 332: A.C. Humphreys-Owen to Stuart Rendal 18th February 1887

[72] Welshpool and Llanfair Railway Act 1887 Ch. clxxxv

[73] Welshpool and Llanfair Railway Plans and sections 1886–87

[74] Welshpool and Llanfair Railway Estimate 23rd December 1886

[75] Welshpool and Llanfair Railway (Abandonment) Act 1892 Ch. ii

[76] ZPER 260 *The Railway Times* 2nd February 1895

[77] ZPER 2 60 *The Railway Times* 5th January, 12th January, 26th January, 9th February 1895

[78] ZPER 2 60 *The Railway Times* 27th April, 15th July, 30th November 1895

[79] ZPER 2 60 *The Railway Times* 30th November 1895

[80] *The Montgomeryshire Express and Radnor Times* 3rd December 1895

[81] *The Montgomeryshire Express and Radnor Times* 24th December 1895

[82] *The Montgomeryshire Express and Radnor Times* 4th February 1896

[83] ZLIB 6 63 The Light Railways Act 1896

[84] *The Oxford Companion to British Railway History* Jack Simmons & Gordon Biddle (Eds) OUP 1997

[85] *The Oxford Companion to British Railway History* Jack Simmons & Gordon Biddle (Eds) OUP 1997

[86] *The Montgomeryshire Express and Radnor Times* 10th December 1895

[87] *The Montgomeryshire Express and Radnor Times* 19th May 1896

[88] *The Montgomeryshire Express and Radnor Times* 7th July 1896

[89] *The Montgomeryshire Express and Radnor Times* 14th July 1896

[90] *The Montgomeryshire Express and Radnor Times* 21st July 1896

[91] *The Oswestry and Border Counties Advertiser* 13th May 1896

[92] *The Montgomery County Times and Shropshire and Mid-Wales Advertiser* 4th July 1896

[93] *The Oswestry and Border Counties Advertiser* 8th July 1896

[94] *The Montgomery County Times and Shropshire and Mid-Wales Advertiser* 8th August 1896

[95] *The Montgomeryshire Express and Radnor Times* 11th August 1896

[96] *The Montgomeryshire Express and Radnor Times* 1st September 1896

[97] Rail 92 65 Promoters meeting with C.S. Denniss 17 September 1896

[98] *The Montgomeryshire Express and Radnor Times* 29th September 1896

[99] Rail 92 65 C.S. Denniss Report to Cambrian Board 26th September 1896

[100] Rail 92 11 Traffic and Works Committee 26th September 1896

[101] Rail 92 65 C.S. Denniss to Dr C.E. Humphreys 29th September 1896

[102] *The Montgomery County Times and Shropshire and Mid-Wales Advertiser* 19th September 1896

[103] *The Montgomeryshire Express and Radnor Times* 6th October 1896

[104] *The Montgomeryshire Express and Radnor Times* 16th December 1896

[105] MT6 781 9 Llanfair and Meifod Valley Light Railway M. Woosnam to Board of Trade 10th December 1896

[106] *The Oswestry and Border Counties Advertiser* 3rd February 1897

[107] MT6 781 9 Llanfair and Meifod Valley Railway Investment by Oswestry Borough Council February 1897

[108] Rail 92 66 Cambrian Solicitor to Board 21st February 1897

[109] Rail 722 1 W&L Promoter's Minute Book 25th February 1897

[110] MT 6 781 9 Llanfair & Meifod Valley Railway Board of Agriculture to Board of Trade 18th May 1897

CHAPTER TWO

ECHOES OF INDIA

IN Welshpool the progress of the proposed railway from Llanfair to Arddleen was watched with interest. When the proposal was discussed by Members of the Borough Council on 14th May 1896 they agreed that the line was unlikely to pay its way and that its promoters would have difficulty in raising the capital required to build it. However, they recognised that although Welshpool had been the natural outlet for the Llanfair district for centuries, if the proposed scheme was successful it would divert trade to Oswestry. Members of the Council decided to establish a small committee to consider the merits of building a railway from Welshpool to Llanfair.[1]

Messrs Moorsam & Ward, Civil Engineers of Manchester and Welshpool, were commissioned to prepare a scheme for a railway between the two towns. The principal considerations for the Committee and their Engineers were to build a line that would be profitable as economically as possible. The proposed railway would not only have to connect with the Shropshire Union Canal, the Cambrian Railways and the L& NW and GW joint railway, but also had to traverse a hilly district and be capable of further extension. A gauge of two foot six inches was recommended because:

1. Less material would be required than if a standard gauge line was built,
2. Sharper curves and steeper gradients would be possible,
3. Savings could be made in cuttings, embankments and the width of the line.

At Welshpool, goods would have to be transferred between the standard and narrow gauge lines. Objections to transhipping merchandise were dismissed on the grounds that it would only apply to a portion of the goods carried; experience on other lines had shown that the cost would not exceed 5d per ton, and that tranship wagons would be available to move large quantities of goods over the railway in standard gauge wagons. The Engineers argued that even on conventional railways some goods were transhipped at junctions.

The proposed railway would start at the Cambrian Railways station at Welshpool, then follow the Smithfield siding and the Lledan brook before crossing the canal by a swing bridge close to the aqueduct. Exchange sidings were to be provided at the canal side. The railway would then run along the side of the brook and the Vicarage grounds to cross Church Street. Five old shops, five black and white cottages, and *The Seven Stars* public house would be demolished to make way for the line between Church Street and Hall Street. The railway would then follow Brook Street as far as Raven Square, from where it would run alongside the Llanfair road as far as Park Drive. The line would run by Nant y Caws, above the Black Mill, and below the Earl of Powis' new cottages at the Glyn before rejoining the Llanfair Road near Sylfaen dairy farm. It would then follow the road to Llanfair except at occasional points where steep gradients had to be avoided. The railway

would reduce the cost of maintaining the Llanfair Road which was said to be the most expensive in the County. Similar schemes in Ireland were thought to have reduced the cost of road maintenance by as much as seventy-five percent.

The cost of building and equipping the line was estimated to be £21,000, while a further £4,000 was required to acquire land and other property, making the total estimated cost £25,000. Projected income amounted to £2,808 per annum with annual working expenses estimated to be £1,872, producing a forecast surplus of £936. The line was thus a good investment for local authorities and other interested parties. The Llanfair & Meifod Valley scheme was dismissed on the grounds that it was of no benefit to Welshpool and involved travelling over greater distances to reach Llanfair's markets than by the Welshpool route. The proposal was adopted by the Borough Council at their meeting in October 1896.[2/3]

Distances between Llanfair and local market towns by the rival routes

	Welshpool & Llanfair	Llanfair & Meifod Valley
Length to construct	9	14
Llanfair to Welshpool	9	20¼
Llanfair to Oswestry	24	22½
Llanfair to Newtown	22	33¼
Llanfair to Shrewsbury via Buttington	28	37

At the beginning of December a public meeting was held in Welshpool to consider the desirability of promoting a light railway from Welshpool to Llanfair. Mr William Forrester Addie, the then Mayor of Welshpool and the Earl of Powis' Agent, told the meeting that a Committee had been formed to look into the matter and had approved plans and estimates for a light railway. He did not think that it was for the meeting to decide the route, the gauge, or whether steam or electricity would be used. What they had to decide was should a railway be promoted in the interest of the town, and if it was, whether they believed that the ratepayers should contribute towards the cost of building it.

Mr Addie advised the meeting to consider what other towns were doing. Oswestry was subsidising Llanfair in order to promote the Meifod Valley line and was also backing another railway to Llangynog. The town's intention was clear; it wanted to increase its trade at the expense of Welshpool. Mr Addie believed that the Light Railways Act had not been enacted to divert trade that had developed over many years between villages and their market towns. It would be inequitable to rate such places to pay for railways that carried their trade to another town. Councils in the district through which the proposed light railway would pass were now able to contribute a quarter of the capital needed to build it, the Government would contribute another quarter and the rest would be satisfied by the issue of shares. The scheme could only be carried out if it received the unanimous support of those present. If they gave their approval the Borough Council would appoint a Committee to promote the line.

Councillor E.O. Jones stated that steps should be taken without delay to promote the light railway. He believed that the scheme would be a success, would benefit Llanfair and the surrounding district, and that the Light Railway Act provided valuable assistance. Four fifths of the livestock from Llanfair came through Welshpool and was sent to south Staffordshire. Their line was the only one that could pay. Major Pryce-Jones reminded the meeting that the construction of the line would bring increased trade to Welshpool. Those engaged in agriculture would be able to get lime, manure and farm implements at a cheaper rate and in shorter time than at present. He believed that if the other scheme was carried out, Montgomeryshire would be rated for the benefit of a town in another county and that was inequitable. After further discussion the meeting endorsed the proposal with great enthusiasm.[4]

On 15th December 1896 Mr Addie called a meeting of landowners to examine the Engineer's plans and discuss the scheme.[5] Under the Chairmanship of the Earl of Powis they agreed to support the proposed railway.[6] At a meeting held on 28th January 1897 it was decided to form a Committee to promote the railway and appoint a Chairman, Solicitor and Engineer.[7] The following day Welshpool Borough Council voted £200 towards the proposed railway's preliminary expenses.[8] On 8th February Mr Addie was appointed Chairman of the Committee, Mr George Harrison was engaged as its Solicitor and Messrs Moorsam and Ward were confirmed as the line's Engineers.[9] Under the terms of their appointment the Engineers were to:

1. Draw up plans, sections and estimates to meet the requirements of the Light Railway Act,
2. Attend all meetings with the Light Railway Commissioners and Board of Trade, and provide evidence and explanations when required to do so,
3. Attend like meetings of the County, District and Parish Councils.[10]

The route refined

When the Committee met on 11th February, its members decided to adopt the Golfa route and accompany the Engineers through the district to confirm the route of the railway. The purpose of the inspection was to ensure that the railway was kept off the turnpike road wherever practical so that the County Council would not object to the scheme.[11]

Following the inspection it was decided that the route recommended by the Engineers from Welshpool station to Seven Stars would be adopted. Beyond Seven Stars the line was diverted to run behind the houses on the north side of Brook Street and the Armoury, before continuing on to Raven Square. Between Raven Square and the independent chapel at Cyfronydd the route shown on the Engineer's plan was confirmed. Thereafter, the line was diverted to follow the south side of the Banwy, keeping as close to the river as possible, until the mill opposite Eithnog Hall was reached. Here the line would cross the river close to the western side

of the mill. It then made its way along the northern bank of the Banwy as far as Llanfair. The railway terminated in the field belonging to Mr John Jehu on the outskirts of the town.[12]

On 18th February the Committee approved the amended route subject to the railway crossing the Banwy at a point fifteen chains east of the mill. Then they instructed the Engineers to contact those landowners whose property was affected by the alterations to the route so that their views could be obtained. After the relative costs of building, equipping and operating standard and narrow gauge railways to Llanfair had been reviewed, it was agreed that a gauge of 2ft 6in should be adopted because it was cheaper than a standard gauge line.[13]

At its meeting on 25th February the Executive Committee discussed ways of raising the capital required to build the line and decided to draw up a prospectus for issue to the public. They agreed to ask the Welshpool members of Montgomery County Council to secure that Council's support for the scheme, either by way of a loan or by subscribing to its share capital. The Committee also decided to ask Welshpool Borough Council to subscribe £8,000 in support of the line. Finally, they resolved to oppose the Llanfair & Meifod Valley scheme and send a notice of objection to the Light Railway Commissioners.[14]

Everard Calthrop takes charge

The adoption of the narrow gauge caused considerable difference of opinion about the practicality of transhipping goods at Welshpool and whether the traffic offered by the district through which the line had been projected could be accommodated. To answer these concerns, Mr Everard Calthrop gave a lecture entitled *Light Railways as illustrated by the Bársi Light Railway and its rolling stock* at Welshpool Town Hall on 24th March 1897.[15] The speaker had worked in India where he became a strong advocate of narrow gauge railways in districts where broad gauge lines could not be afforded or justified. In the sub-continent he formulated a number of principals for the design, construction and operation of such railways, which later became known as *Calthrop's Patent*. The Bársi Light Railway, built in 1896–7 and opened on 18th March 1897 became a showpiece for his theories.[16]

Addressing his audience Mr Calthrop explained that he was in favour of retaining the standard gauge wherever the traffic was large enough to provide a reasonable return on the capital expended. If the traffic was not large enough to make a line of standard gauge pay there were three alternatives:

1. The promoters could guarantee a minimum return on the capital expended and fund any shortfall out of their own resources,
2. The capital cost could be reduced to a level that would support the revenue which would require the adoption of the narrow gauge,
3. They could have no railway at all.

Traffic was a fixed quantity which would be the same whichever gauge was used, so the question to be decided was whether they would have a narrow gauge line or nothing at all. In his experience, estimates that standard gauge light railways could be built for between £2,500 and £3,000 per mile were over-optimistic as the true cost was double those amounts. When the true cost of construction became apparent, many promoters found that the traffic offered was insufficient to make their schemes viable. He believed that four miles of 2ft 6in gauge railway could be built for the cost of one mile of standard gauge railway. Such lines could produce a satisfactory return in districts producing a fraction of the traffic required to make a standard gauge line pay.

Mr Calthrop then showed a series of views of Bársi Railway that passed over great heights, along rocky precipices and by the roadside. This line, which had a gauge of 2ft 6in, utilised existing bridges wherever possible and there had never been a single accident. He also illustrated the rolling stock, explaining that transportation trucks could be used to carry loaded standard gauge wagons weighing up to 20 tons to any station were they where required. Long timber could be accommodated by using wagons that were 25ft long over the headstocks, which, if used in multiple, could carry timber weighing up to 45 tons in lengths that were up to 75ft long.[17]

The day before the lecture was given Messrs Calthrop and Ward had travelled over the route of the proposed railway.[18] On 25th March Mr Addie announced that Mr Calthrop would assist Mr Ward in presenting the case for the railway to the Light Railway Commissioners.[19] Together they drew up the plans, sections and estimates for the proposed Welshpool and Llanfair Light Railway and provided outline specifications for the railway's rolling stock.

The draft light railway order

The draft Light Railway Order was submitted for the Committee's approval at their meeting on 17th April 1897.[20] If authorised by the Light Railway Commissioners and confirmed by the Board of Trade, the Order would give the promoters the power to make, work and maintain a narrow gauge light railway, 9 miles 1 furlong $1\frac{1}{2}$ chains in length, between Welshpool and Llanfair. The railway was to be operated by steam traction. To save costs, all roads would be crossed on the level and a swing bridge would be provided over the Shropshire Union Canal. When the canal company objected to the swing bridge, it was agreed that the line would be carried over the canal and towing path on a bridge that was at least 7ft 6in above the water level. There were only two substantial bridges in the course of the line, Brynelin viaduct at Cyfronydd and the Banwy Bridge near Heniarth Gate. Construction of the railway was to be completed within three years of the Order being confirmed.

The draft Order stated that £26,000 would be raised to build the railway, half of which was to be issued as ordinary shares with the balance being made up of loans and debentures. If required, a further £5,000 could be raised by shares, debentures or a combination of shares and debentures. Local authorities and railway companies with lines in Montgomeryshire were empowered to invest in the undertaking.

It was proposed to appoint nine Directors, although there were powers to reduce the number to a minimum of five or to increase it to a maximum of eleven. Directors had to hold a minimum of thirty £1 shares in their own right.

The draft Order listed the maximum tolls and charges for the carriage of passengers, parcels, livestock, goods and mineral traffic. Although it gave details of the charges for first, second and third class passengers, the company was not bound to provide more than one class of carriage.[21]

On 6th May 1897 the Committee approved the draft Order and decided to send their application for a Light Railway Order to the Light Railway Commissioners together with a cheque for £50 made payable to the Board of Trade.[22] The following day the plans, sections and books of reference were deposited with the Clerk of Montgomery County Council.[23]

Gathering support for the line

While the Engineers prepared their plans and gathered evidence to support the case for the railway, the promoters lobbied councils in the district through which the line passed and canvassed support for the line from private individuals.

In March 1897 Llanfyllin Rural District Council agreed to lend £1,600 to the Welshpool and Llanfair scheme on the condition that its loan was secured on the company's assets.[24] On 3rd April Welshpool Council offered to advance £8,000, half of which was to be invested in shares with the balance as a loan.[25] Montgomery County Council considered an application for funding from both schemes at its meeting on 6th April. The Welshpool and Llanfair promoters asked for £6,000 to be advanced in support of their railway. They emphasised that their route was the shorter and cheaper of the two proposals and that their town was the natural outlet for the Llanfair district. In their opinion the Meifod Valley scheme could not pay and would result in Montgomeryshire people being rated for the benefit of a Shropshire town. Responding, the Meifod Valley promoters stated that their line would be easy to construct and inexpensive to work, would open up a larger district and would receive a larger grant from the Treasury. They asked for an advance of £10,000. Although the supporters of each scheme attempted to limit the funds available to their rival, the Members of the County Council resolved to offer a quarter of the estimated capital cost to whichever scheme was approved by the Light Railway Commissioners.[26/27] On 14th July Forden Rural District Council agreed to provide a loan of £500 towards the Welshpool and Llanfair scheme because they did not wish to see the trade of Welshpool harmed.[28/29] Thus by the time that the Inquiry opened, the promoters could demonstrate that they had substantial backing from the District and County Councils.

Although the Parish Councils could not make contributions towards the proposed railway's capital, their support was canvassed to demonstrate that there was a demand for a railway in the districts that it intended to serve. Support for the rival schemes was divided, with Castle Caereinon, Llanerfyl and Llangadfan passing resolutions supporting the Welshpool scheme,[30] while Guilsfield[31] and Llanfair Caereinion preferred the Meifod Valley proposal. Later Llangadfan passed a resolution supporting the Llanfair & Meifod Valley Railway,[32] and eventually the scheme received the support of eleven Parish Councils. When a delegation of Welshpool promoters addressed Llanfair Parish Council, they were subjected to a robust examination by Dr Humphreys and all the Members present expressed their dissatisfaction with the proposal for a narrow gauge railway.[33]

On 6th May the Committee decided to write to the principal landowners in the district through which the railway had been projected, to ask on what terms they would release land required for the undertaking. Other landowners were approached by members of the Committee or were contacted by letter.[34] Following these appeals, the Earl of Powis, Captain Pryce and Mr R.C. Anwyl agreed to gift land along more than half the line to the undertaking once its draft Order had been confirmed. The land so pledged was valued at more than £2,400.[35/36] The Earl of Powis and Mr Anwyl also offered to subscribe £1,500 and £300 respectively towards the undertaking.[37] While they waited for the Light Railway Commissioner's Inquiry to be convened, the promoters drew up lists of potential subscribers to their undertaking, sought witnesses who would give evidence in support of their scheme, and instructed their Counsel.

AN INDEPENDENT ASSESSMENT OF THE RIVAL SCHEMES

When the Welshpool promoter's application for a Light Railway Order was received by the Light Railway Commission, a briefing paper was prepared comparing it with the Llanfair & Meifod Valley proposal. Although the author was not identified, it seems likely that the paper was written by a member of the Railway Inspectorate. Each scheme was considered to have its own advantages and disadvantages and while it was difficult to decide which was the better of the two, there was a slight preference for the Meifod Valley scheme.

The Welshpool and Llanfair proposal had the advantage of being more direct than the Meifod Valley scheme. The distance from Llanfair to Welshpool by this route was only 9 miles whereas the Meifod Valley scheme was 14 miles long and more than 20 miles had to be travelled to reach the markets at Welshpool and Oswestry. The cost of the Welshpool scheme was estimated to be £21,000 (excluding rolling stock), compared with £42,000 for the Meifod Valley, which was in its favour. However, it traversed six miles of rough, hilly country from which little local traffic could be expected and only passed along the Banwy valley for about three miles, whereas the Meifod Valley scheme ran for about 7 miles along the valleys of the Banwy and Vyrnwy between Llanfair and Meifod. The narrow gauge line approached Llanfair on the opposite bank to which the town stood. This was considered to be an improvement on the Meifod Valley scheme which ran up to the town and so precluded any further extension. The narrow gauge proposal required goods to be transhipped at Welshpool.

The Welshpool and Llanfair scheme had many steep gradients and sharp curves although they were quite acceptable for a narrow gauge line. About 3½ miles out of the nine were on gradients steeper than 1 in 50, one mile being as steep as 1 in 30, and there were curves of 200ft radius. The worst curves were all in the first mile where the railway ran through Welshpool, and the estimated cost allowed for the purchase of land and buildings along this mile appeared to be inadequate. The rest of the line had many curves that could have been eased with a little more expenditure on earthworks, which were very light, as the line ran on the surface in most places. The line would have to be fenced throughout and its level crossings needed to be protected by gates or cattle guards. The four level crossings in Welshpool would require gates and gatekeepers. In contrast the proposed Llanfair & Meifod Valley Light Railway would have no gradient steeper than 1 in 66, had no curve with a radius less than 600ft, was to be fenced throughout and provided with gated level crossings.[38]

THE LIGHT RAILWAY COMMISSIONERS' INQUIRY

At 3.30pm on Tuesday 3rd August 1897 the Light Railway Commissioners opened their Inquiry into the projected light railway schemes to Llanfair at the Board School in the town. The Commissioners were the Earl of Jersey, who had taken great interest in agriculture and was the chairman of the Inquiry; Mr Fitzgerald, a Parliamentary barrister; and Colonel Boughey, a military engineer who had constructed and maintained railways in India. Mr Able Thomas QC MP and Mr Ralph Banks appeared for the Welshpool and Llanfair promoters, while Mr Ellis Jones Griffith MP represented the Meifod Valley scheme's backers. Mr E. Gardner represented the Shropshire Union Railway and Canal Company.[39] Lord Jersey decided to hear evidence in support of the Llanfair & Meifod Valley scheme first because its application for a Light Railway Order had been received before that of the Welshpool and Llanfair.

The Llanfair & Meifod Valley scheme

Mr Griffith began by tracing the history of the unsuccessful attempts to bring a railway from Welshpool to Llanfair over the last quarter century and explained that Llanfair people now looked to a line that connected them with Oswestry. The proposed light railway enjoyed considerable public support within the district through which it was projected. Montgomery County Council had approved it and all the District Councils, with the exception of Forden, had passed resolutions in support of the line. Oswestry Borough Council had promised financial aid. Eleven of the twelve Parish Councils through which the proposed railway would pass also supported the scheme. The dissenting Council was Castle Caereinion, a village that was served more directly by the rival scheme. Support had also been promised by local landowners. When prompted by Lord Jersey, Mr Griffith named those who opposed the Meifod Valley scheme.

The proposed railway followed the Banwy and Vyrnwy valleys to Meifod, then continued to Arddleen where a junction with the Cambrian main line would be made. The railway was well engineered with no gradient steeper than 1 in 66. It would be constructed and worked by the Cambrian Company which would provide three trains a day in each direction between Llanfair and Oswestry. Prudent traffic estimates suggested that the railway would carry 26,000 passengers and 10,400 tons of coal and general merchandise per annum as well as a considerable quantity of livestock.

Mr J.E. Thomas C.E. described the course of the Meifod Valley line. Arddleen had been chosen as the junction with the Cambrian Railways because it was on the Welshpool road in a populous area whose inhabitants wanted a goods station. He knew the district well and thought that the railway would open it up considerably. Under cross-examination he admitted that, although he had considerable experience of building railways, he had only been the principal engineer of one and had no experience of Light Railways. When pressed, he admitted that between Arddleen and Meifod the line was practically parallel with the Llanfyllin to Llanymynech branch and did not know that Arddleen, far from being a centre of population, was only served by two trains a week.

Questioned about the population of the district to be served, Mr Thomas agreed that the population of Sarnau amounted to about 50 people while that of Meifod was about 400. Although the proposed station at Newbridge would serve the upper Vyrnwy valley, the district was sparsely populated with the nearest village, Pont Robert, having a population of only forty. Mr Able Thomas asserted that the real objective of the line was to serve the populous areas around Llanerfyl and Garthbeibio. The Engineer stated that it was hoped to extend the line through those places and onto Dinas Mawddwy. When asked if the district above Llanfair sent its produce to Welshpool, he stated that it went to Oswestry via Meifod, which produced laughter and shouts of 'No, No'. The Engineer then admitted that he had never heard of anyone taking a trap from Oswestry to Llanfair except for special reasons.

Mr C.S. Denniss, General Manager of the Cambrian Railways, gave evidence that the district through which the proposed line would run was rich in timber, pasture and corn growing land, and said that the railway would allow the dairy industry to be developed in a way that was impossible at present. He thought that traffic at Meifod would be increased if the railway was built because agriculture and general trade would be improved and new industries would develop there. The estimated cost of the line was £42,000 to be funded by Local Authority loans totalling £13,500, a Treasury loan of £10,500 and a Free Grant of £10,500, with £7,500 being raised in shares. He estimated that the railway would earn £2,765 per annum from which the Cambrian would retain sixty percent for working expenses. This would leave £1,106 to defray interest and dividend payments of £1,050 and £56 to fund all other costs. Cross-examined, Mr Denniss had to concede that his Directors had been induced to build and work the line because of the extent of Treasury funding. If loans had to be raised at commercial rates of interest, the line could not pay. He also conceded that the draft working agreement with the Cambrian did not bind that company to build the line for £42,000 but was at pains to assure the

Commissioners that his company intended to deal fairly with the Meifod Valley promoters.

Dr Humphreys, the Chairman of the Llanfair & Meifod Valley promoters, stated that meetings had been held in Llanfair, Pontrobert, Meifod, Trefnannau and Arddleen where resolutions in favour of the scheme had been passed unanimously. They had the support of Oswestry Borough Council and Llanfyllin District Council. He believed that they had deposited their scheme before the Welshpool promoters had moved in the matter. Although Llanfair was the terminus of both schemes, no meetings had been held in Llanfair in support of the Welshpool scheme and none of its promoters lived in Llanfair. Local opinion was unanimously in favour of the Meifod Valley scheme.

Mr Banks, acting for Welshpool Borough Council, dismissed Dr Humphreys' contention that Welshpool did not move in the matter of light railways until the Meifod scheme had started. In May 1896, before the Light Railway Act was passed, the Borough Council appointed a Committee to watch the movement in Llanfair. In September they put themselves in communication with the L&NW and Great Western Companies. When cross-examined, Dr Humphreys stated that cattle sold at Llanfair were usually taken through the vale of Meifod to Oswestry which caused much amusement. While he would not accept that most cattle went to Welshpool, he was forced to concede that some were taken to the town because it was nearer to Llanfair. Dr Humphreys later admitted that most goods for Llanfair came through Welshpool and that most of the Llanfair district's produce passed through the town. After a good deal of questioning he agreed he did not know anyone in Llanfair who made Oswestry their market town.

Support for the Meifod Valley scheme

Mr J.M. Jones, Mathrafal, stated that he had to cart lime from Porthywaen a distance of 13 miles. Farmers from Garthbeibio were in an even worse position as they had to cart lime for between 16 and 18 miles. The land required a great deal of lime and hauling it cost more than the lime itself. Coal and feedstuffs were collected from Llansantffraid. Livestock were driven to Oswestry or to Llansantffraid in bad weather from where they were sent on by rail. Butter was sent to Oswestry and Shrewsbury. Plans for a dairy factory at Meifod had to be abandoned because there was no railway there. When Mr Abel Thomas pointed out that his farm would be about a mile from the Welshpool and Llanfair line, Mr Jones replied that he knew the road between Meifod and Pontsychoed. The hill there was very steep and too long to take a load up it. It was an extraordinary hill! Mr Joseph Richards, Lower Hall Meifod, stated that all his produce went in the direction of Arddleen or Llansantffraid and that Welshpool was the wrong way altogether. Local people wanted to go to Oswestry. The Vicar of Meifod, the Rev J.W. Jones, said that the village was the centre of a large agricultural district that included 2,000 acres of timber which could be brought down the line. Mr Proudley, a dealer in butter, eggs and poultry, stated that his produce was sold at Oswestry which involved a round trip of

Memoranda

AS TO

PROPOSED LIGHT RAILWAY

FROM

WELSHPOOL TO LLANFAIR.

The passing of the Light Railway Act, 1896, has brought prominently before the public the question of a Railway to connect Welshpool with Llanfair, and a Committee of the Members of the Town Council were appointed to consider how such a line would affect the interests of Welshpool.

A Scheme was prepared at the request of the Committee, by Messrs. Moorsam and Ward, Civil Engineers, Manchester and Welshpool, which has been approved of by this Committee.

The considerations which have guided the Committee and Engineers in the preparation of this Scheme have been :—

1.—Cheapness of Construction—all other suggested lines for this District having proved abortive mainly in consequence of the difficulty in raising the necessary Funds.

2.—The Usefulness—of such a Railway, how to make it pay, and one that will be of advantage to the County at large.

In considering the Cheapness of Construction, "the Gauge" has occupied the attention of the Committee, and bearing in mind that this Railway has not only to deal with the Cambrian Railways, the London and North-Western and Great Western Joint Railway, and the Shropshire Union Canal Company, but must be a line suitable for a mountainous district, and in view of further extension a "Gauge" of 2ft. 6in. is suggested as being the most useful of all, mainly on the following grounds :

(a) Less weight of material required.

(b) That quicker curves and steeper gradients may be adopted to allow of securing the traffic, which at present is chiefly conducted on the Main Road.

(c) A saving in forming cuttings and embankments, and less width of land required.

Objection may be taken to Transhipment, but this can only affect a portion of the goods to be carried, and the experience on other successful lines of a similar "Gauge" has been that the cost of this work has not exceeded 3d. to 5d. per ton, and appliances are provided for transhipping large quantities at once.

Even with ordinary gauge lines, transhipment occurs with part of the goods at the junction of the Railways.

The Plans prepared by Messrs. Moorsam and Ward show the line starting from the Cambrian Railways Station at Welshpool, following the Smithfield Siding and the Lledan Brook, crossing the Canal at the "Aqueduct" by a small swing bridge, the Canal being at this point only seven feet wide, and this will enable sidings to be provided by the Canal side.

The Railway then follows the side of the Brook and the Vicarage Grounds, crossing Church Street on the level, and continuing along a New Street to be opened between Church Street and Hall Street, entailing taking in 5 old Shops now occupied by Messrs. Rowlands, Williams, Owen, Quinn, &c., &c., as well as 5 old Black and White Cottages, and the projecting Public House know as the "Seven Stars."

It is obvious that such a New Street would be of great advantage to the Town, doing away with an old and narrow Street and dangerous corners.

The Railway will then follow the Back Road to Raven Square, widening this Road, and covering the Brook where required.

The Railway then follows the side of the Llanfair Road to the Park Drive, then will go past the Black Mill, Nanty Caws, below the New Cottages at the Glyn recently erected by Lord Powis, and join the Main Road near Sylfaen Dairy Farm, after which the Line would follow the side of the Road all the way to Llanfair except at occasional points to escape steep gradients.

A Line so constructed, following the Main Road will, without doubt, save the County a considerable sum per annum in maintaining the most expensive Road in the County, the experience in Ireland, where a similar line has been so constructed, has effected a saving of 75 per cent. in the maintenance of the Road.

A careful Preliminary Estimate has been prepared by the Engineers, giving the cost of the Line at £21,000, which includes Construction, Equipment, Telephone, Engines, &c., Machinery for Transhipping, and Buildings at Welshpool and Llanfair, and with the addition of £4000 for Land and other Property, would make a total of £25,000 to complete the Line ready for working.

Another Line is being promoted from Llanfair through Meifod, joining the Cambrian Railway at the Arddleen, obviously of no advantage to Welshpool, and even for the inhabitants of Llanfair, would entail what is shown in the following table, so that a person attending the said markets would have to travel 226 miles on the Llanfair-Meifod Railway, and only 166 miles on the Welshpool and Llanfair Railway.

	Llanfair & Welshpool Railway.	Llanfair & Meifod Railway.
Length to construct ...	9 Miles	14 Miles
Llanfair to Welshpool ...	9 "	20¼ "
" Oswestry ...	24 "	22⅞ "
" Newtown ...	22 "	33¾ "
" Shrewsbury via Buttington	28 "	37 "

A moderate estimate of the income derivable from such a Line, based upon previous experience should at least provide £6 per week per mile giving a total per annum of ...   £2,808

Deduct working expenses at £4 per mile per week ...   £1,872

Showing a Balance of ...   £936

or equal to about 4 per cent. on the capital. With such a result the Local Authorities interested need fear no risk in providing money for the construction of such a Railway.

The memorandum proposing the Welshpool and Llanfair Light Railway. Source: Rail 722 1

36 miles by road. Cross-examined, he stated that he could not sell his butter at Welshpool. Asked if it was bad butter, he replied that it was good enough for Oswestry.

Mr John Jehu, a Llanfair miller and corn merchant, said he received 500 tons a year from Welshpool for which he paid 6s per ton hauled. The Meifod Valley line would serve the area up to Garthbeibio. Most farmers of the district sold their poultry to hucksters who took it to Oswestry. He did not know any hucksters that went to Welshpool, although local farmers went there. Under cross-examination, he agreed that the trade of Llanfair came through Welshpool although it was not *with* Welshpool, and that the wealth of the Llanfair district came mainly from Llanerfyl and Garthbeibio. Llanfair shop-keepers, for their own reasons, did not want a direct con-nection with Welshpool.

Mr Whitfield, an auctioneer from Oswestry, gave evidence that cattle from the lower Meifod valley formed a large pro-portion of the stock sold at Oswestry and had to be driven along roads to Llansantffraid. When challenged he gave the names of several customers from the Meifod and Newbridge districts, but admitted that only about one eighth of the stock sold by his firm came from the area. He also stated that he was not aware of Llanfair cattle being consigned from Welshpool. When cross-examined by Mr Banks, he agreed that his firm obtained stock from Welshpool, Montgomery and other stations down the line to Aberystwyth, and that on the previous Wednesday between twenty and thirty truck loads of cattle were sent from Welshpool to Oswestry.

Mr Thomas Edwards, Mayor of Oswestry, stated that the Borough Council had agreed to advance £2,500 in support of the scheme and that Oswestry people would take up one thousand £1 shares. He knew the district between Arddleen and Oswestry and that people living there sent their produce to Oswestry. He believed that stock worth about £50,000 per annum came from the district served by the proposed railway. Cross-examined, he agreed that his Council's objective in supporting the Meifod Valley scheme was to secure part of this trade to its market. He believed that Oswestry was the natural outlet for Llanfair.

Opposition by landowners ...
The Meifod Valley scheme was opposed by three large land-owners. Mr E. Gandy for the trustees of the Hayhurst-France estate stated that both the owners and tenants opposed the scheme. They were served by the railway at Llanstantffraid from where there was a good County Council road to Meifod. Several tenant farmers carted their produce to Welshpool market. In his opinion the railway ran on the wrong side of the Vyrnwy valley which was sparsely populated below Meifod so the line could not pay. The estate would have to be compelled to sell the land required for the railway and would demand payment for the severance of its land. Captain Mytton also opposed the scheme because it severed his estate. The line cut through thirty-eight fields and he could not conceive of any change in the proposed route that would be acceptable. He was not prepared to sell his land voluntarily. Captain Mytton asserted that between Meifod and Arddleen the line would

only serve a few farms and could not possibly pay. He also objected to the level crossings near Trefnannau because they were near to the school and would be a danger to local children. Mr R.C. Anwyl opposed the line because it ran close to Eithnog Hall which belonged to his wife. The railway would sever the property from the river where there was a boathouse. A considerable acreage of timber near the line would have to be felled and the enjoyment of the property would be ruined. He also opposed the line as a taxpayer because he did not think that it was viable.

... An existing undertaking ...
Mr Gardner, representing the Shropshire Union Railway and Canal Company, stated that his client had given instructions to oppose the Meifod Valley scheme, but on the previous day its promoters had agreed to build an interchange siding at Arddleen. If the siding was provided the Shropshire Company would withdraw its opposition. However, Mr Denniss for the Cambrian Railways opposed the provision of the siding because it would divert traffic from the railway.

... and the promoters of the Welshpool and Llanfair Light Railway
Mr Able Thomas, appearing for the Welshpool and Llanfair promoters, conceded that a railway through Meifod would benefit the village. However, from the evidence presented, it was clear that although a considerable quantity of produce from the Llanfair district went to Oswestry, most of it passed through Welshpool. Traffic originating from the district between Meifod and Arddleen could not support the proposed line and Mr Thomas contended that the only way of making the line pay was to secure traffic from Llanfair and the sur-rounding districts. It was monstrous that the promoters of the Meifod Valley scheme should attempt to divert this traffic from Welshpool to a town in a different county. Furthermore, landlords had not given reasonable facilities over six of the fourteen miles of railway.

Mr Thomas' view was supported by Mr Banks who sub-mitted that the objective of light railway inquiries was to consolidate traffic and not to dislocate it. The trade of Gar-thbeibio, Llangadfan and Llanerfyl had always gone through Welshpool which was the natural outlet for Llanfair and the surrounding district. Welshpool was at the centre of a large agricultural area, and buyers attended its market from all over the country. Llanfair shopkeepers were anxious that their business should not be diverted to Welshpool and so they were attempting to divert traffic from the district to an English county. If they succeeded, dealers from Shrewsbury and the Midlands would cease to come to Welshpool and, by the time their railway failed, the damage would be done and the dealers would not return.

The Welshpool and Llanfair scheme
Evidence in support of the Welshpool and Llanfair proposal was heard on the second day of the Inquiry. Mr Able Thomas described the course of the line and then called Mr Addie, the chairman of the Welshpool promoters. Mr Addie stated

Deposit. Board of Trade

Welshpool and Llanfair Light Railway,

MONTGOMERYSHIRE.

ESTIMATE OF PROPOSED LIGHT RAILWAY.

RECEIVED 11 MAY 1897 № 4962 BOARD OF TRADE

Whether Single or Double

Line No. 1 — Single.

Length of Line—9 Miles, 1 Furlong, $1\frac{1}{2}$ Chains.

Gauge—2 feet 6 inches.

	Cubic Yards.	Price per Yard.	£ s. d.	£ s. d.
EARTHWORKS:				
Cuttings Rock	3880	3/-	582 0 0	
„ Soft Soil	37,551	1/4	2503 8 0	
„ Roads	160	2/6	20 0 0	
				3105 8 0
Embankments, including Roads, Cubic Yards 33,720				
Bridges, Public Roads			none.	
Accommodation Bridges and Works				275 0 0
Viaducts (Bridges over Canal and over River Banwy) ...				800 0 0
Culverts and Drains				614 0 0
Metallings of Roads and Level Crossings				567 0 0
Gatekeepers' Houses at Level Crossings				...
Permanent Way, including Fencing— Miles 9, Furlong. 1, Chains. 1·50, Cost per Mile. £950				8682 0 0
Permanent Way for Sidings and Cost of Junctions ...				1257 0 0
Stations				1390 0 0
				16,690 8 0
Contingencies 10 per Cent.				1669 0 0
Land and Buildings				2950 0 0
				£21,309 8 0

Calthrop & Ward

Engineers.

Source: MT6 1081 3

that he had assessed the impact of the railway on the Earl of Powis' property and the district through which it would pass. The proposed line would be of great benefit because it would tap a district of some 81,280 acres with a rateable value of £38,000 that had been in need of a railway for many years. As the Chairman of the promoters he had been guided by the following reasons:

1. Large and important fairs were held at Llanfair which was a convenient place for the disposal of the stock of the district which were mainly store cattle,
2. Welshpool was the natural outlet for the produce of the district beyond Llanfair as well as that between Welshpool and Llanfair,
3. Welshpool was served by the Cambrian, L&NW and Great Western companies and had better railway facilities than Arddleen which was served by the Cambrian alone. Thus the produce of the district served by the proposed Welshpool and Llanfair Light Railway could be placed with consumers more quickly and cheaply than by the Llanfair & Meifod Valley route via Arddleen,
4. The narrow gauge was more suited to the district, could be built at less cost to ratepayers, had a better chance of proving a financial success, and was less likely to be a financial burden to the ratepayers,
5. A standard gauge line would cost nearly twice as much as the proposed railway without any additional advantages being gained. He was advised that transhipment between the standard and narrow gauge was now an easy matter,
6. It would be possible to extend the line to Llanerfyl or Garthbeibio quite easily and relatively inexpensively. The Earl of Powis had agreed to aid the extension financially,
7. Welshpool market was used by most people living between Welshpool and Llanfair and by the Earl of Powis' tenants living between Llanfair and Garthbeibio,
8. The Earl of Powis' main tenants had been consulted and were in favour of the scheme,
9. The Earl of Powis had no antipathy to the Meifod scheme and would be glad to see it built, but as only one railway could be a financial success he had to consider which line would confer the greatest benefits to his property and to the area generally.

Under cross-examination Mr Addie agreed that when the Welshpool Corporation's Light Railways Committee was convened, an Alderman had prior knowledge of the Meifod Valley proposal. In his view, Llanfair was the centre for Garthbeibio, Llangadfan and Llanerfyl from where farmers could send their cattle forward to Welshpool. Store cattle from the Llanfair district was usually sold at Welshpool market rather than Oswestry which mainly dealt with dairy cattle. He was not aware that ninety per cent of the Earl of Powis' tenants had signed a petition in favour of the route via Meifod.

Support for the Welshpool scheme ...
Mr Richard Jones, a partner of Watkin and Jones, wool and seed merchants of Welshpool, gave evidence that agricultural produce from Garthbeibio, Llangadfan and Llanerfyl was sent to Llanfair, and the greater part of the trade from all these places went to Welshpool. The cost of carting coal and lime from Llanfair to Llangadfan was 10d a ton, while timber cost 8d per cubic foot. Similar charges were made for haulage between Welshpool and Llanfair. Under cross-examination he agreed that he occasionally sent goods for Llanfair and beyond via Llansantffraid.

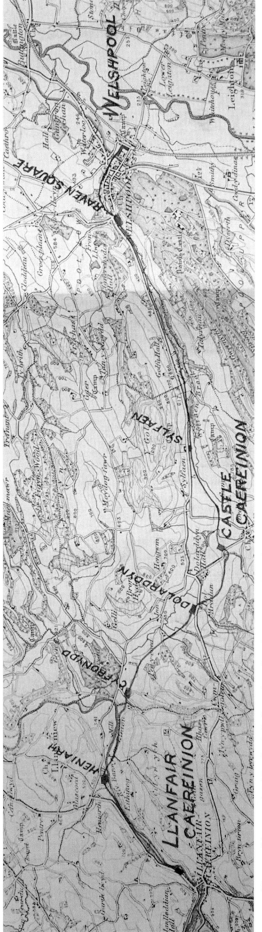

The route of the proposed Welshpool and Llanfair Light Railway that was sent to the Light Railway Commissioners with the promoters' application for a Light Railway Order. The site of Golfa stopping place is not shown but one is proposed at Dolarddyn. Source: MT58 56

Mr Edward Vaughan, Llanerfyl, and Mr Richard Owen who were tenant farmers on the Powis estate, preferred the Welshpool scheme. They sold their cattle and produce at Welshpool as did other farmers in the district, and received coal and lime via the town. Mr Edward Green, The Moors, gave evidence that traffic from Llanfair went through Welshpool. He maintained that Oswestry fairs were no better than those at Welshpool where he sold about three hundred fat cattle each year. Cattle from farms at Trefnannau in the Meifod valley were also sold at Welshpool market. Mr Green believed that the Welshpool line would be of greater benefit to agriculture than one through Meifod which he thought would not pay. A petition from thirty-nine cattle drovers in favour of the line was read, as was a letter stating that Sir Watkin Williams Wynn was in favour of it.

Mr Calthrop stated that he had not constructed any light railways in Britain but had done so in India where there was no one to watch for the safety of the public at level crossings. The method of avoiding transhipment of goods proposed for Welshpool was used successfully in India but had not been used in Great Britain. It had, however, been tested by Liverpool Corporation with great success. Mr Horace Bell, late consulting engineer to the Indian Government, supported Mr Calthrop's evidence and said that in his opinion the Welshpool line would pay. He thought that the cost of constructing the Meifod Valley line was underestimated and did not believe that it could be made to pay because there was insufficient traffic. Indeed, the goods traffic would have to be increased tenfold to make it pay. Mr J.R. Dix, Manager of the Corris Railway, asserted that the Welshpool and Llanfair scheme was more than adequate for the traffic offered by the surrounding district. He had surveyed the area and believed that Welshpool was the natural outlet for the produce of the locality. Mr Dix thought that a line to Welshpool could be made to pay, but that a standard gauge line through Meifod to Arddleen could not, because the traffic was insufficient and Arddleen was nowhere. On the Corris Railway there were no difficulties with regard to transhipment.

... and objections to it

Objections to the scheme were then heard. Mr A.C. Nicholson, an Oswestry surveyor, stated that he had examined the route through Welshpool and estimated that property valued at £6,179 6s 3d would have to be acquired. Cross-examined, he explained that he had been told that eleven properties were required and did not know that the promoters only intended to go through three. To laughter he admitted that he had never valued any property in Welshpool before.

The final submission in support of the Meifod Valley scheme

Once the evidence for the Welshpool scheme had been presented, Mr Griffith addressed the Commission in support of the Meifod Valley scheme. Turning to the agreement with the Cambrian, he suggested that the investing local authorities would not let the Cambrian take advantage of the Meifod Valley scheme as Mr Able Thomas had suggested.

Mr Griffith admitted that the scheme did not have the strong support of the landowners that the Welshpool proposal enjoyed. However, out of thirty-one landowners affected by the scheme, only nine dissented and eight assenting landowners had indicated that they would sell their land in exchange for shares in the railway. He suggested that the dissenting landlords were promoting the rival scheme. When Mr Thomas reminded him that Captain Mytton was not involved with the Welshpool scheme, Mr Griffith retorted that he was giving evidence against the Meifod Valley scheme which amounted to the same thing and that the Treasury would take that into consideration when deciding what constituted 'reasonable support'.

Mr Thomas then intervened again, alleging that the Meifod Valley promoters had no private money because they had only obtained subscriptions of £750 towards the share capital and £9,000 was required. Mr Griffiths assured the Commissioners that if his scheme was sanctioned, the promoters could guarantee that the necessary subscriptions would be found. He stated that the Welshpool scheme required £6,500 from private sources and asked his learned friend how this was to be achieved. Mr Thomas replied that Mr Addie had said that sufficient money would be subscribed to finish the line.

Mr Griffith maintained that no Llanfair traders had spoken in support of the Welshpool scheme and that Llanfair people should be allowed to determine from where they were to be connected to an existing railway. They had chosen the route via Meifod to Arddleen and it was supported by the County, District and Parish Councils. Mr Griffith invited the Light Railway Commissioners to support the public view. Lord Jersey then said that the Commissioners would reserve their decision and the Inquiry ended.[40]

On Saturday 4th September 1897 Messrs Harrison and Winnall received a letter from the Light Railways Commissioners stating that they would, in due course, submit an Order to the Board of Trade authorising the construction of the proposed Welshpool and Llanfair Light Railway. The bells of St. Mary's, Welshpool's parish church, were rung at intervals throughout the day in celebration.[41] The Oswestry Advertiser reported that as opinion at Llanfair was all but unanimously in favour of the Meifod route, it was natural that grave disappointment should be felt there. However, the disappointment would be greatly mitigated by the knowledge that a railway would at last be brought to Llanfair.[42]

Once the Light Railway Commissioners adopted the Welshpool and Llanfair Light Railway as the preferred route, the promoters found that there was much to do. The draft Light Railway Order had to be confirmed by the Board of Trade; the capital required to build and equip the line had to be raised; a working agreement with an existing railway company had to be negotiated so that state aid could be secured; detailed plans and contract specifications had to be drawn up; while a company had to be formed and its Board appointed. Only then could the land needed for the railway be acquired and a contract let to build it. Compared with the rapid advance made over the previous nine months, further progress was painfully slow and over three and a half years were to elapse before the contract to build the line was let.

LIGHT RAILWAY COMMISSIONERS BRIEFING PAPER
PROPOSED WESLSHPOOL AND LLANFAIR LIGHT RAILWAY
9 MILES – 2'6" gauge

This line starts alongside the Cambrian Railways at Welshpool. It runs through part of the town of Welshpool and then generally in a westward direction to Llanfair a distance of slightly over 9 miles. It is promoted by certain private individuals who are proposed to be incorporated for the purpose with a capital of £26,000. The County Council of Montgomery have applied for power to lend £5,000, viz one fourth of the cost of the line and the Town Council of Welshpool has applied for power to lend £4,000 and subscribe for £4,000 in shares. It is proposed to ask the Treasury for a grant of one fourth of the cost of the line.

This scheme proposes to connect Welshpool with Llanfair by a narrow gauge line about 9 miles long. It is to some extent a rival scheme to one that has been before us for the past six months but for which no public inquiry has yet been held as the Town Council of Welshpool, who are interested in the present scheme, asked us to defer consideration of the earlier one until the present one could be placed before us.

The earlier scheme proposes to connect with the Cambrian Railway by a standard gauge railway 14 miles long at a point about 6 miles north of Welshpool (or about half way between Welshpool and Oswestry). By this route Llanfair would be rather more than 20 miles from Oswestry or Welshpool. In fact Oswestry and Welshpool are rival candidates for the traffic of Llanfair by means of the two routes proposed. For the last two miles into Llanfair both routes run in parallel to each other on either bank of the small river Banwy.

Each scheme has its own special advantages and disadvantages, and it is difficult to decide which is the better of the two, though on the whole I am inclined to favour the earlier scheme. The present scheme is a much more direct one for Llanfair, being only 9 miles from Welshpool, whereas the earlier scheme makes the distance 14 miles from Llanfair to the railway at Arddleen, and more than 20 miles to the nearest large market at Oswestry or Welshpool. On the other hand the present scheme is only for a 2ft 6in gauge line with about 3½ miles out of the 9 at gradients steeper than 1 in 50, one mile being as steep as 1 in 30, and with curves of 200ft radius whereas the earlier scheme is for a standard gauge line with no gradient steeper than about 1 in 66 and no curve with a radius less than 600ft. The present scheme goes over a pass more than 200 feet higher than the earlier one, but as the earlier scheme goes down the Vyrnwy valley to a point 100ft vertically lower than the present scheme there is a difference of about 100 feet vertical lift against the present scheme and in favour of the earlier one.

The present scheme is estimated to cost about £21,000 and the earlier one about £41,000 which is in favour of the present scheme; but on the other hand the present scheme traverses six miles of rough hilly country from which little local traffic can be expected and only through about 3 miles of the valley of the Banwy at the Llanfair end, whereas the earlier scheme goes through about 7 miles along the valleys of the Banwy and Vyrnwy between Llanfair and Meifod.

As regards the engineering features of the present scheme, the gradients and curves are severe but not unduly so for a line of this small gauge. The line rises 337 feet in the first three miles from Welshpool, it is then fairly level for about a mile and a half to 4½ miles. It then falls 227 feet in the next 2¾ miles to mile 7¼ and for the last 2 miles it ascends the Banwy valley on easy gradients. The steepest gradient is 1 in 30 of which there is a continuous length of about one mile from mile 1¼ to mile 2¼ with a rise of 175 feet. About 3½ miles out of a total length of 9 miles are on gradients of 1 in 50 or steeper.

The curves are very numerous and sharp. The worst curves are four of 200ft radius, three of 264ft radius and one of 330ft. These are all in the first mile where the railway is curving through the town of Welshpool. But the rest of the line, though not so bad as this, is very much curved and there is very little straight. It seems to me that the line could be straightened out a good deal by a little more expenditure in earthwork.

The earthwork is extremely light and the line is almost everywhere on the surface. The earthwork is estimated to cost less than £350 per mile. If the cost in earthwork was increased to say £500 per mile the line might be very considerably straightened and improved, though curves of 200 feet radius need not be objected to for a line of this gauge.

The maximum speed a line of this gauge and with 200 feet curves should be no more than 15mph. There is nothing about speed in the draft Order.

The rails should not weigh less than 30lbs per yard for which a load of 6 tons might be allowed. There is nothing about this in the draft Order.

There are two bridges on the line; a swing bridge of 80ft span over the Shropshire Union Canal in Welshpool at ¼ mile from the com-

mencement of the line, and a bridge over the Banwy with three spans of 40ft at 7½ miles. There is nothing to show that these bridges have been approved by the persons in charge of the canal or river. The two bridges are estimated to cost a total of £800 for the two.

There are 9 level crossings of public roads. Four of these are in the first mile within the town of Welshpool. The line commences by running for about 100 yards along the side of the road at the back of the Cambrian Railways goods yard, it then crosses this road on a curve by a long skew crossing. It crosses Church Street at 3 furlongs then after going through some houses it runs along a street for about 100 yards. This is a very awkward point as cross streets come into the main street on both sides of the line. After leaving this point the line then goes behind some houses and through gardens for about half a mile, then at about 1 mile, it runs for about 50 yards through an open space called Raven Square where three roads come in on one side of the line and unite into one on the other side of the line, so that all are crossed by the railway. It is proposed to put a station at this point.

There are three places, viz at the commencement, 3¼ furlongs and one mile where the line runs for some little distance along the streets of the town, and at the commencement there hardly seems room, without interfering with the street, for the necessary arrangements for transhipment between this line and the Cambrian Railways. It looks as if the line should have been taken around the outskirts of the town and it certainly seems doubtful if sufficient provision has been made in the estimates for the cost of land and buildings for the mile through the town of Welshpool. The cost of land and buildings for the whole 9 miles of line is only £2,950 which seems wholly insufficient even for the first mile.

There is nothing in the draft Order about fencing or the protection of level crossings, except that Clause 35 of the draft Order provides that the speed at level crossings shall not exceed 5mph. The line will be required to be fenced throughout and the level crossings protected with gates or cattle guards. As the line seems to pass generally through enclosed fields it will be required to be fenced thoughout and the level crossings to be protected by gates or cattle guards. The four crossings in Welshpool will need to be protected by gates and gatekeepers.

Six intermediate stations are shown on the index plan.

The line crosses the Banwy at 7½ miles and approaches Llanfair on the opposite bank to which the town stands. This seems to be an improvement on the earlier scheme which runs up to Llanfair and would be difficult to extend without going right through Llanfair, whereas the present line being on the opposite side of the river could be extended without difficulty.

Clause 2 of the draft Light Railway Order incorporates certain Acts but strikes out several provisions of the Regulation of Railways Act which seem necessary to be included. For instance the law about accommodation works and fencing has been struck out and there is nothing in the draft Order to take its place.

Clauses 8 and 9 of the draft Order state that the gauge will be 2' 6" and that the motive power will be steam or any other power approved by the Board of Trade.

Clause 25 of the draft Order gives the power to any local authority, and Clause 28 to any railway, in the district to subscribe to the undertaking.

Clause 29 of the draft Order provides that the line is to be completed within 3 years.

Clause 30 prescribes the proposed rates for the carriage of goods. These vary between 3½ and 6d per ton mile. Since the rates are very high it would be better to adhere to the standard rates fixed in Tramway Provisional Orders which vary between 2d and 4d per ton mile and are considerably higher than ordinary railway rates.

Clauses 42 and 43 of the draft Order propose passenger fares of 3d, 2d, 1d per mile, but if only one class of passenger is carried the fare must not exceed 2d per mile. This seems reasonable as Clause 50 of the draft Order provides that there shall be a carriage each morning and evening at a rate of 1d per mile.

31 acres of land are required for the line at an estimated cost £2,950 or less than £100 per acre. As remarked above this seems very insufficient to pay for all the land including the land and buildings in Welshpool. The amount of land proposed to be taken seems very small. It is only about 3¾ acres per mile which gives a strip of an average width of only 27 feet which seems hardly sufficient.

The line is estimated to cost £21,309 without rolling stock or £2,300 per mile which seems reasonable except for the probable cost of land and buildings.

Source: MT58 56

[1] *Montgomeryshire Express and Radnor Times* 19th May 1896

[2] Rail 722 1 Memoranda as to proposed light railway from Welshpool to Llanfair

[3] *Montgomeryshire Express and Radnor Times* 20th October 1896

[4] *Montgomeryshire Express and Radnor Times* 6th December 1896

[5] Rail 722 1 W. Forrester Addie Letter calling a meeting of landowners 15th December 1896

[6] Rail 722 1 Promoter's minutes 21st December 1896

[7] Rail 722 1 Promoter's minutes 28th January 1897

[8] *Montgomeryshire Express and Radnor Times* 2nd February 1897

[9] Rail 722 1 Promoter's minutes 8th February 1897

[10] Rail 722 1 Promoter's minutes 25th February 1897

[11] Rail 722 1 Promoter's minutes 11th February 1897

[12] Rail 722 1 Promoter's minutes 18th February 1897

[13] Rail 722 1 Promoter's minutes 18th February 1897

[14] Rail 722 1 Promoter's minutes 25th February 1897

[15] *Montgomeryshire Express and Radnor Times* 30th March 1897

[16] Robert Gratton *The Leek and Manifold Light Railway* RCL Publications 2005 p. 342

[17] *Montgomeryshire Express and Radnor Times* 30th March 1897

[18] *Montgomeryshire Express and Radnor Times* 30th March 1897

[19] Rail 722 1 Promoter's minutes 25th March 1897

[20] Rail 722 1 Promoter's minutes 17th April 1897

[21] MT6 1081 3 Draft Light Railway Order May 1897

[22] Rail 722 1 Promoter's minutes 6th May 1897

[23] NLW Deposit plans and sections Reel 3

[24] MT 6 1081 3 Letter from Llanfyllin RDC 24th March 1897

[25] MT 6 1081 3 Welshpool Borough Council affidavit 3rd April 1897

[26] *Montgomeryshire Express and Radnor Times* 13th April 1897

[27] MT 6 1081 3 Montgomeryshire County Council affidavit 6th April 1897

[28] MT 6 1081 3 Forden RDC affidavit 14h July 1897

[29] *Montgomeryshire Express and Radnor Times* 20th July 1897

[30] *Montgomeryshire Express and Radnor Times* 13th April 1897

[31] *Montgomeryshire Express and Radnor Times* 16th March 1897

[32] *Montgomeryshire Express and Radnor Times* 26th May 1897

[33] *Montgomeryshire Express and Radnor Times* 27th April 1897

[34] Rail 722 1 Promoter's minutes 6th May 1897

[35] Rail 1057 613 Circular appealing for subscriptions totalling £2,500 24th January 1899

[36] Rail 1057 613 The Earl of Powis to HM Lords Commissioners of the Treasury 22nd April 1902

[37] *Montgomeryshire Express and Radnor Times* 8th June 1897

[38] Rail 58 56 Undated briefing paper

[39] *Montgomery and Cardigan County Times* 7th August 1897

[40] MT 58 56 *Montgomery and Cardigan County Times* 7th August 1897, *Border Counties Advertiser* 11th August 1897, *Shrewsbury Chronicle* 6th August 1897

[41] *Montgomeryshire Express and Radnor Times* 7th September 1897

[42] *The Oswestry Advertiser and Montgomeryshire Mercury* 8th September 1897

CHAPTER THREE
SLOW PROGRESS

WHEN members of the Executive Committee met on 28th September 1897 Mr Addie stated that the Light Railway Order would not be received for some time but in the interim a number of provisional arrangements could be made. The first thing to be done was to approach the railway and canal companies to see what support they were prepared to offer. Then they had to get the Engineers to settle the course of the railway so that the Solicitor could make enquiries about the terms on which the land and property required for the railway could be acquired. They could then fix the Engineers and Solicitors terms of appointment. The Committee expressed its willingness to meet the Meifod Valley promoters to see if anything could be done to gain their support.[1/2] A week later Mr Addie reported that a meeting had been held with Mr Thorne of the L&NW and GWR Joint Committee who agreed to bring the matter before his Directors, but no further progress appears to have been made.[3]

Shortly after the Commissioners approved the narrow gauge scheme, Mr Addie contacted Mr Denniss informally to see if the Cambrian Company would admit the light railway to Welshpool station and was told that if a formal approach was made to the company it would be looked upon favourably.[4] On 16th December Mr Ward sent a plan of the proposed light railway terminus at Welshpool to the Committee's Solicitor, Mr Winnall. Mr Calthrop advised that from a passenger's point of view it would be desirable for the narrow gauge line to commence from the Cambrian station, but this would allow that company to impose joint station charges which could be substantial. If the narrow gauge lines were kept to the west of the Smithfield Road and the narrow gauge terminus was established there, joint station charges would be avoided. However, if the Cambrian Company was prepared to let the light railway occupy part of its good yard for a peppercorn rent, that would be quite acceptable. Mr Calthrop also suggested that a standard gauge siding should be brought into the narrow gauge yard so that wagons from the main line could be transhipped onto narrow gauge transportation cars. If the tranship siding was in the light railway's goods yard, joint station charges would be avoided. Until the Cambrian's views on the proposals were known, no further progress could be made.[5]

On 23rd December Mr Winnall forwarded a copy of the plan to Mr Denniss and asked him to meet members of the Executive Committee at Welshpool to discuss the proposed arrangements for the use of the Cambrian station. At meetings held in January and February 1898 Mr Denniss suggested that the Llanfair Company's line should begin in Smithfield Road as originally proposed; offered to construct a platform and waiting shelter in the Cambrian goods yard for which a nominal rent would be charged; and intimated that his company would give favourable consideration to building and

working the light railway.[6/7] On 29th March the Llanfair Directors decided to investigate the terms offered by the Cambrian.[8] Three days later, a deputation consisting of Messrs Addie, Rogers and Winnall met Mr Denniss and Mr Collin, the Cambrian Railway's Chief Engineer, at Welshpool station. Mr Denniss told the deputation that he was prepared to place the following proposals before his Directors:

Construction
The Cambrian Company would build the Llanfair Railway if its Directors could secure the necessary capital. A contract to build the line would be put out to competitive tender, or offered to selected contractors, and Mr Collin would satisfy himself that the line could be built for the amount tendered.

Working the line
The exact proportion of receipts that the Cambrian would require for working the line could not be determined until the nature of the rolling stock was known but would probably not exceed 60%. The Cambrian Company would undertake to arrange through rates by all routes from Welshpool if it could persuade the other railway companies concerned to offer them.

Train services
A clause would be included in the Working Agreement that bound the Cambrian to provide reasonable facilities for the development of the line. If a dispute arose between the two companies, the Light Railway Commissioners would be asked to arbitrate on the matter.

Transhipment
The method adopted for transhipment would be agreed between the two Boards or by Mr Denniss on behalf of the Cambrian Board.[9]

While Mr Denniss' proposals were generally acceptable, the main point of contention was the proportion of gross receipts that the Cambrian proposed to retain for working the line. Although Mr Addie offered 57% of the gross receipts, the Cambrian was implacable and the smaller company was forced to accede to its wishes.[10] The Cambrian Traffic and Work's Committee endorsed Mr Denniss' proposals on 29th June 1898, adding that the percentage of gross receipts that their company retained would be reconsidered after it had worked the line for five years.[11]

The first directors are appointed

The Executive Committee continued to manage the light railway's affairs until March 1898 when the amended draft Light Railway Order was received from the Light Railway Commissioners.[12] On 19th March the Earl of Powis, Capt. A.R. Pryce, Mr Anwyl, Dr Gill and Mr Hilton became the first Directors of the Light Railway and Welshpool Borough Council was invited to appoint its nominees.[13] The Borough's first nominees were Messrs Addie, Rogers and Jones. At the first meeting of the Board the Earl of Powis was invited to become the Chairman of the company with Capt. Pryce as his Vice Chairman. The Directors expressed their thanks to Mr Addie for his energetic support as Chairman of the undertaking since its inception and he continued to be the driving force behind the light railway throughout its early years.[14]

NEGOTIATIONS WITH WHITEHALL AND THE CAMBRIAN

At the May Board the Directors decided to apply to the Treasury for a special grant under Section 5 of the Light Railway Act 1896 and to negotiate a Working Agreement with the Cambrian. Mr Winnall was instructed to apply for the Treasury Grant, while Mr Addie and the Solicitor were asked to conduct the negotiations with the Cambrian.[15]

The Treasury grant

For an award to be made under Section 5 of the Light Railways Act 1896 the following conditions had to be satisfied:

1. The line had to be constructed, maintained and worked by an existing railway company,
2. Financial support was required from the local authorities, landowners and other interested parties in the district through which the line would run,
3. The Board of Agriculture had to certify that the line would be beneficial to agriculture in the district that it served.

In June 1898 the Cambrian agreed to work the line, while support from the local authorities had been secured as part of the preparations for the Light Railway Commissioner's Inquiry. A certificate confirming that the railway would benefit agriculture in the district that it served and could not be constructed without special assistance from the state was issued by the Board of Agriculture on 26th August.[16]

The Treasury Committee appointed to consider applications for special advances under Section 5 of the Light Railway Act examined the Llanfair Railway's case on 3rd December. At this time the cost of building the line was estimated to be between £27,000 and £28,000.[17] The Committee recommended that a grant of £7,000 should be awarded in aid of the line on the understanding that the promoters would acquire the necessary land and buildings for no more than £3,000 and would raise £21,000 from the local authorities and private individuals. An undertaking that the Cambrian Railways would work the line for 99 years was also required. The grant would be payable once the Board of Trade issued a certificate stating that the railway was open for traffic and that a sum of £14,000, exclusive of the value of the land gifted by the landowners, had been spent on the line.[18] On 20th December 1898 Mr Winnall received a letter from the Board of Trade confirming that the application had been successful.[19]

The working agreement

Although the Cambrian had agreed to work the Llanfair Railway, a working agreement setting out the terms for its construction, maintenance and operation had to be drafted and then agreed by the two companies. In July 1898 Mr Winnall asked Mr Denniss to prepare the draft heads of agreement and by August it was in the hands of the light railway's Solicitor.[20/21] The draft working agreement included a clause stating that if the working expenses exceeded 60% of the gross receipts, the light railway would compensate the Cambrian for its loss. Mr Winnall insisted that it had always been the promoters' understanding that 60% was the maximum proportion of the receipts that was payable to the Cambrian and asked for the offending clause to be redrafted.[22] On 19th August Mr Denniss assented to his request.[23]

In October the Llanfair Directors asked Alfred Aslett, the General Manager of the Furness Railway, to advise them on the draft working agreement. Mr Aslett, once the Cambrian Railways' Secretary and General Manager, wrote to Mr Denniss to ask for his Director's consent to the proposed arrangement and it was given.[24] Following consultation with Mr Aslett, the draft working agreement was revised and on 9th December it was sent to Mr Dennis for his approval. When Mr Collin examined the working agreement, he found the Llanfair Company had inserted a clause that required his company to pay the Contractor's monthly certificates but would not be reimbursed by the light railway until the line had been completed. Another clause required the Cambrian to compensate the Llanfair Company if building work continued after the agreed completion date. The Engineer recommended that both clauses should be revised or struck out.[25] Although Messrs Addie and Winnall made repeated attempts to meet Mr Denniss to discuss the draft working agreement before 10th January 1899, when the Llanfair Railway Directors were due to meet, they were unable to do so.[26]

When the Directors met on 10th January 1899 they must have felt that their railway would soon become a reality. Treasury and local authority funding amounting to £19,100 had been promised, pledges to take up 8,400 £1 Ordinary shares had been received,[27] and a provisional Light Railway Order had been issued by the Light Railway Commissioners. The Board decided to raise £10,000 by the issue of shares, so they called a public meeting and sent a circular to all persons likely to assist the railway, inviting them to invest in the line. Mr Addie was asked to approach Messrs Collin and Calthrop to understand the terms on which they would be prepared to act as the light railway's Engineer and Consulting Engineer respectively.[28] Two days later Messrs Addie, Winnall, Denniss and Collin met at Barnstaple where an inspection of the Lynton and Barnstaple Railway had been arranged for the following day.[29] During the visit to Barnstaple the amendments to the working agreement were discussed and in the following weeks progress was made to resolve the points of disagreement between the two companies.

In April the Board of Trade inserted a clause into the Light Railway Order that gave its officials the power to reduce the rates charged for the carriage of goods and minerals once the railway had been open for five years.[30] Fearing that this might reduce the revenue received by the Cambrian to a sum less than the cost of working the line, Mr Parry-Jones the company's Solicitor, inserted a clause into the working agreement

Lynton and Barnstaple Railway.

MANAGER'S OFFICE.

Pilton Bridge,

Barnstaple, Jan.y 5 1899

Dear Sir

I beg to acknowledge receipt of yours of the 4th instant re inspection of this line and have much pleasure in offering to do all that I can to enable you to obtain any information you desire.

As you remark I have little engine power to spare but I can arrange as follows:— leave Barnstaple by the 10·0 am train for Lynton arriving there at 11·32. See Lynton station and Terminus and leave there by train at 12·8 arriving Blackmoor station at 12·43., Then by trolley down the grade stopping as often as you like and at each station arriving at Chelfham at 2·0 to 2·30 pm. I will have an engine & coach there to bring us in by about 3·40 or earlier.

If this will suit you I shall have pleasure in accompanying your party, & by this method you will miss only one station namely Wooda Bay which is an exact copy of Blackmoor

Yours faithfully

Frank Chanter

C. S. Denniss Esq
Huntley. Bishops Teignton.

P.S. If not I will try & arrange a special

Welshpool and Llanfair Light Railway Company.

Incorporated by the Welshpool and Llanfair Light Railway Order, 1899.

Directors:

The Right Hon. The Earl of Powis, Chairman.
Capt. A. R. Pryce, Cyfronydd, Welshpool, Deputy Chairman.
R. C. Anwyl, Esq., Eithnog, Llanfair, and Llugwy, Machynlleth.
J. C. Hilton, Esq., Glynhiraeth, Llanfair.
W. Forrester Addie, Esq., Powis Castle Estate Office, Welshpool.   } Nominated by
David Jones, Esq., Mayor of Welshpool.   } the Welshpool
W. A. Rogers. Esq., Broad Street, Welshpool.   } Corporation.

CAPITAL:

10,000 Shares of £1 each - - £10,000

In addition to the above Capital, the Treasury have made a Free Grant of £7,000, and the County Council and other Authorities have agreed to advance £12,100.

Issue of Share Capital at Par.

Payable 2s. 6d. per Share on application, 2s. 6d. per Share on allotment, and by further calls of not exceeding 5s. per Share at intervals of not less than three months with the option of payment in full on allotment.

Form of Application

To be filled up and signed by the person in whose name the Shares are to be allotted.

To the Directors of
THE WELSHPOOL AND LLANFAIR LIGHT RAILWAY COMPANY.

GENTLEMEN,

I request you to allot me _____ Shares of £1 each in the above-named Company, upon which I have paid to your Bankers the sum of _____ being the required Deposit of 2s. 6d. per Share, and I hereby agree to accept the same, or any smaller number that may be allotted to me, and I authorize you to register me as the holder of the Shares so allotted to me, and engage to pay the further instalments when due.

Usual Signature _____

Name (in full) _____

Address _____

Occupation or Description _____

Date _____ 1899.

The Welshpool and Llanfair Light Railway Company.

RECEIPT FOR DEPOSIT.

Received this _____ day of _____ 1899.

on account of The Welshpool and Llanfair Light Railway Company, the sum of _____ being a deposit of 2s. 6d. per share on _____ shares in the above-named Company.

For LLOYDS BANK, LTD.
For NORTH AND SOUTH WALES BANK LTD.

£ : :   [STAMP.]

This Form should be sent ENTIRE when filled up to Lloyds Bank. Welshpool, or to the North and South Wales Bank, Welshpool or Llanfair with the amount of the Deposit, not later than 19th DECEMBER, 1899.

WELSHPOOL,
24th January, 1899.

Welshpool and Llanfair Railway.

Dear Sir,

As you are probably aware, the Light Railway Commissioners have authorized the construction of a Light Railway from Welshpool to Llanfair.

The total sum required for carrying out the undertaking is £30,000 which it is proposed should be provided as follows:—

FREE GRANT from the Treasury		£7,000
LOANS from Local Authorities—		
Montgomery County Council	£6,000	
Welshpool Corporation	4,000	
Llanfyllin Rural District Council	1,600	
Forden Rural District Council	500	
		12,100
SHARES. 10,900 Shares of £1 each		10,900
	TOTAL	£30,000

Towards the Share Capital of £10,900 the following sums have already been promised:—

Welshpool Corporation	£4,000
The Earl of Powis	1,500
Sir Watkin Williams-Wynn, Bart	500
Captain Pryce	500
H. R. E. Harrison, Esq.	500
J. C. Hilton, Esq.	400
R. C. Anwyl, Esq.	300
J. M. Howell, Esq.	200
W. A. Rogers, Esq.	100
J. Jehu, Esq.	100
Other smaller Subscriptions	300
	£8,400

leaving the sum of £2,500 still to be obtained.

The Earl of Powis, Capt. A. R. Pryce, and Mr. R. C. Anwyl have in addition to the Subscriptions mentioned above intimated their intention of making a **Free Gift of their Land**, which represents rather more than one half the total length of the line.

Terms are being arranged with the Cambrian Railways Company for that Company to construct the Line and to work it for 60 per cent. of the gross receipts.

From a careful estimate of the traffic that can be reasonably looked for, and having regard to the **Gift from the Treasury**, a net revenue is confidently anticipated sufficient, after providing the interest on the contributions by Local Authorities to pay substantial dividends upon the share capital. It will thus be seen that the position is extremely favorable to the success of the undertaking.

The Treasury Free Grant of £7,000 is conditional upon the sum of £2,500 being subscribed, and we feel that it is unnecessary for us to point out the extreme importance of raising this small amount at once by local effort, in order to secure the substantial contribution in question, and we therefore confidently appeal to you for your assistance in making up the share capital that still remains to be subscribed.

We shall be obliged if you will let us hear from you at your earliest convenience, and if you will address your reply to Messrs. Harrison and Winnall, Solicitors, Welshpool, who will be pleased to furnish any information with regard to the undertaking.

We are, Dear Sir,
Yours truly,

POWIS,
Chairman;

A. R. PRYCE,
Deputy Chairman.

Source: Rail 1057 613

that allowed his company to recover any losses, caused by the enforced reduction in rates, from the Llanfair Company.[31] By the end of September the only unresolved issue concerned the renewal of rolling stock which the Cambrian eventually agreed to fund.[32] On 14th December the Cambrian's Traffic and Works Committee gave instructions that the working agreement should be sealed, and the Llanfair Company followed suit in on 1st March 1900.[33/34]

The Light Railway Order

The draft Light Railway Order received from the Light Railway Commission in March 1898 was a far more substantial document than the one prepared for the Public Inquiry, primarily because it included many clauses for the protection of the canal company, road authorities and various utilities.[35] Before construction of the railway could begin, the provisions in the Order had to be agreed by the owning and working companies, and any amendments had to be approved by the Light Railway Commissioners. The Order would then be forwarded to the Board of Trade for confirmation.

At the end of May 1898 a copy of the draft Order was sent to Mr Dennis who forwarded it to Mr Collin and Mr Corfield, the Cambrian Solicitor, for review and comment.[36] Mr Collin recommended that the width of the Banwy bridge should be increased to 14 feet so that the Cambrian's goods wagons could be carried over the line on transportation wagons. The Engineer also suggested that the proposed canal siding should be maintained by the Shropshire Union Company over whose land it passed, and not by the light railway. In his view the clause giving the canal company reasonable accommodation for the interchange of traffic needed to be clarified.[37] Mr Corfield advised Mr Denniss that there was nothing in the draft Order that was prejudicial to his company's interests.[38] The draft Order was returned to Mr Winnall on 5th July with a request that a copy should be made for Mr Denniss' personal use.[39]

On 9th January 1899 Mr Winnall sent Mr Denniss a copy of the provisional Order issued by the Light Railway Commission and asked him to review the document with Mr Collin. The Commissioners were willing to consider representations to amend the Order received by 21st January. Mr Collin's only issue was that a level crossing in Welshpool had to be protected by gates that closed across the road and the railway. Since they would be difficult to fix, he had arranged to meet Mr Winnall to discuss the matter.[40] It seems probable that Mr Parry-Jones, the Cambrian's newly appointed solicitor, reviewed the Light Railway Order at about the same time and drew Mr Denniss' attention to the clauses that permitted the Shropshire Union Company to interchange traffic with the Llanfair Railway at Welshpool.[41] Mr Denniss then contacted Mr Winnall and gave his reasons for objecting to the clauses. He was told that they had been inserted into the Order to remove the Shropshire Company's opposition to the light railway and could not be revoked.[42] When Mr Winnall met Mr Parry-Jones in March, he asserted that if the Cambrian objected to the Shropshire Union clauses the Llanfair Railway

scheme would almost certainly fail.[43] However, Mr Denniss insisted that the matter would have to be considered by the Cambrian Directors at their next meeting.[44]

When the difficulty with the Shropshire Union clauses was reported to the Traffic and Works Committee on 10th April, Mr Denniss declared that he had not been aware of the Shropshire Union clauses until January when he had immediately informed the Llanfair Company's Solicitor that they were detrimental to his company's interests. The tapping of the light railway by the canal was made less serious because the proposed connection was to be made at Welshpool. Traffic arising on the Llanfair Railway would thus be carried along its entire length before it could get onto the canal but the Cambrian would suffer to some extent.[45] Having considered the matter, the Directors decided to have nothing further to do with the Llanfair Railway until the offending clauses had been revoked and their decision was conveyed to Mr Winnall.[46]

On 2nd May Messrs Addie and Winnall met Messrs Denniss and Parry-Jones to enquire whether the Cambrian Directors could be persuaded to change their minds. After Mr Denniss explained the reasons for his company's objections to the Shropshire Union clauses, he said that his Directors' decision was final. However, his company was prepared to explain its position to the Board of Trade and would assist the Llanfair Company in persuading the Board's officials to strike out the offending clauses. If this was done, his company would be prepared to build and work the light railway.[47] The Llanfair Board met two days later and decided to ask the Shropshire Union Railways and Canal Company to build and work their railway but the Shropshire Company would not entertain the proposal. On 2nd June Mr Winnall wrote to Mr Parry-Jones setting out the Llanfair Railway's position and asking if the Cambrian Directors would receive a deputation from the Llanfair Board. He reminded Mr Parry-Jones that if his company was seen to cause the Llanfair scheme to fail, it would be very damaging to the Cambrian's interests in the districts that the line intended to serve.[48] When the Earl of Powis, Capt. A.R. Pryce and Mr Addie met members of Traffic and Works Committee at Welshpool on 1st July 1899, they were informed that the Cambrian Directors would not reconsider their decision.[49]

The Cambrian's objection was referred to the Board of Trade who forwarded it to the Light Railway Commission on 15th June.[50] The representatives of the Llanfair, Cambrian and Shropshire Companies were summoned to a meeting of the Commissioners on 11th July to explain their respective positions.[51] On the 19th the Commissioners ruled that, since the traffic interchanged between the canal and light railway could not possibly be of a serious character, the clauses should be deleted from the Light Railway Order which was then returned to the Board of Trade.[52]

Once the provisional order had been received, the Board's officials gave the Shropshire Company the opportunity to challenge the Light Railway Commissioner's proposal. In the interim Mr Denniss advised Francis Hopwood, Assistant

Secretary of the Railway Department at the Board of Trade, that if the clauses remained, his company would not be prepared to work the light railway and the scheme would fail.[53] Shortly afterwards Mr Denniss wrote to Mr Hopwood stating that he had learnt that the Shropshire Company did not intend to oppose the deletion of the clauses.[54] On 17th August Mr Hopwood replied that nothing had been heard from the Shropshire Company and shortly afterwards the clauses were struck out.[55]

In April 1899 the Board of Trade began their appraisal of the Light Railway Order. Lt. Col. Yorke of the Railway Inspectorate recommended that the maximum speed permitted should be reduced to 20 miles an hour, because of the narrow gauge, and that the speed should be reduced from 15 to 10 miles an hour on all curves of less than five chains radius. The Order proposed that rails weighing 35lbs per yard should be used, but Col. Yorke thought that they would be too light.[56] He recommended that rails weighing not less than 41¼lbs per yard should be used because this was the standard fixed by the War Office for military railways of two feet six inches gauge and by the Indian Government for similar lines.[57] The Inspector's recommendations were conveyed to the Llanfair Railway's Parliamentary Agent on 15th April.[58] The Board's conditions were eventually accepted by the Cambrian and Llanfair Companies and the Light Railway Order was amended accordingly.[59] At the end of August, copies of the local authority resolutions pledging financial support to the light railway were sent to the Board and on 8th September 1899 it confirmed the Welshpool and Llanfair Light Railway Order.[60/61]

PREPARATIONS TO LET A CONTRACT TO BUILD THE LINE
New plans and estimates
When the Llanfair Directors met on 30th September 1899 they learned that Mr Collin was willing to become the com-

Welshpool and Llanfair Light Railway.

RECEIVED 3 0 NOV. 1900 No. 14475

AMENDED ESTIMATE OF THE PROPOSED LIGHT RAILWAY

RAILWAY No. 1.
Length of Line. Miles. F. Chs. 9 1 1·50 SINGLE LINE.

	Cubic Yards.	Price per Yard. s. d.	£ s. d.	£ s. d.
EARTHWORKS—				
Cuttings—Rock	3,000	3 6	525 0 0	
„ Soft-Soil	61,000	1 4	4,066 13 0	
Roads				
TOTAL			4,591 13 0	4,591 13 0
Embankments, including Roads	Cubic Yards			
Bridges, Public Roads	Number			
Accommodation Bridges and Works				3,973 11 0
Viaducts and Bridges				1,899 12 6
Tunnel				
Culverts and Drains				1,350 6 0
Metallings of Roads and Level Crossings				600 0 0
Gatekeepers' Houses at Level Crossings				
Permanent Way, including Fencing, and heavy Permanent Way through Streets				
	Miles F. Chs. 9 1 1·50 at	Cost per Mile. £ s. d.		10,926 10 0
Permanent Way for Sidings and Cost of Junctions				1,500 0 0
Stations				2,000 0 0
				£26,841 6 6
Contingencies	10 per Cent.			2,688 13 6
				£29,530 0 0
Land and Buildings	A. R. P.			2,950 0 0
				£32,480 0 0

(Signed),
A. J. COLLIN,
ENGINEER.

Source: MT6 1084 4

ESTIMATED COST OF CONSTRUCTION NOVEMBER 1900		
	£	£
Engineers Estimate including land		32,480
Add: Rolling stock		8,100
Engineers fees	1,624	
Legal and other expenses	1,000	2,624
Total estimated cost		£43,204

Source: Rail 722 2

pany's Chief Engineer if suitable terms could be agreed.[62] Subsequently his remuneration was set at $5\frac{10}{2}$% of the cost of the work and he was instructed to prepare a detailed survey of the course of the line. Mr Collin asked for a payment of £500 if the railway was abandoned after he had prepared the plans but was asked to reconsider his fee. Messrs Addie and Rogers were instructed to negotiate a suitable settlement with the Engineer.[63]

In March 1900 a Works Committee consisting of the Chairman, Vice Chairman and Messrs Addie, Jones and Rogers was appointed to confer with the Engineer and deal with any matters arising as the plans were prepared.[64] When Mr Collin met the Committee on 4th May to report progress with his survey, he was instructed to prepare plans of the line near Seven Stars showing the properties required to secure the best route and to send a copy to the Town Clerk of Welshpool.[65] The Engineer was also asked to draw plans showing the land required from the Rev. Pughe and to negotiate a price for it, but the clergyman refused to treat with the company and a route that avoided his land could not be found.[66/67] When the Llanfair Board threatened to take steps to remove the protection provided by the 1899 Order, Mr Pughe agreed to negotiate and his land was conveyed to the railway in August 1901.[68/69/70]

On 1st October 1900 Mr Collin presented a revised estimate of the cost of building the line to the Directors. This showed that the cost of construction exclusive of rolling stock, legal expenses and his fee had risen from £21,309 to £32,480, the principal increases being in the cost of the earthworks, bridges and permanent way.[71] Mr Herbert Jones, the Cambrian Railway's Locomotive Superintendent, advised the Directors that rolling stock costing £8,100[72] was required to work the line, while legal expenses and the Engineer's fees were estimated to be £2,624, bringing the total cost of constructing and equipping the line to £43,204.[73] From these estimates it was clear that the company required considerably more capital than the £29,100 that had been secured.[74]

Raising more capital

Recognising that the district through which the proposed railway would run was not affluent, the Directors decided to apply to the Treasury for additional state aid,[75] and to ask the Light Railway Commissioners to sanction an increase in the authorised capital of the undertaking.[76] On 5th November 1900 the Earl of Powis wrote to the Lords Commissioners of the Treasury appealing for further grant aid, attributing the increases disclosed by the new estimate to exceptional rises in the price of labour and materials.[77] The appeal was successful and on 11th December Treasury officials confirmed that the Free Grant would be increased by £7,500 and that it was offered on the same terms as the previous award.[78]

When the Board met on 27th November it approved a draft Amendment Order that proposed to increase the ordinary share capital by £8,000, the Treasury Grant by £7,500 and contributions from the local authorities by £3,250. The draft Order gave the company powers to borrow £3,000 and

---

THE EARL OF POWIS' APPLICATION TO INCREASE STATE AID TO THE RAILWAY 1900

WELSHPOOL & LLANFAIR LIGHT RAILWAY COMPANY

WELSHPOOL

5th November 1900

My Lords

As Chairman of the Welshpool and Llanfair Light Railway Company I have the honour to submit the following facts for your consideration.

The Company was incorporated by the Welshpool & Llanfair Light Railway Order 1899 with a capital of £6,000 in addition to any shares that might be subscribed for by the County Council or by the Welshpool Corporation. The Order also authorised various local authorities to contribute sums amounting to £16,100 and your Lordships have agreed to aid the line by a free grant of £7,000.

The whole of the Share Capital has been subscribed and agreements, under seal, have been entered into with the various local authorities for securing their contribution authorised by the Order. The amount available for capital expenditure is therefore as follows: -

	£	£
Shares subscribed for by Landowners and others	6,000	
Shares subscribed for by Welshpool Corporation	4,000	
		10,000
Advances by Local Authorities by way of loan: -		
Montgomery County Council	6,000	
Welshpool Corporation	4,000	
Llanfyllin Rural District Council	1,600	
Forden Rural District Council	500	12,100
Free Grant		7,000
Total		£29,100

The Engineers of the Cambrian Company, who have undertaken to construct and work the Light Railway, have completed their detailed plans, sections, specifications and quantities for construction and now report that, owing to the exceptional increase in the price of labour and materials since the original estimates were formed, it will be quite impossible to construct and equip the line for the sum upon which the original calculations were based.

It is now estimated that at least an additional £10,000 must be provided to ensure the completion of the Railway.

Owing to the exceptional circumstances of the District, which have already been brought before your Lordships, the Directors feel that they have practically exhausted the whole of the support that can be reasonably expected from the locality and think that it will be impossible for them to carry the scheme into effect unless your Lordships can see your way to supplement the Grant in aid of the line which has been already promised.

Under the circumstances I am requested by the Directors to bring the matter before your notice as a matter of extreme urgency to the locality in the hope that you might favourably consider the position.

I am also requested to enquire whether your Lordships would be pleased to receive a deputation from the Directors who would be happy to attend for the purpose of laying the whole of the facts before you.

I have the honour to be

Your obedient Servant

POWIS

The Lords Commissioners
Her Majesty's Treasury

Source: Rail 1057 613

Welshpool and Llanfair Light Railway Company.

Incorporated by the Welshpool and Llanfair Light Railway Order, 1899.

CAPITAL:

10,000 Shares of £1 each (already Subscribed)	£10,000
5,000 do. (Present Issue)	5,000
	£15,000

With a Free Grant from the Treasury of £14,500, and advances by the Montgomery County Council and other Local Authorities, to be secured by Debentures, amounting to £15,360.

ISSUE OF £5,000 SHARE CAPITAL AT PAR.

Payable 2s. 6d. per Share on application, 2s. 6d. per Share on allotment, and by further calls of not exceeding 5s. per Share at intervals of not less than three months, with the option of payment in full on allotment.

Directors:

THE RIGHT HON. THE EARL OF POWIS, CHAIRMAN.
Capt. A. R. PRYCE, D.L., Cyfronydd, Welshpool, DEPUTY CHAIRMAN.
R. C. ANWYL, Esq., D.L., Llugwy, Machynlleth.
J. C. HILTON, Esq., Glynhiriaeth, Llanfair.
W. FORRESTER ADDIE, Esq., Powis Castle Estate Office, Welshpool.
DAVID JONES, Esq., High Street, Welshpool,
W. A. ROGERS, Esq., Broad Street, Welshpool

} For the Welshpool Corporation.

Bankers:

LLOYDS BANK, Limited, Welshpool Branch; and the NORTH & SOUTH WALES BANK, Welshpool and Llanfair Branches.

Solicitors:

Messrs. HARRISON & WINNALL, Welshpool.

Engineer:

Mr. A. J. COLLIN, C.E., Oswestry, Engineer to the Cambrian Railways Company.

Secretary:

Mr. JOHN EVANS, Broad Street, Welshpool.

Prospectus.

Object of the Company. The Company was incorporated by the Welshpool and Llanfair Light Railway Order, 1899, for the purpose of constructing and working a Light Railway from Welshpool to Llanfair. The length of the line is about nine miles and it will connect at Welshpool Station with the Railways of the Cambrian and North-Western Companies.

Gauge. The gauge will be 2 feet 6 inches. By the adoption of the narrow gauge the cost of heavy bridges, cuttings, and embankments, which a line of standard gauge would entail, is avoided, and a further saving in the initial cost will be effected by crossing all roads on the level.

Free Grant. The Directors have succeeded in obtaining a **Free Grant of £14,500** out of the fund set aside by the Treasury to aid Light Railways. This very substantial contribution towards the Capital is an absolutely free gift, and is equivalent to upwards of one third of the estimated cost of the line, and places the Company in the exceptionally fortunate position of having to earn a return on only two-thirds of the sum expended in construction.

Gifts of Land. The Company has been further substantially aided by gifts of land from several of the principal landowners, and the **land for more than half the length of the line** is thus obtained **without cost.**

Local Authorities. The Montgomery County Council, the Welshpool Corporation, and the Llanfyllin and Forden Rural District Councils have agreed to aid the Company by advances under the Light Railways Act at such rate of interest as they may themselves borrow on the security of their Rates, and the Welshpool Corporation in addition subscribe £4,000 to the Share Capital.

Working Agreement. The Company have entered into an agreement with the Cambrian Railways Company for the construction and working of the line, under which the Cambrian Company undertake to work and maintain the Railway for a term of 99 years for 60 per cent. of the gross receipts.

Net Revenue Receipts. **A net revenue is therefore assured** of 40 per cent. of the gross receipts, and a very moderate traffic only will suffice to secure a substantial return upon the small Capital of the Company.

Estimate of Traffic. The General Manager of the Cambrian Railways Company has furnished the following estimate:—

> The Cambrian Railways Company,
> Secretary and General Manager's Office,
> Oswestry, February 19th, 1901.
>
> Dear Sir,
>
> WELSHPOOL AND LLANFAIR LIGHT RAILWAY.
>
> I have pleasure in informing you that having looked carefully into the matter of the probable traffic which might be reasonably expected to arise on this Railway, I have drawn up the following estimate:—

Coal and other Minerals	...		£500
Grain, Manure, and other Goods	...		1,505
Passengers, 25,000 at 1/-	...	...	1,250
Parcels and Luggage	...	...	150
			£3,405

This is equivalent to a gross revenue of £65 9s. 7d. per week, or £7 3s. 2d. per mile of Railway per week.

Of this total of £3,405, £2,043 would be required to pay the working expenses, leaving a balance of £1,362 net revenue. As I understand only £1,252 is required to pay fixed Charges and give 4 per cent. on the Ordinary Shares, a very fair margin is left for contingencies, and from the experience of traffic on the Cambrian and other railways, and having regard to the population and other conditions in the district through which the railway will pass, I think you will be justified in anticipating that the estimate which I have made is not by any means excessive.

> Yours truly,
> C. S. DENNISS.

Reasons for Delay. The whole of the original issue of Share Capital was subscribed, but owing to the high prices that have recently prevailed for labour and all classes of material, the Directors were obliged to delay the work of construction.

Tender accepted. On the recommendation of the Light Railway Directors the Cambrian Company have now let the contract for construction to the well-known contractor, Mr Strachan of Cardiff, who has already commenced operations. The additional Capital now issued is required to complete the equipment of the line, and such additional Capital will rank equally with that already subscribed.

No Preliminary Expenses. The preliminary expenses connected with the promotion of the undertaking up to the date of the Local Inquiry held by the Light Railway Commissioners have been paid by the Welshpool Corporation.

Agreements. In addition to the before mentioned agreement with the Cambrian Railways Company, agreements have been entered into with the Local Authorities for securing the amount of their contributions, and with Landowners for the purchase of land, and applicants for shares shall be deemed to have notice of these agreements.

Application for Shares should be made on the form enclosed with the Prospectus and sent with a remittance for the amount payable on application to the Bankers of the Company. In case no allotment is made to any applicant, the deposit will be returned in full.

Prospectuses and Forms of Application for Shares can be obtained from the Company's Secretary, Bankers, or Solicitors.

Copies of the Order of the Light Railway Commissioners can be seen at the Office of the Solicitors to the Company.

WELSHPOOL,
MAY, 1901.

WELSHPOOL AND LLANFAIR LIGHT RAILWAY CO.

Prospectus.

Issue of £5,000 Share Capital at par.

Source: Rail 1057 613

allowed the Cambrian to subscribe up to £1,000 in the undertaking even though Mr Denniss had made it clear that his company would not invest in the line.[79/80/81/82] Mr Winnall was instructed to lodge an application to increase the company's capital with the Light Railway Commissioners by 30th November,[83] and shareholders approved the draft Order in January 1901.[84] When the Commissioners reviewed the draft Order, they confirmed the increases in the Treasury Grant and the contributions from the local authorities, but they reduced the proposed increase in the ordinary share capital to £6,000 and gave the company powers to borrow up to £4,000. The rate of interest payable on the local authority loans was increased from 3 to $3\frac{1}{2}$%. On 2nd August 1901 the provisional Amendment Order was sent to the Board of Trade for confirmation which was given on 22nd September 1901.[85]

The 1899 Light Railway Order gave the company powers to issue an additional 5,000 £1 shares with the approval of the Board of Trade. These shares had not been issued when the application for the Amendment Order was made, which may explain why the Light Railway Commissioners did not increase the company's share capital by the amount proposed by the Directors. On 18th April the Llanfair Board decided to issue the shares and a prospectus was published in May 1901.[86/87/88]

The search for a contractor

In December 1900 the Works Committee met Mr Collin who reported that although the contract plans would not be ready for six weeks, the land plans could be completed and sent to members of the Committee within a fortnight. The Engineer advised against advertising the tender for the construction of the line until February 1901 when the prices were likely to be more favourable.[89] On 21st December the Directors instructed their Solicitor to issue 'Notices to Treat' to landlords whose property was required by the railway and to make arrangements to deposit £1,000 with the Paymaster General[90] so they could exercise the powers conferred by the Light Railway Order.[91]

When the land plans and specifications were reviewed by the Works Committee on 25th January 1901 they decided that greater provision for unloading livestock was required at the Smithfield. The alignment of the railway was amended slightly at Seven Stars, requiring the acquisition of the old malthouse as well as the public house and Cyfronydd station was re-sited.[92] Subsequently alterations were made to the route through Morris' yard in Welshpool[93] and the line was diverted around the south side of Dolrhyd Mill in accordance with Mr Anwyl's wishes.[94] Mr Collin's assistant, Mr Byron, gave assurances that the contract specifications and schedule of quantities would be completed by 14th February so that tenders for the construction of the line could be obtained and submitted to the Directors for their approval as quickly as possible.[95/96] The contract was advertised at the end of February and Mr Collin offered to show Contractors over the route of the railway on 1st March. Tenders had to be returned to Mr Denniss by 19th March.[97]

The Board met on 20th March to assess the six tenders that had been received. Mr Collin explained that items such as permanent way materials, buildings and equipment had been excluded from the specifications and quantities supplied to the contractors because he thought that it would be cheaper to let the work locally. The Works Committee were instructed to make such enquiries as were thought necessary into the three firms with the lowest tenders so that the Llanfair

WELSHPOOL AND LLANFAIR LIGHT RAILWAY.

TO CONTRACTORS.

THE DIRECTORS of the Cambrian Railways Company are prepared to receive TENDERS for the Construction of a Light Railway, about 9 miles long, 2ft. 6in. gauge, commencing at the bottom of the Company's Station Approach at Welshpool and terminating at Llanfair Caereinion, all in the County of Montgomery. Plans can be seen, and copies of Specification and Quantities obtained, at the Office of Mr A. J. Collin, Engineer to the Welshpool and Llanfair Light Railway Company, Oswald Road, Oswestry (Opposite the Cambrian Railways Station), on and after February 25th, 1901. A charge of two guineas will be made for each copy of the Quantities, which will be returned on receipt of a bona-fide Tender. Sealed Tenders endorsed "Tender for Welshpool and Llanfair Light Railway" to be forwarded by post to Mr C. S. Denniss, Secretary, Cambrian Railways, Oswestry, so as to be received on the morning of Tuesday, March 19th, 1901.

The Directors do not bind themselves to accept the lowest or any Tender, or to pay any expenses attending the same.

The Engineer will be prepared to accompany Contractors over the route of the Railway on Friday, March 1st, 1901.

C. S. DENNISS, Secretary, Cambrian Railways Co.
J. EVANS, Secretary, Welshpool and Llanfair Light Railway Co.

Oswestry, February 18th, 1901.

NET COST OF TENDERS TO BULD THE WELSHPOOL AND LLANFAIR LIGHT RAILWAY

Tendered by		£
Cleveland Bridge Co.		32,382
A. Braithwaite		26,353
Holme & King Ltd	Liverpool	25,583
H. & M. Nowell	Leeds	25,350
J. Strachan	Cardiff	23,675
Engineer's estimate		22,325
N. Jones & Co.	Manchester	20,696

The amounts tendered and the Engineer's estimate exclude the cost of permanent way materials, buildings and equipment.

Source: Rail 722 2

Company could come to terms with one of them. Messrs Collin and Hilton undertook to assist the Committee in their deliberations. It was decided to ask Mr Denniss to make enquires about the financial standing of Messrs N. Jones & Company, whose tender was the least expensive, and the nature of the work that the firm had carried out. A suggestion that the line should be worked by electric traction, made by a firm of Liverpool electrical engineers, was left on the table. The Directors agreed to meet on 1st April to consider the Works Committee's report on the standing of the contractors.[98]

When the Board met on 1st April it was reported that Messrs N. Jones & Company's financial standing was unsatisfactory and it was agreed that the firm's tender could not be accepted. The Directors decided to recommend acceptance of Mr Stachan's tender to the Cambrian Company, on condition that he would buy 1,000 £1 ordinary shares in the light railway company.[99] On 3rd April John Evans, the Light Railway's Secretary, received a telegram from Mr Denniss stating 'Strachan accepts shares. My Board agree to his having the contract'.[100] Mr Denniss confirmed his telegram by letter and enquired how the share and other capital required to fund the railway's construction would be raised.[101] Mr Evans replied that the sums promised by the Treasury and Local Authorities, which amounted to more than the contract price, would be allocated to pay Mr Strachan.[102] At last construction of the railway appeared to be imminent.

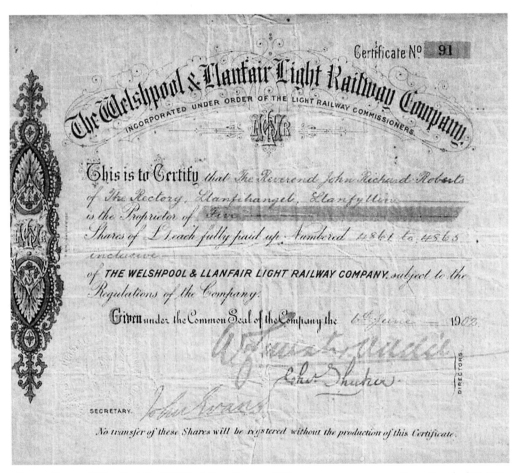

Share certificate for Welshpool and Llanfair Light Railway Company 1902.   *Source: Powysland Museum*

[1] *The Montgomeryshire Express and Radnorshire Times* 5th October 1897
[2] Rail 722 1 W&L Executive Committee 28th September 1897
[3] Rail 722 1 W&L Executive Committee 5th October 1897
[4] Rail 92 66 C.S. Denniss to Cambrian Board 21st September 1897
[5] Rail 1057 613 F. Ward to Harrison & Winnall 16th December 1897
[6] Rail 722 1 W&L Executive Committee 11th February 1898
[7] Rail 1057 613 A.J. Collin to C.S. Denniss 18th February 1898
[8] Rail 722 1 W&L Board 29th March 1898
[9] Rail 1057 613 Memorandum of meeting 1st April 1898
[10] Rail 1057 613 Notes by C.S. Denniss 17th June 1898
[11] Rail 1057 613 Cambrian Traffic and Works Committee Minute 8042
[12] The *Montgomery County Times and Shropshire and Mid-Wales Advertiser* 3rd March 1900
[13] Rail 722 1 W&L Promoters Committee 10th March 1898
[14] Rail 722 1 W&L Board 19th March 1898
[15] Rail 7221 W&L Board 11th May 1898
[16] MT 6 1081 3 Board of Agriculture Certificate date 26th August 1898
[17] MT 6 1081 3 Treasury minute 1884/98 15th December 1898
[18] MT 6 1081 3 Treasury minute 1884/98 15th December 1898
[19] Rail 1057 613 Harrison & Winnall to C.S. Denniss 20th December 1898
[20] Rail 1057 613 Harrison & Winnall to C.S. Denniss 2nd July 1898
[21] Rail 92 67 C.S Denniss to Cambrian Board 5th August 1898
[22] Rail 1057 613 Harrison & Winnall to C.S. Denniss 17th August 1898
[23] Rail 1057 613 Harrison & Winnall to C.S. Denniss 19th August 1898
[24] Rail 1057 613 A. Aslett to C.S. Denniss 14th October 1898
[25] Rail 1057 613 A.J. Collin to C.S. Denniss 15th December 1898
[26] Rail 1057 613 Harrison and Winnall to C.S. Denniss 9th December 1898
[27] Rail 1057 613 W&L Prospectus 24th January 1899
[28] Rail 722 1 Board 10th January 1899 p.29
[29] Rail 1057 613 C.S. Denniss to F.W. Chanter 4th January 1899
[30] MT6 1081 3 Note on Board of Trade facing sheet 6th April 1899
[31] Rail 1067 613 J. Parry-Jones to C.S. Denniss 1st May 1899
[32] Rail 722 W&L Board 14th November 1899
[33] Rail 1057 613 Cambrian Traffic and Works Committee Minute 5475 14th December 1899
[34] Rail 722 2 W&L Board 1st March 1900
[35] Rail 722 6 Light Railway Order 1899
[36] Rail 1057 613 Harrison & Winnall to C.S. Denniss 14th June 1898
[37] Rail 1057 613 A.J. Collin to C.S. Denniss 15th July 1898
[38] Rail 1057 613 H.C. Corfield to C.S. Denniss 11th July 1898
[39] Rail 1057 C.S. Denniss to Harrison & Winnall Re draft Light Railway Order 5th July 1898
[40] Rail 1057 613 A.J. Collin to C.S. Denniss 14th January 1899
[41] MT 6 1081 3 Draft Light Railway Order S.31 (9)&(10)
[42] Rail 92 68 C.S. Denniss to Cambrian Board 10th April 1899
[43] Rail 1057 613 J. Parry-Jones to C.S. Denniss 8th March 1899
[44] Rail 1057 613 C.S. Denniss to J. Parry Jones 8th March 1899
[45] Rail 92 68 C.S. Denniss to Cambrian Board 10th April 1899
[46] Rail 92 68 C.S. Denniss to Cambrian Board 30th June 1899
[47] Rail 92 68 C.S. Denniss to Cambrian Board Memorandum of meeting held on 2nd May 1899
[48] Rail 92 68 Harrison & Winnall to J. Parry-Jones 2nd June 1899
[49] Rail 1057 613 Cambrian Traffic and Works Committee Minute 8354
[50] MT6 1081 3 Light Railway Commissioners to Board of Trade 19th July 1899
[51] Rail 92 68 Letter from the Secretary of the Light Railway Commission to C.S. Denniss 22nd June 1899
[52] MT6 1081 3 Light Railway Commissioners to Board of Trade 19th July 1899
[53] Rail 1057 613 C.S. Denniss File note re conversation with Francis Hopwood 28th July 1899

[54] Rail 1057 613 C.S. Denniss to F. Hopwood 11th August 1899
[55] Rail 1057 613 F. Hopwood to C.S. Denniss 17th August 1899
[56] *The Leek and Manifold Railway* Robert Gratton. Rails weighing 35lbs per yard were used on the Bársi and Leek and Manifold railways
[57] MT 6 1081 3 4th April 1899
[58] MT 6 1081 3 Board of Trade to Bircham & Co. Amendments to the draft Order 5th April 1899
[59] Rail 722 6 Light Railway Order 1899 S.52 (2)
[60] MT6 1081 3 Resolutions by Local Authorities in Montgomeryshire in support of the line
[61] Rail 722 5 Light Railway Order 1899
[62] Rail 722 2 W&L Board 30th September 1899
[63] Rail 722 2 W&L Board 14th November 1899
[64] Rail 722 2 W&L Board 1st March 1900
[65] Rail 722 2 Works Committee 4th May 1900
[66] Rail 722 2 W&L Board 1st October 1900
[67] Rail 722 2 Works Committee 5th December 1900
[68] MT 6 1084 4 Amendment Order : Light Railway Commissioners report to Board of Trade 2nd August 1901
[69] Rail 722 2 W&L Board 8th July 1901
[70] Rail 722 2 W&L Board 29th August 1901
[71] Rail 722 2 W&L Board 1st October 1900
[72] Rail 1057 613 C.S. Denniss to Harrison & Winnall 1st November 1900
[73] Rail 722 2 W&L Board 27th November 1900
[74] Rail 1057 613 Earl of Powis to HM Treasury 5th November 1900
[75] Rail 722 2 W&L Board 1st October 1900
[76] Rail 722 2 W&L Board 27th November 1900
[77] Rail 1057 613 Earl of Powis to H.M. Treasury 5th November 1900
[78] MT 6 1081 3 H.M. Treasury to Harrison & Winnall 11th December 1900
[79] Rail 722 2 W&L Board 27th November 1900
[80] MT6 1084 4 Light Railway Commissioners Report (not dated)
[81] MT 6 1084 4 Light Railway Commissioners report to Board of Trade Re Amendment Order 3rd August 1901
[82] MT 6 1084 4 Amendment Order 22nd September 1901
[83] Rail 722 2 W&L Board 27th November 1900
[84] *The Montgomery County Times and Shropshire and Mid-Wales Advertiser* 2nd February 1901
[85] Rail 1057 613 C.S. Denniss to Harrison & Winnall 3rd December 1900
[86] Rail 722 2 W&L Board 18th April 1901
[87] Rail 722 6 W&L Balance Sheet 31st December 1901
[88] Rail 1057 613 Prospectus for the issue of 5,000 £1 shares at par May 1901
[89] Rail 722 2 Works Committee 5th December 1900
[90] Rail 722 5 Light Railway Order 1899 S.85
[91] Rail 722 2 W&L Board 21st December 1900
[92] Rail 722 2 Works Committee 25th January 1901
[93] Rail 722 2 W&L Board 1st April 1901
[94] Rail 722 W&L Board 18th April 1901
[95] Rail 722 2 Works Committee 25th January 1901
[96] Rail 722 2 W&L Board 31st January 1901
[97] *The Montgomery County Times and Shropshire and Mid-Wales Advertiser* 2nd March 1901
[98] Rail 722 2 W&L Board 20th March 1901
[99] Rail 722 2 W&L Board 1st April 1901
[100] Rail 722 2 W&L Board 18th April 1901
[101] Rail 722 2 W&L Board 18th April 1901 Letter from C.S. Dennis dated 3rd April 1901
[102] Rail 92 70 C.S. Denniss to Cambrian Board 1st May 1901 quoting a letter from John Evans 23rd April 1901

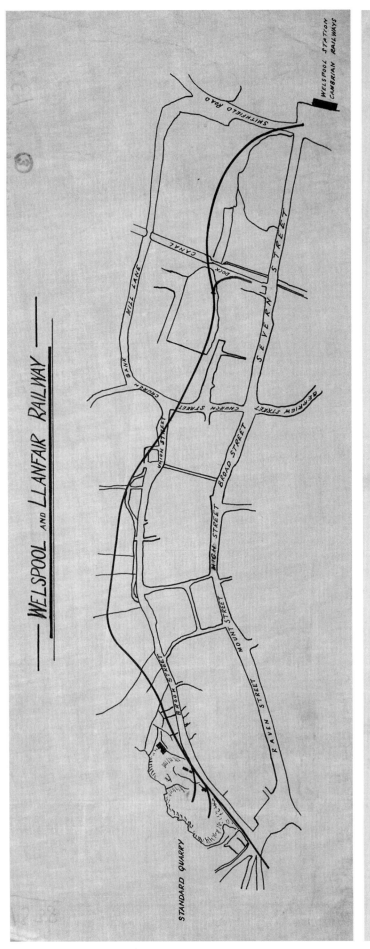

WELSPOOL AND LLANFAIR RAILWAY

STANDARD QUARRY

WELSPOOL STATION
CAMBRIAN RAILWAYS

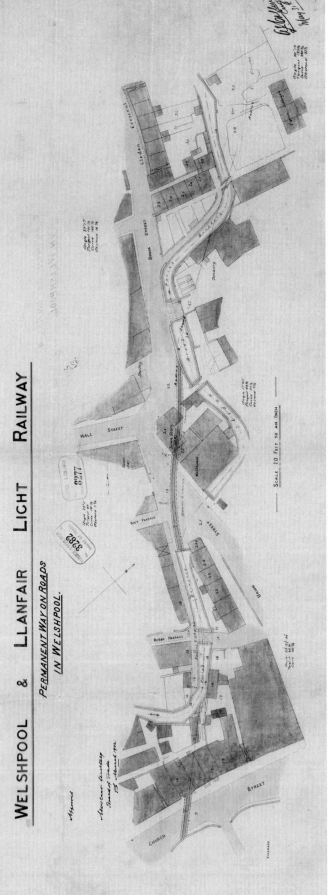

WELSHPOOL & LLANFAIR LIGHT RAILWAY

PERMANENT WAY ON ROADS IN WELSHPOOL.

Scale 20 Feet to an Inch.

CHAPTER FOUR

BUILDING THE LINE

THE Directors hoped to open their railway to the public before 7th September 1902 when the three years allowed for the construction of the line ended.[1/2] At the April Board Mr Addie stated that the Contractor could take posession of about three miles of land required for the railway whenever he needed it.[3] Mr Collin reported that Mr Bailey Hawkins, the Cambrian Deputy Chairman, could secure a favourable price for rails and the Directors agreed that he should act on their behalf. In June Messrs Guest, Keen & Nettlefold's tender for eight hundred tons of Bessemer steel rails and fishplates was accepted.[4] The Directors also decided to apply to the Treasury for the payment of state aid in instalments as the work proceeded.[5] In May Messrs Bircham & Co., the company's Parliamentary agent, applied to the Treasury for payment of the Free Grant in two instalments.[6] Treasury officials agreed to make the first payment when the Board of Trade was satisfied that expenditure of £14,500 had been incurred. The balance would be payable on the production of the Board of Trade certificate stating that the line has been completed and opened for public traffic.[7]

In Welshpool the railway ran along Smithfield Road for about sixty-seven yards[8] and crossed three public roads on the level within the course of a mile.[9] Plans for the permanent way along the road and over the level crossings had to be approved by the Board of Trade and Montgomery County Council. On 31st May 1901 Mr Collin sent plans and a section of the road crossings in Welshpool to the Board of Trade for its approval. He intended to use flat-bottomed, grooved rails weighing 75lbs per yard that were carried on a concrete bed nine inches thick. Between the rails and on either side of them for eighteen inches the roadway would be carried on granite setts.[10]

When the Board's officials received the plans, they seem to have been uncertain about how to proceed and eventually asked if the County Council had approved the Engineer's proposals.[11] An amended design using rail weighing 45lbs per yard carried on 6ft × 9in × 4½in sleepers with a macadamed roadway was submitted to the Borough and County Councils in December 1901. Members approved the plans once they had been assured that the railway company would maintain

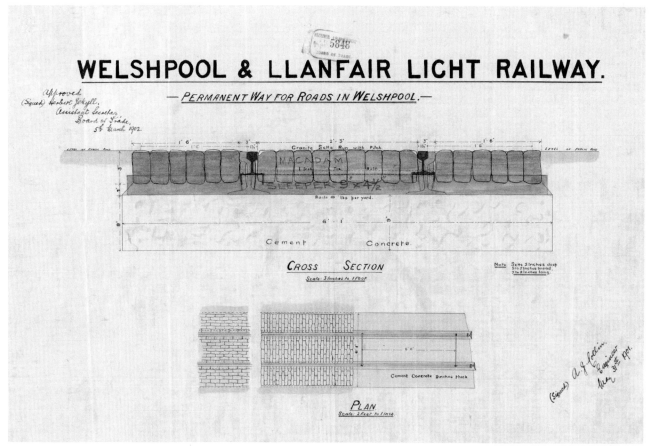

Source: MT6 11504

The Seven Stars Inn at the junction of Union Street, Hall Street and Brook Street was demolished to make way for the railway. Its name was perpetuated by the first halt from the terminus at Welshpool which was close to the town centre.

POWYSLAND MUSEUM

the crossings in perpetuity, that the road surface on the crossings would be no more slippery than on other parts of the highway, and that horses would be unable to catch their hooves in the rails.[12/13] Amended plans and sections were sent to the Board of Trade on 26th February 1902 and approved on 5th March.[14]

CUTTING THE FIRST SOD

In April 1901 the Directors invited Viscount Clive, the Earl of Powis' young son, to cut the first sod of the new railway and appointed a Committee to make the necessary arrangements.[15] The Committee decided that the ceremony would be held in Col. Hutchins' field on Thursday 30th May and that Capt. Pryce would present a silver spade to Viscount Clive.[16] The spade, bearing the engraved inscription *Presented to the Right Hon. the Viscount Clive by the Directors and Shareholders of the Welshpool and Llanfair Light Railway Company on the occasion of his cutting the first sod of that railway at Welshpool 30th May 1901*, was supplied by Mr David Lloyd and cost £18.0s.9d.[17] Messrs Collin and Strachan agreed to provide a suitable wheelbarrow. The Secretary, Mr John Evans, met the Mayor of Welshpool and the Chief Constable of Montgomeryshire to make arrangements for a procession from the Town Hall to the Col. Hutchins' field.[18] A paragraph was inserted in local newspapers advising that the ceremony would start at 1.00pm and that admission was free.[19]

On 30th May Welshpool was lavishly decorated to celebrate the cutting of the first sod of the new railway. At 12.30pm the Mayor and Corporation met at the Town Hall where they were joined by the Mayors of the other Montgomeryshire boroughs and a number of gentlemen from the surrounding district. After a few minutes delay, they processed along Broad Street and Seven Street to the field where the first sods were to be turned. By kind permission of Sir Watkin Williams Wynne, the procession was headed by the band of the Montgomeryshire Yeomanry Cavalry who had come from an encampment at Wynnstay. A pavilion had been erected in Col. Hutchins' field where many ladies had assembled by the time the procession arrived. The four sods to be cut were placed in front of the pavilion and when turned formed the letters WLLR.

At one o' clock the Powis Castle carriage, drawn by two splendid bays and proceeded by an outrider in livery, drew up to the cheers of the crowd. The party consisted of The Earl and Countess of Powis with Viscount Clive, Major-General the Hon. W.H. Herbert, Mrs Herbert, Lady Margaret Cholmondesley and Miss Lucy Herbert. In Capt. Pryce's absence through illness the party was welcomed by Mr J.C. Hilton and the Countess was presented with a bouquet of flowers by Miss Collin, the daughter of the Cambrian Railways' Chief Engineer.

Mr Hilton presented a silver spade to Lord Clive, remarking that they were there on business that was very important for Welshpool and even more so for Llanfair. There had been many attempts to make a railway from Welshpool to Llanfair but all had failed for the want of money. However, he believed that they would be successful this time because the Gov-

ernment had been very generous in providing a free grant; the local authorities had been supportive in their funding; while the Earl of Powis and other landowners had done everything that they could by giving land. Recognising the importance of the line to the district that it would serve, the Directors had decided to commence construction before the share capital had been fully subscribed. Mr Hilton believed that now the light railway's supporters saw they were in earnest, the unissued shares would soon be taken up. He wished Lord Clive a long and happy life and hoped that in the coming years the spade would remind him of the important work that he had inaugurated that day.

Mr Strachan asked Viscount Clive to accept a wheelbarrow of oak with heavy silver mountings. Remarking on the splendid weather and the presence of the Earl, Countess and their son he suggested that the auspicious circumstances in which they were beginning might be taken as an augury of the success of the enterprise. He had no doubt that the railway would be properly built and that it would be profitable. With Mr Collin's assistance Viscount Clive then cut the first sod to loud applause. After each sod was cut, he pushed the wheelbarrow up an inclined plane and tipped the contents over. Once the sods had been turned, the band played *God save the King*. Speaking on behalf of his son, the Earl thanked the Directors for the gift of the spade and Messrs Strachan and Collin for the wheelbarrow. He hoped they would remind Viscount Clive of the first light railway to be authorised under the Light Railways Act and trusted that as the years went by the railway would be a great success.

The procession then reformed and returned to the Town Hall. At two o'clock, by kind invitation of the Earl and Countess, over two hundred people were entertained to lunch in the assembly room and many toasts were drunk. Mr A.C. Humphreys-Owen, by now the Chairman of the Cambrian Railways, proposed the toast *Success to the W&L*. He reminded those present that it was over thirty years since the first scheme to build a railway from Welshpool to Llanfair had been proposed. All previous attempts to reach Llanfair were made by private endeavour but the light railway would be made through the united efforts of those interested as private persons and the great public bodies who represented the ratepayers of the county and the tax payers of the country. While there were some who doubted the wisdom of state interference in these matters, Mr Humphreys-Owen thought that in this instance it was fully justified. He spoke warmly of the generosity of the landowners who for the most part had parted with their land at a very reasonable price, and also thanked the local authorities and the Treasury for the funding that they had provided. Mr Humphreys-Owen concluded by expressing his gratitude to the Directors of the Cambrian Railways who, by agreeing to work the line, made its construction possible.

The Earl of Powis responded by reminding those present of the generosity of the Cambrian Company who had agreed to work the line for sixty percent of the receipts, and to Messrs Collin and Jones for their energies in connection with the line. He believed that without Government assistance, it would be impossible to make the railway. In Ireland the Government had seen the great value of making light railways and they had been prepared to extend that value to the remoter parts of Britain. Mr Collin congratulated the Directors on awarding the contract to the well-known Contractor, Mr John Strachan of Cardiff. He felt confident that the work would be done conscientiously and that they would get full value for their money so that in a few months they would be celebrating the driving in of the last spike. Shortly afterwards the proceedings were concluded and the company dispersed.[20/21]

PLANNED FUNDING MAY 1901	
	£
Shares : By Private Individuals	11,000
By Welshpool Corporation	4,000
	15,000
Local Authority Loans	15,350
Treasury Free Grant	14,500
Total funds	£44,850
Sources: MT6 108 4 and Rail 722 2	

BUILDING THE FORMATION

By the end of May a considerable quantity of the Contractor's machinery had arrived at Welshpool.[22] On 1st June, work began to remove approximately six thousand cubic yards of material from a field next to the Smithfield so that a station yard could be made there. A start was also made on the earthworks from the Smithfield to a point near New Drive crossing, a distance of a little over one and a half miles. Repairs to the walls of the Lledan brook, over which the railway would run, were practically complete by the end of June when work to build the canal bridge abutments began.[23]

Excavation of the station yard was nearly finished by early August, by which time approximately three thousand sleepers had been delivered. Between the Smithfield and Raven Square the earthworks were practically complete. Work on the first mile of Golfa bank, two cattle creeps and a culvert was well in hand and fencing was being erected as far as Sylfaen. In Welshpool the rebuilding work at the Tannery and most of the property alterations had been completed. Work on the retaining wall at Rock Cottage was well in hand and the abutments of the canal bridge were almost complete.[24]

Negotiations to buy *The Seven Stars* inn were protracted. Although the company reached a settlement with the tenant Miss Smout in July, the owner Mrs Dowthwaite would not agree a price for the property.[25] In September Mr Addie reported that the company's offer of £1,155 had been rejected and that the vendor asked for £1,200, to which price the Directors reluctantly acceded.[26] Although agreement was reached with Mrs Dowthwaite's solicitor, the lady refused to confirm the arrangement, so on the last day of October the Board resolved to refer the matter to arbitration if full agreement was not reached within three days.[27] The property was conveyed to the company in January 1902[28] and demolished shortly afterwards.[29]

During the summer, work began on the construction of the Banwy bridge. In August the Board heard that the stone being used was of a perishable nature and the matter was referred to the Cambrian. The following month Mr Collin inspected the work done and gave instructions that it should be taken down and rebuilt.[30] Work on the other major bridge on the railway, Brynelin viaduct, started in the autumn.[31] Difficulty was experienced in establishing a stable base for the foundations, requiring the excavation of eight feet of soft blue clay before gravel was encountered. The foundations were then filled with concrete to ground level.[32]

By the beginning of October most of the larger cuttings had been started and several of the smaller ones had been completed. The construction of several cattle creeps had started and some were ready for arching. Work had also begun on a culvert near Castle Caereinion station and the river wall at Llanfair. In Welshpool the boundary wall along the vicarage grounds had been built, while the weighbridge office at Standard Quarry had been removed as it was in the way of the railway. Approximately one quarter of a mile of line had been laid with ballast ready for the sleepers and rails.[33] Although the first consignment of rails was received in November,[34]

Work had started on the first mile of Golfa bank by August 1901. Here workmen were building one of the cattle creeps at the bottom of the bank. RALPH CARTWRIGHT COLLECTION

Workmen excavating the shallow cutting of the summit of the line between Golfa and Sylfaen using picks and shovels. Spoil was removed in wheelbarrows and loaded into the Contractor's wagons which were pulled by horses until the formation could accommodate locomotives. RALPH CARTWRIGHT COLLECTION

Cuttings and embankments were kept to the necessary minimum to reduce expenditure on the earthworks. Here one of the cuttings was being excavated. Again the reliance on manual labour is evident. RALPH CARTWRIGHT COLLECTION

work on laying the permanent way did not commence until the following month.[35]

In winter the Lledan brook often flooded the neighbourhood adjacent to *The Seven Stars*. In November Welshpool Borough Council complained that the new bridge erected over the brook near Tipton's Well was of insufficient capacity to carry rain water in times of flood, and that a larger arch was required.[36] The matter was referred to Mr Collin who reported that although the arch near the Tannery Yard had dealt with flood water satisfactorily on two occasions, after careful consideration he believed that the arch was insufficient to allow exceptional flood water to pass and he recommended that it should be taken down and ironwork substituted as on other sections of the brook. The Board asked the Engineer to prepare a plan and estimate for the work and to see if a sewage pipe could be fitted lower down in the bed of the brook.[37] The plans were approved by the Works Committee in February 1902 when Mr Collin offered to pay the cost of rebuilding the bridge which was estimated to be £200.[38]

In December Mr Collin reported that the earthworks and fencing were proceeding in a satisfactory manner and that several cattle creeps were in a forward state. The superstructure of the canal bridge had been inspected at the maker's yard and was now ready for erection.[39] Except for painting, the bridge was completed early in January 1902.[40] The steelwork required to bridge the Lledan Brook was inspected on 9th December[41] and it had been erected by the middle of February.[42]

For much of January and February all masonry and concrete work ceased because of the severe weather but fair progress was made with the earthworks. By mid February the cuttings near Golfa were almost complete. Once they were finished, the Contractor could lay temporary rails as far as the top of Golfa bank. Earthworks were in hand in various places between three and six miles. The line through Welshpool was expected to be completed by the end of February. Although it had been a difficult section to build, very few complaints had been received from people living close to the line.[43]

Major Druitt visited the line on 18th February to inspect the progress of the work.[44] He reported that about half of the formation had been completed; bridgework in Welshpool was practically complete and was in hand at the principal bridges in the country; and one and a half miles of track had been laid. The company had incurred expenditure of £12,916 on this work and had acquired property costing £5,000. There was clear evidence that reasonable support had been provided by the local authorities and landowners.[45] The inspector's assessment of the works was reported to the Lord Commissioners of the Treasury in support of the Llanfair Company's claim for payment of the first instalment of the free grant which was received on 2nd April 1902.[46]

When the Board met on 20th February, a letter was read from Mr Collin reporting progress on construction of the railway. He stated that Major Druitt was satisfied with the progress of the works and that if the weather was favourable for the next few months the line might be ready for final inspection by the Board of Trade in July or early August. This was earlier than expected, so Mr Collin advised his Directors

---

PRELIMINARY INSPECTION
18th February 1902

RAILWAY DEPARTMENT
Board of Trade
Richmond Terrace
Whitehall
London SW
22nd February 1902

Sir

I have the honour to report for the information of the Board of Trade that, in compliance with the instructions contained in your Minute of the 6th February, I have inspected the works in progress on the Welshpool and Llanfair Light Railway and also enquired into the assistance and facilities given by Landowners and local authorities for the construction of the said light railway.

As regards the progress of the works I walked over a portion of the line and examined all the principal bridges and viaducts in the course of construction on the whole line, which is 9 miles 1 furlong and 1½ chains in length, accompanied by Mr Collin the Engineer of the Cambrian Railways who is also the Engineer of the Light Railway and Mr Addie, agent to Lord Powis, one of the Directors of the Light Railway.

About one half of the formation has been done and about 1½ miles of rails laid and spiked to the sleepers but not yet ballasted up. About one half of the fencing has been completed. The bridge over the Shropshire Union Canal in Welshpool is practically completed and the steel joists for carrying the railway over the Lledan Brook are in position. The viaduct at Brynelin consisting of six masonry spans has been commenced and the foundations of six out of the seven piers are laid. The abutments and piers for the bridge over the river Banwy are finished. There are about three miles of rails, and sleepers for about five miles of line, on the ground.

I attach a statement supplied to me by Mr Collin the Engineer marked 'A' showing expenditure to date which amounts to £12,916, and in addition a sum of £5,000 has been paid for the purchase of land necessary which was not contributed free (see page 5 of the information supplied to me by Messrs Harrison and Winnall the solicitors to the light railway marked 'B'). I can therefore recommend the Board of Trade to certify that a sum of more than £14,500 has been expended on the construction of, and purchase of land for, the said light railway.

With respect to the statutory paragraph re assistance by local landowners and local bodies I attach a statement 'B' supplied to me by Messrs Harrison and Winnall in which will be seen:

Page 1 shows free gifts of land by landowners that has an estimated value of £2,400, the largest portion given by Lord Powis extending over about half the length of the line.

Page 2 gives contributions given by local authorities with the amounts paid and amounts still due. These have all been increased in amount since the schedule to the Memorandum of Agreement with the Treasury was drawn up by clause 2 of the Amendment Order 1901.

Page 3 gives shares, with amounts paid, subscribed by the public, and page 4 shares subscribed by Local Bodies.

From this it would appear that the requirement of the statutory paragraph re reasonable assistance has been carried out, although the amount expended in the purchase of land £5,000, is considerably in excess of the £3,000 originally laid down.

I may add that I was informed that the rolling stock and engines are under construction and that it is hoped to open the line next August.

I have etc
E Druitt
Major RE

Source: MT6 1612 2

to press for the delivery of the rolling stock by the anticipated date of inspection because two locomotives and a carriage would be needed to test the bridges.[47] Although two locomotives had been ordered from Beyer Peacock in October 1901,[48] when the Works Committee met in March its members were astonished to find that the plans for the locomotives were incomplete and that work to build them had not started.[49] The builders indicated that the locomotives would not be ready for eight or nine months and possibly longer, so the Earl of Powis wrote to press them for an early delivery date.[50]

THE EARL OF POWIS' APPLICATION TO THE TREASURY FOR INCREASED STATE FUNDING 1902

WELSHPOOL & LLANFAIR LIGHT RAILWAY COMPANY

WELSHPOOL

22nd May, 1902

My Lords,

By the request of the Directors of the Welshpool & Llanfair Light Railway Company I, as Chairman of the Board, have the honour to bring the following matter to your notice in the earnest hope that it may receive your favourable consideration.

At the outset I may mention that previous appeals have been made on behalf of the Company to the Treasury, and that your Lordships have already voted a sum of £14,500 by way of Special Grant in aid of the line. This generous subsidy is greatly appreciated by all interested in the promotion of the railway, but unfortunately, owing to the following circumstances, it has become absolutely necessary to make a further appeal for assistance.

At the time the last application was made to the Treasury amended Estimates were submitted showing a total approximate expenditure of £43,204. With extreme difficulty the Directors succeeded, with the aid of the Free Grant, in providing within a very few pounds the whole of this amount, made up as follows: -

	£	£
Free Grant		14,500
Contributions by Local Authorities by way of loan: -		
Montgomery County Council	7,000	
Welshpool Corporation	5,000	
Llanfyllin Rural District Council	2,600	
Forden Rural District Council	750	
	15,350	
By Welshpool Corporation : shares	4,000	19,350
Shares subscribed by landowners and others		9,292
Total		£43,142

Under these circumstances the Promoters felt justified in proceeding with the work. Notices to treat were accordingly given to the landowners in February, 1901 and shortly afterward the Contract for construction of the Railway was let to Mr J. Strachan of Cardiff. Rapid progress has been made, and the Engineers of the Company state that the line will be completed and ready for inspection by the Board of Trade by the end of August next.

As the work is now nearing completion the Directors are able to accurately ascertain the total cost of the Undertaking, and find that although every possible care has been taken to keep within their limit the actual expenditure will exceed the estimates by a sum of about £7,000. The excess above the estimate is shown in the detailed Statement that I have the honour to submit herewith.

In addition to the subscribed capital of the Company free gifts of land to the value of upwards of £2,400 have been made by myself and other owners of property for the purposes of the Undertaking, which, if added to the actual expenditure would represent a total of £52,671.

As has already been brought to your Lordship's notice, the country to be served by the line is a large, but poor agricultural district, sparsely populated, and where the inhabitants have very limited means. For many years past repeated attempts have been made to obtain railway communication, and although in some cases the necessary Parliamentary powers have been obtained, the schemes have invariably fallen through by reason of the failure to obtain the capital for the construction of the line.

The Directors feel that it is quite impossible for them to raise the deficit of £7,000 in the locality, and I desire therefore respectfully to urge very strongly upon your Lordships the importance of some further assistance being given by the State towards the completion of a line which must prove of inestimable advantage to the agricultural interest of the locality.

If your Lordships can see your way to make up the Free Grant to one-third of the total cost, which would be equivalent to a further payment of £3,000, I am authorised by the Directors to state that they will be prepared to find the balance needed to complete and equip the line.

Should your Lordships not be prepared to grant this request, might I be permitted to enquire whether the Treasury would be disposed to advance a sum of £3,000 by way of loan on easy terms?

I am,
My Lords,
Your obedient Servant,
POWIS

Source: MT6 1081 3

THE EARL OF POWIS REPORTS PROGRESS ON THE LINE

The third annual general meeting of the proprietors of Welshpool and Llanfair Light Railway Company was held in Welshpool Town Hall on Wednesday 26th March 1902. Addressing the meeting the Earl of Powis said that much had been accomplished since the first sod had been cut on 30th May 1901. The contract had been let to John Strachan of Cardiff for completion by 1st September next. Work had progressed very satisfactorily, half the earthworks and fencing were complete, and the bridges in the town over the canal and Lledan Brook were ready for painting. Given good weather Mr Collin the company's Engineer believed that the line could be ready for inspection by the Board of Trade in July or August.

Terms had been agreed with the landowners without it being necessary to resort to arbitration, although some negotiations had proved to be difficult. The Directors were extremely indebted to Mr Addie for the trouble he had taken in making the necessary arrangements with the landowners. All land and property required for the line was now in the hands of the Contractor. The cost of land in Welshpool had been £3,598 and in the country £2,047, making £5,645 in total. Surplus land at Seven Stars had been sold to the Town Council for £200 so that the road could be widened. The cost of land would have been much greater if three Directors had not gifted land to the company as Mr Noel Turner had also done. Other gentlemen had accepted shares in part payment for land.

Loans had been arranged with the local authorities at rates of interest between 3½ and 3¾%. Unfortunately rates of interest had increased since the war in South Africa had begun. Since May subscriptions of £3,292 had been received towards to a new issue of five thousand £1 shares. The Earl had pleasure in reporting that Mr David Davies, Plas Dinam, had invested £1,000 in the company but expressed regret that the issue had not been fully subscribed. A further £5,000 or thereabouts would have to be raised to complete and equip the line. The exact amount would be known once the railway had been completed.

Source: The Montgomery County Times and Shropshire and Mid-Wales Advertiser 29th March 1902

Mr Collin inspected the line on 8th April and found that the work was progressing satisfactorily.[51] During the month the permanent way had been laid and ballasted for the first $2\frac{1}{2}$ miles and a start had been made to erect the walls of Brynelin viaduct.[52] By 10th July the permanent way had been laid for $6\frac{1}{4}$ miles and there was a good stock of rails at Welshpool. The cuttings had either been finished or gulleted as far as Brynelin, while beyond the viaduct the earthworks were in an advanced state as far as the River Banwy. One arch of the viaduct was nearly turned and work on three others was in hand. The girders for the Banwy Bridge had arrived at Welshpool and it was hoped to erect them during the month.[53] By the beginning of August the rails had been laid as far as the Banwy Bridge some $7\frac{1}{2}$ miles from Welshpool. At the bridge the girders had been fixed in position and, as soon as the deck had been laid, the permanent way would be carried forward. Brynelin viaduct was almost finished while the fencing and earthworks were in a forward state.[54]

When Welshpool Borough Council met in August the Mayor reported that the railway had reduced the width of Brook Street near Rock Cottage so that two vehicles could only pass with difficulty.[55] The matter was referred to Mr Byron, the resident engineer, who met the Borough Surveyor to resolve the matter.[56] At the same meeting Alderman Morris called attention to the dangerous state of the railway near his premises. The girders over the Lledan brook had been left uncovered and two ladies leaving his home fell between the gaps.[57] Nothing was done about the matter and in 1906 Mr Morris wrote to the railway company warning of the danger that the bridge posed to pedestrians.[58] The brook was partly enclosed in 1907 but was not fully boarded over until 1911.[59/60]

By the last days of August the Contractor's track reached Llanfair. Interviewed by *The Montgomery County Times*, Mr Strachan said he hoped that the Board of Trade inspection of the railway would take place at an early date and that the line would be opened for goods traffic at the end of September. Passenger services could then start a month later. Mr Strachan hoped that when Lord Kitchener visited the Earl of Powis in September he would travel over the line with his host and the railway's Directors.[61]

By the end of September all the earthworks had been completed except for the slopes to three of the cuttings, while sidings had been put in at most of the stations. Unfortunately one of the Contractor's engines failed during the month,

Brynelin viaduct nearing completion in the summer of 1902 with the Contractor's track running across it.   W&LLR PRESERVATION CO.

stopping work on ballasting the line.[62] On the last day of September the first wagon of coal was hauled from Welshpool to Llanfair by one of Mr Strachan's engines.[63] Three days later the Directors, accompanied by Cambrian officials and Mr Winnall, made their way over the line in an open wagon fitted with benches. The Director's journey was not without incident as one of the Contractor's locomotives failed on the way, but eventually the special train reached Llanfair where it was welcomed by some of the townsfolk. At the suggestion of Mr J.C. Hilton, the passengers retired to *The Wynnstay Arms* where they toasted the railway with champagne. On returning to the station, they boarded their improvised carriage and returned to Welshpool without incident.[64] More than fifty years after Brunel's proposed Worcester & Porthdinlleyn Railway had been projected through Llanfair, it seemed that the town would soon get a railway of its own.

Work on the Banwy Bridge was begun in 1901 and was completed in the summer of the following year. The temporary water tank on the left held water for the Contractor's locomotives. One of these engines, Strachan No. 8, features in the centre of the bridge.   POWYSLAND MUSEUM

Strachan No. 3, a standard gauge 0–4–0 saddle tank built by the Hunslet Engine Company in 1885, was used on the Welshpool and Llanfair contract. Here the locomotive was standing on temporary track in the Llanfair Railway yard at Welshpool with the Smithfield behind it. During the construction of the light railway, Mr Strachan unloaded a great deal of his plant from the Smithfield siding and transhipped a considerable quantity of spoil and other materials from it.
NLW W&LR archive

SHORT OF TIME AND MONEY

In March 1902 the Work Committee asked Mr Collin to estimate the cost of the completing the railway.[65] When the estimate was received, the Committee reported that a further £6,542 was required to complete the line because:

1. More rock had been encountered than anticipated,
2. The prices of rail fastenings and sleepers had increased,
3. The line had to comply with the Board of Trade's regulations for block signalling,
4. Property costs in Welshpool were greater than anticipated.

The Works Committee recommended that the sum required should be raised by making an application for £3,000 to the Treasury, issuing 3,000 £1 shares, and reducing expenditure on buildings and equipment by £500. The Committee's recommendations were adopted by the Directors at their meeting on 22nd May.[66]

When the Earl of Powis wrote to the Lords Commissioners of the Treasury to appeal for further assistance, he explained that £43,142 had been raised to build the line but that the estimated cost of completing it was now £50,271, leaving a deficiency of £7,129. The line would serve a poor agricultural district and for this reason the Directors believed that it would be impossible to raise £7,000 locally. However, if the Treasury would contribute a further £3,000, then they would be prepared to find the balance.[67] Having reviewed the Earl's letter, Board of Trade officials considered that his application was likely to succeed, so they arranged a meeting between the promoters and a Treasury Committee on 11th June 1902.[68] The meeting was successful and on 21st June a letter was received from the Treasury stating that the Free Grant had been increased by £3,000.[69]

In July it became clear that the railway would not be completed by 7th September 1902 so the Directors instructed their Solicitor to apply to the Board of Trade for a six month extension of time.[70] Statutory notices were placed in the *London Gazette* and *The Montgomery County Times* advising that the application was to be made on or by 1st September and that any objections should be sent to the Board of Trade by 23rd August. No objections having been received by the due date, on 6th September 1902 Board of Trade officials agreed to extend the time allowed for the completion of the line to 8th March 1903.[71]

Equipping the line

When the Board met to review Mr Collin's plans for the termini and stopping places on the railway, their deliberations were guided by the need to make economies. They decided to make the savings that were required by working the railway with one engine in steam, thus reducing the cost of signalling, and providing less accommodation at the termini. At Welshpool, the carriage shed, waiting room and pit outside the engine shed would be dispensed with, and the size of the tranship shed would be reduced, while Llanfair would lose its engine shed. The plans for the stopping places were approved without any amendments being made.[72]

Mr Denniss objected to the reduced accommodation, so in July the Board agreed to build a carriage shed that could hold two carriages, to provide a pit outside the engine shed and to build a tranship shed that could accommodate two Cambrian wagons.[73] In August a tender was awarded to the Clyde Structural Iron Co. for the construction of the locomotive and carriage sheds at a cost of £280 on the condition that additional lights were provided in the side of the engine shed. At the same time, plans were approved for station buildings and warehouses at the termini, a tranship shed at Welshpool and waiting huts at Castle Caereinion, Cyfronydd and Heniarth.[74] The following month the contract to build them was awarded to Mr T.J. Evans of Welshpool at a cost of £300.[75] In November an agreement was sealed for the lease of land in Welshpool goods yard that was required for the tranship shed and station building.[76]

Although the Board decided not to build an engine shed at Llanfair, a water tank was required there, so in August the Works Committee authorised the construction of a ram to extract water from the river.[77] When no suitable site could be found at Llanfair it was decided to abstract water at Dolrhyd instead, and a tank and pump costing £50 was erected near the bridge over the mill race.[78] At Welshpool water was supplied from the town main to water columns next to the engine and tranship sheds.[79]

Messrs Saunders' tender to equip the line with the electric telegraph was accepted at the July Board.[80] After negotiations with the company, a price of £300 was agreed and the following month the firm were awarded the contract to interlock the points.[81]

THE STRUGGLE TO COMPLETE THE LINE

In August Mr Collin obtained the forms required to apply for the inspection of the railway by the Board of Trade.[82] When work on ballasting the line was halted because one of Mr Strachan's engines failed, it was decided to hire *The Earl* which had arrived at Welshpool on 2nd September, and up to twenty of the wagons received in October, to the Contractor.[83/84] The hire agreement was approved by the Llanfair and Cambrian Boards in October.[85] At the September Board Mr Collin reported that the line would be ready for inspection on 1st November and that a date during the third week of November could be fixed for the formal opening.[86] On 3rd October Mr Evans contacted the Board of Trade stating that the line would be ready for inspection on 3rd November 1902.[87] However, at the beginning of November the line was still being ballasted and tie bars were being fitted to the curves of less than six chains radius to stop *The Earl* from spreading the track.[88] Where the line passed over the Lledan Brook it was decided to fit check rails as an additional safeguard.[89] The telegraph poles and wires had been erected but the telephones had not been installed as the buildings had not been completed, but the interlocking of the points was progressing satisfactorily.[90] On 14th November Mr Evans wrote to the Board of Trade to advise officials that the railway was not sufficiently complete to warrant an inspection.[91]

Mr Collin arranged to go over the line on 26th November but both the Contractor's locomotives had broken down and he was only able to inspect the works at Welshpool. Following discussions with John Strachan junior and Mr Byron, the Engineer concluded that it would take a month to complete the line if the weather was favourable. Unfortunately, severe weather was experienced; at first there were heavy downpours that caused slips in some of the cuttings and then hard frosts interfered with work on the line. By 8th December the work required to complete the line included back filling the station yard at Llanfair, top ballasting for a length of three miles, metalling some of the station yards, interlocking the points at two of the stations, and the final lifting of the rails.[92] The bad weather continued until early January and nothing could be done to complete the work ready for the Board of Trade inspection.[93]

Problems with couplings ...

In the first week of November the last two wagons loaded with stone became detached from a train twenty or thirty yards after it had started from a ballast siding and ran down the incline towards Welshpool.[94] Fortunately someone at the Standard Quarry noticed them and they were turned into the siding where they crashed into some rocks and were badly damaged.[95] On 10th November six wagons became detached from the engine. In both cases it was alleged that the couplings had broken, but when the matter was investigated Mr Jones found that on neither occasion did the couplings break. He suggested that on the first occasion the couplings had not been attached properly, while on the second a chain had been used to attach the trucks to the engine.[96] Mr Jones recommended that as a precaution against future breakaways all rolling stock should be fitted with side chains.[97]

On 19th November a test train consisting of an engine, four wagons and a brake van ran as far as Castle Caereinion. When the wagons were hauled no difficulties were experienced, but when the train was propelled the wagon next to the engine derailed on five occasions, even when travelling at speeds as slow as two miles an hour. However, the couplings did not become detached nor did they break. Mr Jones concluded that the derailments were due to the incomplete state of the permanent way.[98] Although Mr Collin conceded that the gauge was not as true as on an old line, he could find nothing that would cause the wagons to mount the rails. He noted that derailments occurred on both straight and curved track and it was the wagon next to the engine that usually derailed. The Engineer stated that Mr Strachan had told him that the couplings were too stiff and caused the wagons to cant when they passed around the curves.[99] *The Montgomery County Times* was more incisive, reporting that anyone who cared to examine the couplings could see that there was insufficient play for the wagons to pass around the many curves on the railway, and that two wagons standing on a curve could not be coupled up properly. The paper insisted that modifications were required urgently.[100]

... and doubts about timber and livestock traffic

On 19th December members of Montgomery County Council considered a request from the Light Railway's Directors to defer the payment of interest and principal on its loan. Although the request was granted, when the matter was discussed, Col. Pryce-Jones and Dr Humphreys alleged that the railway could not carry timber or livestock and that such traffic would still have to pass along the main road after the railway opened. When Mr Addie attempted to repudiate the allegations, Dr Humphreys intervened, saying that when he had attempted to sell long timber on his property the prospective purchaser was told by Cambrian staff at Oswestry that only short lengths of timber could be carried over the light railway, and for this reason his sale had failed.[101] Although Mr Denniss gave assurances that both categories of traffic could be carried by the railway, his statement was not thought to be entirely convincing because he did not say that long timber would be dealt with.[102] Thus confidence that the line would meet all the requirements of the district was severely shaken, allowing Dr Humphreys to dismiss it as a ridiculous toy railway.[103]

Ready for traffic at last?

By December 1902 the Directors were anxious to ensure that the Board of Trade authorised the opening of the line to the public before the time allowed for its completion expired.[104] At the December Board Mr Collin stated that the line would be ready for inspection in the month of January and the Directors decided to make a preliminary inspection of the line with Cambrian officials on 21st and 22nd January. Mr John Evans was instructed to contact the Board of Trade with the object of having the line inspected on 27th or 28th January

---

THE LAST DAYS OF THE LLANFAIR BUS

When work on building the railway reached Llanfair some bus drivers attempted to reduce the journey time. Unfortunately this proved too much for some of the vehicles and a number of accidents occurred. On 3rd September 1902 a bus was returning from Welshpool when a spring broke at Heniarth. Rather than wait for a replacement vehicle many of the passengers walked home, some muttering "*Thank heaven the railway is coming.*"

Although the bus was slow and inconvenient many Llanfair people depended on it. Mr T.J. Jones was a bus driver for over thirty years, and when he suffered a stroke many of the townspeople were dismayed. Mr Jones was taken to Welshpool Infirmary on 23rd October 1902 where he seems to have made a partial recovery as he was mentioned in a speech to diners celebrating the opening of the line. Capt. Pryce remarked that it was very sad that the opening of the line would result in the disappearance of such landmarks as Johnny Jones and the Llanfair bus. Although poor Johnny had not been in the best of health the Captain was pleased to be able to announce that Mr Denniss and the Cambrian Company had helped to look after him. Anyone who had seen a perspiring man leading four horses drawing a heavy load up the Llanfair Road must have felt that some other form of locomotion would be a vast improvement.

Source: The Montgomery County Times and Shropshire and Mid-Wales Advertiser 13th September 1902, 25th October 1902, 4th April 1903

Llanfair Railway and Welshpool Reservoir   Photo by A. Thomas   E. Jones, Stationer, Welshpool

An early view of the railway near the site of Golfa station, with the line carried high above the Black and Upper Pools. The sleepers are of irregular length and do not appear to have been ballasted, suggesting that this view predates the opening of the line for public traffic. If this is so, the locomotive was probably working a Contractor's train.

A. THOMAS

1903.[105] On 21st January the Board of Trade was told that the line could be inspected after the 31st of the month,[106] but the inspection by the Cambrian officials was postponed until work on the permanent way had been completed.[107]

On Monday 26th January a trial run to Llanfair with one of the engines and the recently delivered carriages was attempted, but the train became detached from the locomotive in Welshpool yard and the rest of the day was spent making adjustments to the couplings. The following day another attempt was made, but after passing through Welshpool the engine became derailed on a curve and the front bogie of the first carriage dropped between the rails. Once both vehicles had been re-railed, the journey to Llanfair continued without incident.[108] News that a special train was on its way caused considerable excitement in Llanfair because until then only the Contractor's engines had been seen at the terminus. The train was expected at 1pm but arrived about two hours later to be greeted by a cheering crowd. During the wait local wags suggested that the wind was delaying the train's progress or that it was hauling long timber and could not pass around the curves. The Vicar, Mr Evan Jones, and Mr Richard Humphreys, North & South Wales Bank, accompanied Mr Collin on the return journey as far as the Banwy Bridge. Both gentlemen enjoyed the trip, the Vicar declaring that travelling on the new railway was quite as easy as on many of the great lines.[109]

Major Druitt inspects the line

The line was inspected by Major Druitt on 3rd February but he was unable to report that the railway had been completed to his satisfaction.[110] Although the Inspector found that the permanent way would be fit for traffic once his recommendations had been implemented, he declared that until the couplings had been modified so that they were free to move when a train was on a curve, the railway would be a danger to the public who used it.[111] Once the Inspector's report had been received, John Evans wrote to the Board of Trade to assure its officials that Major Druitt's recommendations were being attended to. He also requested a meeting with the Inspector to discuss Mr Jones' proposals for modifications to the couplings.[112] Major Druitt visited the railway again on 20th February to inspect the couplings and the permanent way. The couplings were found to work satisfactorily but check rails still had to be fitted on some curves of 3 chains radius, wheel guards were required on the bridges over the Lledan Brook and River Banwy, and tie bars and proper super-elevation were needed on the sharpest curves. He recommended that the Board of Trade should sanction the line to passenger traffic subject to an overall speed limit of 15mph while the formation consolidated, this being reduced to 4mph where the railway crossed public roads in Welshpool and 5mph over the reverse curves at Golfa and on the curves by Dolrhyd mill.[113]

BOARD OF TRADE INSPECTION
3rd February 1903

RAILWAY DEPARTMENT
Board of Trade
Richmond Terrace
Whitehall
London SW
6th February 1903

Sir

I have the honour to report for the information of the Board of Trade that, in compliance with the instructions contained in your Minute of 22nd January 1903, I have inspected the Welshpool and Llanfair Light Railway constructed under the provisions of the Order of 1899.

This light railway consists of a single line 9 miles 11½ chains in length, gauge 2ft 6in, and the motive power is steam.

Land has been purchased for an additional line of rails.

The width at formation level is 10ft 6in on embankments and 9ft in cuttings.

The rails are flat-bottomed steel rails 30ft in length weighing 45lb per yard secured to the sleepers by dogspikes and at the joints soleplates are used, and the rails secured by three dogspikes. The rails are joined by fishplates of the usual kind with four fish bolts. The sleepers are of creosoted Baltic fir 6ft × 9in × 4½in laid 3ft centre to centre. The ballast is of broken stone and river gravel laid to a stated depth of 5 inches below the underside of the sleepers.

The deepest cutting has a depth of 15ft, and the highest embankment a height of 29ft. The sharpest curve has a radius of 3 chains and the steepest gradient is 1 in 30 in one place continuous for one mile in length.

The fencing is mostly of post and wire, with seven wires, the height of the top wire being 4ft 6in, and there are the usual strengthening posts at intervals. Some post and rail fencing is also used of the same height; and in Welshpool along the Lledan Brook some unclimbable fencing has been employed.

The drainage is of the usual description.

There are 15 underbridges and one overbridge on the line.

Of the underbridges one, viz that over the Banwy River, is of three spans each 40ft on the skew with masonry piers and abutments, and steel girders under each rail; one viz over the Shropshire Canal is of steel plate girders and cross rolled joists, one span of 33ft 4in on the skew; three are of brick arches of 8ft span or less; and ten are formed by timber baulks under each rail and are of spans varying from 4ft to 10ft 6in. There are also wooden baulks carrying the rails across the gaps forming the cattle guards at either side of the roads where gates are not provided at the public level crossings.

There is one masonry viaduct of six spans of 22ft 6in each and three viaducts over the Lledan Brook, the line being carried directly over the course of the brook for some little distance by means of longitudinal rail bearers supported by cross girders (rolled joists) which in turn rest on the masonry sides of the stream. There are about 45 of these joists of varying span, the longest being 17ft 3in.

All the steel girders, joists, baulks etc have sufficient theoretical strength and proved fairly stiff under test load, but a few of the rolled a joints over the Lledan Brook need their bearings attended to.

There are two culverts of 3ft and 4ft diameter respectively, of substantial construction and they appear to be standing well. There are no tunnels.

There are eleven public road level crossings and the railway runs along the side of Smithfield Road for the first three chains of its length. Of the level crossings, three are furnished with gates shutting across the railway but not across the road, and the remainder have cattle guards and the usual notices on the roads, but these notice boards have still to be provided for Bebb's Passage, Bushell's Lane near Raven Square, and b the road adjoining Cyfronydd station.

With the exception of the roads in Welshpool, across which the Corporation of Welshpool have fixed the speed at 4 miles an hour under the powers conferred in them by Clause 52(3) of the Order, the only important road crossed on the level is that adjoining Castle Caereinion station whose gates are provided so that the train will stop on either side of it, and over the rest of the level crossings a speed of 10 miles an hour may be allowed. The gates across the railway at Castle Caereinion are hung to open inwards and not across the high road. It would be an improvement if they were hung to open across the road which is on a fairly steep gradient as they would then be visible to cyclists or people in charge of vehicles, and also the person opening the gate could attract the attention of such people. I do not think that Sections 46 to 48 of the Railway Clauses Act 1845 apply to the Order.

There are the following stations on the line viz

1. Welshpool station	at the commencement.
2. Welshpool	at 0m 33c.
3. Raven Square	at 1m 0c.
4. Golfa	at 2m 66c.
5. Castle Caereinion	at 4m 66c.
6. Cyfronydd	at 6m 57c.
7. Heniarth Gate	at 7m 54c.
8. Llanfair Caereinion	at the termination.

At 1 and 8 there are booking offices and waiting rooms, at 5, 6 and 7 there are shelters. All stations are furnished with gravel platforms at rail level.

There are the following sidings and loops on the line all of which are worked from ground frames consisting of two levers each of which are controlled by the train staff for the whole line, as it is worked by one engine in steam only viz

1. Exchange siding points at Welshpool station.
2. Loop siding at the goods yard.
3. & 4. A double frame of four levers working the up facing point at the loop siding and the point leading to the goods yard.
5. Standard Quarry siding not yet connected up.
6. & 7. The loop points at Golfa Station.
8. Sylfaen siding facing to up trains.
9. & 10. The loop points at Castle Caereinion station.
11. & 12. The loop points at Cyfronydd station.
13. & 14. The loop points at Heniarth station.
15. The facing point at Llanfair station loop, the points at the termination of the line for the engine to run around its train being worked by hand.

The interlocking of these 15 ground frames was correct but the sidings at 5 are not ready and the left hand tongue of the facing points c should be secured and the right hand one clamped to the stock rail if passenger traffic is commenced before the sidings are ready. There was also not quite sufficient clearance between the main line and the siding opposite the trap points at Sylfaen siding. The sidings at Heniarth and d Llanfair stations should be slewed further away from the running line at these points. A buffer post is required at the termination of the line at Llanfair station.

At Cyfronydd station the pit of the cattle guard at the road adjoining e the station requires draining.

The following requirements are also necessary in addition to points a to e viz

f. Check rails to be furnished on all sharp curves situated on high banks.

g. Wheel guards have still to be fixed on the bridges over the River Banwy and over the Lledan Brook.

h. The top ballast requires breaking up and the sleepers require additional packing in places.

j. On some curves sufficient gauge has not been given to allow the engines, which have a fixed wheelbase of 10ft, to get round without there being considerable strain in the outer rail as they grind heavily against it, and all sharp curves of 3 chains should be tied to their proper gauge by steel ties.

k. The speed of the trains on the sharp reverse curves below Golfa station not to exceed 5 miles an hour at present.

The rolling stock purchased for this railway are as follows:

Two engines of six wheels coupled, gross weight 19½ tons with a weight of between six and seven tons on each of the three axles.

The passenger carriages are on bogies with a 4ft 6in wheelbase, bogies 24ft centre to centre, and the total length over the headstocks is 35ft. They have entrances at both ends with side steps and they appear suitable.

The carriages and the goods trucks are fitted with centre buffer couplings with Norwegian hooks, but at present no side play has been given to the couplings on the engine or on the trucks, although some has been given on the carriages. I was unable to see them in use so cannot say if the hooks will form a satisfactory coupling, but it would be dangerous to use the couplings as at present fitted owing to the want of sideplay, as they would be very liable to cause derailments when a train was on the sharp curves that are very numerous on this line. Some modification by which the rigid auto buffer couplings are quite free to move when the train is on a curve is absolutely necessary.

Under these conditions I do not feel able to recommend to the Board of Trade that the Light Railway has been completed to their satisfaction although with the requirements a to j inclusive completed, the permanent way would be fit for traffic. But in any case the conditions regarding the payment of the balance of the grant will not be fulfilled until the line has been opened for public traffic.

Until the couplings above mentioned have been modified I consider the opening of the railway would be attended with danger to the public using it.

> I have etc
> E Druitt
> Major RE

Source: MT6 1150 4

SECOND BOARD OF TRADE INSPECTION
20th February 1903

RAILWAY DEPARTMENT
Board of Trade
Richmond Terrace
Whitehall
London SW
21st February 1903

Sir

In accordance with the wishes of the Welshpool and Llanfair Light Railway I visited that line again on the 20th instant and inspected the couplings which now appear to work quite satisfactorily. The amount of sideplay for the sharpest curves, and vertical play for the changes of gradient, seem to be quite sufficient and I can recommend them for sanction.

I also went over the line again with a train that consisted of the following: engine, bogie carriage, two covered trucks, three open trucks and a brake van which when loaded will comprise an ordinary mixed train on this line and as most of the requirements of my report of the 6th instant have been carried out I made a re-inspection of the line to save another visit.

As soon as the Engineer can report the completion of the check rails around all the 3 chain curves, that wheel guards have been fitted to the bridges over the Lledan Brook and River Banwy, and that the gauge ties and proper super-elevation have been provided for the sharpest curves, I can recommend the Board of Trade to sanction the line to passenger traffic subject to the following special restrictions viz

a) A maximum speed of 15 miles per hour over any part of the line. (This restriction can be removed at the discretion of the company's Engineer once the formation has got consolidated.)

b) The further restrictions of speed laid down in Clause 52 of the Order.

c) A speed of 5 miles an hour when passing over the sharp reverse curves south of Golfa, and also those at Dolrhyd Mill.

Before opening for passenger traffic it will of course be necessary to see that all the facing and trap points of the sidings are connected up to the ground frames as they are at present disconnected for the convenience of the Contractor.

The attention of the Company should be should also be called to Clause 28(4) regarding the gates at level crossings.

Although the line is I consider safe for passenger traffic with the speed restrictions imposed above, yet as the earthworks are new and will settle while consolidating, care must be taken to keep the line true to gauge by constant attention to packing the sleepers and supplying more top ballast when required.

I have asked the Cambrian Railways (the working company) to apply for the usual permission to work mixed trains on the line.

> E Druitt
> Major RE

Source: MT6 1150 4

On 3rd March Mr Collin reported that the work required by Major Druitt had been completed and an application was made to the Board of Trade for the certificate that allowed the railway to be opened to the public.[114] It was issued on 4th March[115] and the railway opened for goods traffic on 9th March. Unfortunately, this was the day after the period allowed for the completion of the railway, so a further extension of time was applied for and granted.[116] For the opening, Oswestry works supplied forty wagons sheets, twenty wagon ropes, two hand trucks, two parcels trucks and two platform lorries.[117] During the first week 254 tons of coal, fertilisers and general merchandise were carried, all the traffic being taken from Welshpool to Llanfair.[118/119] In the first three weeks of operation 756 tons of goods were received, yielding receipts of £138 18s 3d, and 14 tons were forwarded by the railway, producing revenue of £3 7s 0d.[120]

Llanfair traders threaten to boycott the railway
Once the railway opened, Llanfair traders found that it was more expensive to send goods over the line than to carry them by road. On 20th March they sent a petition to Mr Denniss asking him to reduce the rates charged for the carriage of goods over the line. Mr Denniss replied that when a new railway opened it was difficult to forecast the revenue that the line would generate and that in fixing the rates he had to take into account the cost of working the line. He regarded the existing rates as being tentative and drew the petitioner's attention to the substantial reductions that had been made in recent days.

Mr Denniss' response did not placate the Llanfair traders because the new rates were still more expensive than those charged by carters. A meeting was called on the day before the official opening of the line, at which the traders decided that until such time that the Cambrian offered competitive rates for the carriage of freight over the light railway, they would have their goods sent to Welshpool by the L&NW line, or by the canal, and would then carry them to Llanfair by road. A resolution was passed deploring the reductions made by Mr Denniss and he was asked to consider the matter very seriously. The traders called for substantial reductions in the rates with the object of making the conveyance of goods to Llanfair by rail less expensive than by road. Copies of the petition were sent to Mr Denniss and Mr Humphreys-Owen. A committee chaired by Mr Levi Jones, the town's Postmaster, was formed to confer with Mr Denniss or any other official of the Cambrian company.[121]

THE OPENING CEREMONY
On 27th February the Directors decided to hold a public luncheon to celebrate the opening of the line to passengers on Tuesday, 31st March 1903 and a committee was appointed to organise the celebrations. However, the opening ceremony was postponed until Saturday 4th April to enable the Earl of Powis to be present.[122] A circular letter was sent to all shareholders advising them about the meal, while those who had subscribed more than £15 to the undertaking were given free

MRS. DAVIES of Haulfan, Llanfyllin, desire to THANK most cordially all who hav so kindly sympathised with her in her sad bereave ment.
Dated, 9th March, 1903.

CAMBRIAN RAILWAYS

PUBLIC NOTICE.

THE LINE BETWEEN
WELSHPOOL AND LLANFAIR
IS NOW OPEN
for Goods, Mineral, and Live Stock Traffic.
Rates and other information may be obtained from the Company's Agents at Welshpool and Llanfair, or from Mr W. H. Gough, Traffic Superintendent, Oswestry.

GOOD FRIDAY TRAIN SERVICE.

ON GOOD FRIDAY, April 10th, a Special Service of Trains will be run on all parts of the line, with the exception of the Kerry Branch. Full particulars as to the times of the trains may be obtained at any of the stations, or from Mr W. H. Gough, Traffic Superintendent, Oswestry.

passes to travel on the opening day. Two hundred tickets giving admission to the termini were printed for shareholders without free passes. The Chief Constable was requested to provide two constables at Welshpool and three at Llanfair.[123] Mr Herbert Jones was asked to ensure that the locomotive was suitably decorated and it was agreed that the train crew would receive gratuities but not refreshments. At Llanfair a local committee was appointed to decorate the town, while members of the Parish Council were invited to a reception at the station where champagne and biscuits would be served.[124] On 27th March a trial run was made with one of the locomotives and the three carriages. A representative of *The Montgomery County Times* who travelled on the train noted that the day was fine and the journey through the beautiful scenery was very pleasant. The carriages were described as comfortable, almost luxurious, there being a remarkable absence of vibration.[125]

The morning of the 4th was wet but in the main streets of Welshpool and at the station the many flags and streamers provided an abundance of colour. The special train was drawn up at the Smithfield Road terminus headed by *The Countess* which was decorated with red and green muslin, red rosettes

Near Golfa Station

Near Llanfair Station

Welshpool Terminus

Near Melin Dolrhyd

The special train run to celebrate the opening of the line on 4th April 1903 seen at the Welshpool and Llanfair station in Smithfield Road. The light railway's Directors and representatives of the Cambrian Railways can be seen behind the last carriage. POWYSLAND MUSEUM

and daffodils. The Prince of Wales' feathers were placed on the front and back of the engine and the motto *Success to the W&LLR* was carried in white letters along the sides of the boiler. By 11am a crowd of several hundred people had gathered in Smithfield Road to watch the train depart. A special train arrived from Oswestry with the Cambrian officials, and the Earl of Powis drove up in a dog cart to a warm welcome from the crowd.

At a few minutes after 11.15 the train departed to the cheers of the spectators and passengers. They were accompanied by a fusillade of exploding detonators that had been placed on the rails. The train was welcomed by cheering crowds at Church Street and along Brook Street. At Standard Quarry small charges of dynamite were detonated as the train passed. The train paused near Llanerchydol Gates to pick up some late passengers, then steamed away from the town. Country people gathered at the stopping places along the line to cheer the special on its way, while at Cyfronydd Captain Pryce, who lived nearby, joined the train. More detonators had been placed on the line near Llanfair and when the terminus was reached it seemed as if the whole town had turned out to welcome the travellers.

In Llanfair the church bells were rung from nine o'clock to celebrate the opening of the railway and, despite the driving rain, flags had been hung from many houses. The Llanfair brass band played suitable selections in the town before making their way to the station to greet the special as it arrived. At the main entrance to the station a huge arch covered with evergreens and surmounted by flags had been erected. At the gate opening onto the pathway to the booking office, a second arch carried the word *Welcome* and thirty yards from the platform end a third arch had been built over the line.

The travellers were welcomed by the Chairman of the Parish Council Mr W.A. Jehu who reminded his audience of the many attempts that had been made to bring the railway to Llanfair. Some people had entertained doubts about the nature of the new railway and the way it was to be worked, but the traffic that had passed over the line in recent weeks seemed to indicate that it would be a success. He thanked the Earl of Powis and the Directors for all that they had done to promote the line, then wished the railway every success.

The Earl of Powis congratulated the people of Llanfair on obtaining a railway after so many years of waiting. There had been many difficulties to overcome, notably at the Golfa, although raising the money to build the line had been an even greater mountain to climb. In fact, having spent over £50,000, another £2,000 was still required. The railway had been open for three weeks and the returns were very satisfactory, showing very favourable prospects for the future. Reminding his audience that the greater portion of the capital raised did not come from Llanfair, his Lordship appealed to them to do what they could to help raise the additional capital that was needed. Referring to the complaints about the rates charged for carrying freight over the railway, he thought that they would decrease as the railway progressed and that the line would be of great advantage to the district. He concluded by saying that the completion of the railway to Llanfair had been a source of considerable satisfaction to the Llanfair Board and assured his audience that they had no greater friends than the Llanfair Railway Directors.

Addressing the crowd, Mr Denniss said he was confident that the railway would be of great benefit to the district. He believed that the rates that had been put into operation were not necessarily those that would continue to be charged. While the rates were within the parliamentary powers, the Cambrian did not seek to choke off traffic by attempting to make exorbitant charges. It was hoped that the traffic would develop so that the shareholders would have the satisfaction of receiving a substantial dividend, but this would require good accommodation to be provided. The existing accommodation at Llanfair was rather limited and additional capital was required to extend the yard there. Mr Denniss concluded by assuring his audience that his company would do everything in its power to ensure the line was worked to the advantage of the district.

After several more speeches, refreshments were served and the special train returned to Welshpool with several people from Llanfair. It arrived at its destination punctually and was loudly cheered on its return. The travellers then adjourned to *The Oak* for their lunch and more speeches.[126]

Evan Astley of Llanfair recalled the opening day sixty years later. *"I will never forget the day as long as I live. We had any amount of champagne, a good meal and finally a free trip down to Pool. It was wonderful. I was sixteen when I started work on the railway with my father who was a carpenter. We helped to build the station and warehouse at Llanfair and to lay the sleepers and lines"*.[127]

Welshpool and Llanfair Light Railway.

OPENING CEREMONY,
Saturday, 4th April, 1903.

OFFICIAL PROGRAMME.

11-15 a.m.—Special Train will leave Welshpool Station for Llanfair.

(Free Railway Passes—not transferable—will be sent on application to all Shareholders of £15 and upwards).

12-15 p.m.—Reception at Llanfair Station.

1-0 p.m.—Special Train leaves Llanfair.

1-45 p.m.—Special Train arrives at Welshpool.

2-0 p.m.—Public Luncheon at the Royal Oak Hotel, Welshpool. Chairman: The Earl of Powis. Tickets, 3/6 each.

The Directors much regret that the small space at their disposal obliges them to limit the issue of Free Railway Passes.

To ensure seats being reserved at the Luncheon Table, Tickets should be taken at the Royal Oak Hotel, Welshpool, not later than Tuesday, March 31st.

JOHN EVANS.
SECRETARY.

24, Broad Street, Welshpool,
23rd March, 1903.

Source: Rail 1057 613

---

[1] Rail 722 6 W&LLR Light Railway Order 1899
[2] *The Montgomery County Times and Shropshire and Mid-Wales Advertiser* 29th March 1902
[3] Rail 722 2 W&L Board 18th April 1901
[4] Rail 722 2 W&L Board 22nd June 1901
[5] Rail 722 2 W&L Board 18th April 1901
[6] MT6 1081 3 Bircham & Co to The Treasury 1stMay 1901
[7] MT6 1081 3 Treasury and Bircham & Co. 28th May 1901
[8] Rail 1057 613 Application to Light Railways Commissioners 17th April 1897
[9] GWR Central Wales Division Section Appendix March 1943 Llanfair & Guilsfield level crossing 0m 76c p.108
[10] MT 6 1150 4 A.J. Collin to Board of Trade 31st May 1901
[11] MT 6 1150 4 Board of Trade to A.J. Collin 8th June 1901

[12] *The Montgomery County Times and Shropshire and Mid-Wales Advertiser* 21st December 1901
[13] *The Montgomery County Times and Shropshire and Mid-Wales Advertiser* 18th January 1902
[14] MT 6 1150 4 Amended specification approved by Herbert Jekyll 5th March 1902
[15] Rail 722 2 W&L Board 18th April 1901
[16] Rail 722 2 Works Committee 10th May 1901
[17] Rail 722 2 Works Committee 17th May 1901
[18] Rail 722 2 Works Committee 20th May 1901
[19] Rail 722 2 Works Committee 28th May 1901
[20] *The Montgomery County Times and Shropshire and Mid-Wales Advertiser* 1st June 1901

[21] *The Border Counties Advertiser* 5th June 1901
[22] *The Montgomery County Times and Shropshire and Mid-Wales Advertiser* 1st June 1901
[23] Rail 92 70 A.J. Collin to Cambrian Board 3rd July 1901
[24] Rail 92 70 A.J. Collin to Cambrian Board 7th August 1901
[25] Rail 92 70 Rail 722 2 W&L Board 8th July 1901
[26] Rail 92 70 Rail 722 2 W&L Board 26th September 1901
[27] Rail 92 70 Rail 722 2 W&L Board 31st October 1901
[28] Rail 722 2 W&L Board 23rd January 1902
[29] *The Montgomery County Times and Shropshire and Mid-Wales Advertiser* 22nd March 1902
[30] Rail 722 2 W&L Board 26th September 1901
[31] Rail 92 70 A.J. Collin to Cambrian Board 3rd October 1901
[32] Rail 92 70 A.J. Collin to Cambrian Board 12th November 1901
[33] Rail 92 70 A.J. Collin to Cambrian Board 3rd October 1901
[34] Rail 92 70 A.J. Collin to Cambrian Board 12th November 1901
[35] Rail 722 2 W&L Board 20th December 1901
[36] Rail 722 2 W&L Board 28th November 1901
[37] Rail 722 2 W&L Board 20th December 1901
[38] Rail 722 2 Works Committee 3rd February 1902
[39] Rail 92 70 A.J. Collin to Cambrian Board 9th December 1901
[40] Rail 92 71 A.J. Collin to Cambrian Board 13th January 1902
[41] Rail 92 70 A.J. Collin to Cambrian Board 9th December 1901
[42] Rail 92 71 A.J. Collin to Cambrian Board 10th February 1902
[43] Rail 722 2 W&L Board 20th February 1902
[44] *The Montgomery County Times and Shropshire and Mid-Wales Advertiser* 4th February 1902
[45] MT6 1612 2 Major Druitt's report of preliminary inspection 22nd February 1902
[46] Rail 722 2 W&L Board 24th April 1902
[47] Rail 722 2 W&L Board 20th February 1902
[48] Rail 722 2 W&L Board 31st October 1901
[49] Rail 722 2 W&L Works Committee 21st March 1902
[50] Rail 722 2 W&L Board 26th March 1902
[51] Rail 92 71 A.J. Collin to Cambrian Board 15th April 1902
[52] Rail 92 71 A.J. Collin to Cambrian Board 13th May 1902
[53] Rail 92 71 A.J. Collin to Cambrian Board 10th July 1902
[54] Rail 92 71 A.J. Collin to Cambrian Board 7th August 1902
[55] *The Montgomery County Times and Shropshire and Mid-Wales Advertiser* 23rd August 1902
[56] Rail 722 2 W&L Board 28th August 1902, 25th September 1902, 23rd October 1902
[57] *The Montgomery County Times and Shropshire and Mid-Wales Advertiser* 23rd August 1902
[58] Rail 722 3 Works Committee 11th December 1906
[59] Rail 722 3 Works Committee 15th February 1907, W&L Board 23rd September 1907
[60] Rail 722 4 W&L Board 25th July 1911
[61] *The Montgomery County Times and Shropshire and Mid-Wales Advertiser* 30th August 1902
[62] Rail 92 71 A.J. Collin to Cambrian Board 7 29th September 1902
[63] *The Montgomery County Times and Shropshire and Mid-Wales Advertiser* 4th October 1902
[64] *The Montgomery County Times and Shropshire and Mid-Wales Advertiser* 4th October 1902
[65] Rail 722 2 Works Committee 21st March 1902
[66] Rail 722 2 W&L Board 22nd May 1902
[67] MT6 1081 3 Earl of Powis to the Lords Commissioners of HM Treasury 22nd May 1902
[68] MT 6 1081 3 Board of Trade facing sheet 23rd May 1902
[69] Rail 722 2 W&L Board 11th July 1902
[70] Rail 722 2 W&L Board 11th July 1902
[71] MT6 994 First extension of time 1902
[72] Rail 722 2 W&L Board 24th April 1902
[73] Rail 722 2 W&L Board 11th July 1902
[74] Rail 722 2 W&L Board 28th August 1902
[75] Rail 722 2 Works Committee 2nd September 1902
[76] Rail 722 2 W&L Board 27th November 1902
[77] Rail 722 2 W&L Board 26th September 1902
[78] Rail 722 2 W&L Board 27th November 1902
[79] Cambrian Railways Register of water cranes, turntables, travelling and stationary cranes p.93
[80] Rail 722 2 W&L Board 11th July 1902
[81] Rail 722 2 Works Committee 6th August 1902
[82] MT 6 1150 4 A.J. Collin to Board of Trade 11th August 1902
[83] Rail 722 2 W&L Board 2nd September 1902
[84] Cambrian Railways rolling stock register pp. 70–71
[85] Rail 722 2 W&L Board 23rd October 1902
[86] Rail 722 2 W&L Board 26th September 1902
[87] MT 6 1150 4 John Evans to the Board of Trade Statutory notice 3rd October 1902
[88] Rail 92 71 A.J. Collin to C.S. Denniss 29th November 1902
[89] Rail 722 2 W&L Board 27th November 1902
[90] Rail 92 71 A.J. Collin to Cambrian Board 10th November 1903
[91] MT 6 1150 4 John Evans to the Board of Trade 14th November 1902
[92] Rail 92 71 A.J. Collin to Cambrian Board 8th December 1902
[93] Rail 92 72 A.J. Collin to Cambrian Board 13th January 1903
[94] Rail 92 71 H.E. Jones to C.S. Denniss 20th November 1902
[95] *The Montgomery County Times and Shropshire and Mid-Wales Advertiser* 15th November 1902
[96] Rail 92 71 H.E. Jones to C.S. Denniss 20th November 1902
[97] Rail 92 71 H.E. Jones to Harrison & Winnall 24th November 1902
[98] Rail 92 71 H.E. Jones to C.S. Denniss 20th November 1902
[99] Rail 92 71 A.J. Collin to C.S. Denniss 20th November 1902
[100] *The Montgomery County Times and Shropshire and Mid-Wales Advertiser* 15th November 1902
[101] *The Montgomery County Times and Shropshire and Mid-Wales Advertiser* 20th December 1902
[102] *The Montgomery County Times and Shropshire and Mid-Wales Advertiser* 27th December 1902
[103] *The Montgomery County Times and Shropshire and Mid-Wales Advertiser* 24th January 1903
[104] Rail 722 2 Works Committee 13th January 1903
[105] Rail 722 2 Works Committee 22nd December 1902
[106] Rail 722 2 W&L Board 23rd January 1903
[107] Rail 722 2 Works Committee 13th January 1903
[108] Draft report in Beyer Peacock Archive MSI Manchester
[109] *The Montgomery County Times and Shropshire and Mid-Wales Advertiser* 31st January 1903
[110] *The Montgomery County Times and Shropshire and Mid-Wales Advertiser* 7th February 1903
[111] MT6 1150 4 First Board of Trade inspection 6th February 1903
[112] MT6 1150 4 John Evans to Board of Trade 9th February 1903
[113] MT6 1150 4 Second Board of Trade inspection 20th February 1903
[114] MT6 1150 4 A.J. Collin to J. Evans; Harrison & Winnall to Board of Trade 3rd March 1903
[115] *The Montgomery County Times and Shropshire and Mid-Wales Advertiser* 4th April 1903
[116] MT6 994 Second application for an extension of time 8th March 1903
[117] Rail 92 72 Locomotive Superintendent report to Cambrian Board 10th March 1903
[118] *The Montgomery County Times and Shropshire and Mid-Wales Advertiser* 14th March 1903
[119] Rail 92 72 C.S. Denniss report to Cambrian Board 18th March 1903
[120] Rail 92 72 C.S. Denniss report to Cambrian Board 21st April 1903
[121] *The Montgomery County Times and Shropshire and Mid-Wales Advertiser* 4th April 1903
[122] Rail 722 2 W&L Board 27th February 1903
[123] Rail 722 1 Opening Committee 9th to 31st March 1903
[124] Rail 722 1 Opening Committee 9th to 31st March 1903
[125] *The Montgomery County Times and Shropshire and Mid-Wales Advertiser* 28th April 1903
[126] Rail 92 72 *The Salopian and Montgomeryshire Post* 11th April 1901
[127] Down memory lane by diesel *The Montgomeryshire Express* 6th April 1963

Llanfair Railway.

Amount due – 31 May. 1903.

Earthworks.	£8,000.0.0.
Br. Om.18chs.	290.0.0.
Ret.Wall 0.67.	200.0.0.
Steel Wk. Lledan Brook.	750.0.0.
Viaduct 6.67.	1,100.0.0.
Bridge 7.43.	1,000.0.0.
River Wall 8.68.	410.0.0.
Bridge &c. Dolrhyd.	610.0.0.
Culverts & Drains.	1,240.0.0.
Stream Bridges.	365.0.0.
Permanent Way.	7,480.0.0.
Cattle pits.	520.0.0.
Metalling.	490.0.0.
Fencing & Gates.	3,678.0.0.
Stations.	950.0.0.
Accom. Wks.	1,620.0.0.
Sundries yet to come say.	800.0.0.
	£ 29,503.0.0.

Less 2½%		737.0.0.
" Cash.		23,837.5.6.
" Retn.5% on Contract		1,124.0.0.
	£24,290.	25,788.0.0.
	Bal due.	£ 3,715.0.0.

CONTRACTOR'S OFFICE,

222, NEWPORT ROAD,

CARDIFF, 16th. July. 190 3

TELEGRAMS. "STRACHAN, CARDIFF."
NAT. TELEPHONE No 1141

Dear Sir,

Mr. Strachan will be obliged for a payment for the Welshpool & Llanfair Railway. The annexed shows amount agreed by the Engineer who writes that he has passed forward a payment on account of this work.

Yours faithfully,

J. Strachan

C.S.Denniss Esq.

17 JUL 1903

CHAPTER FIVE

THE LLANFAIR JINNY

WHEN the railway opened for passenger traffic on 6th April, crowds flocked to travel to the Welshpool April fair. *The Montgomery County Times* reported that as each train steamed in and out of Llanfair station, large crowds gathered to watch. For some it was the first time in their lives that they had seen a railway train. At Welshpool the 4.55pm departure was unable to accommodate all the people who wished to travel, so a special was run and this too was crammed with people returning to Llanfair. The following Wednesday, members of the committee, formed to protest about the rates charged by the railway company, met Mr W.H. Gough, the Cambrian Railways' Superintendent of the Line, who offered rates that for the most part were comparable to those offered by the road hauliers. By the end of the first week 1,274½ tickets had been issued and 156 tons had been carried over the line. The paper congratulated Mr Griffith and his staff for the able manner with which they conducted themselves.[1] The volume of traffic carried over the line in the first weeks was encouraging, allowing Mr Denniss to report to his Board that if it was maintained the railway would be a distinct commercial success.[2]

Traffic carried over the line from 9th March to 18th April 1903

Week ending	Passengers	Goods	Receipts
14th March	–	254t 9c	£48 14s 9d
21st March	–	255t 5c	£43 19s 5d
28th March	–	254t 15c	£49 11s 3d
4th April	–	Not stated	Not stated
11th April	1,274½	156t 5c	£63 1s 10d
18th April	864½	174t 8c	£56 1s 4d

PAYING FOR THE LINE

The contract to build the railway was made between the Cambrian Railways and Mr Strachan who was paid as the works progressed on receipt of certificates issued by Mr Collin, the Chief Engineer to both the Cambrian and Llanfair Companies. The Cambrian was reimbursed by the light railway company from monies received through the issue of shares, loans from the investing authorities, and instalments of the Free Grant awarded by the Treasury. The contract for the construction of the railway specified that it had to be completed by 1st September 1902[3], but as autumn turned to winter with little prospect of the line opening, the Llanfair Directors became concerned about the escalating cost of construction. In December Mr Collin submitted a revised estimate of the cost of completing the line which was referred to the Works Committee for review. The Committee was also asked to consider how more capital could be raised.[4]

Although the estimated cost of building the line had increased to £25,350[5] and more work had to be carried out before the railway could be opened to the public, further consideration of the matter was deferred until after the official opening of the line, and nothing appears to have been done to raise more capital.[6] When the Board met on 7th April

1903, the Directors asked the Works Committee to canvass for more subscriptions to the share capital before any long-term borrowing was contemplated.[7] The appeal only realised £1,387, so on 1st September the Directors decided to raise £3,000 by an issue of debentures bearing interest at 4½%.[8/9/10] Although the issue was approved by the shareholders on the same day, the prospectus was not issued until the following November.[11]

In May 1903 the Works Committee began to prepare a statement of expenditure incurred in building the railway so that an assessment of the additional capital required could be made and presented to the July Board.[12] In the interim Mr Strachan invoiced the Cambrian for the final payment due on the contract to build the line. The cost of construction was stated to be £29,503 and the Contractor asked for payment of £3,175, this being the balance due to him, together with retention monies totalling £1,124.[13] On 28th July Mr Collin wrote to the Works Committee putting the cost of Mr

WELSHPOOL AND LLANFAIR LIGHT RAILWAY COMPANY

WELSHPOOL

20th April 1904

My Lords

I much regret to have again to appeal to you in the interests of the Welshpool and Llanfair Light Railway Company, of which I have the honour to be Chairman.

It will doubtless be within your recollection that upon the 22nd of May 1902 I addressed a letter to Your Lordships appealing upon the grounds therein set forth for additional aid for the construction of the line and its equipment. In response to this application Your Lordships generously augmented the Free Grant that had been given in aid of the line by a further sum of £3,000.

At this date the Directors were advised that an additional sum of £7,000 was all that was required in order to complete the line and fund the necessary rolling stock and they accordingly undertook to raise by local effort a further £4,000 which, with the £3,000 then asked for, was considered, as the Board had every reason to believe, was properly estimated as being sufficient for the purpose.

In pursuance of this Undertaking, the Directors have succeeded with very great difficulty in obtaining further subscriptions to share capital of £1,500, and they have also by the issue of debenture stock raised a further sum of £3,000, the maximum amount they are authorised to borrow under the Order.

This sum, on the estimates of May 1902, would have been more than sufficient to meet all requirements. It is however with surprise and extreme regret that the Board have ascertained from their Engineer's final certificate a further sum of £5,700 is still required to defray the liabilities in connection with the construction of the line. This has been brought about in a very large degree by the following necessary additional works which were not provided for in the Engineer's estimate of May 1902:-

a) Works ordered by the Board of Trade as follows:- Check rails on curves, Alteration of Sidings to give six foot clearance, Alterations of gauge, Cant and tie-clips, Check rails on the Lledan and Banwy bridges, Strengthening the road to carry locomotives.

b) Additional earthworks in cuttings to give a better slope and drainage, which were found necessary owing to serious slips having occurred.

c) Making and metalling a roadway to Heniarth station

d) Additional works required by the District Council

e) Additional sidings required at Llanfair station to meet ordinary traffic requirements in excess of what was estimated.

Your Lordships are already aware of the difficulties that have been experienced in raising capital for the construction of this railway, and it is a source of gratification to the Directors to be able to report to Your Lordships that since the line was opened the returns have more than justified the expectations of the Promoters, and moreover the traffic proves incontestably how greatly the advantages of railway communication is appreciated in a district which, on account of its poverty, has hitherto been unable to obtain this unquestioned boon.

The line was opened for goods traffic on 9th March 1903 and to passengers on the 6th April and the traffic receipts to the 31st December 1903 are as follows:

	£ s d	£ s d
March		150.13.9
April		29?.14.2
May		268.12.11
June		297. 3.7
Gross receipts		1,007. 4.5
Less: 60% working expenses due to the Cambrian Company		604. 6.8
Net receipts		402.17.9
July	292. 5.4	
August	342.14.9	
September	276. 7.11	
October	262. 9.1	
November	228. 4.2	
December	250. 7.10	
Gross receipts	1,652. 9.1	
Less: 60% working expenses	991. 9.6	660.19.7
Total net receipts for ten months		£1,063.17.4

On the existing Capital of the company, which is made up as follows:-

	£
Loans from Local Authorities	15,350
Debenture Stock	3,000
	18,350
Share capital of which £15,074 has been subscribed	16,000
	34,350

the revenue is sufficient to pay the interest on the loans from the Local Authorities (including redemption), interest on the debenture stock and other fixed charges, and to leave a small sum for division among the shareholders.

For the proper development and successful working of the Railway the following works and additional rolling stock are also urgently needed:-

	Estimated cost
	£
Alteration of signalling and provision of passing places so that more than one Engine in steam may run	880
Platform, goods sidings and metalling the station yard at Castle Caereinion	270
Additional sidings and enlargement of the station yard at Llanfair	215
A third engine	1,600
Timber wagons	440
Additional passenger carriage	235
Total	£3,640

In view of the facts that are hereunder set forth, I venture very earnestly and respectfully to submit to Your Lordships that this Company, which has successfully carried out its engagements and supplied to the locality railway communication in the face of extreme difficulties, has a peculiar claim upon other funds set aside by the State to aid Light Railways, more especially having regard to the fact that owing to its poverty, they [*the Directors*] cannot look for more help from the District served by the line which has already subscribed to the utmost of its ability. I therefore appeal to Your Lordships that such further assistance be given to the Company under Section 5 of the Act, and to express the earnest hope that Your Lordships may be able to see your way to make up the Free Grant to one third of what has now been found, after providing for the additional works needed, to be the actual cost of constructing and equipping the line which would be equivalent of a further grant of £3,500, and that a further sum may be granted to the Company by way of a loan to clear off the existing liabilities and enable the Directors to affect the improvements that are needed to ensure the success of the undertaking. As Your Lordships are aware you are empowered to give assistance by way of Loan as well as by way of Free Grant and it is submitted that the receipts of the line show sufficient security for a loan.

The Directors and Officers of the Company will be pleased to wait upon Your Lordships should You desire it and give any explanations or details with regard to the expenditure that You may require.

    I am My Lords,
      Your obedient Servant
      POWIS
        Chairman

The Lords Commissioners of
His Majesty's Treasury

Source: Rail 1057 613

Analysis of additional expenditure incurred in construction of the line for which a loan of £5,700 was requested

	£
Works ordered by the Board of Trade	1,648
Additional earthworks to present slips in cuttings and drainage	1,531
Making and metalling the roadway to Heniarth station	219
Works required by the District Council and raising the river walls at Dolrhyd and Llanfair	787
Additional siding at Llanfair and water supply	989
Miscellaneous accommodation works	525
Total	£5,699

Strachan's work at £28,910 which was £3,560 more than the previous estimate.[14] When the Directors met on 31st July, they instructed the Works Committee to prepare a report on the cost of building the railway indicating where the cost overruns had occurred and the reasons for them. They also decided to apply to the Treasury for additional funding.[15]

In September 1903 the Board decided to let the application for additional public funds stand over until the exact amount required was known, but it was not until 26th March 1904 that Mr Collin produced the final estimate of the cost of Mr Strachan's contract which he put at £31,160 including additional work valued at £1,907.[16] In April the Directors received the Works Committee's report on the cost of building the line and decided to apply to the Treasury for a loan of £5,700 to fund the extra cost of construction, and asked for a Free Grant of £3,500 to pay for signalling, additional accommodation and more rolling stock.[17] In August the Treasury agreed to offer a loan of £5,700 at $3\frac{1}{4}$% under Section 5 of the Light Railway Act to rank equally with the railway's existing loans and debentures, but the application for another grant was refused.[18] The loan offered was conditional on the Llanfair Company raising funds of approximately £3,700 to put the line in a satisfactory condition, although subsequently assurances that the funds would be raised by 31st December 1907 were accepted.[19] Before the loan could be awarded, a further amendment to the 1899 Light Railway Order was required which was obtained on 1st May 1905.[20]

While attempts where made to assess the cost of building the railway, and to find the additional capital needed to pay for it, the final payment to the Mr Strachan was withheld. The contract between the Cambrian Company and the Contractor contained the provision that 'Any disputes that arise under this contract shall on completion of the works, and not before, be referred to Mr Collin or other Chief Engineer of the Cambrian Company and his decision shall be final'.[21] In April 1904 Mr Collin agreed to meet Mr Strachan to arbitrate on the final payment but before the meeting could take place he declined to act in the matter and subsequently resigned from his position as Engineer to both the Cambrian and Llanfair

A train for Llanfair crossing Union Street before calling at Seven Stars station.

Seven Stars station and cottage. POWYSLAND MUSEUM

Companies.[22] Mr Strachan refused to accept Mr Collin's successor as arbitrator and proposed three alternatives, none of which were acceptable to the Cambrian.[23] He then commenced an action to appoint an independent arbitrator and recover £19,723 that he claimed was owed for additional work on the line.[24] Although the amount claimed was patently unreasonable it proved impossible to arrive at a mutually acceptable settlement without resort to arbitration.[25]

When Mr McDonald, the Cambrian Chief Engineer, re-examined the final contract certificate prepared by Mr Collin he found that £1,509 was due to the Contractor but the Llanfair Directors were only prepared to acknowledge work totalling £976.[26] The Cambrian and Llanfair Companies were advised that Mr McDonald should send the final certificate to Mr Strachan before a summons was issued instructing him to refer the disputed amount to the Engineer who would then arbitrate on the matter. Additionally, a counterclaim of £1,685 should be made against the Contractor for failing to complete the line by the date specified in the contract, and for the use of rolling stock, manpower and materials provided by the

---

A RECORD DAY

Monday 4th May, Welshpool fair day, proved such a wonderful attraction to the country folk of Llanfair and district that the May Day Fair proved a record in the history – short at present – of the new line. The early train left Llanfair at 6.30 carrying fifty passengers for Pool, but this number was nothing compared with the crowd that left the country terminus at 9.40. Over 180 people found 'seats' somewhere in the train although scores had to be content with standing in the vans. So great was the crush at Welshpool at 5pm that the officials had to run two specials which reached shining Llanfair at 9.30pm and midnight respectively. The first special was terribly over crowded and many of the passengers longed for the old buses which even when packed had the fresh air as their canopy. Owing to some misunderstanding the last train was run with very few folks, many of the 'left behinds' having walked from Pool.

Source: The Montgomery County Times and Shropshire and Mid-Wales Advertiser 9th May 1903

Llanfair.   Dolrhyd Weir

The River Banwy near Dolrhyd, a view issued by
the Cambrian Railways at about the time the
railway opened.   CAMBRIAN RAILWAYS

Dolrhyd weir in about 1905. The railway crossed
the entrance to the mill race, then continued along
the north bank of the river.   VALENTINES

Llanfair station shortly after the railway opened for passenger traffic, with station staff and the train crew posed next to the locomotive. The gentleman standing next to the entrance to the station building may have been Mr Barrow Griffith, Llanfair's first station master.

Cambrian and Llanfair Companies.[27] Although this advice was accepted, the Llanfair Company found itself so short of funds that it was forced to ask the Cambrian to pay the amount certified on the final account to the court, pending receipt of the Treasury loan.[28/29]

The action to force Mr Strachan to accept Mr McDonald as the Arbitrator failed so Mr Walter Armstrong, the Great Western Railway's new works engineer, was appointed to arbitrate on the matter.[30] At a meeting held before the Arbitrator on 18th April 1905 Mr Strachan asserted that he was owed £9,877 but because he had not allowed the defendant companies sight of the amount claimed, Mr Armstrong proposed that the Engineers for both sides should meet, examine Mr Strachan's statement, agree as may items as possible, then prepare a schedule of the disputed costs. He also decided to inspect the railway on 12th May and hold a further meeting on 18th May.[31] By the 18th, agreement had been reached to pay Mr Strachan £1,574 but the schedule of disputed costs had not been prepared.[32] Once it was completed, the case came before Mr Armstrong who eventually awarded Mr Strachan £2,565 14s 3d plus costs.[33] The action against Mr Strachan left the light railway with liabilities totalling £4,145, the principal creditor being the Cambrian Company.[34/35] In May 1907 an attempt was made to obtain a Treasury loan so that these liabilities could be discharged and in July a meeting was held with the President of the Board of Trade. Although Mr Lloyd George was sympathetic to the Llanfair Company's application, officials dismissed it on the grounds that the light railway appeared to have reasonable security for the proposed loan, and it seemed likely that a Treasury loan was not warranted by the Light Railways Act.[36]

Further attempts to raise new capital were unsuccessful and the railway was unable to make any significant investment in

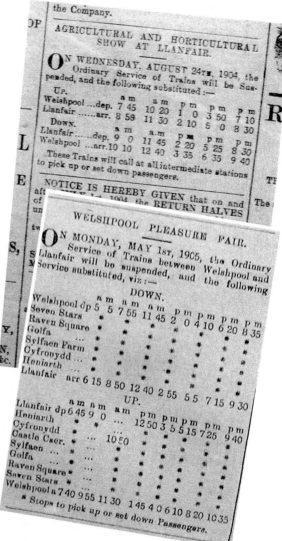

RAILWAY STATION AND COUNTY SCHOOL, LLANFAIR. BY J. W. E.

*Llanfair station and the County Intermediate School
photographed circa 1905. A train composed of the
railway's three carriages is seen at the platform whilst
the sidings were full of open wagons including three
belonging to J.Ll. Peate, a Llanfair coal merchant.
Notice the van underneath the warehouse canopy.
In the next decade the warehouse was extended to
provide additional storage for a farmer's co-operative.
Peate's office can be seen near the station entrance.
The cottages to the left of the station were known as
Nos. 1 and 2 station cottages.*

JOHN WATKINS ELLIS

*No.1 The Earl with a mixed train for Welshpool
photographed at Llanfair with the train crew and
station staff.*

its infrastructure or acquire any new rolling stock.[37] The Llanfair Company remained indebted to the Cambrian for the rest of its existence, making it impossible to declare a dividend on the ordinary shares.[38] In 1908 the local authorities agreed to suspend the periodic repayments of their loan capital for seven years, and in 1915 the waiver was extended for another seven years.[39/40] Although the Treasury loan was due to be repaid on 5th July 1915, agreement was reached that it need not be redeemed until repayment of the local authority loan principal was resumed. When this occurred the Treasury loan was to be repaid on the same basis as the local authority loans.[41/42]

FURTHER DEVELOPMENTS 1903–1922

At the opening ceremony Mr Denniss referred to the need to provide better facilities for goods traffic on the line. He suggested that Llanfair yard should be enlarged so that another siding could be provided.[43] The Llanfair Directors referred the matter to Mr Collin but although Mr Denniss pressed for additional accommodation at Llanfair, no more sidings were added to the station yard.[44] It was not until 1914 that additional wharfage and warehousing was authorised in response to pressure from a local agricultural co-operative.[45]

Shortly after the railway opened, Mr Denniss asked the Llanfair Directors to provide ten or a dozen timber trucks so

Llanfair photographed by J. W. Ellis in about 1905.
DR. W. T. R. PRYCE
COLLECTION

Castle Caereinion shortly after the railway opened.
DR. W. T. R. PRYCE
COLLECTION

Brake vans Nos 1 and 2 with a train of round timber carried on six timber trucks and a flat wagon at Welshpool. This probably formed the test train run on Sunday 22nd October 1906 to see if it was feasible to carry long timber over the railway.
CAMBRIAN RAILWAYS

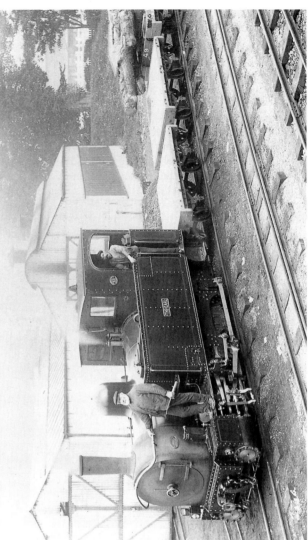

The locomotive and carriage sheds form the backdrop to No.1 The Earl. The two flat wagons were early conversions of open wagons.

that this class of traffic could be catered for, and six single bolster wagons were delivered in March 1904.[46/47] Accommodation in Llanfair yard was severely limited so agreement was reached with Messrs E. O. Jones & Sons to provide a timber siding at Tanllan where a sawmill was established.[48] Formal sanction for the siding's use was given by the Board of Trade on 29th November 1904.[49] Much of the timber carried was sawn into short lengths and at the 1906 Annual General Meeting a shareholder complained that long timber could not pass over the line because of the severe curvature.[50] On 22nd October 1906 a trial train of long timber was run over the line under the supervision of Messrs Gough, McDonald and Jones.[51] The experiment was successful and in February 1907 Messrs Jabaz Barker began to forward long timber from Tanllan. It was anticipated that Mr Barker's traffic would be so heavy that the line would have to be worked in two sections, so in June a signal box was provided at Castle Caereinion. However, although Messrs Barker's traffic was considerable, it did not require the use of a second engine.[52] By 1909 the traffic dealt with at Tanllan had grown to such an extent that the siding could not accommodate both firms' traffic and Mr Barker's timber had to be loaded at Heniarth.[53] Traffic forwarded from the station was sufficient to justify extending the loop in 1911.[54] In 1912 Mr Barker's timber was also loaded at Cyfronydd[55]

In 1907 narrow gauge rails were laid along part of the Smithfield siding at Welshpool so that long timber could be brought into the Cambrian yard[56] and by November 1913 the tranship siding had been extended to form a triangle of narrow gauge lines. In the same year, under pressure from Welshpool Borough Council, the passenger terminus was moved from Smithfield Road into the Cambrian goods yard.[57] In the early 1920s the narrow gauge rails in the Smithfield siding were extended towards Boys and Boden's saw mill, allowing timber from Pen-y-Coed near Cyfronydd to be forwarded to the firm's premises.

TRAFFIC

Detailed statistics showing the traffic carried by the railway only appear to have survived for the years before the Great War. In this period the railway carried between forty-nine and fifty-five thousand passengers each year. Passenger traffic was generally heaviest in the August when Llanfair show was held. On show days the normal timetable was suspended and an intensive service was run between Welshpool and Llanfair. Occasionally disputes were resolved during the journey. Shortly after the line opened, John Roberts and R. Jones admitted having a little scuffle to the annoyance of their fellow passengers. When they appeared before Llanfair Petty Sessions they were each ordered to pay costs of six shillings.[58] In the same period parcels traffic amounted to six or seven thousand items per annum, while between eight and eleven thousand tons of general merchandise and minerals, predominantly coal and lime, were carried each year. From claims for goods lost or damaged in transit it appears that boxes of rabbits were

12.45 p.m., arriving Llanfair at 1.40 p.m.

WELSHPOOL PLEASURE FAIRS.

MONDAYS, APRIL 2ND, & MAY 7TH, 1906.

ON the above Dates the Ordinary Service of Trains between Welshpool and Llanfair will be suspended, and the following Service substituted, viz:—

DOWN	a.m	a m	a.m.	p.m	p.m	p.m	p.m
Welshpool Station dep	5 57	7 55	11 45	2 0	4 10	6 20	8 35
Welshpool Seven Stars ...	a	a	a	a	a	a	a
Raven Square ...	a	a	a	a	a	a	a
Golfa ...	a	a	a	a	a	a	a
Sylfaen Farm ...	a	a	a	a	a	a	a
Castle Caereinion	a	a	a	a	a	a	a
Cyfronydd ...	a	a	a	a	a	a	a
Heniarth Gate ...	a	a	a	a	a	a	a
Llanfair C. arr	6 15	8 50	12 40	2 55	5 5	7 15	9 30

UP.	a.m	a.m	a.m.	p.m	p.m	p.m	p.m	p.m
Llanfair C. dep	6 45	9 0	...	12 50	3 5	5 15	7 25	9 40
Heniarth Gate ...	a	a	...	a	a	a	a	a
Cyfronydd ...	a	...	10 50	a	a	a	a	a
Castle Caereinion	a	...	a	a	a	a	a	a
Sylfaen Farm ...	a	...	a	a	a	a	a	a
Golfa ...	a	...	a	a	a	a	a	a
Raven Square ...	a	...	a	a	a	a	a	a
Welshpool Seven Stars ...	a	...	...	a	a	a	a	a
Welshpool station arr	7 40	9 55	11 30	1 45	4 0	6 10	8 20	10 35

a—Stops to pick up or set down passengers

FOOTBALL MATCHES AT LIVERPOOL.

THE MAY PLEASURE FAIR 1906
The annual May pleasure fair on Monday attracted an unusually large number of merry makers who invaded Welshpool from the surrounding countryside by every mode of conveyance. In contrast to the first few days of the 'merry month' the weather was all that could be desired, and all, whether bent on pleasure, or on business were able to achieve their aims with the minimum of discomfort. Business was perhaps the chief concern in the morning and the streets were crowded with a surging crowd. While the farmers' wives bargained in the shops and at the market, the farmers interested themselves with the buying and selling of stock at the Smithfield or were busy hiring lads and lasses for work on the farm during the next twelve months. Afterwards pleasure was everything. In the Salop Road fairground and the Cock yard there were the usual shooting galleries, merry-go-rounds, cinematograph show and other attractions which were kept going until a late hour. Order was efficiently preserved during the day by a strong staff of police under P.S. Poole and on the whole there was not much rowdyism or drunkenness.

Source: The Montgomery County Times and Shropshire and Mid-Wales Advertiser 7th May 1906

forwarded from Llanfair to Manchester, poultry and rabbits were sent to Birmingham, and butter was dispatched to the Wrexham area. Sugar, clothing and oil cake were received from Liverpool, Manchester and Newtown respectively. After the introduction of the sheep wagons in 1911 livestock traffic increased significantly.[59/60]

TRAIN SERVICES

When the railway opened, three mixed trains were provided on weekdays only. They left Welshpool at 7.50am, 11.40am and 4.55pm and returned from Llanfair at 9.40am, 2.20pm, and 6.30pm.[73] When the summer timetable was introduced on 1st July, a fourth service was provided so that trains now

departed from Welshpool at 7.50am, 11.45am, 3.40pm and 7.10pm, and returned from Llanfair at 9.40am, 2.15pm, 5.50pm and 8.30pm.[74] From May 1906 the midday service from Welshpool was retimed to run an hour later on Mondays. The service of four mixed trains in either direction continued until July 1909 when the last train of the day from Llanfair, by then the 8.00pm departure, became a goods only service allowing the early morning goods train to be cancelled.[75] This change was introduced as part of the economies introduced by John Conacher, the Cambrian Chairman.[76]

From July 1910 an 8.15pm departure from Llanfair was provided on Thursdays to cater for passengers returning to Welshpool using half-day excursion tickets.[77] The following

---

MEMORIES OF WORKING AT WELSHPOOL AND ON THE LLANFAIR TRAIN

Dick Leighton worked as the booking porter at the Llanfair Railway's Welshpool terminus between November 1906 and March 1908 when Mr Tom Pryce was station master. When he started, his wages were 15s for a week of seventy-two hours. His duties included issuing tickets and giving the right away to trains. The guard carried a case of tickets to issue to passengers in between the stopping places.

In between the train arrivals and departures Dick was in charge of the weighing machine where all the merchandise and coal was weighed. The Breezes, a Welshpool coal merchant, and J. & M. Morriss who owned the foundry, were regular customers and the charge was 2d a ton. At the end of the month, Dick had to go to the premises of those people who had used the weighing machine to collect any money that was owing so that he could balance the weighbridge tickets that he had issued with the money received. He also had to make out abstracts of accounts for the L&NWR and Cambrian Railways goods.

Several times Dick had to come out at 5am when an extra train was put on to bring timber down from Llanfair, and many times, owing to the length of the trees, they would throw the wagons off the curves and cause delays. He also remembered sending coal up to Llanfair for J. Ll. Peate.

Every Monday the train was packed and Dick had to travel on it to take charge of the tickets. He remembered what a crowd they had had coming to Welshpool. One of the important passengers was Mr Pickmere who was the Town Clerk of Liverpool. On the journeys up to Llanfair the fireman had to get off the train to open the crossing gates and Dick had to get off to close them. After the train had passed over the crossing, the driver John Williams and the fireman used to look back to see that he was back on the train. More often than not, Dick had to run behind the train because Driver Williams had set off too soon.

A porter at the main line station and Dick decided to form a branch of the Amalgamated Society of Railway Servants at Welshpool. They had to get 20 names to start, so they filled up a form with the names of people who did not intend to join at that time and opened up a branch.

There were occasional mishaps at the station. On 21st September 1906 David Blockley, then a newly appointed guard, gave the driver of *The Earl* the signal to proceed from the carriage shed road towards the catch points when they were open, causing the engine to be turned off the line. Traffic was considerably delayed and the 8.10am train to Llanfair was unable to run that day.

A SUNDAY SCHOOL EXCURSION

The bells of St Mary's Parish Church rang out merrily at 4am on Tuesday 21st July 1908 to wake the church choir, Sunday school and others who wished to join the trip to Aberystwyth. A large number started from Llanfair and were joined by several more at Heniarth station. At Welshpool the excited cries of the town's children could be heard as they made their way to the station. Two special trains departed from Welshpool at 7.00 and 7.15 carrying between 1,300 and 1,400 excursionists in total. They arrived at Aberystwyth between 9.00 and 9.30 and were soon bathing, boating or paddling while some listened to the pierrots on the Castle, the Pier or in the Elysian Grove. Tea was catered for in a capable manner by Mr Powell, Aberystwyth and was served at the Town Hall. The day was beautifully fine and everyone seemed delighted with the outing. The special trains left Aberystwyth at 7.30 and 10.00pm the last one reaching Welshpool at about 12.05am. The travellers for Llanfair caught the earlier service and reached their destination at 11.30pm. Much praise was due to those responsible for the arrangements for the day and especially to the Honorary Secretary Mr J.W. Smith.

Source: The Montgomery County Times and Shropshire and Mid-Wales Advertiser 25th July 1908

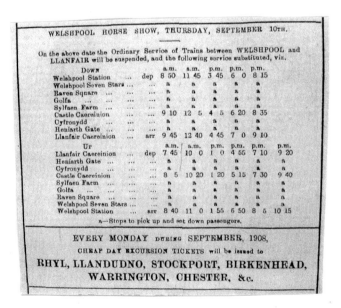

WELSHPOOL HORSE SHOW, THURSDAY, SEPTEMBER 10TH.

On the above date the Ordinary Service of Trains between WELSHPOOL and LLANFAIR will be suspended, and the following service substituted, viz.

Down		a.m.	a.m.	p.m.	p.m.	p.m.
Welshpool Station	dep	8 50	11 45	3 45	6 0	8 15
Welshpool Seven Stars	...	n	n	n	n	n
Raven Square	...	n	n	n	n	n
Golfa	...	n	n	n	n	n
Sylfaen Farm	...	n	n	n	n	n
Castle Caereinion	...	9 10	12 5	4 5	6 20	8 35
Cyfronydd	...	n	n	n	n	n
Heniarth Gate	...	n	n	n	n	n
Llanfair Caereinion	arr	9 45	12 40	4 45	7 0	9 10
Up		a.m.	a.m.	p.m.	p.m.	p.m.	p.m.
Llanfair Caereinion	dep	7 45	10 0	1 0	4 55	7 10	9 20
Heniarth Gate	...	n	n	n	n	n	n
Cyfronydd	...	n	n	n	n	n	n
Castle Caereinion	...	8 5	10 20	1 20	5 15	7 30	9 40
Sylfaen Farm	...	n	n	n	n	n	n
Golfa	...	n	n	n	n	n	n
Raven Square	...	n	n	n	n	n	n
Welshpool Seven Stars	...	n	n	n	n	n	n
Welshpool Station	arr	8 40	11 0	1 55	6 50	8 5	10 15

n—Stops to pick up and set down passengers.

EVERY MONDAY DURING SEPTEMBER, 1908,

CHEAP DAY EXCURSION TICKETS will be issued to

RHYL, LLANDUDNO, STOCKPORT, BIRKENHEAD, WARRINGTON, CHESTER, &c.

No. 2 The Countess *taking on water from the water tower at Dolrhyd.*

year it also ran on Saturdays for the duration of the summer timetable, and ran throughout the year from July 1914.[78/79] For the duration of the summer timetable of 1911, and from July 1912, an evening train ran on Llanfair fair days for the benefit of dealers returning to Welshpool.[80/81] The evening mixed train from Welshpool and return service were discontinued from January 1917, leaving the branch with a passenger service of three mixed trains in each direction.[82] The evening train was reintroduced in May 1920 when it ran on Tuesdays, Wednesdays and Saturdays but had been discontinued by 20th September 1926.[83/84] Thereafter three mixed trains were run in each direction on weekdays only until Saturday 7th February 1931.[85] The passenger service was withdrawn on and from the following Monday.[86]

Market day services and special goods trains

Welshpool livestock market was held on the first and third Mondays of the month and fairs were held at Llanfair on the first Friday of the month. To cater for traffic to Welshpool market it was originally intended to run a service that left the town at 5.30am and returned from Llanfair at 6.40am.[87] However, it only ran on 6th April 1903 because the Llanfair traders asked for, and were given, an early morning train to connect with services for London and Manchester at Welshpool. From 13th April a goods train left Welshpool for Llanfair at 5.15am on Mondays, Tuesdays and Wednesdays and arrived at Llanfair at 6.25am. The locomotive then worked the 6.30 mixed train from Llanfair which arrived at Welshpool at 7.40am.[88] From October 1907 an early morning goods service

also ran when required on Thursdays, Fridays and Saturdays but returned as a goods train.[89] The return working was probably used to haul the timber trains and ran on fifty occasions between October 1908 and April 1909.[90] With the exception of the Welshpool market trains, the early morning services were withdrawn in July 1909.[91] The market day trains were heavily patronised and although attempts were made to persuade the Directors to purchase an additional carriage it could not be afforded.[92] The early morning goods to Llanfair that returned to Welshpool as a mixed train continued to run on the first and third Monday of each month until 15th February 1926. In later years the goods left Welshpool at 5.50am and returned from Llanfair at 7.15am.[93] On Llanfair fair days a mixed train left Welshpool at 5.15am and arrived at Llanfair at 6.25am; the locomotive then worked the 6.30am goods to Welshpool.[94] The service had been discontinued by July 1915.[95]

Fairs, agricultural shows and other special occasions

Annual agricultural shows were held at Welshpool and Llanfair in September and August respectively, while pleasure fairs took place at Welshpool in April and May. On show and fair days before the Great War the ordinary service was suspended and was replaced with a special timetable. The first occasion on which this happened seems to have been for the 1904 Llanfair show when five trains were provided in each direction.[96] For the 1905 show seven return trains were provided together with one trip from Llanfair to Castle Caereinion and back.[97] Seven trains were also provided for visitors to

WELSHPOOL AND LLANFAIR LIGHT RAILWAY
Working expenses, income, net revenue, amounts paid to the Llanfair Company and net profit or loss to the Cambrian company

	1903	1904	1905	1906	1907	1908	1909	1910	1911	1912	1913	1914	1915	1916	1917	1918	1919	1920	1921	1922
	£	£	£	£	£	£	£	£	£	£	£	£	£	£	£	£	£	£	£	£
Locomotive, carriage and wagon department																				
Running expenses																				
Wages of enginemen, firemen etc	348		354	366	366	373	375	364	366	380	376	364	354	371	258					
Coal	109		225	211	233	292	266	224	197	214	253	259	314	415	394					
Water, gas and general stores			26	23	32	19	25	26	34	46	21	18	22	24	45					
Repairs and renewals																				
Wages	49		28	43	51	53	43	9	121	10	26	85	61	20	33					
Materials	41		23	18	39	9	43	6	93	5	18	46	56	18	13					
Carriages and wagon repairs																				
Carriages wages			20	40	20	9	42	5	6	11	11	35	12	21	18					
materials			21	13	5	2	22	2	3	7	7	15	2	44	20					
Wagons wages			39	38	12	15	6	16	12	24	25	20	40	25	57					
materials			68	32	12	5	6	17	22	38	40	10	29	7	39					
War bonus													9	96	120					
Engineer's Department																				
Wages	572		504	461	462	484	474	394	376	426	368	439	409	411	399					
Materials	29		20	31	132	43	47	178	207	76	94	27	48	122	185					
Engine hire and ballasting								78												
Miscellaneous											6	8	6	6	7					
War Bonus													60	131	268					
Traffic Department																				
Wages	244		412	419	412	389	375	338	299	313	319	315	322	325	321					
Materials	28		39	33	41	43	47	50	40	37	34	33	47	34	63					
War Bonus													53	108	233					
Sundries	27		61	65	52	61	37	40	40	43	45	53	54	50	50					
National Insurance Contributions										9	13	13	12	14	13					
Maintenance of Telegraphs	13		19	19	19	19	20	20	19	19	19	19	19	19	19					
Total Expenditure	1,460	0	1,859	1,812	1,888	1,816	1,828	1,767	1,835	1,658	1,675	1,759	1,929	2,261	2,555					
Gross receipts	2,660	3,210	2,921	2,968	2,914	2,907	2,981	2,961	3,046	3,089	3,049	2,937	3,049	3,052	3,054					
Net revenue	1,200	0	1,062	1,156	1,026	1,091	1,153	1,194	1,211	1,431	1,374	1,178	1,120	791	499					
40% of receipts paid to the Llanfair Company	1,064	1,284	1,168	1,187	1,166	1,168	1,163	1,195	1,218	1,236	1,220	1,175	1,220	1,221	1,222					
Profit (Loss) to the Cambrian Company	136		(106)	(31)	(140)	(77)	(10)	(1)	(7)	195	154	3	(100)	(430)	(723)					

WELSHPOOL AND LLANFAIR LIGHT RAILWAY
Analysis of Gross Income

	1903	1904	1905	1906	1907	1908	1909	1910	1911	1912	1913	1914	1915	1916	1917	1918	1919	1920	1921	1922
	£	£	£	£	£	£	£	£	£	£	£	£	£	£	£	£	£	£	£	£
Passengers	1,167	1,353	1,365	1,407	1,323	1,284	1,265	1,239	1,227	1,214	1,318									
Parcels	109	220	177	181	177	171	185	190	182	185	193									
General merchandise	852	1,058	736	723	824	871	936	923	1,016	883	766									
Minerals	522	566	632	641	569	548	557	551	521	714	656									
Livestock	10	12	10	15	20	31	35	54	95	88	91									
Miscellaneous		1	1	1	1	2	3	4	5	5	25									
Gross receipts	2,660	3,210	2,921	2,968	2,914	2,907	2,981	2,961	3,046	3,089	3,049									

WELSHPOOL AND LLANFAIR LIGHT RAILWAY
Traffic Analysis

	1903	1904	1905	1906	1907	1908	1909	1910	1911	1912	1913	1914	1915	1916	1917	1918	1919	1920	1921	1922
Passengers (Nos.)	46,452	55,057	55,272		54,362	53,550		50,260	49,470	49,128	55,474									
Parcels (Nos.)	3,592	6,293	5,839		6,205	6,357		6,915	7,171	7,127	7,376									
General merchandise (Tons)	3,526	4,589	3,263		3,313	3,622		3,787	3,861	3,742	3,107									
Minerals (Tons)	4,405	4,639	5,403		4,849	4,715		4,830	4,445	7,742	6,101									
Livestock (Wagons)	26	33	29		55	84		146	155	335	346									

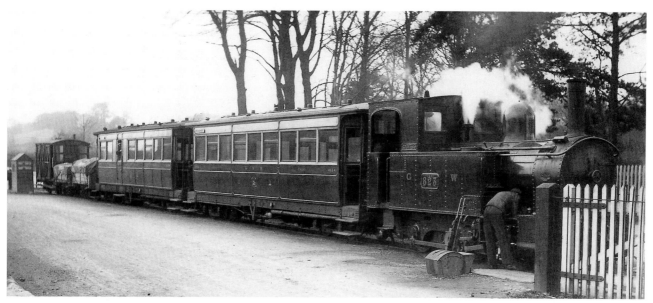

No. 823 Countess *waiting for time at the passenger terminus in Welshpool goods yard with a service for Llanfair. Welshpool Yard No.1 ground frame, situated to the left of the gatepost, controlled access to the tranship siding.*

Welshpool show.[98] The following year seven trains were run in connection with the Welshpool pleasure fairs and Powys Eisteddfod but only six trains were run on Llanfair show day.[99/100/101] On such occasions trains were run over the line from as early as 5.05am until as late as 10.35pm.[102]

Special trains were often well patronised and the railway could not cope with demands placed on it. The Welsh National Agricultural show was held at Welshpool on 9th and 10th August 1911 and on the second day 450 passengers travelled over the railway. A great many people had to cycle or hire traps because the railway could not carry them which led a *County Times* correspondent to ask whether an additional carriage should be provided for the profit of the shareholders and comfort of the public.[103]

Journey times and timetables

When the railway opened, seventy minutes were allowed for the journey between the termini.[104] Train speeds were increased from 3rd December 1904 allowing the journey time to be reduced to fifty-five minutes in each direction.[105] With the introduction of the winter timetable in October 1911 the journey time from Llanfair to Welshpool was reduced to fifty minutes, but reverted to fifty-five minutes for the duration of the summer timetable from 1912 to 1916.[106/107] From October 1916 until the closure of the line to passenger traffic, a journey time of fifty minutes became the norm for Up trains.[108/109]

The first public and working timetables did not show the times at which trains called at any of the intermediate stations, and it was not until July 1906 that they showed when trains would call at Castle Caereinion. Passengers wishing to join the train at stations between the termini were expected to signal to the driver and tell the guard where they wished to alight. Dolarddyn crossing was recognised as a stopping place

from 1st July 1904. On Mondays all trains stopped for passengers travelling to or from Welshpool while on other days a stop was made for picnic parties.[110] From 8th July 1929 Dolarddyn was given the same status as the other intermediate stopping places.[111] Trains also stopped near Dolrhyd Mill for the benefit of Mrs Anwyl's tenants.[112]

GOVERNMENT CONTROL AND THE GROUPING

On 4th August 1914 the Cambrian and Llanfair Companies came under Government control which continued until 15th August 1921. The Railways Act of 1921 saw both undertakings placed in the Western Group. The Great Western Railway paid £20,000 in cash for the light railway which, together with compensation received for the period of Government control and its cash balances, enabled the Debenture holders to be paid 90% of the nominal value of their stock, the Treasury and local authorities to receive 81% and 80% respectively of their loan principal, while the shareholders were paid 4s 11d for every £1 share held.[61] When the shareholders met for the last time on 14th December 1922 they passed a resolution urging the Great Western to convert the railway to standard gauge so that the great expense of transhipment could be avoided.[62] The Welshpool and Llanfair Light Railway became part of the Great Western Railway on 1st January 1923.

THE GREAT WESTERN TAKES CHARGE

The most obvious change in ownership was that the locomotives and rolling stock were repainted in the new owner's livery. In 1923 No.1 was renumbered 822 while No.2 became 823 and had its name shortened to *Countess*. In June 1923 the Traffic Committee voted £203 for improved goods transfer facilities at Welshpool but nothing is known about the nature

No. 822 The Earl waiting with a mixed train at Llanfair Caereinion in 1925, by which time a single carriage was sufficient for the traffic offered on all but fair and show days. The corrugated-iron structure to the right of the locomotive was a urinal.
A.W. CROUGHTON, Cty. MICHAEL WHITEHOUSE

A Thornycroft A1 bus waiting outside the Lion Hotel, Llanfair on a Welshpool to Dinas Mawddwy service.   GREAT WESTERN RAILWAY

of the work carried out. In October the carriages were fitted with incandescent lighting and received steam heating apparatus during the following month, which was doubtless appreciated by passengers who were accustomed to the dim light provided by oil lamps and unheated carriages.[63] In December six new timber trucks were ordered for the line, the order being completed at Swindon during the following August. In 1924 the Great Western applied to Welshpool Borough Council to straighten out the line of rails between Welshpool and Raven Square stations. The application was referred to the Buildings Sub-Committee but no more was heard about it.[64]

The return of the Llanfair bus

The Great Western pioneered the operation of road motor services and by 1923 had begun to develop bus routes in the area formerly served by the Cambrian Railways. In May 1925 an agreement was reached with Crosville Motors who undertook not to open up services in the Oswestry and Welshpool areas and on 27th July 1925 the Great Western began to run buses to Llanfair.[65] There were two services in each direction from Oswestry that ran via Llansantffraid and Meifod. The morning service terminated at Llanfair but the

afternoon bus continued on to Welshpool. On Saturdays there was an evening service that ran from Oswestry to Meifod and back. The first service of the day to Welshpool originated at Dinas Mawddwy and connected with the morning bus from Oswestry at Llanfair. At midday the Dinas bus ran from Welshpool to Llanfair and back, before retuning to Dinas Mawddwy in the afternoon. Later in the afternoon the Oswestry bus retuned from Welshpool via Llanfair. When first introduced, the Welshpool services ran via Cwm Goleu and Castle Caereinon but a handbill dated January 1926 shows that they had been rerouted along the main road.[66/67] The road motor services were run subject to the condition of the road and in adverse weather they could be altered. When seating capacity was limited, passengers using the bus in connection with train services and those travelling to more distant points on the route were given preference. Parcels and goods not exceeding one hundredweight could also be conveyed by bus between stations and the company's Road Motor Parcel Agents.[68]

By 1930 there were three return journeys between Oswestry and Llanfair every weekday. The journey between the termini took an hour and a half. On Mondays a service was provided from Oswestry to Welshpool that ran via Heniarth. There were three daily return services between Welshpool

Llanfair — 1m. 29c. — Heniarth — 1m. 77c. — Cyfronydd — 1m. 75c. — Castle — 1m. 19c. — Sylfaen — 9m. 3c. — Golfa — 1m. 68c. — Raven Square — 1m. 73c. — Seven Stars — 37c. — 35c. — Welshpool

*RECEIPTS—YEAR 1925.

* As shown on Station Traffic Statement; see note on page 2 of Report.

STATION.	PASSENGER. £	PARCELS. £	GOODS. £	TOTAL. £	1924 TOTAL. £	INCREASE OR DECREASE. £
Welshpool (Branch only) ..	750	298	—	1,048	1,129	— 81
Llanfair ..	501	417	2,544	3,462	3,537	— 75
	£ 1,251	£ 715	£ 2,544	£ 4,510	£ 4,666	— £ 156

TOTAL .. .. £ 2,544

EXPENDITURE.

TRAFFIC DEPARTMENT STAFF—PAYBILL FIGURES.

Station.	1924.	1925.
Welshpool	£ 435	£ 435
Llanfair	356	382
	£ 791	£ 817

	£	PERCENTAGE OF TRAFFIC RECEIPTS. *
TOTAL ..	817	18.12

LOCO. DEPARTMENT, ENGINE AND TRAIN RUNNING EXPENSES.

Coaching (Coal consumption..35.7..lbs. per mile). Total £ 1,081.   Maintenance, Renewal and Working Cost } 21.90 per mile.

Freight (Coal consumption..35.7..lbs. per mile). Total £ 2,476.   Maintenance, Renewal and Working Cost } 23.65 per mile.

	£	
TOTAL ..	3,557	78.87
ENGINEERING DEPARTMENT, MAINTENANCE AND RENEWAL ..	1,930	42.79
SIGNAL DEPARTMENT, MAINTENANCE AND RENEWAL ..	138	3.06
CLOTHING	10	.22
FUEL, LIGHTING, WATER AND GENERAL STORES ..	5	.11
RATES	45	.99
TOTAL	£6,502	† 144.16

† NOTE.—No general charges (Abstract E. of Annual Report) nor cost of supervision, advertising, printing, etc. (Abstract D. of Annual Report) have been included in this Statement. In the 1925 Annual Report these items = 8.98% of Traffic Receipts.

The percentage of maintenance, renewal and working expenses to Traffic receipts for whole system = 83.63%.

PASSENGER TRAFFIC WORKED BY:—

Branch Train: (Narrow gauge : 2 ft. 6 in.)
3 " Mixed " Trips each way daily.
1 " Mixed " Train—3 times weekly.

Engine stabled at Welshpool.

SIGNALLING ARRANGEMENTS:—

Wooden Staff.
One Engine in Steam.

ALTERATIONS MADE OR PROPOSED IN WORKING ARRANGEMENTS:—

Reduce Train Service and Branch Hours to 8 per day.
Withdraw Station Master from Llanfair.

GOODS TRAFFIC WORKED BY:—

Mixed Trains.

Goods Tonnage : forwarded and received 1925 :—

		Principal traffic consists of:
Coal and Minerals ..	5,639 }	Coal, Roadstone, Lime, Grain
General Goods ..	2,579 }	

Daily average of wagons dealt with :—

	forwarded	received
Coal and Minerals ..	—	5
General Goods ..	3	4

RULING GRADIENT

1 in 30 ....

Length ....

1925
1,368 cans of milk.
344 trucks of live stock by goods train.

Estimated Annual Value of Savings £ 6,502

2-26 (17)

Source: Rail 250 736

No. 823 Countess *passing Bronybuckley with the 9.35am mixed train from Llanfair on 6th April 1926.*   LCGB, KEN NUNN COLLECTION

and Llanfair, of which one continued to Dinas Mawddwy while another terminated at Garthbeibio. On Saturdays there was an additional late service from Welshpool. The scheduled journey time from Welshpool station to Llanfair was 44 minutes.[69] In July 1930 the GWR merged its bus undertaking in north and central Wales with Wrexham and District Transport, and a new company, Western Transport, took over the operation of services to Llanfair. Western Transport became part of Crosville Motors on 1st May 1933 and the GWR received a $12\frac{1}{2}$% stake in the merged undertaking.[70]

The branch line review

In 1926 the Assistant Superintendent of the Line, H.L. Wilkinson, reviewed the performance of fifty-three branch lines assessing their system of operation and financial viability using data collected for the year to 31st December 1925. The Llanfair Railway was included in the review because it was a self-contained, secondary branch line. In 1925 three mixed trains ran over the branch in each direction every weekday, there being an additional evening service on Tuesdays, Wednesdays and Saturdays. The principal traffic consisted of coal,

roadstone, lime and grain. Mr Wilkinson concluded that serious consideration should be given to closing the branch because working, maintenance and renewal charges were considerably greater than the receipts. The value of rail traffic lost by closing the line was unlikely to be equivalent to the cost of working and maintaining it. Road services could be used to carry parcels and the lighter goods traffic, leaving road hauliers to carry the heavier traffic such as coal, from Welshpool or Llansantffraid stations. If closure was not an option, Mr Wilkinson recommended that consideration should be given to abolishing the post of Station Master at Llanfair and reducing the train service to eight hours a day so that the line could be worked by a single set of men. Such a service was unlikely to meet the needs of local people, so as an alternative, the line could be worked by a split shift or the hours of a single set of men might be extended. Although the branch survived the 1926 review, the deteriorating economic climate and increased competition from road transport meant that it was always vulnerable to closure.[71] Despite the mounting losses made by the branch, the locomotives were given new boilers in 1929–30.[72]

7183.

No. 822 The Earl passing through the narrow gauge yard at Welshpool with a mixed train for Llanfair. Three sheep wagons, with their sides removed, are seen on the loop whilst the Great Western cattle wagons on the left had been stabled on the Smithfield siding. c. 1930.

THE WITHDRAWAL OF THE PASSENGER SERVICE

Once the bus service became established, passengers generally found it quicker and more convenient than the railway even through the fares were more expensive. On Welshpool market days the trains continued to be well patronised because passengers could store their market baskets in the carriage gangways. By 1931 eighty passengers travelled from Llanfair to Welshpool on Mondays and a further twenty joined the trains en route, but on other days some trains ran without any passengers.[113] In January 1931 the Great Western gave notice that the passenger service would be withdrawn on and from Monday 9th February 1931.[114] The decision to withdraw the service seems to have been taken quite quickly and was not reported to the Traffic Committee until 12th February, some five days after the last passenger train ran.[115]

A notice announcing the closure of the line to passengers appeared in *The County Times* on 31st January barely eight days before the last passenger train ran, so local people and their representatives had little opportunity to object to the loss of the service.[116] On 2nd February Mr D.W. Evans, Clerk to Llanfair Parish Council, wrote to Mr James Milne, the Great Western's General Manager, asking why a passenger service could not be provided if goods trains continued to be run. Mr Evans stated that local people were seriously con-

cerned that the slender facilities already offered would be reduced and did not believe that road services could satisfy the needs of the district. He asked for confirmation that fares charged by Western Transport would be no greater than those offered by the railway.[117] Two days later Mr J. Ben Davies, Town Clerk of Welshpool, wrote to the Great Western Secretary objecting to the withdrawal of the passenger service and proposing that, at a minimum, a market day service should be operated on Mondays. However, the company would not reconsider its decision to withdraw the passenger service.[118]

The last passenger train was hauled by *Countess* on Saturday 7th February. As on the opening day, it was wet, but in contrast to the crowds of cheering townsfolk that greeted the first departure, the last train passed over the line almost unnoticed.[119] A leader in *The County Times* argued that the construction of the railway had been funded in large measure

Train and station staff at Llanfair on the last day of the passenger service. 7th February 1931.

29/1/1931.

GREAT WESTERN RAILWAY.

Welshpool & Llanfair Branch. Abermule & Kerry Branch.

THE GREAT WESTERN RAILWAY COMPANY give NOTICE that owing to the losses which are being incurred on the Welshpool and Llanfair and the Abermule and Kerry Branches, the Passenger Train facilities now afforded by the Company will be WITHDRAWN on and from FEBRUARY 9th, 1931.

The WESTERN TRANSPORT COMPANY will arrange compensatory ROAD PASSENGER SERVICES on the WELSHPOOL AND LLANFAIR BRANCH.

The Great Western Company will continue to afford facilities for the CONVEYANCE OF PARCELS, MERCHANDISE & MINERALS over the two Branches.

Particulars of the arrangements may be obtained from the Company's local representative.

JAMES MILNE, General Manager.

Paddington Station, London. W.2., January, 1931.

Telegraphic Address:-
MANAGER, PADDINGTON STATION, LONDON.

Great Western Railway

General Manager's Office,
Paddington Station,
London, W.2.

Paddington
7000
Exten. 349.

G.1.57,312(10)

19th February, 1931.

Dear Sir,

I am in receipt of your letter of the 18th instant enclosing copy of resolutions of your Council and a petition in regard to the withdrawal of the passenger train facilities between Welshpool and Llanfair. I need hardly say that the Company much regret that present circumstances have rendered it necessary to close this line to passenger traffic but, as the business is not sufficient to cover the cost of operating, it is felt there is no alternative but to do so, particularly having regard to the fact that the route is now served by the Western Transport Company's omnibuses. It is thoughtthat the omnibus service will meet all the requirements of the District but if experience shews that additional facilities are necessary, arrangements will be made for the service to be augmented.

Yours faithfully,

J. Ben Davies, Esq.,
Town Clerk's Office,
WELSHPOOL.

Source: Powys County Archive Office

Broad Street, Welshpool.
VALENTINES

by the district and it was in a special sense the property of the locality. Although the line had never paid a dividend it was of great service to the communities that it served and should receive special consideration.[120]

In Welshpool the Municipal Association organised a petition urging the Borough Council and Mr Henry Warwick, the Great Western's Divisional Traffic Manager, to press for a passenger service on market days, show days and Saturdays. The petitioners asserted that on market days the buses did not provide an adequate service and that their fares were excessive. They noted that the Great Western provided passenger services between Welshpool and Llanfair by train and bus, and attributed the cause of the losses on the train service to the reduction in rates charged since the line was acquired by the company. In Llanfair a large number of people were said to be dependent on the railway to get their produce to the markets at Welshpool and beyond.[121]

On Friday 13th February Mr John Eddowes, the Mayor of Welshpool, and representatives of the Municipal Association met Mr Warwick who explained the reasons underlying the decision to withdraw the passenger service. Faced with rising costs and the loss of traffic to road transport, the Great Western was compelled to seek economies. The introduction of the eight-hour day meant that two sets of men were required to work trains on the branch, and a Railway Clearing House Committee had compelled the company to offer return tickets at the price of a single ticket. This had caused the revenue to fall by 37% which only funded half the locomotive department's expenses. Since the line had become part of the Great Western, the rates offered for through traffic to Llanfair were the same as those to Welshpool, so the company received no extra revenue for carrying through traffic on to Llanfair. Members of the delegation contended that the fall in receipts was due to the Great Western's actions and that people living in the district served by the railway would prefer to pay the

higher rates that were in force before amalgamation than lose the line. Mr Warwick agreed to consider the Association's proposals for a service on Welshpool market days.[122]

When the Borough Council met on 18th February its Members discussed the Municipal Association's petition protesting at the closure of the railway to passengers. They passed a resolution reminding the Great Western that the railway had been built to develop agriculture in the district. In their opinion the closure of the line to passengers would inconvenience local farmers and damage the markets at Welshpool and Llanfair. Copies of the Association's petition and the Council's resolution were sent to the Ministry of Agriculture and Fisheries, the Ministry of Transport and Mr Clement Davies, the Member of Parliament for Montgomeryshire, with a request that they take up the matter with the Great Western and use their best endeavours to bring about a partial restoration of the passenger service.[123] On the 19th Mr James Milne, the Great Western's General Manager, acknowledged the receipt of the petition and resolution, expressed regret that it had been necessary to close the line to passenger traffic, and drew attention to the bus service provided by the Western Transport Company.[124]

Later in the month Mr Warwick told the Municipal Association that a market day service could not be provided while the eight-hour day was in operation. About a hundred people used the line on Mondays but only half of them returned to Llanfair by the 12.50pm train. Without a second train the number of people travelling would be reduced by half so the service would not be viable. Supplying a second train crew for a service later in the afternoon would result in further losses. If the branch was operated as a mineral line, considerable savings in maintenance could be made because the Board of Trade's requirements for passenger traffic could be dispensed with. The Association's representatives contended that the Cambrian had agreed to work the line for ninety-

Llanfair station yard with the 'back road' filled with dropside wagons and one of the covered vans. The crane was rated to lift 2 tons 10 cwt.

Sylfaen halt and farm, photographed on 8th October 1931, eight months after the line was closed to passengers.

nine years and that the Light Railways Act made no provision to close railways that had been built under its provisions. Although the Municipal Association urged the Borough Council to seek Counsel's opinion on the matter, no further action appears to have been taken.[125]

Protests to Whitehall also proved to be futile. In June Mr Eddowes reported that the Ministry of Agriculture took the view that the matter was essentially one for the Ministry of Transport and would not intervene. Herbert Morrison, the Minister of Transport, had written to Mr Clement Davies M.P. stating that although he had taken up the matter with the Great Western, he could not compel the company to restore the passenger service. Mr Davies wrote that the Great Western might have put a motor train on the line instead of introducing a bus service on the road, so increasing the cost of local rates without providing a better service to the public.[126] Mr Eddowes concluded that there was nothing further that the Council could do.[127] While attempts where made to restore the passenger service, the carriages were taken to Swindon where they were eventually broken up.

GOODS ONLY

After the line closed to passengers, the former waiting room at Llanfair was used as a store for animal feeds while the goods warehouse continued to be rented by a local farmer's co-operative. By the mid 1930s there was an acute shortage of covered accommodation at the station. Growth in the volume of agricultural merchandise dealt with at Llanfair justified the provision of a galvanised iron lock-up shed that was brought into use in December 1937. At about the same time the veranda on the former waiting room and booking office was removed to allow road vehicles access to the new store.

SOME LIGHT ON A LIGHT RAILWAY
THE WELSHPOOL AND LLANFAIR – A LITTLE KNOWN
GREAT WESTERN LINE

Welshpool was just the place for a holiday. Reasonably accessible to keep one pleasantly interested; and nicely set among the beautiful mountains of Montgomeryshire. There was just one drawback. It proved to be the terminal station of the Welshpool and Llanfair Light Railway. That sounds little enough. But walk down the main street; hear a whistle and a bell; stand back to allow a quaint little train to fuss across the road; be told that it is called "the ghost train". Then imagine a mind that cannot resist "a story" and the drawback will be realised.

Immediately I had watched that little train puff away into the heart of Montgomeryshire I realised that one day I must go with it. And so it turned out. At 11am the following morning I was there. *The Earl* (which works a fortnight about with *Countess*) was still juggling with wagons in the station yard, its air of importance somewhat marred by the fact that its "puff" was about as full blooded as a parson's sneeze! And even at that the wagons stood but a shade higher than my shoulder and were tared at 1 ton 4cwt.

There seemed to be time to look around the premises. The light railway has transhipping facilities in the yard of the Great Western station, and there was at one time a booking office. Much of the other equipment is still in use. The engine shed, for example, where the 2ft 6in pits are so narrow that a fat man – or even a portly one – could never fall into them. Inside was the *Countess* who sat primly aloof while I ran the rule over her. She is an 0–6–0 tank, with outside cylinders and a roomy cab; the pricker was just about as long as my arm, and I was deciding just how much bigger the fireman's shovel was than its household contemporary, when a shout warned me that we were ready to be away. It was exactly 11.25am.

A few minutes later, while I searched for the least uncomfortable spot on the wooden seat in the brake van, we joggled past the old stock shed, cattle pens, and goods store. The line threaded its way most ingeniously through the back yards of Welshpool; in places we could *almost* have lit Mrs Evan's gas stove with a match that we could almost have taken from Mrs Jones' kitchen on the other side. Certainly our speed would hardly have prevented it, so steep is the gradient up through the town.

The train is scheduled to run on three days a week, but the traffic is sufficient to justify a trip on most days. In any case, those wives of Welshpool who live on the route are unlucky because wash-Monday is always a Llanfair day – which means that they must take down their washing for the train to pass.

At certain road crossings there are protecting gates; the train stops, and the fireman descends and opens the first gate. He then leads the train across the road, to an accompaniment of whistle and clanging bell, and after opening the far gate, remounts the footplate. The guard brings up the rear of this unusual procession, and closes both gates behind the train.

I soon found that I had grievously misjudged *The Earl*. When the occasion demanded he could puff with a good manly puff. And occasion did demand, for in those first two miles out of Welshpool, we ascended 300 feet up the Golfa pass, finishing with a final half mile at 1 in 30.

There are few level stretches all the way to Llanfair. In places, the line seems to have been pushed up on the hillside quite needlessly. The guard whispered the promoters of the line found themselves in an awkward position: they were unable to secure much of the land they would have liked and, on the other hand, they felt a natural reluctance to refuse gifts of land from other sources. Their efforts to make the best of the double difficulty resulted in deviations that were not helpful, either from a constructional or from an operating point of view.

The contractors seem to have worked on the economical principle of not making the banks too high, nor the cuttings too low, with the result that looking back from the van we could see the line sliding away in deliciously unconventional corrugations – that was where the line was straight enough. At many parts of the route it wiggled and twisted about among the hills to such an extent that we could not see even 100 yards of it. Now crawling along the valley with the river, then up the hillside into the tree tops; usually a gallop down towards the valley again, with the brakes hissing as we ran, for it had come onto rain. But up or down, curved or straight, the line passed through some of the most attractive scenery that even these Welsh mountains can show.

There was never anything very remarkable about our speed. In the early days of the line there was a general restriction of 15 mph. Now it is 20, but as you cannot develop anything of a speed on up-gradients, and as there are few level stretches, and as a little white board decorated with a curt "5" or "10" bobs up every time a favourable gradient comes along, there is not much in that! Motorists passed us – and smiled; cyclists seemed to regard us as a useful pacemaker.

I began to be aware of several rather unusual features about this jolly little railway. The guard had made noises at me several times; it sounded like "station" but I could see nothing. As we slowed down and approached Castle Caereinion he did it again. "Station" it was, and before he left the van he jabbed this thumb over my shoulder. And there it was – a tiny hut on the ground level, three sided and with the shoulder to shoulder capacity for about six people. It was painted black, which recalls the fact that one of the old stations in Welshpool is now an undertaker's workshop.

There is a signal box at Castle Caereinion, although there are not, nor never were, any signals. This was the crossing station for trains in the old days, and it was here that the train staff – it is of course, a single line – was exchanged. The day I travelled was a big day for Castle Caereinion – there were two trucks of coal to be dropped. When we left, they were standing remotely in the siding, looking as if they had been there for years. And there was nothing about this beautiful but isolated valley to suggest they might not be there for many more years, until the guard returned and informed me that there was a coal merchant lurking somewhere in the vicinity, who would be busy before we had gone very far.

Near Castle Caereinion is the site of one of the ancient castles of Powysland. In the 12th century it was the scene of a bitter family feud which ended when a nephew of the owner (they weren't too dutiful in those days!) carried the castle by assault, set light to it, and thoughtfully hurled his uncle into the flames.

The Llanfair line is intersected by many level crossings; each is protected by shallow pits extending from fence to fence under the permanent way, and topped by wide spaced metal bars. The effect of these grids is to prevent cattle from wandering onto the line. Nevertheless, sheep sometimes manage to worm their way through the fences onto the track; and on occasion the train has been brought to a standstill while the crew have chased them from the line.

The line passes over a fine stone viaduct at Brynelin, which comes just after Cyfronydd station, and then gets badly mixed up with the Banwy River. At Melin-dol-rhyd-y-defaid – the English translation is "the mill of the meadow at the ford of the sheep" and the everyday name is Dolrhyd Mill – the river seems to be all round and under the line. There are few places on the Great Western system where trout can be seen playing in the water within a yard or two of the train, but this is one!

A few minutes later we arrived at Llanfair Caereinion; it was exactly 12.30pm. Llanfair Caereinion – to hear the music in the name it must be heard as it slides off a Welsh tongue – has been called the most prosperous town in Montgomeryshire. High on the hillside stands the church. What else can be seen from the station is a gathering of good sound roofs – the sort of roofs that cap respectable houses. At any rate, this is a splendid centre for a delightful countryside; the Llanfair Valley and the Berwyn Mountains, the Breidden Hills, the Rhiw Valley and Lake Vyrnwy are all conveniently reached. And so is Gibbet Hill where, in 1735, Hugh and Margot Jones and their two sons were hung in connection with the disappearance of a number of travellers who had been unlucky enough to select the lonely inn on Bryn Penarth as a lodging place for the night.

The station buildings at Llanfair Caereinion are worthy of the place. There is a good sound booking office and a waiting room (now used as a store for agricultural feeding stuffs); stout accommodation for goods traffic; cattle pens; a useful little crane and no platform.

Suspecting that Llanfair Caereinion might not be too good a place on a wet day, I asked the guard how long we stayed. "Oh, we do what we have to do" was his cryptic reply. I went out into the teeming rain to watch the doing. The incoming load had been disposed off and the sidings were now being "dressed" all three of them. This operation involved the engine in frequent trips into the countryside with a number of wagons. Presently there would be a smudge of smoke against the drenched Welsh Hills, and a wagon would appear, turning and twisting through the points until it reached its appointed berth. After our guard had dripped round in the rain, manipulating points and making signals to the invisible driver, for a matter of thirty minutes, he looked around with an appraising eye, nodded, and said "very tidy" then left me to spend the next ten minutes with the driver – he in a cab that looked delightfully dry and cosy; myself in the rain. I heard that the little Llanfair engines were built by Beyer, Peacock & Co.; that they thrived on hard work and uphill pulling, and were very comfortable to drive – virtues that found me strangely unappreciative as the rain dripped relentlessly down my neck. I heard also that they were maintained from Oswestry and taken for a ride on flat trucks if it became necessary for them to go into the shops for repair.

At 1.5pm we started back on a journey which proved to be uneventful, except for a stop for water at Dolrhyd Mill. In the old days this was a somewhat lengthy process, as it meant pumping water from the river into the tank before the engine could be "watered". There was a time when the proceeding was watched with keen enjoyment by the passengers particularly on market days when the train consisted of three coaches full of farmers and country folk, and two vans full of their baskets. The ordinary trains carried passengers and freight. They made four trips up and down and took 55 minutes in each direction. Tickets were issued on the train and there was always a rush to secure seats in the smoking compartment – which accommodated four! The other favourite spot on the train was in the gangway, which gave a magnificent view of the passing countryside. But today the passenger traffic is gone; the coaches are no more; and the Welshpool and Llanfair Light Railway is little more than a ghost that flits sometimes through the memories of the people who once greeted it with such enthusiasm.

F. G. RICHENS *Great Western Railway Magazine*
September 1937

Although there was insufficient warehousing at the station, the company refused to provide more space because of the uncertainty about the future of the line. It was not until March 1940 that additional warehousing space was provided in the form of a Cambrian Railways carriage body.[128] After the war the bodies of a clerestory coach and a passenger brake van were installed at Llanfair to provide more covered storage.

At Welshpool, plans to remove the siding serving the former carriage shed were drawn in November 1937 and it had been removed by the following August. The former carriage shed saw further use as a road transport garage. The narrow gauge siding to the saw mill appears to have lasted until the early 1940s but was not mentioned in the 1943 Sectional Appendix. The connection to the Smithfield siding had been removed by 1949 and part of the former carriage siding had been reinstated. In December 1949 a power-operated crane for transferring goods between standard and narrow gauge stock was tried for a few days.[129]

After the line closed to passenger traffic, the timber shelter at Seven Stars was used as a coffin maker's workshop while the waiting hut at Sylfaen was sold in 1933. The corrugated iron waiting huts at other intermediate stations were retained until the last days of the goods service. At Castle Caereinion the frame was removed from the box and the signals were recovered.

Attempts to secure more traffic

Merchandise arriving at Welshpool in private owner wagons for places served by the Llanfair branch had to be transhipped into narrow gauge stock. In 1936 a charge of 10d per ton was made for transhipment while a further charge was made for the use of the light railway's wagons and vans. In an attempt to counter the growing threat of road competition, the Divisional Traffic Research Committee proposed that the hire charges should be dispensed with, but because of the volume of coal traffic, the proposal required the approval of the Great Western's Mineral Traffic Manager. Since no complaint had been received regarding the hire charges made for coal traffic, the position was deemed to be satisfactory, but it was agreed they could be abolished for all other classes of traffic. The annual revenue foregone as a result of this initiative was estimated to be 9s 6d.[130]

Driver George Jones taking a goods train hauled by No. 822 The Earl *towards Llanfair & Guilsfield level crossing.*

Welshpool exchange sidings and the tranship shed seen from Smithfield Road. 16th April 1938.

FREDERICK LE MANQUAIS

The narrow gauge yard at Welshpool showing the connection to the Smithfield siding on which a line of Great Western cattle wagons had been stabled. The connection to the former carriage shed had been lifted as it was then used as a road transport garage. 16th April 1938. FREDERICK LE MANQUAIS

The line climbed out of the narrow gauge yard to cross the Montgomeryshire arm of the Shropshire Union Canal. Notice the platelayers trolley between the standard gauge Smithfield siding and the narrow gauge lines. 16th April 1938. FREDERICK LE MANQUAIS

At Raven Square the railway crossed the roads to Guilsfield and Llanfair. This view shows the line running along one side of Brook Street towards the town centre and the main line station. The house on the corner of Brook Street and Raven Square was once occupied by a Mr Bushall who sued the Standard Quarry Company when its roof was damaged during blasting operations. 16th April 1938.

FREDERICK LE MANQUAIS

No. 823 Countess at Llanfair with a train for Welshpool on 29th May 1941. The grounded Cambrian carriage body was used as a warehouse for Messrs Silcock's animal feeds.

W.A. CAMWELL

The following year the Traffic Research Committee also attempted to secure more livestock traffic to rail by providing a loading ramp at Cyfronydd.[131] A similar ramp was also provided at Castle Caereinion at a date as yet unknown. In 1937 two cattle wagons built by the Great Western for use on the Vale of Rheidol line were re-gauged for use on the Llanfair branch.[132] From 1942 to 1947 livestock specials were run on a regular basis between July and December. With very few exceptions the special trains ran on Tuesdays, usually conveying sheep for destinations in north western England. On average five hundred beasts were conveyed on each occasion, requiring more than one trip over the line.[133]

Special trains

Despite the loss of the passenger service the line attracted the attention of railway enthusiasts and the curious. The line was the subject of an illustrated article in the September 1937 issue of the *Great Western Magazine*. Reports in the railway press noted that the locomotives where kept in spotless condition and that they worked alternate fortnights.[134/135] By 1945 they were worked on alternate weeks. In 1947 both engines were reported to be in poor condition.[136/137]

In July 1949 the first passenger train for eighteen years was organised by the Birmingham Locomotive Club when special trains were run on successive Saturdays. Between July 1949 and November 1956 nineteen special trains travelled over the line, their passengers riding in open wagons fitted with benches removed from the platforms at Welshpool station. Private individuals who applied to the Welshpool station master to ride on the train were allowed to do so once an indemnity form had been signed and a second class return ticket purchased. They usually travelled in the guard's van.

[1] *The Montgomery County Times and Shropshire and Mid-Wales Advertiser* 11th April 1903
[2] Rail 92 12 CS Denniss to Cambrian Board 21st April 1903
[3] MT6 994 11 Harrison and Winnall to Board of Trade 17th July 1902
[4] Rail 772 2 W&L Board 17th December 1902
[5] Rail 772 2 W&L Works Committee 22nd December 1902
[6] Rail 722 2 W&L Board 23rd January 1903, 27th February 1903
[7] Rail 772 3 W&L Board 7th April 1903
[8] Rail 1057 613 Capital receipts 24th June 1903
[9] MT 6 1612 2 Memorandum 10th May 1907
[10] Rail 722 3 W&L Board 31st July 1903
[11] Rail 1057 613 Harrison & Winnall to CS Denniss 2nd September 1903
[12] Rail 722 3 W&L Works Committee 5th May 1903
[13] Rail 1057 613 Strachan to CS Denniss 16th July 1903
[14] Rail 772 2 Works Committee 22nd December 1902
[15] Rail 722 3 W&L Board 31st July 1903
[16] Rail 1057 613 Harrison &Winnall to CS Denniss 2nd September 1903
[17] Rail 1057 613 Earl of Powis to HM Treasury 20th April 1904
[18] MT6 1612 2 HM Treasury to the Earl of Powis 4th August 1904
[19] MT6 1612 2 HM Treasury to Bircham & Co 31st October 1904
[20] MT 6 1350 1 Amendment Order 1905
[21] MT6 1612 2 Memorandum re Welshpool & Llanfair Railway 10th May 1907
[22] Rail 1057 617 A.J. Collin to C.S. Denniss 23rd April 1904
[23] Rail 92 73 C.S. Denniss to Board 8th June 1904
[24] Rail 1057 617 Harrison & Winnall to Le Brasseur & Oakley 23rd August 1904
[25] MT 6 1612 2 Memorandum re Welshpool & Llanfair Railway 10th May 1907
[26] Rail 92 73 C.S. Denniss to Cambrian Board 11th October 1904
[27] Rail 1057 617 Le Brasseur & Oakley to H&W 1st September1904
[28] Rail 92 73 C.S. Denniss to Cambrian Board 11th October 1904
[29] Rail 92 73 C.S. Denniss to Cambrian Board 2nd November 1904
[30] Rail 92 75 C.S. Denniss to Board 5th April 1905
[31] Rail 92 75 C.S. Denniss to Cambrian Board 3rd May 1905
[32] Rail 92 75 C.S. Denniss to Cambrian Board 7th June 1905
[33] Rail 92 77 Cambrian Board Copy of Mr Armstrong's Award dated 14th June 1906
[34] Rail 722 3 Report of the Works Committee W&L Board 23rd March 1907
[35] MT 6 1612 2 Memorandum re Welshpool & Llanfair Railway 10th May 1907
[36] MT6 1612 2 Re deputation to the President of the Board of Trade 1st July 1907
[37] Rail 722 3 W&L Board 23rd September 1907, 7th August 1908
[38] Rail 253 765 GWR Grouping papers
[39] Rail 722 3 W&L Board 7th August & 28th September 1908
[40] Rail 722 4 W&L Board 21st June 1915
[41] Rail 722 4 W&L Works Committee 15th April 1914
[42] Rail 722 4 W&L Board 21st June 1915

[43] Rail 722 3 W&L Board 5th May 1903
[44] Rail 92 78 Cambrian Board 2nd January 1906
[45] Rail 772 4 27th April 1914
[46] Welshpool Borough Council minutes 13th May 1907
[47] NLW WL C 14 General Manager and Traffic Manager 14th and 20th October 1913
[48] Rail 722 3 W&L Works Committee 7th July 1904
[49] Cambrian Railways rolling stock register
[50] Rail 722 3 W&L Board 20th April 1904
[51] MT6 1302 Llanfair (Tanllan siding) 1904
[52] The Montgomery County Times and Shropshire and Mid-Wales Advertiser 8th September 1906
[53] The Montgomery County Times and Shropshire and Mid-Wales Advertiser 3rd October 1906
[54] Rail 1057 619 J Conacher to CS Denniss 24th November 1909
[55] Rail 722 3 W&L Works Committee 17th May 1909
[56] Rail 722 4 W&L Works Committee 3rd June 1911
[57] Rail 722 4 W&L Works Committee 14th October 1912
[58] The Montgomery County Times and Shropshire and Mid-Wales Advertiser 6th June 1903
[59] Rail 722 5 Shareholders minute book
[60] Rail 92 95 & 96 Schedules of claims against the Cambrian Railways 1920–21
[61] Rail 722 4 W&L Board 14th December 1922
[62] Rail 722 5 Shareholders special general meeting 14th December 1922
[63] GWR carriage registers 4001–5000, 6001–7000
[64] Welshpool Borough Council Minutes 23rd December 1924
[65] Railway Motor Buses and Bus Services in the British Isles 1902–1933 v.2 John Cummings OPC 1980 pp.132–138
[66] Rail 936 59 Timetable road motor cars and omnibuses 21st September 1925
[67] Rail 936 60 Road alterations January 1926
[68] Rail 936 59–64 GWR Road Motor and Omnibuses services
[69] Roadway motor coach & motor bus time tables England and Wales 15th April to 14th May 1930
[70] Railway Motor Buses and Bus Services in the British Isles 1902–1933 v.2 John Cummings OPC 1980 pp.132–138
[71] Rail 250 736 Great Western Railway Report on Branch Lines
[72] David Hyde cited in Llanfair Railway Journal No. 157 October 2000 pp. 12, 13, 16
[73] Supplement to The Montgomery County Times and Shropshire and Mid-Wales Advertiser 4th April 1903
[74] Rail 923 26 Cambrian Railways public timetables 1903
[75] Rail 923 33 Cambrian Railways public and service timetables 1909
[76] Rail 92 84 C.S. Denniss to Cambrian Board 9th June 1909
[77] Rail 923 34&35 Cambrian Railways public and service timetables 1910
[78] Rail 923 36&37 Cambrian Railways public and service timetables 1911
[79] Rail 923 41 Cambrian Railways public and service timetables 1914
[80] Rail 923 36&37 Cambrian Railways public and service timetables 1911
[81] Rail 923 38&39 Cambrian Railways public and service timetables 1912
[82] Rail 923 44 Cambrian Railways public and service timetables 1917
[83] Rail 923 47 Cambrian Railways public and service timetables 1920
[84] Rail 937 145 GWR No.14 Service timetables 20th September 1926 and until further notice
[85] Rail 937 155 GWR No.14 Service timetables 22nd September 1930 and until further notice
[86] The Montgomeryshire Express and Radnor Times 3rd February 1931
[87] Supplement to The Montgomery County Times and Shropshire and Mid-Wales Advertiser 4th April 1903
[88] The Montgomery County Times and Shropshire and Mid-Wales Advertiser 11th April 1904
[89] Rail 923 30&31 Cambrian Railways public and service timetables 1907
[90] Rail 92 84 C.S. Denniss to Cambrian Board 9th June 1909
[91] Rail 923 33 Cambrian Railways public and service timetables 1909
[92] Rail 722 4 W&L Board 2nd May 1913
[93] Rail 937 144 GWR Supplement to service timetables Nos. 12, 13, 14 and 15 March 1926
[94] Rail 923 26 Cambrian Railways service timetables 1903
[95] Rail 923 42 Cambrian Railways public and service timetables 1915
[96] The Montgomery County Times and Shropshire and Mid-Wales Advertiser 24th August 1904
[97] The Montgomery County Times and Shropshire and Mid-Wales Advertiser 17th August 1905
[98] The Montgomery County Times and Shropshire and Mid-Wales Advertiser 2nd September 1905
[99] The Montgomery County Times and Shropshire and Mid-Wales Advertiser 17th March and 7th May 1906
[100] The Montgomery County Times and Shropshire and Mid-Wales Advertiser 28th June 1906
[101] The Montgomery County Times and Shropshire and Mid-Wales Advertiser 18th August 1906
[102] The Montgomery County Times and Shropshire and Mid-Wales Advertiser 17th March and 7th May 1906
[103] The Montgomery County Times and Shropshire and Mid-Wales Advertiser 12th August 1911
[104] Supplement to The Montgomery County Times and Shropshire and Mid-Wales Advertiser 4th April 1903
[105] Rail 92 76 C.S. Denniss to Cambrian Board 2nd February 1905
[106] Rail 92 86 S. Williamson to Cambrian Board 4th October 1911
[107] Rail 923 Cambrian Railways public and service timetables 1912–1916
[108] Rail 923 Cambrian Railways public and service timetables 1916–1920
[109] Rail 937 GWR public and service timetables 1923–1930
[110] Rail 923 & 937 Cambrian and GWR public and service timetables 1904–1928
[111] Rail 937 152 GWR public and service timetables 8th July–22nd September 1929
[112] Rail 1057 622 Dolrhyd Mill 1903–1922
[113] The Montgomery County Times and Shropshire and Mid-Wales Advertiser 7th February 1931
[114] The Montgomeryshire Express and Radnor Times 3rd February 1931
[115] Rail 250 458 GWR General Manager's report to Traffic Committee 12 February 1931
[116] The Montgomery County Times and Shropshire and Mid-Wales Advertiser 31st January 1931
[117] The Montgomery County Times and Shropshire and Mid-Wales Advertiser 7th February 1931
[118] GWR Superintendent of the Line's Office to J. Ben Davies Town Clerk 6th February 1931
[119] The Welshpool and Llanfair Light Railway Lewis Cozens 1951
[120] The Montgomery County Times and Shropshire and Mid-Wales Advertiser 7th February 1931
[121] The Montgomery County Times and Shropshire and Mid-Wales Advertiser 7th February 1931
[122] The Montgomery County Times and Shropshire and Mid-Wales Advertiser 14th February 1931
[123] Welshpool Borough Council minutes 18th February 1931
[124] James Milne General Manager GWR to J. Ben Davies 19th February 1931
[125] Welshpool Borough Municipal Association's report 25th February 1931
[126] Welshpool Borough Council minutes 17th June 1931
[127] The Montgomeryshire Express and Radnor Times 23rd June 1931
[128] NLW Welshpool and Llanfair Archive GWR era papers
[129] The Montgomery County Times and Shropshire and Mid-Wales Advertiser 31st December 1949
[130] Rail 250 718 CWD Traffic Research Committee Minutes 23rd April – 21st October 1936
[131] Rail 250 718 CWD Traffic Research Committee Minutes 2nd November 1937
[132] Great Western Railway Goods Wagons A.G. Atkins, W. Beard, R. Tourret. Tourret Publishing 1998 p. 422
[133] Rail 279 48–51 Oswestry TMO Operating and commercial weekly train notices 1942–1945
[134] SLS Journal July 1935 No.125 p.186
[135] Railway Observer v.10 1938 No.115 p.308
[136] Railway Observer v.15 1944/5 No.196 p.214
[137] Railway Observer v.17 1947 p.177

CHAPTER SIX

A JOURNEY ALONG THE LINE

The Llanfair Railway passenger station was situated in the main-line goods yard at Welshpool. Passenger facilities were confined to a gravelled platform at ground level, a booking office cum waiting room and a solitary gas lamp. The running line gave access to the tranship siding and shed. The toe of the points for the shed road lay under the white gate which formed the boundary between the goods yard and Smithfield Road. The points here were worked by Welshpool yard No. 1 ground frame. 8th October 1931.
R. K. COPE

THE Welshpool and Llanfair branch was part of the Oswestry Traffic Inspector's district. Except on those very rare occasions when Castle Caereinion signal box was open, the branch was worked by one engine in steam. The train staff was painted red and lettered Welshpool and Llanfair. The Annett's key attached to the staff was used to work the ground frames at the sidings and stations on the branch.[1]

When the railway opened, the maximum speed permitted over the line was 15 mph[2] but this was later increased to 25mph.[3] The new maximum speed limit was introduced on 3rd December 1904 when journey times were reduced by 15 minutes[4] following a survey of the line by Mr J. Williamson, the Cambrian Railways' Assistant Engineer.[5] In August 1927 the maximum permitted speed was reduced to 20mph,[6] and in 1939 a further reduction to 15mph was made.[7] There were numerous permanent speed restrictions along the line, notably through Welshpool, at level crossings without gates in the countryside, and on curves of less than five chains radius.

The branch was in the Welshpool Permanent Way Inspector's district.[8] Mr Edward Williams, who worked as a platelayer

on the branch from 1911 to 1931, recalled that a staff of ten platelayers once worked on the line, there being two gangs of five men that worked on either side of Castle Caereinion. Mr Williams' hours were from 6 am to 5.30 pm and he often had to walk four miles to work. Starting at sixteen shillings a week, he was paid £2 8s 0d in 1931. By 1930 the line was maintained by a gang of five men[9] and after the passenger service was withdrawn in February 1931 it was reduced to three.[10] Jack Williams, Les Dunning and Ivor Broxton worked on the line during the last week of the goods service.[11]

In December 1940 a four-wheel motor trolley which seated four people was delivered to the railway. Built by D. Wickam & Co. of Ware, it was used by the Permanent Way gang to travel to wherever they were working on the line.[12] When they reached their workplace, the trolley was lifted from the rails and stored so that it did not foul the line. The gang had absolute occupation of the branch from a point near the trolley shed at Welshpool to the terminus at Llanfair until 10.30 am and from 4.00 pm on weekdays except Mondays.[13]

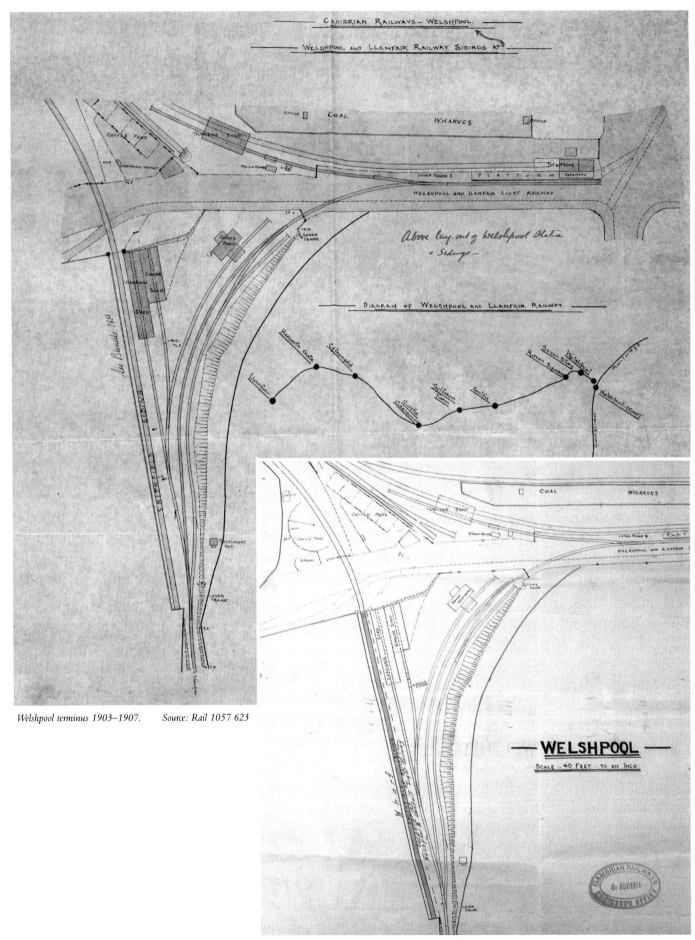

Welshpool terminus 1903–1907.   *Source: Rail 1057 623*

WELSHPOOL 0m 0c

The first detailed proposals for Welshpool terminus were made by Messrs Calthrop and Ward in December 1897. Their preferred option was to keep all narrow gauge lines and the standard gauge tranship siding on the western side of Smithfield Road so that large joint station charges could be avoided. However, if the Cambrian was willing to let the light railway occupy part of its station yard for a peppercorn rent, as was done in India, that would be just as acceptable. Following meetings between Mr Denniss, the Cambrian Railway's General Manager, and the Llanfair Railway promoters, proposals were made to site the waiting shed and passenger platform in the standard gauge goods yard.[14]

No further progress was made until the contract to build the line had been let. By this time Mr Collin, the Cambrian Railways' Chief Engineer, had succeeded Messrs Calthrop and Ward as the Llanfair Railway's engineer. On 20th February 1902 the directors gave Mr Collin authority to obtain tenders for the construction of the buildings at stations on the line.[15] At Welshpool it was intended to provide a waiting room, warehouse, engine shed, carriage shed and a tranship shed. However, following a review of the railway's finances, it became clear that economies were required, so it was decided to reduce the size of the tranship shed and to dispense with the pit outside the engine shed, the waiting room and the carriage shed.[16]

The decision to reduce the accommodation at Welshpool did not find favour with Mr Denniss, who wrote to the Llanfair Directors urging them to provide a carriage shed capable of holding two coaches, insisted that a pit outside the engine shed was essential and suggested that the Engineer should attempt to build a tranship shed capable of holding two standard gauge wagons at reduced cost.[17] Mr Denniss' advice was accepted by the Llanfair Directors who also reconsidered the question of providing a waiting room at the terminus. They decided to provide a waiting shed with a veranda on the site occupied by a coal office which was removed to the south end of the coal wharf.[18] The contract to build the engine and carriage shed was awarded to the Clyde Structural Iron Company,[19] while the waiting shed, warehouse and tranship shed were erected by Mr T.J. Evans of Welshpool.[20]

In August 1902 authority was given to procure two standpipe type water columns for use at Welshpool.[21] One was erected by the engine shed and the other was situated in the goods yard[22] next to the tranship shed.[23] This column seems to have been removed by the Great Western and had gone by 1938.[24] A three inch hydrant was provided in the engine shed. Water was supplied by Welshpool Corporation at a cost of £200 per annum, it being estimated that between 10 and 12 million gallons would be used annually.[25]

THE TERMINUS 1903–1907

Trains started their journey to Llanfair from the south-west corner of the Cambrian Railways goods yard at Welshpool. When the railway opened, the passenger platform was on the edge of Smithfield Road at road level, while the station building was just inside the goods yard next to the entrance. The railway ran along the side of Smithfield Road for about sixty-seven yards before swinging across it to enter the narrow gauge yard. Just before the line crossed the road, a siding left the running line and continued to the tranship shed. Access to the tranship siding was controlled by a two-lever ground frame that stood by the roadside. One lever worked the facing point lock while the other moved the point blades.

The tranship shed was a timber-framed structure with a pitched roof. The roof, the upper two thirds of the sides and the upper part of the gable end were clad with corrugated iron sheets. A standard and a narrow gauge siding ran through the shed which protected merchandise from the weather whilst it was being transhipped. A wagon weighbridge was provided on the narrow gauge siding a few yards before the entrance to the tranship shed.

On Monday 6th October 1902 workmen erecting the tranship shed narrowly avoided serious injury. While they were sheltering from a heavy shower underneath some cattle wagons, a Cambrian engine began to shunt the wagons. The workmen scrambled to safety but one of their number called Charles Gambell, a married man of 23 Powell's Row, failed to get a foot away in time and a wheel passed over it. Happily his comrades rescued him before another wheel could touch him. Mr Gambell was immediately carried home on a stretcher where his injuries were attended to. Although his foot was badly crushed, within the week he was said to be making steady progress.[26]

Having crossed Smithfield Road and entered the narrow gauge yard, the running line passed between the loop and the warehouse siding. Access to the loop was controlled by a two-lever ground frame. The warehouse was a timber-framed structure with a double pitch roof clad with corrugated iron. A canopy supported on pillars protected the rail-side entrance to the warehouse, while the yard-side entrance was sheltered by a canopy that was cantilevered out from the roof. A ramp used for loading and unloading livestock stood close to the western end of the warehouse.

At the western end of the yard the loop rejoined the main line, while the line that threw off the carriage shed and engine shed sidings before continuing to the warehouse, joined the main line by a trailing connection. Access to the loop and siding was controlled from a four-lever ground frame. The points leading to the carriage and engine sheds were operated

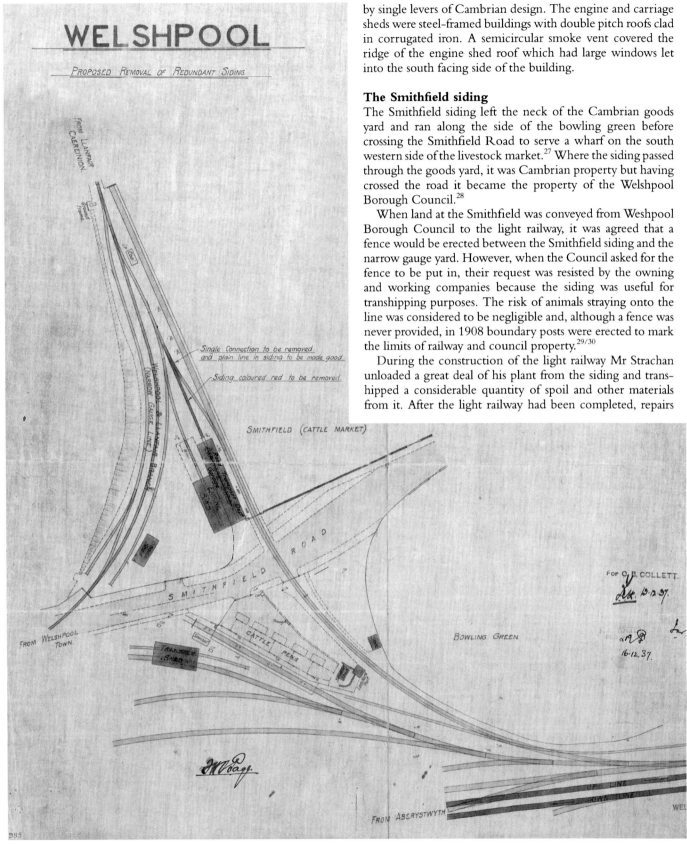

WELSHPOOL

Proposed Removal of Redundant Siding.

FROM LLANFAIR CAEREINION.

Welshpool & Llanfair Branch (NARROW GAUGE LINE).

Single Connection to be removed and plain line in siding to be made good.

Siding coloured red to be removed.

SMITHFIELD (CATTLE MARKET)

SMITHFIELD ROAD

FROM WELSHPOOL TOWN.

CATTLE PENS

BOWLING GREEN

For C. B. COLLETT.
15.12.37.

16.12.37.

FROM ABERYSTWYTH

Welshpool Yard in 1937.

by single levers of Cambrian design. The engine and carriage sheds were steel-framed buildings with double pitch roofs clad in corrugated iron. A semicircular smoke vent covered the ridge of the engine shed roof which had large windows let into the south facing side of the building.

The Smithfield siding

The Smithfield siding left the neck of the Cambrian goods yard and ran along the side of the bowling green before crossing the Smithfield Road to serve a wharf on the south western side of the livestock market.[27] Where the siding passed through the goods yard, it was Cambrian property but having crossed the road it became the property of the Welshpool Borough Council.[28]

When land at the Smithfield was conveyed from Weshpool Borough Council to the light railway, it was agreed that a fence would be erected between the Smithfield siding and the narrow gauge yard. However, when the Council asked for the fence to be put in, their request was resisted by the owning and working companies because the siding was useful for transhipping purposes. The risk of animals straying onto the line was considered to be negligible and, although a fence was never provided, in 1908 boundary posts were erected to mark the limits of railway and council property.[29/30]

During the construction of the light railway Mr Strachan unloaded a great deal of his plant from the siding and transhipped a considerable quantity of spoil and other materials from it. After the light railway had been completed, repairs

Source: NLW W&LR archive

estimated to cost £350 were needed on that part of the siding that was within the standard gauge goods yard. While the repairs were being carried out, the opportunity was taken to ease the acute curve where the siding ran along the side of the bowling green so that the Cambrian's larger locomotives could pass along it.[31]

That part of the siding belonging to the Council also required attention after being used by Mr Strachan. The Cambrian first refused to work its locomotives into the siding and then gave notice that it would not allow its wagons to enter the siding until it had been repaired. Mr Strachan refused to contribute to the renovation of the siding, claiming that he had paid the Cambrian £160 to use it, so in 1904 the Council demanded that the railway company carry out the necessary repairs. At a meeting between representatives of the two parties in January 1905 Mr Denniss indicated that his company was prepared to put the siding in good order and offered to pay £5 per annum for its use. The offer was rejected by the Council who threatened to padlock the gate that gave access to their siding to prevent the Cambrian from using it. The matter was eventually resolved in January 1906 when the siding rental was fixed at £7 10s 0d per annum for a period of five years from 25th March.[32] The agreement was renewed for a further five years in 1911[33] and for fifty years by the Cambrian Railways Act of 1913.[34]

Towards the end of 1906 Mr Jabez Barker a Shrewsbury timber merchant, gave notice that he required a stacking ground at Welshpool station for the accommodation of timber loaded at Llanfair.[35] In February 1907 plans were drawn proposing that the stacking ground should be sited in the Cambrian goods yard between the cattle pens and the Smithfield siding. It would be connected to the light railway by a siding

that left the carriage shed road, then ran along the Smithfield siding.[36] The work was carried out by the following May but without any variation being made to the 1899 Light Railway Order or the agreement of the Borough Council over whose land part of the siding ran.[37] In January 1909 an agreement to pay the Council a nominal sum for the use of its land was sealed.[38] Retrospective authority to carry out the work and give the light railway running powers over the Smithfield siding for a period of fifty years was provided by the Cambrian Railways Act 1913.[39]

ALTERATIONS TO THE PASSENGER TERMINUS

In 1906 Welshpool Borough Council made proposals to widen Smithfield Road and move the passenger station into the Cambrian goods yard but the Llanfair Directors were unwilling to carry out the work.[40] All attempts to move the terminus from the road were resisted by the owning and working companies until the Council threatened to turn the light railway off the Smithfield siding once the agreement made in 1909 expired.[41/42] The Cambrian Railways Act 1913 gave the Llanfair Company the power to relocate their Welshpool terminus and to remove the rails serving the old passenger terminus from Smithfield Road.[43] It was intended to start the alterations on 27th October 1913 and to complete them within a week to ten days at an estimated cost of £100. The waiting shed was removed to the south end of the coal wharf and was partitioned to provide a booking office and accommodation for the weighbridge clerk. The standard gauge tranship siding was cut back to make room for the passenger platform, while the platform road was moved into the goods yard, making it necessary to realign the Smithfield Road crossing. An unclimbable iron fence was erected between the

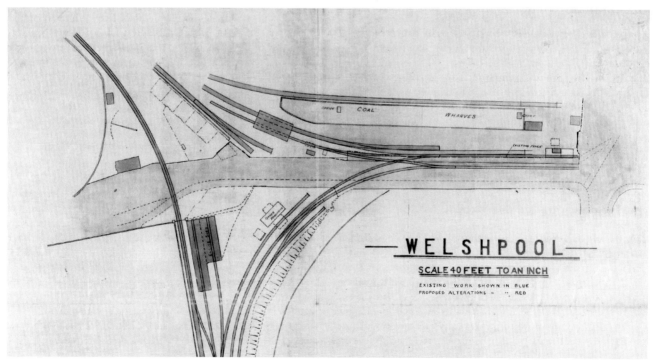

Alterations to the passenger terminus 1913.

Source: NLW W&LR archive

The saw mill as it appeared in 1942–1943. The building with the double pitch roof was once Lord Powis' warehouse but when photographed it was used as an auxiliary stable for the horses that hauled Boys and Boden's timber wagons. The windows on the gable end and the side overlooked the railway, so the Great Western charged the company five shillings per annum for the enjoyment of the light and air that it provided. The crane by Butters Brothers of Glasgow had a jib that was 100ft long and became a local landmark. Its legs were mounted on concrete plinths that were about 10ft tall. Mr Boden recalled climbing the thirty feet to the top of the sheerlegs to fix a cable that had become displaced. The gantry crane features between the stable and the mill. The hopper next to the mill roof was part of a system to extract dust, while the chimneys served two cross tube boilers.
Cty H.W. BODEN

road and railway.[44/45] It seems likely that the tranship siding was extended to meet the narrow gauge line in the Smithfield siding thereby creating a narrow gauge triangle at about this time.

While the work was carried out, trains started and terminated in the narrow gauge yard at a point opposite the engine shed. New burners were fitted to the gas lamps in the yard for the safety of passengers joining or alighting from the trains. During the alterations the tranship shed could only be reached via the Smithfield siding and a platelayer was stationed in the Cambrian yard to join up and disconnect the rails when access to the tranship shed was required.[46] Which rails were joined up and disconnected is not clear, but two Great Western plans state that the narrow gauge rails which crossed the standard gauge cattle siding could be removed when they were not required.[47] The alterations to the passenger terminus were completed by 19th November 1913.[48]

Further expansion and then decline
In 1916 Boys and Boden opened their British Sawmills next to the Cambrian main line at Welshpool. In 1920 negotiations commenced with the Cambrian to convey 5,000 tons of timber over the light railway, but this required the narrow gauge line to be extended from the north-eastern tip of the triangle to a point near the sawmill. Messrs Boys and Boden offered to fund half the cost of the work but the Llanfair Railway could not afford to pay for its share of the work or for the new timber trucks that were needed. An application

for public funding was made to the Ministry of Transport, but was refused because the traffic was not considered to be of national importance. The Ministry then approached Mr Williamson, the Cambrian Railways' General Manager, to see if his company would provide the necessary funding. At a meeting with officials from the Ministry, Mr Williamson explained that the Llanfair Railway was already severely indebted to his company and that his Directors were unlikely to advance the amount required. However he offered to advance £140 towards the cost of the siding if the Llanfair Company would pay the Cambrian a rebate of 7d per ton on Messrs Boys and Boden's traffic until the cost of the siding had been extinguished. The Llanfair Railway's Directors agreed to the proposal which was approved by the Cambrian Directors on 3rd November 1920.[49] The date that siding came into use is not known and it was left to the Great Western to build the new timber wagons which arrived on the branch in 1924.

A plan drawn in November 1937 shows that the narrow gauge rails which crossed the standard gauge cattle siding had been removed, but the sawmill siding was still in situ.[50] By this time the carriage shed was used as a road motor garage and the siding leading to it had been removed by April 1938.[51] The siding to the sawmill is not mentioned in the 1943 Sectional Appendix, nor is it shown on the GWR closure plans that were drawn in November 1947 although the narrow gauge connection to the Smithfield siding remained.[52] This connection had been removed by July 1949 by which time part of the carriage shed siding had been reinstated.[53]

BOYS AND BODEN

The mill was served by a private siding that was shunted twice a day. Wagons could be unloaded or loaded using the hand or gantry cranes. In the late 'forties and 'fifties, off-cuts from the mill were loaded into a wagon that was shunted to the firm's siding in the downside yard where there was a charcoal kiln. The kiln was of Belgian manufacture and on its journey to Welshpool fell into a dock while being unloaded at an east coast port. It was recovered by divers.

Cty H.W. BODEN

Boys and Boden was founded by two cousins, Harry Boys Boden and Frank Albert Boys, at Darlaston and was trading by 1895. The principal business was the supply of oak scantlings to the railway industry. During the Great War the company decided to move closer to the source of the Montgomeryshire oaks on which the business depended.[1] In 1915 the company was offered the lease of a site at Welshpool, between the Shropshire Union Canal and the Smithfield.[2] However, in May 1916 a 6½ acre site was acquired next to the Cambrian Railways' main line at Pentrefelin and by June a siding had been laid in. Under the supervision of Mr. Pierson, engines and plant were laid down and by the autumn the site was used as a saw mill. The firm employed about fifty men and boys locally, preference being given to disabled servicemen, and many teams of horses were engaged in hauling timber from various parts of the county.

In November 1916 a large shed measuring 120ft in length was under construction. Standing on sixteen iron stanchions each weighing about half a ton, the shed was being clad with corrugated-iron sheets. At about 4pm on Monday 16th November a hurricane lifted most of the stanchions and their concrete beds, or snapped them at their base, so that the shed was thrown onto its side. Six men working inside the shed managed to get clear but one of the girders fell onto a cart to which a horse was harnessed and it sustained a bruised leg. Much of the iron-work was twisted and so rendered useless. The cost of the damage was estimated to be between £300 and £400, and considerable delay was incurred with the construction.[3/4] Despite the setback, the mill was fully operational by 1917.[5]

In 1920 a proposal to connect the saw mill to the Welshpool and Llanfair Light Railway was considered by the line's Directors, but the cost of the works was beyond their Company's means.[6] The narrow gauge was extended from the northern end of the triangle towards the saw mill in the early 1920s. In 1921 the lease on the Darlaston premises expired, so on 8th June the plant and machinery were put up for sale by auction.[7] Mr Stanley Davies, whose timber business traded as E.O.

Occasionally timber trains were run for Messrs Boys and Boden. This one was photographed on the down side of station bridge, Welshpool. The group includes Mr H. D. Boden, Station Master H.E. Watson, Timber Inspector Jim Laker, Jack Roberts and Harold Davies. The locomotive, a class '2021' 0-6-0 tank engine, had moved from Paddington to Oswestry on 6th July 1923 and remained in the Central Wales Division until it was withdrawn on 15th March 1951. The photograph must have been taken after August 1934 when No. 2075 was fitted with pannier tanks.

Cty H.W. BODEN

Messrs Boys and Boden moved to Welshpool so that their business would be closer to the source of Montgomeryshire oak on which it depended. One such oak is seen on the stacking ground that the company acquired from Stanley Davies in 1930. The gentleman to the right of the trunk may have been the Great Western timber inspector. The Ruabon wagon was probably delivering coal for gassing at Welshpool gas works. The engine shed was demolished in 1932 to make way for a siding that served Midland Tar Distillers' tar works.   Cty H.W. BODEN

Jones & Sons, ceased trading in 1927 and their premises at Welshpool and Tanllan were acquired by Boys and Boden in 1930.[8]

Round timber from estates that were up to sixty miles south of Welshpool, near to the mid-Wales coast, and on the Shropshire borders was brought to the town by road, rail, and occasionally canal. Before the outbreak of the Second World War, horse teams were used to haul timber for distances of up to ten miles, but for longer journeys the load was taken to the nearest station and forwarded to Welshpool. During the war horses were largely replaced by motor vehicles, Messrs Wynns of Newport being hired to haul the heaviest loads. However, two horses were retained for haulage around the town until the late 1950s.

On at least two occasions special trains were run for Messrs Boys and Boden's traffic. Timber was loaded using rail-mounted hand cranes or, if the traffic justified it, a steam crane would be provided. Loading timber from the lineside required total possession of the line, so the trains were run on Sundays. Mr Harry W. Boden, grandson of Mr H.B.

A circular saw and rack bench were used to cut long timber. The saw was set in the floor and the piece that was being sawn was placed on a steel bench that ran on rollers and was drawn forward by a rack. Timber for sawing, was stacked at the far end of the bench. The crane used to lift it onto the bench is seen next to Tommy Davies and Gwen Pugh, both of whom were sawyer's mates. Scantlings, sawn components for railway wagons, had been stacked to the left of the nearest rollers.

Cty. H.W. BODEN

Small trees and large off-cuts were sawn into rail key blanks. The wheelbarrow was used to take the blanks for machining into finished keys. The people involved in this work were Jack Thomas (labourer), George Perking (sawyer), unknown, and Freddie Smith (sawyer).

Cty. H.W. BODEN

These sawn blanks had been stacked before they were machined into ferrules on the belt-driven lathes by the wall. The balata belts were driven from overhead shafts powered by a gas engine that ran on producer gas made using wood shavings and sawdust. During the war the lathes were operated by local women including Muriel Charles, Gladys Simmons, Glenys Owen and Sybil Evans. The gentleman was the foreman Harry Gardener.
Cty H.W. BODEN

Boden, remembers travelling to Trawscoed and Garth with timber loaders from Oswestry, Montgomery and Caersws. He went to measure the timber and ensure that it was of the quality required but often helped load the trunks, working as 'doger on'. This involved judging where to attach the dogs to a trunk so that it was properly balanced during the lift and could be slewed onto the bogie bolster with relative ease.

When hand cranes were used, the loaders were keen to raise the load to the minimum height necessary to clear the side of the bolster and then slew it onto the wagon. Judging the height was quite difficult and often the lift was halted prematurely. Usually a maximum of three bolsters could be loaded during a possession. If a steam crane was being used, the driver was also keen to minimise the number of adjustments to the gears, jib or position of the crane. Once at Trawscoed, after several miscalls, an exasperated steam crane operator decided to judge the height required himself, much to the consternation of the loaders who were there to guide him.

When Boys and Boden moved to Welshpool, the firm dealt in English and foreign timber, and was a railway stores contractor.[9] Round timber was sawn at the mill to produce wagon components including solebars, headstocks, middle bearers, longitudes, diagonals, and rails that were supplied to companies such as Wagon Repairs Ltd. Rail keys, treenails and ferrules were also produced for customers, particularly those with large internal railway systems. Products for the coal mining industry were also made at the saw mill including chocks, lids, and cover boards. In 1930 a builder's merchants department was opened.[10] Postwar shortages of oak and the decline of the railway and coal industries led the company to develop its builder's merchant business and the manufacture of staircases.

The mill also produced components for the mining industry including cover boards which were being cut on circular saws in the centre of this view, which includes Mr Bishop, Gwen Pugh, Tony Harris, George Bluewett and Bert Thomas.
Cty H.W. BODEN

[1] Boys Boden 100 years of Service Supplement to *The County Times*
[2] Rail 92 91 Cambrian Board 30th March 1915
[3] *The Montgomeryshire County Times and Mid-Wales Advertiser* 17th November 1916
[4] Rail 92 91 Cambrian Board 7th June 1916
[5] Boys Boden 100 years of Service Supplement to *The County Times*
[6] Rail 722 4 Board 6th August 1920
[7] Boswell & Tomlins sale catalogue
[8] Per the deeds to the property
[9] *The Montgomeryshire County Times and Mid-Wales Advertiser* 4th July 1925
[10] *The Montgomeryshire County Times and Mid-Wales Advertiser* 12th July 1930

Harold Bluewett swaging teeth on a band saw that was 25ft long in the saw doctor's shop. Mr Bluewett and other key workers moved to Welshpool from Darlaston when Messrs Boys and Boden transferred their business to Welshpool.
Cty H.W. BODEN

The Cambrian Railways station and forecourt. The standard gauge goods yard was to the left of the forecourt. PATRICK KINGSTON

The former passenger terminus on 9th July 1949. The presence of the platform trolley and seats from the main-line station suggest that preparations were in hand for the second of the Birmingham Locomotive Club's special trains. The point controlled by Welshpool Yard No. 1 ground frame is set for the running line that curved to cross Smithfield Road. The line on the left made its way to the tranship shed. J.I.C. BOYD, Cty. ROBERT HUMM

The line left the standard gauge yard and swung across the Smithfield Road to reach the Llanfair Railway yard.   H. B. TOURS

No. 822 making its way over Smithfield Road level crossing and into the main-line yard at Welshpool. The tranship shed was occupied by standard and narrow gauge wagons.
A.W.V. MACE

102

No. 822 on the tranship siding collecting loaded wagons before commencing the journey to Llanfair. 12th October 1951. F.W. SHUTTLEWORTH

The tranship siding and shed.　　　NRM S. P. HIGGINS COLLECTION

The tranship shed, showing the end of the narrow gauge siding with its stop block and the standard gauge entrance to the shed. 4th June 1953.

In 1907 a third rail was laid along part of the Smithfield siding to allow the Llanfair Railway access to the Cambrian goods yard. In the winter of 1937–1938 new cattle pens were built on the site of the stacking ground and the rails were enclosed in concrete. The site is now listed.
MIKE LLOYD

Cattle pens and mixed gauge track c.1938.
PHOTOMATIC

The narrow gauge siding was extended towards Boys and Boden's saw-mills. The extension left the Smithfield siding near the throat of the main-line goods yard and continued around the perimeter of the bowling green.
PHOTOMATIC

F.W. SHUTTLEWORTH

The empty stock for the SLS special train being propelled across Smithfield Road into the Cambrian yard by No.823. 19th June 1954.

No. 822 leaving the main-line yard with a train for Llanfair on 14th May 1952.

N.K. HARROP

The entrance to the narrow gauge yard next to Welshpool's Smithfield with cattle and sheep wagons stabled on the warehouse siding and a goods brake van on the headshunt at the end of the loop. 12th October 1951.

F.W. SHUTTLEWORTH

The east end of the narrow gauge yard as it appeared on 8th October 1931. The point in the foreground gave access to a run-round loop on which wagons were often stabled because of a shortage of siding accommodation at Welshpool. The siding on the right served the goods warehouse, beyond which the cattle ramp can be seen.
R.K. COPE

The narrow gauge yard with the cattle loading ramp (right) and part of the engine shed (left). The presence of a line of horseboxes on the standard gauge Smithfield siding suggests that a horse sale may have been taking place in the Smithfield.
R.K. COPE

On 14th May 1952 Norman Harrop photographed No. 822 on the running line in the narrow gauge yard. The locomotive could have been shunting open wagons or returning with a train from Llanfair. N. K. HARROP

No. 822 shunting open wagons in the narrow gauge yard. The two cattle wagons were occupying their customary position by the goods shed, while in the main line yard a covered van has been left on the tranship siding. A.W.V. MACE

During a pause in shunting, the guard was checking the coupling between No. 822 and the first wagon. N. K. HARROP

The engine and carriage shed were supplied by the Clyde Structural Iron Co. for the opening of the railway. After the passenger service had been withdrawn, the carriage shed was used as a road motor workshop. L&GRP

The interior of the narrow gauge engine shed at Welshpool on 3rd November 1956.

F.W. SHUTTLEWORTH

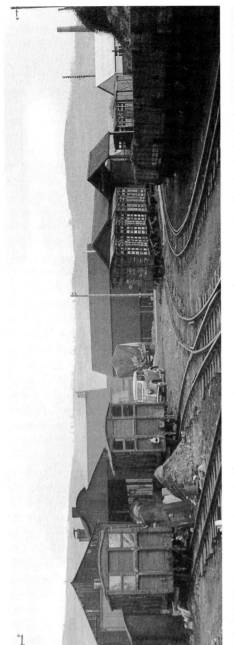

The narrow gauge yard seen from the coal stage, showing, from left to right, the truncated siding that once led to the carriage shed, the engine shed road with one of the goods brake vans outside the shed, the warehouse siding with cattle vans next to the warehouse, the running line and loop.
R.W. KIDNER

Stock awaiting further use in the Llanfair Railway yard.

No. 822 at the coal stage while Driver Joe Davies and other railwaymen were setting the world to rights. It was probably market day as there was plenty of activity in the Smithfield. 14th May 1952.

N.K. HARROP

The Smithfield siding was built to service the livestock market but was later used for the exchange of traffic between the main line and the light railway A mineral wagon loaded with locomotive coal can be seen behind No. 822. 14th May 1952.

N.K. HARROP

In contrast to the earlier views, the narrow gauge yard appears to be almost deserted. A van had been stabled on the loop and sheep wagons were standing on the stub of the former carriage shed siding. 10th April 1946.

Locomotive coal for the Llanfair Railway was delivered using the Smithfield siding. In this view coal had been transferred from the standard gauge wagon to the light railway's coaling stage. The warehouse siding passed the coaling stage before throwing off a short siding on which sheep wagons had been stabled, and then a line leading to the engine shed. A brake van is seen on the running line whilst a van and several wagons covered by tarpaulins have been left on the loop. The ground frame in the foreground was Welshpool yard No.3 groundframe which controlled the entrance to the warehouse siding and the loop.

J.E. NORRIS

The narrow gauge yard, looking towards Llanfair from the engine shed, on 15th September 1956. Two vans and some wagons were standing on the loop. The running line ascended the bank before crossing the canal. Near the coal stage, the line that threw off the carriage and engine shed sidings before continuing as the warehouse road, joined the main line. The Smithfield siding and wharf were adjacent to the livestock market.

NGRS

The line left the narrow gauge yard and climbed towards the canal bridge on a gradient of 1 in 33. The 5mph speed restriction through the town was imposed in 1939–1940. 3rd November 1956.

No. 822 *The Earl* brings the 2.15pm train from Llanfair down the bank from the canal bridge. The permanent way gang's trolley was kept in the hut to the right of the train. 24th August 1948.   H.C. CASSERLEY

WELSHPOOL YARD TO SEVEN STARS

The railway climbed out of the narrow gauge yard towards the canal bridge on a gradient of 1 in 33. In 1939–1940 a permanent speed restriction of 5mph was imposed through the town section and a speed restriction board was erected at 0m 10c.[54] Having reached the girder bridge that carried the line over the Shropshire Union Canal, the gradient eased to 1 in 134 as the railway ran between the Vicarage fields and the Lledan brook on its way to Church Street level crossing.

When the railway was proposed, the then Vicar, the Rev. Grimaldi Davies, regarded it as a great nuisance and asked £1,550 for the strip of land that was needed for the line. Following prolonged negotiations, the price was reduced to £823 12s 0d.[55] As part of the purchase agreement, the company agreed to build a stone water closet with a slate roof to replace one that had been demolished to make way for the line, make a stone boundary wall twelve inches thick and

Driver Percy Evans taking a goods train to Llanfair up the bank to the canal bridge.
PHOTOMATIC

Three schoolboys watching No. 822 taking the daily train to Llanfair over the canal bridge. 31st March 1953.

*On 11th May 1949 No. 823W Count-
ess drifting over the canal bridge with a
train of sheeted open wagons from Llanfair.*
P.M. ALEXANDER

*The railway approached Church Street on
a slight curve. At this point the boundary
with the vicarage field was fenced with iron
railings. 14th September 1956.*
R.M. CASSERLEY

The approach to Church Street level crossing.   P. MARSHALL, Cty. ROBERT HUMM

eight feet high from the vicarage entrance for fifty yards, and thereafter provide an unclimbable iron fence five feet high. Shrubs and trees were eventually planted by the wall to protect the Rev. Davies' privacy.[56] To minimise the amount of land used, the railway followed the course of the Lledan brook closely and there were curves of three chains radius on this part of the line.[57]

Church Street was one of the main thoroughfares in Welshpool so gates were fixed across the railway at the level cros-

sing.[58] Two properties on the west side of the street had to be demolished to make way for the line.[59] In about 1903 a three-storey building was erected next to the railway by Mr Henry Smith,[60] a local plumber. By the 1930s the property was occupied by Barclay's grocery and baker's shop.[61] The bakery was built on a very restricted site behind a shop on the opposite side of the railway and vehicles requiring access to it had to travel over the line. When trains for Llanfair were brought to a stop in front of the level crossing, the fireman, who was

The railway seen from Church Street level crossing, looking towards the terminus. The wall on the left was constructed at the insistence of the Vicar of Welshpool to ensure his privacy.

The gate on the south side of Church Street protected the line from the incursions of small boys and animals.
AUTHOR'S COLLECTION

Guard Dick Morgan shutting the gate across the line at Church Street on 21st April 1950.

NLW, GEOFF CHARLES COLLECTION

responsible for opening the gates, had to check that there were no vehicles fouling the line by the bakery before stopping the traffic on Church Street and calling the train onto the crossing. This having been accomplished, he returned to the footplate, leaving the guard to close the gates. In the Up direction a stop board was erected at 0m 30chains where drivers had to stop and satisfy themselves that were no vehicles on the line before proceeding to the level crossing.[62]

From Church Street level crossing the line ran above the course of the Lledan brook for about 50 yards.[63] It was carried on longitudinal rail bearers that were supported by cross girders which rested on the masonry sides of the stream. The cross girders also supported a wooden deck so that the brook was completely enclosed. This section of the line was full of character as the railway ran across Bebb's Passage; squeezed past Armada Cottages, a terrace of half timbered houses with

The 11.30 train for Llanfair crossing Church Street and about to pass through the narrow gap between Harnell's ladies outfitters and Barclay's the bakers. The goods wagon still carried the last Great Western wagon livery. 12th October 1951.
F.W. SHUTTLEWORTH

The narrow gap between Barclay's grocery and baker's shop (left) and Harnell's dress shop (right) is apparent in this view from the brake van. The baker collected flour from the old iron minks at the main-line station and delivered it by van to his bakery, which can be seen above the stop board. This meant that he had to pass over the line for a few yards. Usually such trips were made at times when it was known that the line would be clear, but occasionally a returning special found its path blocked by his van. Up trains stopped at the stop board so that the driver could check that the line was clear, while the fireman left the footplate to open the gate on the other side of Church Street, halt road traffic and call the train on.
H.C. CASSERLEY

Between Church Street and Union Street the railway squeezed between premises that predated it. To minimise the amount of property that had to be acquired for the construction of the line, the railway ran above the course of the Lledan brook for part of its length carried on longitudinal rail bearers supported by cross girders that rested on the masonry sides of the stream. When the line opened, the brook was open to the elements but, under pressure from local people and the Borough Council, it was gradually boarded over, as can be seen in this 1950s view.

R.S. CARPENTER
COLLECTION

Beyond Barclays the railway was carried along the course of the Lledan Brook on steel joists that supported longitudinal rail bearers and a wooden deck. Bebb's Passage crosses the railway in the middle distance, beyond which is Armada Cottages, a row of half-timbered cottages. 14th September 1956.

R.M. CASSERLEY

The daily goods train rumbling along the Lledan viaduct past Armada Cottages. When trains ran, washing was in danger of being covered in smuts.

P.B. WHITEHOUSE Cty. MICHAEL WHITEHOUSE

The 11.30am train for Llanfair, halted briefly at Seven Stars level crossing while a shooting brake was moved off the line. Austin lorry registration FOA 381 was parked opposite Ballard's Garage. 12th October 1951.   F.W. SHUTTLEWORTH

No. 822 waiting on the Union Street while staff from Ballard's Garage move a car parked on the line. The garage was decorated to celebrate the coronation of Queen Elizabeth II. 4th June 1953.

dormer windows that were dwarfed by a three-storey stone house at its western end; then passed a shop to reach Seven Stars, an open area at the junction of Union Street, Brook Street and Hall Street.

The railway crossed Union Street by an oblique level crossing that was the site of a fatality on 18th March 1902. At about four a clock that morning a train, carrying sleepers for use near Standard Quarry, left the Smithfield hauled by one of Mr Strachan's 0–4–0 tank engines. Seven men were riding on the locomotive there being four on the footplate and three on the front buffer plank. John Williams of Mermaid Passage, Welshpool, was riding on the left-hand side of the buffer

plank as the train made its way through the town at between three and four miles an hour. Mr Williams and three of his companions had started work at 6 am on the previous day. When the train was near the site of *The Seven Stars* inn, he stepped off the locomotive but tripped and fell in front of the engine, bringing it to a halt. The driver, George Sankey, put the engine into reverse but Mr Williams was already under it. Later that morning his body was recovered and taken to his former home. Returning a verdict of accidental death, the Coroner's Jury recommended that the Contractor should post notices stating that unauthorised persons were not allowed to ride on his locomotives.[64]

The site of Seven Stars station seen from a Welshpool-bound train. The Ballard's Morris 8 CDA 324 features in front of Seven Stars Cottage, beyond which the roof of the former waiting shelter can be seen.
A.W.V. MACE

SEVEN STARS 0m 34c

Seven Stars took its name from the public house that had been demolished to make way for the railway.[65] The halt was close to the town centre and the Town Hall markets and was expected to be well used. Before the railway opened, Mr Dennis asked the Llanfair Directors to provide covered accommodation at the halt so a room in Seven Stars cottage was used as a waiting room.[66/67] The rest of the property was let to the Cambrian Railways and by 1912 was occupied by one of the company's guards. In April 1912 the Cambrian terminated its lease of the property because it required major repairs, and it was sold to Mr Edward Davies, a local

builder.[68/69] In October the Works Committee accepted Mr Evan Davies' offer to build a shelter, designed by the Earl of Powis' builder Mr Riddell, at a cost of £24 17s 0d.[70] After passenger services were withdrawn, the shelter was converted into a workshop where Mr Harry Morris made coffins.[71/72]

Passengers occasionally tried to join or leave trains while they were still in motion despite a notice advising them to wait until the train had stopped. On 2nd December 1904 Absolom Evans of Gungrog Lane, Welshpool, attempted to board a carriage as a train was leaving Seven Stars. Although Guard John Pritchard told him to stand back, Mr Evans tried

Traffic on the line increased when petrol rationing was introduced following the outbreak of the 1939–1945 war. Here No. 823 Countess is seen with a train consisting of four cattle wagons, five open wagons and a brake van at Seven Stars station. 29th May 1941.

W.A. CAMWELL

to get into the guard's van as it passed him, missed his footing and fell headlong into the brook. To add insult to injury he was prosecuted by the Cambrian and fined five shillings.[73]

The Cross Foxes on the corner of Union and Hall Street was once a busy stabling inn. On market days carts and traps were parked on the side of Union Street or even on the railway from where they had to be removed as a train approached.[74]

In later years the carts and traps were replaced by cars awaiting attention at Ballard's garage. During the goods-only period, Seven Stars served as a convenient refreshment stop for certain crews when they returned to Welshpool. The train was stopped in front of the level crossing, then the crew walked across the road to enjoy a pint in *The Cross Foxes* or *The Crown* before continuing to Welshpool station.[75]

A train from Llanfair passing Nelson Place. The gas lamp was provided by the light railway at the request of the Borough Council who were concerned that pedestrians might fall into the Lledan Brook which was later boarded over.

H.B. TOURS

Having crossed Union Street, the line swung to the right as it began the climb towards Bronybuckley. Calthrop and Ward's original proposal was to take the railway along Brook Street to Standard Quarry as the Welshpool Railway of 1818–1854 had done, but this route was rejected by the Promoters who feared that it would antagonise the County Council. AUTHOR'S COLLECTION

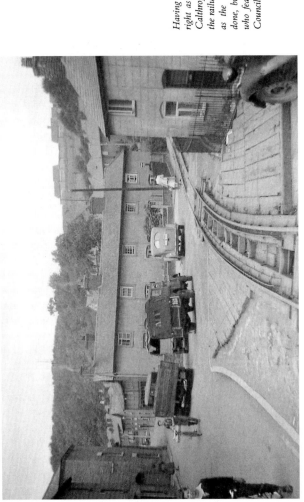

The line between Bronybuckley and Seven Stars was used as an unofficial footpath. Beyond Gardens level crossing, a lady is seen making her way into the town. 14th September 1956.
R.M. CASSERLEY

SEVEN STARS TO RAVEN SQUARE

The railway left the halt and swung away from Brook Street to climb towards Bronybuckley on a gradient of 1 in 30. Messrs Calthrop and Ward had intended to follow the road but this route was rejected by the promoters who feared that it would not find favour with the County Council. Having passed between Lledan Crescent and the Tannery, the line ran through gardens and allotments on land that fell away in the direction of Brook Street. In 1937 work started on the Bronybuckley estate which was built on the site of the allotments. A new level crossing of the same name was put in at 0m 48½c to provide access to the estate.[76] The gradients eased beyond the Armoury level crossing as the line ran through a sinuous reverse curve to rejoin Brook Street near Rock Cottage. From Rock Cottage the railway ran along the side of the road, passing the entrance to Standard Quarry on its way to Raven Square.

No. 822 taking five wagons and a brake van up the bank from Seven Stars to Bronybuckley.
A.W.V. MACE

No. 822 The Earl *with the 2.15pm from Llanfair passing between the gardens of houses at Bronybuckley on its way back to Welshpool yard. 24th August 1948.*
H.C. CASSERLEY

Bronybuckley level crossing was a late addition put in to serve a new housing estate. The line also served as a footpath, as can be seen here. Beyond the crossing the railway climbed, past the notice advertising excursions to Blackpool as it made its way towards the Armoury level crossing and Raven Square. 14th September 1956.   R.M. CASSERLEY

At the Armoury level crossing the railway left the Bronybuckley estate and swept through a sinuous reverse curve to join Brook Street near Rock Cottage. 14th September 1956.
R.M. CASSERLEY

The railway at Quarry Cottage crossing on 6th August 1949. The cottage is seen above the retaining wall. The railway ran alongside Brook Street, passing the entrance to Standard Quarry as it made its way to Raven Square.
JOHN ALSOP COLLECTION

No. 822 The Earl *passing the retaining wall near Quarry Cottage level crossing with the 2.15pm train from Llanfair. The lamp was provided for the benefit of people using the footpath that crossed the line. The back of the train was crossing the entrance to Standard Quarry. 24th August 1948.*   H.C. CASSERLEY

The site of the Standard Quarry Company's siding photographed on 6th August 1949.   JOHN ALSOP COLLECTION

No. 823 taking a train from Llanfair past the site of the Standard Quarry Company's siding.

STANDARD QUARRY AND THE WELSHPOOL RAILWAY

A quarry at the Stondart or rock seems to have been established before 1800. In 1810 the quarry was enclosed under the provisions of the Enclosures Act, ownership passing to the Earls of Powis. A small portion was set aside as a public quarry and £300 was awarded as compensation for the extinction of the Public Rights. This sum was vested in Trustees who used it for the lighting of the town.

In 1797 The Montgomeryshire Canal opened from Llanymynech to Berriew. It was authorised by an Act of 1794 which gave the proprietors of quarries situated within three miles of the canal powers to construct railways or roads to the waterway. At first stone was carted to the canal but in 1818 a railway was built from the quarry to a wharf between the Lledan aqueduct and Pont Howell which carried Seven Street over the canal. The line may have been laid as a plateway and was later relaid with edge rails designed to suit the existing chairs and blocks.

From the quarry the railway followed the route of Brook Street as far as Hall Street. It then followed the course of the Lledan Brook, crossing the stream near Church Street where there was a level crossing in much the same position as the one later occupied by the Welshpool and Llanfair Light Railway. The railway then followed the course of the Lledan Brook before terminating at the canal wharf. It does not seem to have been as successful as the nearby Crickheath tramway and by 1854 it had fallen out of use.[1]

At the time that the Welshpool and Llanfair Light Railway was under construction Mr James Baker was the lessee of the quarry. In July 1901 the weighbridge and smithy at the quarry were taken down to make way for the line. The replacement buildings were still incomplete in the early part of the following year, so Mr Baker wrote to the light railway company to ask that they be put in good order. The Llanfair Board instructed their Engineer to carry out the required work on the weighbridge immediately.[2] In October 1902 the Board paid Mr Baker's executors compensation of £2 18s 8d for the loss of use of the smithy and weighbridge. The Engineer was also instructed to carry out further work on the smithy and weighbridge that had been requested by Mr William Barker and macadam the road at the quarry entrance.[3]

In 1902 Mr Strachan, the light railway's Contractor, used stone from the quarry to ballast the line. Mr Joseph Bushall, whose house was on the corner of Raven Square and the Back Road, wrote to the Town Council complaining that blasting at the quarry was dangerous.[4] The Mayor, Mr Charles Shuker, said that he had been informed that a rock had been thrown as far as *The Raven Inn* where it had smashed into several pieces, some of which weighed as much as four and a half pounds. The Town Clerk wrote to the Inspector of Mines and Quarries about the matter.[5]

In 1903 the site was leased by the Standard Granite Company and up-to-date methods of quarrying were introduced. Early in 1904 an Ingersoll-Sergent drill replaced hand drilling and more powerful explosives were used. On occasions up to 1,000 tons of stone was blasted from the quarry face in a single operation. A stone crusher worked by a gas engine was introduced at about the same time.[6] In December 1904 proposals were made to lay a siding adjacent to the Smithfield Siding to enable stone from the quarry to be transhipped into standard gauge wagons but the matter did not proceed any further.[7]

The noise caused by the drill and crusher was far greater than hitherto and it was alleged that the vibration produced by quarrying operations caused structural damage to houses in the neighbourhood. Stone was thrown into the surrounding neighbourhood and on one occasion came through the roof of Mr Bushall's house in Raven Square. From time to time the quarry company promised to remedy the nuisance but did nothing to improve the matter. In December 1906 Mr Bushall and Mr G.D. Harrison brought an action against the quarry company.[8] The Judge appointed a referee, Mr Lloyd Jones, who drafted regulations

The Standard Quarry Company's siding 0m 67c

During the construction of the line, the Resident Engineer, Mr Byron, had an office at the quarry. When the railway first opened, there was a loop here[77] but the connection at the Llanfair end was removed and may have been re-used elsewhere. Before the passenger service was withdrawn, any traffic from the quarry for stations to Llanfair was collected from the siding by the engine of the 8.10 am train, taken to Welshpool yard and attached to the train. Traffic for Welshpool was picked up by trains from Llanfair. When shunting was performed at the siding, the engine had to be placed at the Welshpool end of the train.[78] The date that siding was taken out of use is not known but the quarry is believed to have ceased its operations by 1939.

A Llanfair bound train crossing the entrance to Standard Quarry on the approach to Raven Square. Although the line ran alongside Brook Street, there was no boundary fence 14th May 1952.
N.K. HARROP

designed to reduce the nuisance caused by the quarrying operations to an acceptable level while allowing the quarry to be worked efficiently. Only one stone breaker, enclosed in a building or substantial shed, could be used at a time and then only between the hours of 7am and 5pm. The use of mechanical rock drills was forbidden and the depth of shot holes was restricted to a maximum of twelve feet. Rock being blasted was to be restrained by a chain net covering all shot holes and any contiguous rock likely to be ejected by the charge. The regulations were accepted by the plaintiffs and the defendant.[9]

In 1906 the Cambrian Railways Chief Engineer tendered for the supply of ballast from quarries that were connected to its railway, but the price offered by the Standard Quarry Company was too expensive.[10] By 1912 the only traffic from the quarry carried by the Llanfair Railway was destined for stations west of Raven Square. Granite forwarded from Welshpool by rail was carted to the Cambrian station where it was tipped into standard gauge wagons. Competition in the market for road stone forced the quarry company to look for a more economical way of carting their traffic to the station. The proprietors considered buying a traction engine, but before doing so asked the Cambrian to quote rates for conveying their traffic to Welshpool station over the light railway using their own and railway company wagons. The company was prepared to buy its own wagons and guarantee traffic of not less than 5,000 tons per annum if a rate could be agreed. Mr Williamson recommended that his company should charge 3d per ton if the quarry company's wagons were used and 4½d per ton if the Llanfair Railway's wagons were used.[11] However, no agreement appears to have been arrived at and the quarry company did not own any narrow gauge wagons.

The quarry is believed to have ceased its operations by 1939.[12]

[1] *Early Railways of the Ellesmere and the Montgomeryshire Canals*, A. Stanley Davies *Transactions of the Newcomen Society* v. XXIV 1943–44 and 1944–45 pp.141–146

[2] Rail 722 2 W&L Board 24th April 1902

[3] Rail 722 2 W&L Board 23rd October 1902

[4] Welshpool Town Council Minute Book 1901–1903 Dangerous blasting at Standard Quarry 15th August 1902

[5] *The Montgomery County Times and Shropshire and Mid-Wales Advertiser* 23rd August 1902

[6] *The Montgomery County Times and Shropshire and Mid-Wales Advertiser* 8th December 1906

[7] Rail 722 3 W&L Board 21st December 1904

[8] *The Montgomery County Times and Shropshire and Mid-Wales Advertiser* 8th December 1906

[9] *The Montgomery County Times and Shropshire and Mid-Wales Advertiser* 27th July 1907

[10] Rail 92 78 Engineer to Board 11th June 1906

[11] Rail 92 87 S. Williamson to the Cambrian Board 5th July 1912

[12] *Early Railways of the Ellesmere and the Montgomeryshire Canals*, A. Stanley Davies *Transactions of the Newcomen Society* v. XXIV 1943–44 and 1944–45 pp.141–146

This train is seen approaching Llanfair and Guilsfield road level crossing. The kerb stones had been painted white in an attempt to make them more visible during the blackout. 29th May 1941.
W.A. CAMWELL

RAVEN SQUARE 0m 72c

Raven Square halt was between the end of the quarry siding and the Llanfair & Guilsfield Road level crossing.[79] It was no more than a gravelled area between the railway and the road. The railway then crossed Bushell's Lane to reach the level crossing. Although two main roads met at Raven Square and the crossing was a long one without gates, no special instructions were issued for it. As at other level crossings in Welshpool, drivers were instructed to keep a sharp look out and be prepared to come to a stand without fouling the crossing.[80]

On the evening of 8th September 1904 a fatal accident occurred at Raven Square. The 7.10 pm train to Llanfair had been delayed by half an hour for the benefit of passengers attending a horse show at the Smithfield. At about 8 pm the train, consisting of three carriages and a brake van, had almost crossed the road when two men were seen running from *The Raven Inn*. They attempted to board the train although the guard, John Pritchard, told them to keep back. Herbert Astley, an underkeeper on the Powis estate, managed to board the train successfully but the other man John Powell, a rabbit catcher from Cwmcefn, Castle Caereinion, overbalanced and fell between the first and middle carriages, causing the leading bogie of the second carriage to derail. Had it not been for the vigilance of the fireman, who was looking back and immediately brought the train to a stand, the carriage would have headed into the Nant y Caws brook. After a delay of

No. 822 taking its train across the Guilsfield Road on 12th October 1951.
F.W. SHUTTLEWORTH

about an hour, the passengers were moved into the first carriage and taken on to Llanfair. Mr Powell's body was then recovered from underneath the second carriage which was re-railed by 11 pm that night. When an Inquest was held at Welshpool Town Hall on 10th September, Mr Astley said that he had attended the horse show with Mr Powell. Although they had visited several pubs in the town and had not eaten that day, Mr Astley maintained that they were both sober enough to look after themselves. The Coroner's jury returned a verdict of death by misadventure.[81/82]

R.M. CASSERLEY

The 11.30am to Llanfair passing the 'normal speed' board on the beginning of the climb towards Golfa on 14th September 1956.

A goods train approaching New Drive crossing.

P.B. WHITEHOUSE Cty. MICHAEL WHITEHOUSE

RAVEN SQUARE TO GOLFA

After Raven Square the town was left behind as the railway passed through parkland belonging to the Llanerchydol and Powis estates. Four chains beyond the level crossing the line reached milepost 1 where the permanent speed restriction of 5mph ended and the ascent of the Golfa incline began.[83] The railway climbed continuously for over 1¾ miles to reach Golfa station, more than a mile of the ascent being on a gradient of 1 in 29. On the way the line crossed New Drive on the level, then climbed along the northern edge of Glyn Golfa.

On 24th January 1908 two platelayers were coming down the line on a trolley when, owing to slippery rails, the brake failed to act. The trolley soon gathered speed and rushed down the line at a great rate. One man jumped off but when Thomas Breeze, who was holding the brake lever, tried to do likewise, he was dragged along the sleepers for five or six yards. Mr Breeze was taken to the Victoria Nursing Institute where it was found that he had cuts and bruises to his face. His right leg was much contused and the muscles injured but no bones were broken. Mr Breeze was expected to make an excellent recovery. The trolley ran as far as the top of the town and then turned over. Fortunately nobody happened to be on the line at the time.[84]

Below Golfa Hall the line passed through a plantation on reverse curves of three chains radius. When proposals for the

F.W. SHUTTLEWORTH

The 11.30am train for Llanfair crossing a cattle creep at the lower end of Golfa Bank. 12th October 1951.

railway were published, the Rev. G. R. G. Pughe, the Vicar of Mellor near Blackburn, objected to the course of the line where it passed through his property. To pacify him, a clause was inserted into the 1899 Light Railway Order preventing the compulsory purchase of his land where it was needed for the railway.[85] Mr Collin attempted to find a route that avoided the clergyman's property, but the line would have had to run along the edge of the valley with the formation on an embankment seventy-six feet above the Black and Upper pools which provided Welshpool with drinking water. This deviation was considered to be dangerous as the embankment would be liable to slippage[86] so an alternative route was devised that took as little of Mr Pughe's land as possible.[87] When the

clergyman still refused to negotiate, the Llanfair Company[88] threatened to insert a clause into the 1901 Amendment Order that would remove the protection granted by the 1899 Order.[89] This persuaded him to treat with the company who paid £300 for the narrow strip of land needed for the line.[90]

Above the reservoirs the railway clung to the side of Glyn Golfa. While the line settled, debris from the railway was washed into one of the pools, so in 1905 a setting tank was built at the foot of the slope to catch any falling material.[91] Beyond the upper reverse curves the line emerged from woodland, allowing a last glimpse of the reservoirs and the wooded upper reaches of the Powis estate. The gradients eased to 1 in 55 as the line approached Golfa station.

On Golfa bank.
JOHN ALSOP COLLECTION

GOLFA 2m 67c

For many crews the halt at Golfa provided an opportunity to attend to the fire and restore boiler pressure after the exertions of the last mile and three quarters. The station was a rather remote spot that served a few scattered farms on the Powis Estate and was built in consideration for the conveyance of land required for the railway.[92]

The accommodation provided at Golfa was typical of that seen at other stations between Raven Square and Llanfair. The platform consisted of a gravelled area 80ft in length at rail level situated next to the running line. The waiting hut, which was open on the platform side, had a timber frame and a single pitch roof that were clad with corrugated iron sheeting.

Entry to the loop was controlled by ground frames that had two levers and were placed at its extremities. The ground frames were locked by the Annett's key that was attached to the train staff. The loop served as a siding for local traffic. A Great Western plan of the branch dated 10th July 1925 states that the points were clipped, spiked and padlocked but the date that the work was carried out is not recorded and the loop was still in situ when the line closed.

In summer the occasional picnic party alighted at Golfa. In 1958 Mrs Painter recalled that when she was a child her family took the train as far as Golfa and picnicked there. The fare was a penny for children and two pence for adults.[93]

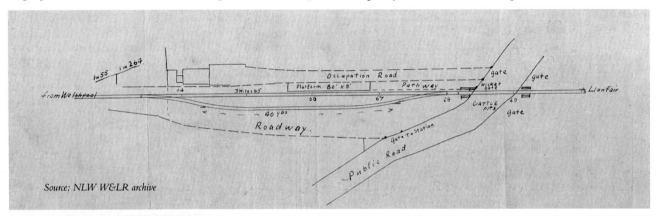

Source: NLW W&LR archive

Golfa station seen from the east end points, looking towards Llanfair. 6th August 1949.

JOHN ALSOP COLLECTION

A train for Llanfair hauled by No. 822 at Golfa.
G. F. BANNISTER

Golfa loop, waiting shed and the west ground frame on 6th August 1949.

JOHN ALSOP COLLECTION

GOLFA TO SYLFAEN

The railway crossed Cwm Lane by a level crossing without gates. After nearly half a mile on gradients of between 1 in 111 and 1 in 37, the summit of the line was reached just beyond mile post 3$\frac{1}{4}$. The line then fell rapidly towards Sylfaen halt on gradients of 1 in 87 and 1 in 33.[94]

On 28th September 1903 a wagon attached immediately behind the last carriage of the 9.40am from Llanfair to Welshpool became derailed as the train approached Golfa summit.

The derailment was caused because one of the wheels broke, part of it being found about 470 yards from Sylfaen siding. There were platelayers working about forty or fifty yards from the siding but they did not notice anything untoward as the train passed. The guard attributed the fracture to a flaw in the wheel, but when it was examined, no flaw could be detected and the cause of the failure could not be explained.[95]

The road and railway ran next to each other at the summit of the line. Notice the photographer standing on the road close to the summit as this Llanfair-bound train was approaching.

N.K. HARROP

Golfa summit, looking towards Llanfair on 6th August 1949. The heavier section rail came from the Tanat Valley Light Railway.   JOHN ALSOP COLLECTION

SYLFAEN 3m 57c

The halt was situated on the opposite side of the main road to Sylfaen dairy farm. Working timetables refer to the stopping place as Sylfaen Farm until July 1913 when it was renamed Sylfaen Halt.[96] When the line opened there was no covered accommodation for intending passengers and, although a shelter was requested in 1905,[97] it was not until August 1914 that a timber waiting shed of Cambrian design was provided.[98/99/100] After the closure of the line to passengers, it was sold to Llanfair Rural District Council and removed on 30th November 1933.[101]

Sylfaen siding served the nearby farm. It was facing to trains for Llanfair and was worked by a two-lever ground frame that was locked by the train staff.[102] In May 1912 the gates across the line at Sylfaen were in an unsatisfactory state of repair and the Cambrian Engineer was asked to attend to them. In the 1920s milk for London was forwarded from the halt.[103]

On Tuesday 2nd January 1951 No. 823 was derailed near Sylfaen farm while working a train for Llanfair. The leading and trailing wheels came off the road but the rest of the train was unaffected and the crew were not injured. The cause of the derailment was attributed to snow and ice.[104]

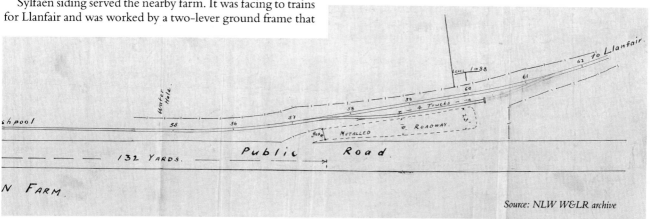

Source: NLW W&LR archive

The overgrown siding at Sylfaen. The right-hand point blade appears to be clipped. 6th August 1949.

JOHN ALSOP COLLECTION

SYLFAEN TO CASTLE CAEREINION

The mid-day train from Welshpool near milepost 4. 24th August 1948.

H. C. CASSERLEY

At Sylfaen the railway turned away from the main road heading south-west along a stream that fed the Black and Upper Pools. In winter the watercourse was occasionally used as an emergency water supply when the tank near Llanfair failed. Crews who nursed their engine back from Llanfair were faced with the unenviable task of replenishing the tanks a bucketful at a time.[105] At four miles the line passed a large oak and began to turn towards the west along Cwm Curve where the gradient increased to 1 in 38 as the line approached Coppice Lane. To the south Pen-y-Foel with its ancient hill fort towered above the line.

A derailment occurred near Coppice Lane on 11th October 1923. A train consisting of an engine, one of the composite carriages, an open wagon, covered van No. 6, a cattle wagon and a brake van was approaching the crossing from Welshpool when the rear wheel set of the covered van mounted the rail, breaking an axleguard. The site was surveyed the day after the derailment.[106]

The railway crossed Coppice Lane on the level, then fell towards Castle Caereinion on a ruling gradient of 1 in 33. At 4m 52½c the line passed under the only accommodation over-bridge on the railway as it ran through the cutting that led to the station. In 1903 the Trustees of David Bebb alleged that the bridge was insufficient for their needs, and alterations costing £5 0s 0d were made.[107/108] In 1932 proposals were

made to replace the bridge using girders that were lying at tunnel yard, Newport.[109] However, the matter did not progress and the bridge was replaced by an accommodation crossing sited at the eastern end of the cutting that led to Castle Caereinion station.

No. 822 passing Sylfaen with the daily goods to Llanfair.

G.F BANNISTER

CASTLE CAEREINION 4m 61c

Montgomeryshire's motto is Powys Paradwys Cymru – Powys the paradise of Wales. *Here No. 822 is seen at Castle Caereinion amongst the rolling hills.*

G. F. BANNISTER

Castle Caereinion station was about half a mile from the village that it served. The view along the Banwy valley from the station was one of the most attractive on the line. On clear days Cader Idris and the mountains around Dinas Mawddwy could be seen in the distance.

The first proposal for accommodation at Castle Caereinion included platforms on the running line and loop, a siding facing to trains bound for Llanfair, a small goods shed and an office.[110] Predictably, given the railway's shaky finances, such generous accommodation never materialised. When the railway opened, a platform at rail level and a small shelter were provided next to the running line which threw off a loop that was used as a siding for local traffic.[111]

Shortly after the line opened, Castle Caereinion Parish Council wrote to complain that where footpaths crossed the line the stiles could not be used and that in one case no stiles had been provided.[112] The matter was referred to the Engineer who reported that he had inspected the stiles and found that there was no cause for complaint, but that he had been unable to find the footpath for which no stiles had been provided.[113]

In 1906 Mr Jabez Barker sought to move about 70,000 cubic feet of timber from Llanfair to Welshpool. Mr Baker stated that the woodland had to be cleared quickly and it was his belief that more than one train would be required each day. If the railway company could not accommodate his needs,

all or part of the timber would have to be removed via Dinas Mawddwy for conveyance over the Mawddwy Railway. This arrangement would have suited the Cambrian Company better because the route via Cemmes Road was longer than the one via Llanfair. It appeared that in the interests of the Llanfair Railway there was no option but to run special trains for Mr Baker's traffic which would cross service trains at Castle Caereinion.[114]

On 27th November 1906 Mr Dennis wrote to the Llanfair Company proposing that a passing place be provided at Castle Caereinion at an estimated cost of £160. If the traffic was secured, timber weighing approximately 1,400 tons could be carried over the line, yielding gross revenues of £350, of which £140 would pass to the light railway company. At a meeting on 28th December the Works Committee assented to the work being carried out at their company's expense. The first trains carrying Mr Barker's timber ran in February 1907, the traffic being worked in the early morning, before the first service of the day left Welshpool.[115]

The new works were inspected by Col. Druitt in June 1907. The Inspector reported that although the interlocking and signalling arrangements were satisfactory, the points and signals were still not connected to the signal box. It was intended to work the line on the staff and ticket system combined with the absolute block telegraph system. Block

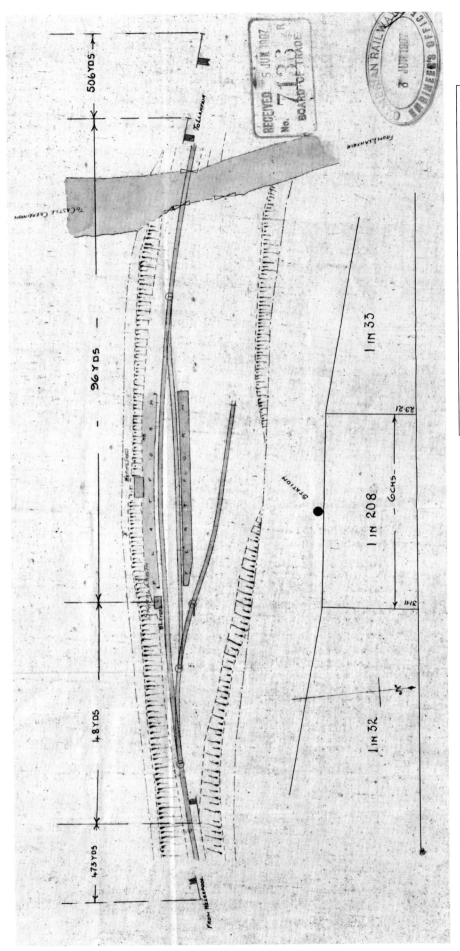

Source: MT6 1632 2

Estimate of the cost of converting Castle Caereinon Station into a crossing place for passenger trains

Quantity	Description of work	Unit cost	£	s	d	£	s	d
2	Taking out traps and relaying as points	5/-		10	0			
1	New crossing laid	£3/-/-	3	0	0			
1	Trap point	10/-		10	0			
55 cu yds	Permanent way in siding	12/-	33	0	0	37	0	0
	Forming platform		1	10	0	1	10	0
	Erecting stock signal frame with shelter	£3/-/-	12	0	0			
	No. 9 lever locking frame		27	0	0			
2	Home signals 20ft 0in high fixed complete	£9/-/-	18	0	0			
2	Distant signals 20ft 0in high fixed complete	£9/-/-	18	0	0			
200 yds	Point rodding on rollers fixed complete	2/6	25	0	0			
950 yds	Signalling wire on stakes	-/2	7	18	4	107	18	4
	Providing staff and staff boxes	£3/-/-	3	0	0	3	0	0
						149	8	4
	Contingencies					10	11	8
	Total					£ 160	0	0

Source: Rail 92 80

No. 822 passing between the signal box and overgrown loop at Castle Caereinion with the 2.15pm train for Welshpool. In the fields above and below the line the harvest was underway. 24th August 1948.
H.C. CASSERLEY

signals were to be transmitted by telephone rather than by block instruments, using the phonopore instruments that had been installed at Welshpool, Castle Caereinion and Llanfair. Col. Druitt sanctioned the use of the new works subject to the points and signals being connected up, the receipt of a copy of the regulations for working the line, and a new undertaking as to the mode of working the railway signed by both the owning and working companies.[116]

A copy of the regulations was sent to Col. Druitt that September. In his covering letter Mr McDonald, the Cambrian Railways' Chief Engineer, stated that it was only intended to use the station as a crossing place when ballasting and maintenance work made this necessary, and that trains would normally be worked on the principle of one engine in steam. During normal working, the points would be disconnected from the signal box and worked from the ground frames, but when the station was used as a passing place the points would be connected to the signal box and disconnected from the ground frames.[117]

Col. Druitt approved the proposed arrangements, recommending that when the line was worked as a single section the existing train staff should be used, but that when it was worked in two sections, train staffs, of different shapes and colour, should be used for each of the two sections. When the line was worked as a single section, the train staffs for the Welshpool to Castle, and Castle to Llanfair sections were to be locked away, as was the Welshpool to Llanfair staff when the station was used as a crossing place. This procedure was required to avoid any misunderstanding about the mode of working that was in place.[118]

The cost of the work at Castle Caereinion exceeded the Engineer's estimate by £30, the additional expenditure being attributed to the provision of repeaters for the distant signals which could not be seen from the box.[119] In 1908 the Cam-

Castle box, rarely used and in need of paint.
BOB BARNARD

WORKING CASTLE BOX IN 1907

In April 1907 John Wynne Jones joined the Cambrian Railways Company as a porter in the goods department at Welshpool. On 25th November of that year he was sent to Castle Caereinion to operate the signal box. The reason for opening it was that the permanent way was being re-ballasted. This operation required two engines to be on the line at the same time, one for the ordinary service and the other for the ballast train. The two services required a crossing place at Castle. Although trains crossed at the station John could not remember if there were signals there. John closed the box on 31st December 1907 and resigned from his employment with the Cambrian in June 1909.

Recounted to Henry Gunston in 1966 via Mike Christensen

Castle Caereinion station, seen from the west end of the loop. The wooden ramp was used to load livestock.   W&LLR PRESERVATION CO.

MEMORIES OF CASTLE BETWEEN THE WARS

Castle Caereinion was the largest place between Welshpool and Llanfair to be served by the railway. Dilys Griffiths, whose relatives lived at Tyn Llan farm, recalled that the community was quite self sufficient, there being a church, chapel, school, post office shop, blacksmith and pub in the village. The shop was very important to village life and at one time a tailor had occupied one of the upstairs rooms. The shop keeper dealt in coal, lime and fertilisers that were brought up from Welshpool by rail. Wagons were left at Castle station, their contents unloaded and taken back to the village by horse and cart. Dilys remembers seeing a large pile of coal in the shop garden, while lime and fertiliser were stored in nearby sheds.

Children attending the County School at Llanfair travelled there by train and Dilys' uncles told her that if they were late, and the driver saw them running down the bank to the station, he would stop the train on the level crossing so that they could climb on board.

On Mondays, farmers' wives from the district served by the railway would take the train into Welshpool to sell their produce and when Dilys was a small girl she used to accompany her mother to market. She remembered that in spring the banks of the road leading down to the station were full of cowslips. The light railway's carriages had slatted seats which faced inwards and large baskets filled with butter, eggs and poultry were placed in the central gangway for the duration of the journey. The baskets often contained live birds and Dilys was rather anxious that they would peck at her legs as she found her way to a seat. Most of the passengers alighted at Seven Stars and made their way to Broad Street. Here stalls had been set up along one side of the street between the Town Hall and the Cross. Dealers would walk up and down the stalls asking what price was asked for the produce offered, but would never make an offer until quite late in the day. This forced prices down because the traders could not afford to return home with unsold produce. After the passenger service was withdrawn, a market day bus ran from Castle to Welshpool via the Waterloo Road.

brian proposed to add the cost of the work to the Llanfair Railway's capital account and to charge interest each half year.[120] When the light railway company protested that the crossing place had never been used, Mr Dennis replied that his company had been able to keep pace with the delivery of timber without bringing a second engine into use, and that the speed at which the timber was brought to Llanfair for delivery at Welshpool could not have been foreseen.[121] Further protest was made by the Earl of Powis in his capacity as Chairman of the light railway and in 1909 the matter was investigated by John Conacher, the Cambrian Chairman. The outcome of the inquiry was very damaging to Mr Denniss who left the Cambrian the following year, while the Llanfair Railway secured a reduction in the interest rate charged on the cost of the works from 5% to $2\frac{1}{2}$%.[122]

In May 1910 certain sections of the line required ballasting with stone from Standard Quarry and a ballast train was required. To carry out the work efficiently, it was proposed to cross the ballast and service trains at Castle Caereinion. However, Mr McDonald deemed it politic to obtain the consent of his Director's before opening the signal box.[123] The frame is thought to have been removed from the signal box after the passenger service was withdrawn and the signals probably went at the same time. The siding is believed to have been in existence for about twenty years.[124] The telephone

Castle gates with the line disappearing towards Llanfair. Charlie Jones lived in the bungalow on the right and kept his traction engine in the station yard.   J.E. NORRIS

was still in situ in the early 1960s and used to ring during thunderstorms.[125]

In 1946 Mr Charles Jones entered into an agreement with the Great Western that allowed him to keep his threshing machine and traction engine at Castle Caereinion station. The annual rent was fixed at two guineas per annum which increased to £3 from 1st July 1948.[126] Mr Jones lived in the bungalow by the level crossing and before he retired the traction engine was used to provide the power for threshing clover. Drivers on the Llanfair Railway and Mr Jones used to cast envious eyes on each other's steam engines until an arrangement was reached whereby Mr Jones 'had a go' on the footplate while the locomotive drivers worked his traction engine.[127] By 1956 the traction engine was in rather a forlorn state, for although the mechanism above the boiler was apparently well preserved, the chimney was badly corroded and appeared to be ready to fall off.[128]

Charlie Jones' traction engine, a Burrell compound, No. 3812. 30th June 1956.
H.C. CASSERLEY

No. 822 climbing Dolarddyn bank on its way to Castle Caereinion on 12th October 1951.

F.W. SHUTTLEWORTH

CASTLE CAEREINION TO CYFRONYDD

At the west end of the station the railway crossed the road leading to Castle Caereinion village by a level crossing. The gates were normally closed across the railway and were opened by the fireman for the passage of a train. The road was on a hill and curved slightly before reaching the railway, so firemen were required to satisfy themselves that there was no approaching traffic before calling the train onto the crossing. Once the train had passed over the level crossing, it was stopped a little way along the line so that it did not foul the road and the guard could shut the gates. The line continued along Dolarddyn bank on a falling gradient of 1 in 32.

At Dolarddyn the railway crossed the Cwm Goleu road on a level crossing without gates, over which a permanent speed restriction of 10mph was in force.[129] Until the introduction of the 1929 summer timetable, trains stopped at Dolarddyn crossing on Mondays to pick up or set down passengers travelling to or from Welshpool. On other days they would stop at the crossing for picnic parties. From 9th July 1929 trains stopped at the crossing every weekday if requested to do so. Passengers were charged the same fares as those boarding at Cyfronydd.[130/131]

Dolarddyn was reported to be the site of a collision between a train and a car on 17th June 1932. The train had stopped before the level crossing and was making its way over the road when a motor car, driven by Mr. Albert Hamlet, Oswestry hit the locomotive. The motor car, which was carrying a funeral party, was completely wrecked and its four occupants had a miraculous escape as the car was practically cut in two. One of the party, Mr. Richard Williams of Penrhos, was trapped in the car and once released was taken to the Victoria Memorial Hospital, Welshpool, where he was detained with injuries to his foot. Mr. Williams was taken to hospital by a travelling salesman and his chauffeur who witnessed the accident.

From Dolarddyn the railway continued through open countryside. At 6m 1¼c it crossed Idanfawr [sic] Lane,[132] a poorly drained farm track which became a quagmire in wet weather. In 1940 John Rowlands, who farmed at Hydan Fawr, collided with *Countess* while driving a tractor over the crossing. Luckily he was thrown clear but his tractor was destroyed and No. 823's frames were cracked, necessitating major repairs.[133] About a quarter of a mile from Cyfronydd the line reached Pen-y-Coed from where timber was forwarded to Messrs Boys and Boden's British Saw Mills at Welshpool in the early 1920s.[134]

White Bridge with the railway running down Dolarddyn bank on its way to Cyfronydd. 6th August 1948.   JOHN ALSOP COLLECTION

CYFRONYDD 6m 57c

Cyfronydd station served a few houses, farms and Cyfronydd Hall which was the home of Captain A. R. Pryce,[135] the Llanfair Railway's Deputy Chairman. The station was built where a minor road crossed the railway, the platform and waiting shed being situated between the west end of the loop and the level crossing. The platform was merely a gravelled area extending for eighty feet at rail level. The waiting shed was a timber-framed structure with a single pitched roof clad with corrugated iron. Entry to the loop was controlled by ground frames with two levers. When the railway opened, the loop was used as a siding for local traffic but by the 1950s it was used to stable the surviving timber trucks and the sheep wagons.[136/137]

Soon after the railway opened, an ancient oak tree at Cyfronydd was struck by lightening and fell across the line shortly after the last train of the day had passed. The next day's early morning goods train was detained at the site until the line was cleared. When the tree fell, it severed the telegraph wire which took over a day to repair.[138]

In 1912 Mr Jabez Barker contracted to clear woodland on the Maesmawr Estate. To secure Mr Barker's timber traffic, the working and owning companies agreed to widen the entrance gates at the station and erect his crane at an estimated cost of between £12 and £15. Forty percent of the cost was to be contributed by the Llanfair Company with the balance being provided by the Cambrian.[139]

After the passenger service was withdrawn in 1931 the railway still dealt with parcels traffic. Parcels could be left or collected from the shelters and this may explain why they lasted until the line closed. The shelter at Cyfronydd was demolished by the permanent way gang in the final week of the goods service.[140] By November 1937 a wooden ramp for loading livestock had been erected opposite the shelter in support of the District Traffic Manager's attempts to secure all available livestock to rail transport.[141]

Cyfronydd station and loop seen from the east end points, looking towards Llanfair on 6th August 1949.   JOHN ALSOP COLLECTION

The basic accommodation provided at Cyfronydd was characteristic of the intermediate stations between Raven Square and Llanfair. In 1912 authority was given to widen the entrance to the station so that timber from the Maesmawr estate could be brought to the station and forwarded to Welshpool.

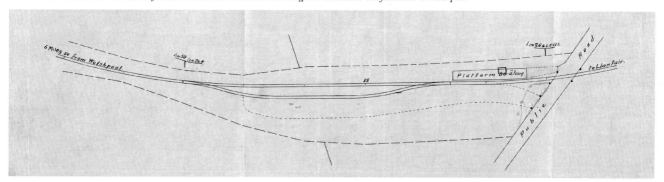

Source: NLW W&LR archive

No.822 at Cyfronydd waiting for the fireman to flag it across the level crossing. Although the locomotive had lost its name plates, it carried an Oswestry (89A) shed plate on the smokebox door. 12th October 1951. F.W. SHUTTLEWORTH

Sheep wagons stabled on Cyfronydd loop.

NRM, S. P. HIGGINS COLLECTION

A train for Welshpool passing the waiting shed at Cyfronydd shortly before the line closed.
A.W.V. MACE

Cyfronydd photographed from the level crossing at the west end of the station on 8th August 1949.
JOHN ALSOP COLLECTION

CYFRONYDD TO HENIARTH

The railway crossed the road by a level crossing without gates, then ran through a cutting to reach Brynelin viaduct that crossed Nant Cwmbaw on six masonry arches. On 4th May 1914 *The Earl* broke an axle while crossing the viaduct and passengers had to complete the rest of the journey by foot.[142] At first the railway ran on a shelf cut into the hillside above the river before descending to the valley floor on a gradient of 1 in 50. It then passed through open countryside and was never far from the river. A little under a mile from Cyfronydd the railway turned towards the River Banwy and crossed it on a plate girder bridge of three spans that were carried on masonry piers and abutments.

The railway crosses Brynelin viaduct as it makes its way to Llanfair.
JOHN ALSOP COLLECTION

No. 822 standing on Brynelin viaduct west of Cyfronydd with the Locomotive Club of Great Britain special of 23rd June 1956. The viaduct crossed a farm track and a minor tributary of the River Banwy.
R.E. VINCENT

The railway at the Kink between Cyfronydd and Heniarth. The line was never far from the river on this section and dropped steeply to the valley floor.
RA/L. & E. THOMAS, JOHN ALSOP COLLECTION

The Kink, looking towards Cyfronydd.   RA/L. & E. THOMAS, JOHN ALSOP COLLECTION

Near Heniarth the railway left the south bank of the Banwy and crossed the river on a bridge of three spans carried on masonry piers and abutments. 6th August 1949.
JOHN ALSOP COLLECTION

The Locomotive Club of Great Britain ran a special train over the line on 23rd June 1956. Here it is seen crossing the Banwy Bridge on the outward journey.
CHRIS GAMMELL

Having crossed the Banwy Bridge, the 11.30 train for Llanfair is seen making its way along the embankment leading to Heniarth station. 12th October 1951.

F.W. SHUTTLEWORTH

When Mr Collin reviewed the plans for the Banwy Bridge in 1898, he suggested that the minimum width should be increased from thirteen to fourteen feet so that the Cambrian's goods wagons could be carried over it on transporter wagons.[143] During the construction of the bridge the Llanfair Directors expressed concern about the perishable nature of the stone being used to build the piers and abutments.[144] Having inspected the bridgework, Mr Collin gave instructions that the work done should be taken down and rebuilt.[145] At a subsequent inspection the Engineer recommended that the piers should be well cemented to protect the stone from the weather.[146] In 1904 it was found that one of the piers had been seriously undermined by the river. During the summer the foundation was repaired at a cost of £50, the low water making it possible to carry out the work with relative ease.[147] In 1929 the transverse timbers were renewed at a cost of £167. Inspections carried out during the 1930s found the bridge to be in good condition.[148] In the early 1950s work was carried out to secure the piers.

No. 823 Countess *drifting along the embankment leading to the Banwy bridge with a train consisting of five wagons and a van. The timber wagons stabled on Heniarth loop were awaiting further use. 29th May 1941.*

W. A. CAMWELL

HENIARTH 7m 55c

The station was near the end of a lane that led from the main road to Heniarth Mill. When the railway opened, the station was called Heniarth Gate but became Heniarth from July 1913.[149] The platform and waiting shed were situated between the west end of the loop and the level crossing. The loop was on a curve at the end of an embankment that led from the Banwy Bridge. Entry to the loop was controlled by the east and west ground frames.[150] In Great Western days it was used to stable timber trucks.[151] Although the loop was still in situ in the summer of 1949,[152] by 1956 the points at both ends had been removed although the rails remained.[153]

On Monday 6th October 1902 Mr John Weaver, the fireman of one of Mr Strachan's engines, crushed both legs when shunting trucks at Heniarth. When getting onto the engine he was caught between a piece of earth and the locomotive which was travelling very slowly. If he not had been holding onto the engine's handrail very tightly, he would have been drawn under the trucks. By the following Saturday Mr Weaver was reported to have made a partial recovery.[154]

When Mr Richard Jones sold the land needed for the railway, he stipulated that the lane leading to the mill should be lowered and the gradient improved. For much of its length the lane was in a cutting with hedges on either side and it was necessary to widen it so that the gradient could be eased. The work was expensive, costing £219 12s 10d, and drew complaints that Mr Collin had misunderstood the nature and extent of the work that had been agreed with Mr Jones.[155] By 1907 no repairs had been made to the lane since the railway opened so Mr W.A. Rogers, the then mill owner, asked that it should be put into good repair.[156] Mr Denniss agreed to carry out the work at his company's expense on the understanding that in the future the cost of maintaining the lane would be shared between the railway and the owner of the mill.[157]

On 14th May 1909 Mr Denniss wrote to the Llanfair Secretary stating that Mr Jabez Baker was no longer able to load timber at Llanfair timber siding. Mr Barker was prepared to load his timber at Heniarth if a sleeper crossing costing £10 was provided at the station. If the work was not carried out he would forward his timber to Welshpool by road transport. The Works Committee agreed to have the work carried out provided that the cost did not exceed £10 and that the cost of any repairs to the lane arising from the passage of Mr Barker's traffic would be borne by the Cambrian Company.[158]

Heniarth east ground frame was situated near the end of the embankment leading from the Banwy Bridge. 6th August 1949.   JOHN ALSOP COLLECTION

No. 823 Countess *at Heniarth on 5th September 1950 with four cattle wagons, five loaded open wagons and a guard's van.* JOHN ALSOP COLLECTION

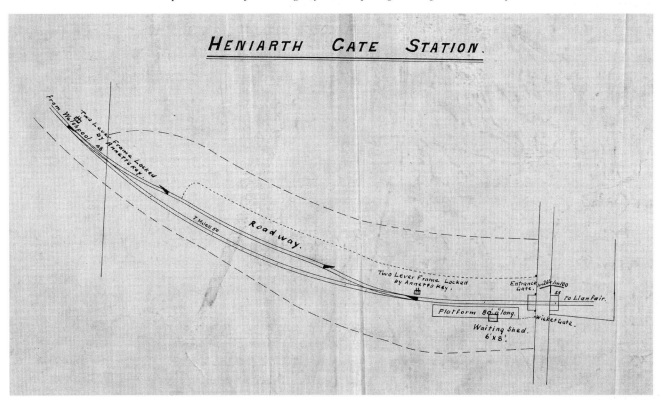

Heniarth waiting shed still in situ twenty years after the last public passenger train ran. A Tyers two-lever ground frame controlled the entry to the west end of the loop. 12th October 1951.   F.W. SHUTTLEWORTH

These terms were agreed by the Cambrian and the sleeper crossing was provided.[159] In May 1911 with the prospect of more timber traffic being handled at the station, the Cambrian asked for the Llanfair company's agreement to extend the loop at an estimated cost of £27. The Works Committee consented to the work being carried out once the traffic had been secured, and offered to contribute £20 towards the work.[160]

Timber loaders were working at Heniarth under the supervision of Inspector Allen on 24th July 1911. Reginald Glover of Oswestry was operating the crane when the Inspector called out that a small boy was in difficulties below the Banwy bridge. When Mr Glover reached the spot, he saw Ellis Jones

of Glasgoed Villa lying on the riverbed in about six feet of water. He dived into the pool and recovered the child but could not resuscitate him. The Coroner, Dr C.E. Humphreys, praised the timber loader's prompt action and recommended that children should be taught how to swim. The jury endorsed the Doctor's recommendation and returned a verdict of accidental death.[161]

Milk traffic was dealt with at Heniarth. In January 1916 the Llanfair directors decided to spend 30s 0d on improving facilities to handle milk at the station. They also asked Mr Williamson to persuade Mr Willis to send his milk traffic by rail instead of by road.[162]

Here No. 822 The Earl had paused on the main line before continuing along the curve leading to the Banwy Bridge. The land to the right of the loop was used to stack and load timber but became increasingly overgrown in later years. 24th August 1948.
H.C. CASSERLEY

No. 822 The Earl at Heniarth waiting for Henry Casserley to take a photograph of fireman Gibby Owen and driver Joe Davies. One of the two remaining Swindon-built timber trucks is seen standing on the now overgrown loop. 24th August 1948.
H. C. CASSERLEY

HENIARTH TO DOLRHYD

The railway ran across Heniarth Mill level crossing and made its way along the northern bank of the Banwy towards Dolrhyd Mill.[163]

At Heniarth the line crossed a lane leading from the main road to the mill. This picture shows No.822 approaching the level crossing on 12th October 1951.

F.W. SHUTTLEWORTH

DOLRHYD
8m 13½c

The mill curves seen shortly after the line opened and on 6th August 1949.   JOHN ALSOP COLLECTION

When the line was planned it was intended to pass to the north of Melin-dol-rhŷd-defaid.[164] This would have taken it very close to the miller's house and over the cartway from the mill to the main road, so at Mr R.C. Anwyl's request the railway was diverted to the south side of the mill.[165] The diversion created one of the most picturesque sections of the line as the railway wound its way between the river and the mill race on an embankment pitched with stone. The line passed the mill on curves of five chains but at the Llanfair end it left the mill race on a curve with a radius of three chains.[166] A speed limit of 5mph was imposed along the curves.[167]

Dolrhyd flag station
Although Mr Anwyl was a director of the light railway and his wife had given land at Dolrhyd for the construction of the line, he became very demanding with regard to the provision of accommodation works. Mrs Anwyl owned Eithnog Hall, which was situated between Dolrhyd and Llanfair on the southern bank of the Banwy. Her husband attempted to make the provision of a flag station, consisting of a shelter with a gravelled area at ground level, a condition of the conveyance of the land to the railway. The proposed halt was to be built opposite the Eithnog boathouse landing and paid for by Mrs Anwyl's Trustees.

When the railway opened, Mrs Anwyl's land had not been conveyed to the light railway, so its solicitor asked for the Cambrian's agreement to Mr Anwyl's request, pointing out that since trains stopped near the mill to pick up water his request was not unduly onerous. Mr Denniss agreed that trains could stop at the halt until such time as his company gave notice that its continuance was detrimental to its interests. The land was conveyed to the light railway on 31st July 1903 but no mention of the flag station was made in the conveyance, nor was any attempt made to build a shelter at the halt.[168]

On 17th July 1903 W.H. Gough, the Cambrian Railways Superintendent of the Line, wrote to Mr Pryce, the Welshpool station master, giving him authority to stop trains near Eithnog for the benefit of the Anwyls and their tenants. Mr Gough also agreed that trains could stop near the mill for the benefit of its occupant, Mr Thomas, who was one of Mrs Anwyl's tenants.[169] Some trains must have called at Dolrhyd before these arrangements were put in place, for on 13th July 1903 Guard Evan Humphreys was reduced to the position of assistant warehouseman at Oswestry for conveying four sacks of potatoes from Dolrhyd Mill to Raven Square without making a proper charge for them.[170]

The issue of providing a platform and shelter was raised in December 1908[171] and again in August 1912,[172] but although the owning and working companies agreed that they should be provided at the Anwyls' expense, the work was not put in hand.[173] Enquiries made in August 1912 by Mr Thomas Pryce, the Welshpool Station Master, and Guard John Pritchard found that on Mondays it had been customary to stop by the old water tank for the occupants of the mill. However, since the new water tank had come into use, the stop was made on the Heniarth side of the mill. The stop near the boathouse saw occasional use by servants from Eithnog whilst on Saturdays laundry in hampers was picked up or set down there. Another of Mrs Anwyl's tenants, Miss Thomas who lived at Tanybryn, expected the train to stop between the mill and the boathouse. Thus in the quarter of a mile from the mill to the new water tower a train might stop up to four times. Mr Pryce recommended that one stop should be made by the site of the old water tower and his recommendation was adopted by Charles Conacher, the Cambrian Traffic Manager.[174]

In June 1920 the Anwyls attempted to sell Eithnog Hall and the question of their tenants' rights to stop trains at Dolrhyd was brought to the attention of Samuel Williamson, the Cambrian General Manager. After protracted cor-respondence, Mr Anwyl accepted the same terms that had been agreed in C.S. Denniss' time.[175] Much to his annoyance, Mr Williamson found that trains continued to stop on either side of the mill and train staff were instructed to make a single stop opposite the Eithnog boathouse.[176] When informed of this decision, Mr D.O. Jones, the mill owner, wrote to Mr Williamson stating that the new residents of Eithinog only made occasional use of the halt but that when they did, it had been his practice to join them so that the train did not have to stop twice.[177]

Floods at Dolrhyd

The line near Dolrhyd was prone to flooding after periods of heavy rain so in 1903 Mr Collin obtained Mr Anwyl's consent to remove gravel from the river bed at Dolrhyd for use as ballast.[178] On Wednesday 9th September 1903 the Banwy washed the bottom ballast away for about 60 yards and traffic was suspended until about one o'clock by which time the platelayers had made the line safe again.[179] The river was over the line again in the early hours of Tuesday 27th October 1903 when it washed the ballast from under the sleepers. On this occasion the platelayers, who were up early, soon put matters right and the 5.15am from Welshpool was able to get through to Llanfair.[180]

At Dolrhyd the line ran between the mill race and the River Banwy. Here No. 823 is seen easing its way along the mill curves with a train for Welshpool. The shed to the right of the locomotive housed the water wheel.
ADRIAN VAUGHAN COLLECTION

Dolrhyd mill with the 1.30pm train rounding the mill curves. 12th October 1951.

F.W. SHUTTLEWORTH

The Llanfair Jinny passing Dolrhyd weir with the return service to Welshpool. 12th October 1951.

F. W. SHUTTLEWORTH

On 2nd December 1912 Mr Bertram Ashcroft and Miss Jennie Vaughan, who were employed at Eithinog Hall, lost their lives while attempting to cross the Banwy in a punt. They had intended to catch the 2.15 train from Llanfair to Welshpool where a Church Defence meeting was being held. The usual procedure was to pull the punt across the river using a line of fencing wire stretched from a beam in the boat house to a sycamore tree on the opposite bank. On the day in question the Banwy was in full spate, the occupants lost control of the punt and were swept over the weir to their deaths. The alarm was raised by Miss Mary Thomas, Tan-ybryn, who saw the punt go over the weir. Although a thorough search of the river was made, it had to be abandoned at dusk. The following morning the punt was found near Meifod some six miles downstream of the weir. Later in the day Miss Vaughan's body was recovered from the salmon pass at Henllan Mill. Mr Ashcroft's body was found in a pool below Pontsycoed five days later. The Coroner's Jury recommended that the crossing to Dolrhyd mill halt should be moved away from the weir and provided with stronger wire.[181/182]

On Thursday, 10th February 1920, the worst floods for thirty-four years washed away the permanent way for half a mile near Dolrhyd, detaining the last train of the day at Llanfair. The train crew had to be taken back to Welshpool by motor car. The following morning, the permanent way gang was dispatched to repair the damage done to the line and throughout the day trains could only run as far as Brynelin from where passengers had to proceed by foot to a point above Dolrhyd where they were met by the train that had been detained at Llanfair on the previous evening. On Wednesday, parcels were dispatched by motor car. By Thursday, the line was repaired and normal services were restored.

At milepost 8¼ the line left Dolrhyd mill on a curve with a radius of three chains. Livestock made incursions on to the railway occasionally, as in this case where cows can be seen on the line.   NRM S. P. HIGGINS COLLECTION

THE WATER TOWER

In August 1902 the Works Committee approved their Engineer's plans for the water supply at Llanfair but the site proved to be unsuitable, so an alternative was sought. The following month the Board agreed that a water tank and pump costing £50 should be provided at Dolrhyd.[183] Water from the millrace was pumped by hand into a wooden tank holding 1,177 gallons. This arrangement was never satisfactory, so in 1911 the tank was moved to a point 570yds closer to Llanfair where it could be filled by gravity from a stream on land owned by Mr John Richard Jones, Tanllan.[184/185] By an agreement dated 1st November 1911 Mr Jones was paid £4 10s 0d per annum for the water abstracted from his land.[186] The tank at the mill curves was removed in January 1912. While it was being recovered, a gust of wind blew it over and two workmen were injured. One of them, Mr R Challinor, a joiner, fractured a thigh and suffered severe injuries to his ankle. Station master James Davies and a guard provided first aid until Dr Humphreys arrived and eventually the injured man was transferred to Oswestry Cottage hospital.[187/188]

The Great Western replaced the Cambrian tank in October 1928. On Tuesday the 23rd at about 6.30pm a special train left Welshpool for Llanfair carrying the replacement tank. The following day the wagon onto which the tank was loaded was attached to the 9.35am mixed train from Llanfair and was

MIKE LLOYD

detached about half a mile east of Llanfair so that it could be unloaded by staff from the Locomotive Department. When unloading had been completed, they pushed the wagon back to Llanfair yard. It was anticipated by the time the 12.50pm from Welshpool arrived at the water tower, unloading would have been completed and the wagon would be back at Llanfair.[189] A pilotman was in charge of both trains between Llanfair and the site.

The water tower erected by the GWR in 1928.   NRM S. P. HIGGINS COLLECTION

A train for Welshpool at rest by the water tower to replenish the locomotive's water tanks on 14th September 1948.
JOHN MEREDITH, Cty.
ROBERT HUMM

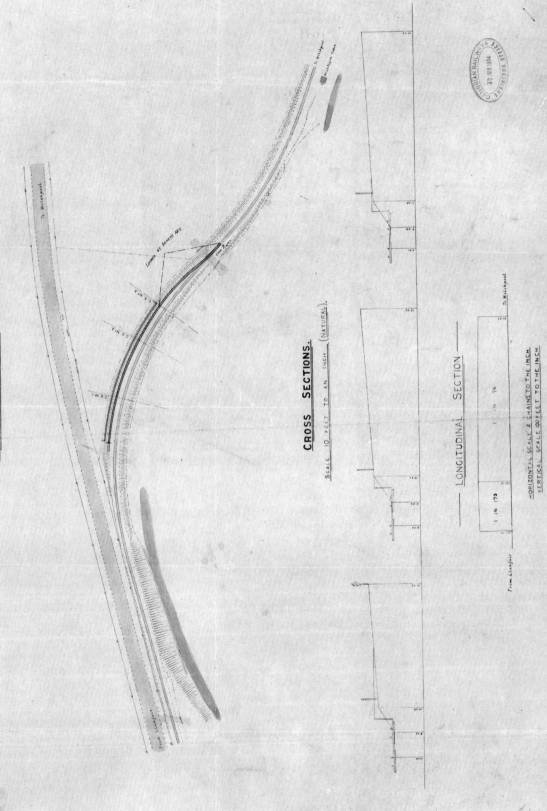

CAMBRIAN RAILWAYS.

WELSHPOOL & LLANFAIR BRANCH.

PROPOSED TIMBER SIDING NEAR LLANFAIR.

— SCALE 40ᶠᵗ TO AN INCH. —

CROSS SECTIONS.

SCALE 10 FEET TO AN INCH (NATURAL).

— LONGITUDINAL SECTION —

HORIZONTAL SCALE 2 CHAINS TO THE INCH
VERTICAL SCALE 100 FEET TO THE INCH

DOLRHYD TO LLANFAIR

From Dolrhyd the railway ran along the northern bank of the Banwy on easy gradients. At $8\frac{3}{4}$ miles the line swung away from the river on a gradient of 1 in 76 as the line approached Tanllan where a timber siding was provided in 1904.

The railway passed Tanllan on a reverse curve then straightened to run parallel with the main road before entering Llanfair Caereinion station on a gentle curve. The station was about a third of a mile from the town centre.

LLANFAIR TIMBER SIDING 8m 60c

In 1903 Messrs E.O. Jones & Sons acquired a considerable quantity of round timber which they began to haul to Welshpool by road. Mr Denniss persuaded Messrs Jones to load their timber at Llanfair on the understanding that a siding with a suitable wharf and hard standing would be provided. A plan of the proposed siding and wharf was drawn by the Cambrian's Engineer who estimated that the work would cost £130. While Messrs Jones were not prepared to pay the full cost of the work, the firm offered £70 that was to be refunded by a rebate of 3d per ton on its timber traffic.[190]

On 18th April 1904 Mr Denniss submitted the proposal to the light railway company offering to construct the wharf and siding at Tanllan. He indicated that the Cambrian was prepared to incur the Llanfair Railway's proportion of the cost on the understanding that the company would repay it when in a position to do so. The proposal was accepted by the Llanfair Directors at their meeting on 20th April.[191] Messrs Jones agreed to send all their traffic from the Llanfair district by rail. The rate to Welshpool was 6s 6d per ton of which the light railway company's portion, before the rebate, was 2s 7d.[192]

At the end of June, work on the siding was sufficiently advanced to allow Mr Denniss to write to the Board of Trade to say that it was ready for inspection. However, it was not until 29th November that formal sanction to use the siding was received. The siding, which had points facing to trains running to Llanfair, was worked from a ground frame with two levers locked by Annett's key. Owing to the steep gradient, all shunting operations had to be conducted with the engine at the Welshpool end of the train.[193]

In 1906 Mr Jabez Barker applied to bring long timber to Llanfair for loading at Tanllan. There was some doubt that long trees could be carried safely, so on Sunday 22nd October 1906 a special train carrying 65ft long trees was taken over the line without incident. Mr Barker's traffic began in February 1907 and continued until April 1909 by which date a total of 1,665 tons had been carried over the line by special trains that ran in the early morning before the passenger service began.[194] In 1909 Messrs Jones was unable to accommodate Mr Barker's traffic at Tanllan as well as their own, so arrangements were made to load Barker's traffic at Heniarth

because there was no other place at Llanfair that timber could be loaded without incurring considerable expenditure.[195]

Mervin Peate, recalling his childhood in the 1920s, spent many hours with friends at the old saw mill at Tanllan. "Full grown trees were brought in on horse-drawn timber carriages and we watched them being sawn into lengths on a rack bench powered by a portable steam engine. They would go down to Welshpool by rail on long bolster wagons. In the evenings we would play on the rack bench, being carried along on the rollers while our friends turned the handle".[196]

Reece Pryce's memories of playing at the water tower
Reece Pryce's father farmed at Tanllan Farm near Llanfair. Reece and his brothers often played by the water tower and sometimes on it. Although the tank was fully enclosed, there was a door in the top which gave access for maintenance. Reece's mother was worried that one of her boys would fall into the tank and drown. The brothers wondered what the big wheel under the tank was used for, and thought it was probably used to pump water into the tank. Trains stopped at the tower on the return journey to Welshpool so that the fireman could water the engine. Occasionally the driver and guard would cut pea sticks from the smaller trees that had sprung up along the river bank. On such occasions the train was held there for some time.

Llanfair yard viewed from the station throat with open wagons full of coal waiting to be unloaded. The van body on the former passenger platform was used to store animal feeds as was the goods warehouse that was enlarged in 1914–15.

J.E. NORRIS

LLANFAIR CAEREINION
9m 4c

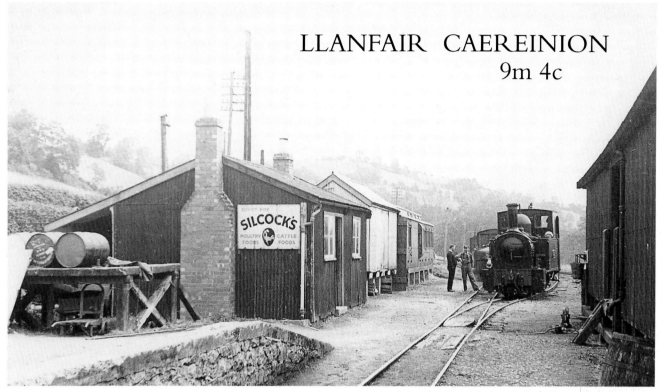

The station, seen from the buffer stop, with the extended warehouse of 1914–15, known as the Long Shed, to the right and the former booking office cum waiting room on the left. The old station building was used as a store by this date and lost its verandah so that carters could obtain access to the stores on the platform. The galvanised iron shed provided in 1937 to relieve the acute shortage of warehouse space is seen here between the station building and the coach body. 24th August 1948.

H.C. CASSERLEY

In keeping with the light railway ethos, very basic accommodation was provided at Llanfair station. The earliest plan shows a platform road with a loop that threw off a siding which served the warehouse. The station building, goods warehouse and weighing machine office were at the Llanfair end of the yard. The buildings were erected by Messrs J. Astley and Sons and were completed at the end of October 1902.[197] A wooden ramp for loading cattle was provided next to the headshunt and there was a cast iron urinal near the Welshpool end of the platform.[198] The proposed engine shed had to be abandoned through lack of funds.[199] Although it was intended to provide a water tower at the terminus, it proved impossible to find a reliable water supply.[200]

At the preliminary inspection of the line Mr Denniss was concerned to find that only one siding had been provided at the station and he insisted that another should be laid in so that the anticipated traffic could be accommodated. Mr Collin therefore gave instructions for the work to proceed on the siding, known as the back road, at a cost of £85.[201/202/203]

Access to the loop at the Welshpool end was provided by a two-lever ground frame locked using the Annetts key on the train staff. The point at the Llanfair end of the loop did not require a facing point lock as passenger trains terminated a few yards before it. The loop threw off two sidings: the back

road that ran along the southern boundary of the yard, and the warehouse road which passed behind the warehouse. A crane rated to lift up to 2 tons and 10 hundredweights was provided next to the warehouse siding.[204]

The station building was 25ft long and 15ft wide with a small extension at the back at the Llanfair end.[205/206] It had a timber frame and a double pitch roof that were clad with corrugated iron, a veranda on the platform side, and gable ends that were decorated with rather plain wooden finials.[207] The building accommodated a booking and parcels office, and a waiting room. These rooms were heated by cast iron stoves whose stovepipe chimneys protruded from the roof.[208] By 1948 brick chimneys projecting from the gable ends had been provided.[209]

The platform, built to rail height and surfaced with gravel, was 120ft long.[210] It was furnished with oil lamps, rustic bench seats and a running-in board to designs seen at other stations on the Cambrian. Electric lighting was provided from January 1915.[211]

Until 1914 the warehouse was quite small, being 30ft long by 12ft wide.[212] It was a timber-framed structure with a double pitched roof clad in corrugated iron. A canopy supported by two pillars stood above the railside entrance and provided shelter for merchandise as it was transferred to or from railway

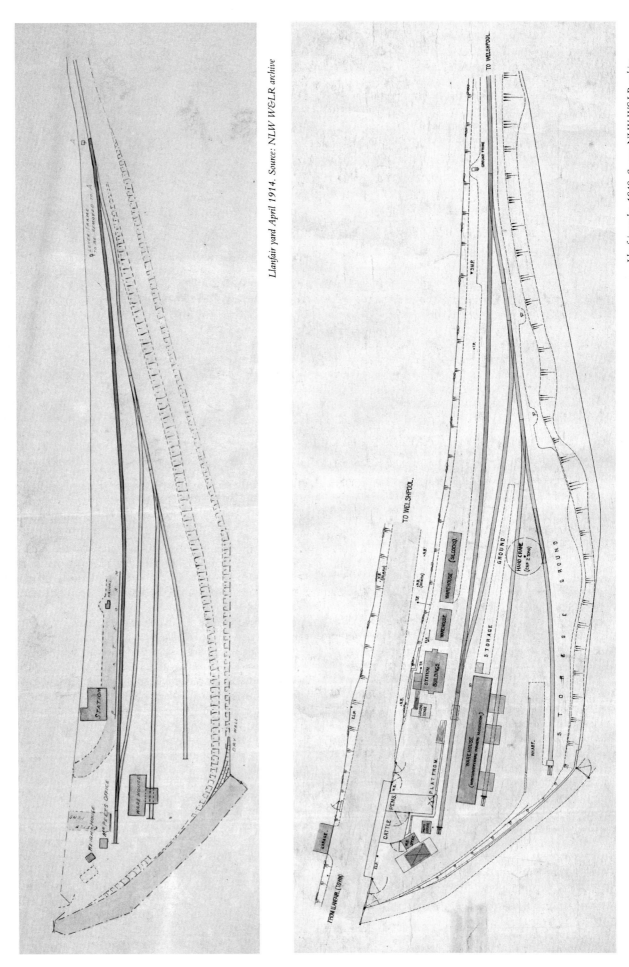

Llanfair yard April 1914. Source: NLW W&LR archive

Llanfair yard c. 1940. Source: NLW W&LR archive

vehicles. Unlike the warehouse in the narrow gauge yard at Welshpool, the roadside entrance was not protected by a canopy.[213/214]

The weighing machine office was a timber-framed structure clad in corrugated iron with a single pitch roof.[215] In later years the office was clad with weatherboards and had a double pitched roof suggesting that the earlier structure was either replaced or rebuilt.[216] This may have occurred in 1937 when the old weighbridge was replaced by a 15ton cart weighbridge from Caerphilly. The replacement weighbridge was overhauled at Welshpool in June 1937 and the pit required for the table was dug and concreted in July. The work was completed, inspected and tested by 29th August 1937.[217]

Limited siding accommodation ...
Shortly after the line opened, Mr Denniss wrote to John Evans, the Llanfair Railway's Secretary, stating that he believed the accommodation provided at Llanfair would be insufficient for the traffic that was expected at the station. Mr Denniss suggested that the yard should be backfilled along its southern boundary, the back siding slewed, and another provided.[218] The cost of the work was estimated to be £215.[219] Mr Evans replied that the light railway had insufficient funds to carry out the work and asked what terms Mr Denniss could offer if his company carried out the work. The Cambrian offered a loan at 4½%, the principal to be repaid from the proceeds of an issue of debenture stock. These terms were rejected by the light railway Directors who decided to defer further consideration of the matter until their Engineer's final certificate for the construction of the railway had been received.[220/221/222]

In 1906 Mr Denniss reported that Mr J.E. Thomas of Oswestry had bought a sizeable stand of timber in the Llanfair district, but that it had been taken to Welshpool by road because Llanfair yard was very congested. There was no storage space for coal and loaded wagons stood at the station for days, resulting in poor utilisation of rolling stock. The cost of backfilling the yard and providing an additional siding was estimated to be £170. The light railway Directors asked the Cambrian to do the work on their behalf on the understanding that payment would be made as soon as their company had sufficient funds, but the working company would have nothing to do with the proposal. The deadlock was not broken until 1914 when farmers in the Llanfair district threatened to set up a collection and delivery service using motor lorries based at Llansantffraid.[223]

In December 1913 Mr Charles Garfitt and Mr Vaughan of Llanerfyl, representing the Farmers Cooperative Society, called on Mr Williamson. The deputation stated that their Society intended to order all manures, seeds, feedstuffs, implements, coal and lime to Llansantffraid station from where deliveries would be made to farms in the upper Vyrnwy and Banwy valleys. Messrs Garfitt and Vaughan suggested that the Cambrian could run the lorry service, but also stated that they were in negotiation with the Great Western with a view to inducing that company to put on a service from Oswestry to Garthbeibio. Mr John Evans reported that the proposed service would collect produce from farms for sale at Oswestry.

Both the working and owning companies were extremely concerned about the potential loss of traffic to the light railway.[224]

... and inadequate storage
Enquiries instigated by the Cambrian Board found that the Farmers' Co-operative Society were proposing to use Llansantffraid station because the goods warehouse at Llanfair station was too small for their needs and there was insufficient wharfage to store coal. The limited accommodation at Llanfair caused considerable delay to wagons belonging to the light railway company and to J.L. Peate, a Llanfair coal and lime merchant. The situation could be remedied, and Llanfair selected as the distribution centre for the surrounding district, if the goods warehouse was extended and the existing siding accommodation improved at an estimated cost of £120 and £15 respectively.[225]

Since the improvements were required urgently, the Cambrian Board proposed to pay for them on condition that the Llanfair Company would agree to repay the cost in equal instalments over five years with no interest being payable on the outstanding balance. At the request of the Earl of Powis the Works Committee met on 19th February to consider the Cambrian's proposal, but deferred further consideration of the matter until a plan showing the proposed work had been prepared and they had received Mr Addie's views on the matter.[226]

The Works Committee met Messrs Williamson, McDonald, and Gough at Llanfair in April 1914 when the matter was discussed at length.[227] Acting on the advice of their Works Committee the light railway Directors sanctioned the proposed work subject to agreement that £50 was payable on completion of the work, the balance was to be repaid over 10 years, and that no interest was to be charged on the outstanding balance.[228] Mr Williamson accepted these conditions which were ratified by his Directors.

When the work was executed it became necessary to move the point at the Llanfair end of the loop towards Welshpool by approximately 50ft so that the warehouse extension could be accommodated. This increased the length of the headshunt slightly and it is possible that the landing at the end of the line was put in at the same time as the other alterations. The back road was slewed towards the southern boundary of the yard so that a coal wharf could be accommodated.[229] On 21st June 1915, the Llanfair Secretary reported that the improvements at the station had been completed at a cost of £133 15s 9d.[230/231]

New demands for warehouse space
In 1936 R. Silcock & Son rented the former waiting room as a store for their animal feeds and the Montgomeryshire Farmers Association occupied the warehouse. Growth in the volume of animal feeds and fertilisers dealt with at the station led to an acute shortage of warehouse accommodation, so on 4th October 1937 authority was given for the provision of a lock-up shed measuring 20ft by 8ft made from galvanised iron and mounted on brick piers. The lock-up shed, which was built

The station yard seen from Pool Road with the warehouse and back roads full of wagons and coal merchants loading bagged coal onto their lorries. There were coal storage grounds behind the back road and between the warehouse road and the loop. Additional storage was now provided by two coach bodies and a 40ft passenger brake van.

R.W. KIDNER

Having dressed Llanfair yard, The Earl was waiting here with a return service for Welshpool. The clerestory coach body had been placed in front of the Cambrian brake third to provide additional storage, but the 40ft van body did not arrive until the following year. 24th August 1948.

H.C. CASSERLEY

The station yard as it appeared on 18th October 1951. The van and coach bodies were used to store animal feedstuffs.   F. W. SHUTTLEWORTH

on the Welshpool side of the station building, was brought into use at the end of December.[232] That month authority was given to remove the veranda from the station building and fill the track to rail height to allow road vehicles to obtain access to the lock-up shed.[233]

In January 1938 the feasibility of providing a 40ft carriage body or a standard warehouse to accommodate Messrs Silcock's merchandise was contemplated[234] and a suitable site was found on the former passenger platform beyond the lock-up hut. The feasibility of extending the warehouse onto the coal wharfs between the loop and warehouse road was also investigated but was rejected because it was felt that the coal merchants would move out of the yard and their traffic would be lost to road haulage.[235]

By July additional storage was needed urgently. Warehousing and checking Messrs Silcock's stock required Welshpool-based staff to travel to Llanfair which was costly and inconvenient, while the former waiting room was not vermin proof. Although two cats were kept at the station, stocks of animal feed were continually being damaged. To remedy the problem, the new lock-up hut was used to store Messrs Silcock's goods while the former waiting room became the railway's warehouse.[236] Although the company's representatives pressed the Chief Goods Manager for additional storage

at Llanfair, their wishes were not acceded to because of the uncertainty about the line's future.[237]

In July 1939 merchandise was being retained in covered vans for longer than the stipulated time because of the shortage of warehouse space at Llanfair. Mr Watson, the Welshpool station master, reported that until new storage was provided, the practice would have to continue.[238] In November authority was given to install the body of brake third No. 4137 at Llanfair for use as a warehouse for Messrs Silcock's traffic.[239] The carriage, once Cambrian Railways No. 275, was built by Ashbury in 1898 as a tricomposite with luggage cupboards and a coupé end. It was converted to a brake third in July 1910 and withdrawn in November 1938. The body was moved to Llanfair, where it was placed on brick piers on 27th February 1940, and was brought into use on 4th March.[240]

Additional warehouse accommodation was provided after the Second World War. At its meeting on 29th March 1946 the Traffic Committee agreed to provide more storage accommodation for Messrs Silcock[241] and the body of a clerestory brake composite was moved to Llanfair at some time between April 1946[242] and August 1948[243]. More storage was provided by a 40ft passenger brake van body that was brought into use by July 1949.[244]

Goods traffic was healthy in the years following the end of the 1939–1945 war. The warehouse road (left) and the back road (right) appear to be filled to capacity. The principal traffic seems to be coal.
KIDDERMINSTER RAILWAY MUSEUM

A ground frame at the east end of Llanfair station gave access to the yard. This view shows No. 822 shunting coal wagons on the warehouse road.

WORKING AT LLANFAIR

Ted Lewis came from a railway family. His uncle, Bill Lewis, was the Bridge Inspector at Caersws and he was related to a Station Master who served at Blaenau Festiniog. Ted joined the GWR at Welshpool in 1945 as a lamp boy, having attended an interview at Moat Lane. On Mondays they would change the lamps at the Forden end of the station, while those at the Buttington end were dealt with on the following day. Later, they changed eight lamps daily. From 1947 to 1949 he was a National Serviceman, returning to Buttington because there was no vacancy at Welshpool. During his time at Buttington, Ted lodged in the crossing keeper's house at Buttington Gates. When a vacancy for a lamp boy arose at Welshpool, Ted was able to return there. He subsequently became a passenger shunter and a guard.

Ten people were needed to work the Llanfair branch. They were the train crew, that is a driver, fireman and guard; two porters at the tranship shed in Welshpool yard; two porters at Llanfair; and a permanent way gang of three. The two tranship porters were Mr Lightfoot and Mr Morgan. Mr Lightfoot, who lived on the Long Mountain, only had one hand but could shovel coal remarkably quickly. The permanent way gang consisted of a ganger, Mr Jones, and two lengthsmen, one of whom was a Mr Gough

In 1945 the two porters who worked at Llanfair were Mr Foulkes and Mrs Astley (later Mrs Davies). Mr Foulkes, a Grade 1 Porter, was in charge of the station and Mrs Astley assisted him. Her duties included delivering parcels around the town. Mr Foulkes, who lived in a white cottage near Pontsycoed, suffered from a skin complaint and sometimes had to take time off work. During such enforced absences he would repair bicycles.

Ted was sent to help out at Llanfair in Mr Foulkes' absence and was paid 1s 6d 'basket allowance' when working away from Welshpool. To get to Llanfair, Ted usually caught the bus, although sometimes he went there by train. On one occasion when Mr Foulkes and Mrs Astley both had to be relieved, he cycled the nine miles to Llanfair on a tandem with Cliff Vaughan, a parcel porter from Welshpool.

Ted's duties at Llanfair included washing out the cattle pens on Mondays (which was market day in Welshpool), issuing weighbridge

tickets to local coal merchants and delivering parcels around Llanfair using a hand cart. Officially parcels were delivered within a one mile radius of the station, but the limit was sometimes ignored as in the case of Mr Tong, who lived at Llwyn Onn. Bacon, in sacks, was delivered to Mr Davies, The Stores at the top of Bridge Street. Whenever Ted delivered to Eddie Davies' mum, he was given 6d. Freddie Jones, who ran a grocer's shop, used to collect his parcels from the station, including boxes of Palethorpe's pork pies. He would open a box, then sell pies to the station staff. He wore khaki coloured clothes and was a great walker. Parcels for the villages beyond Llanfair, such as Foel, Llangadfan and Llanerfyl, were carried by bus.

The Montgomeryshire Farmers Association had depots at Llanfair, Welshpool and Newtown. The firm used the Long Shed at Llanfair to store their feedstuffs. They also dealt in coal. Their warehouseman at Llanfair lived in the house next to the station and was known as 'Lucky Jim'. Bibby and Silcox sent animal feeds to Llanfair by train, where they were transferred to old coach bodies that were used as warehouses. Orders for animal feeds received from local farmers were collected from the station and delivered by road. Deliveries were made to a wide area around Llanfair including Foel, Llangadfan and Llanerfyl. Ifor Williams, Pont Robert, drove the delivery lorry. He is remembered as a very nice man who was always in a hurry. Ifor employed a driver, Glyn Roberts, who drove the milk lorry that collected churns from local farms and delivered them to the creamery at Kilkewydd.

Coal merchants included Morgan Brothers, Peate Brothers, who owned Dolgoch mill in Llanfair, and Ifor Jones, Dolrhyd mill. The Morgans and Peates owned stock lorries which took beasts to Welshpool market on Mondays. There were three Peate brothers, Bert, Mervyn and Aidan. Mervyn later ran a café at Fairbourne. Peate's had an office in the yard near the weighbridge. Ifor Dolrhyd did not use sacks to bag coal, preferring to use any thing suitable that was to hand.

Ted enjoyed working at Llanfair because 'they were such lovely people'.

Ifor Williams' lorry EP 7656 waiting to leave Llanfair yard with bags of animal feed for delivery to farms in the Banwy and Vyrnwy valleys. 12th October 1951.

F.W. SHUTTLEWORTH

The landing at the west end of the station was one of the improvements made to station accommodation at Llanfair following pressure from the farming community. The strong links between farming and the railway are evidenced by the plough and roller awaiting collection on the landing whilst a cattle wagon is seen at the end of the head shunt next to the loading ramp. The hut nearest to the cattle wagon was Peate's office and the weighbridge office stood next to it. H.C. CASSERLEY

Having dressed Llanfair yard this train was waiting to return to Welshpool. Silcock's enamel sign on the former booking office advertised the firm's products which were stored at the station before distribution to farms in the district. A.W.V. MACE

After the line closed to all traffic, the old booking office, galvanised iron shed and coach bodies continued to be used to store fertilizers and animal feeds.
MIKE LLOYD

The cattle pen with a cattle wagon awaiting loading next to it. Peate's office is seen between the cattle wagon and the weighbridge office. 8th September 1951.
F. W. SHUTTLEWORTH

SOME LLANFAIR TRADERS
The Peates

Mr J Lloyd Peate, Glaneinion, Llanfair Caereinion established a business as a coal and lime merchant in 1889–90. After the railway opened the firm traded from the station yard, its office being situated behind the cattle pens near to the weighbridge hut. The firm also rented part of the coal wharf and owned five narrow gauge and three standard gauge coal wagons.[248]

J.Ll. Peate took W.D. Peate into the business and the firm traded as J.Ll. & W.D. Peate until the 31st May 1936. In the 12 months ending April 1936 the firm received 1,535 tons of coal at Llanfair. A new agreement was drawn up between the GWR and W.D. Peate & Sons in August 1936 and a ledger account was opened. When the firm incorporated as W.D. Peate & Sons Ltd a new agreement was signed with the Railway Executive which came into force on 30th October 1950. W.D. Peate & Sons were the Great Western and the Railway Executive's carting agent at Llanfair, delivering merchandise from the station to communities in the upper Vyrnwy and Banwy valleys. By the 1940s the firm had become a livestock and road haulier and was the local agent for BOCM.[249]

W.D. Peate & Sons had ledger accounts at Welshpool, Barry Docks and Derby (Mineral Accounts section). Authority to open the Barry and Derby accounts was given on 31st October 1950. The account at Barry was for coal freight. Payment of the Barry and Welshpool accounts could be made by one cheque but a separate cheque was needed for the London Midland Region.[250] Peate's received coal, grain, oil cake, cement, bricks and building materials at Llanfair. In 1955 coal came from collieries at Onllwyn, Aberdare, Mountain Ash, Bolsover, Madley and Ifton.[251]

The Montgomeryshire Farmers Association

The Montgomeryshire Farmers Association originated as the Farmers Supply Association Limited, Corn and Seed Merchants, of Church Street, Welshpool. In April 1904 the firm traded at sixteen stations in Montgomeryshire.[252] After the Great War Bill Burgess was the Association's warehouseman at Llanfair.[253] In 1939 the Association held ninety square yards of covered storage accommodation in the warehouse at Llanfair for which a charge of £23 12s 6d per annum was made.[254] By 1953 most of the firm's traffic in general merchandise was carried by road,[255] although their coal and basic slag was still received by rail. In 1955 the Association's coal was forwarded from Pantyffynon and Mountain Ash.[256]

Morgan Brothers

Morgan Brothers were coal, builders and agricultural merchants based in Llanfair.[257] They held a tenancy at the station coal wharf and by 1954 delivered animal feeds from R. Silcock & Son's warehouse.[258] In 1952 it was estimated that between forty and sixty deliveries were made from the station each week.[259]

R. Silcock & Son

R. Silcock & Son signed a tenancy with the Great Western on 12th October 1936 by which they rented twenty square yards in the former waiting room at Llanfair for the storage of oil cake pending its distribution to local farmers.[260] In 1937 226 tons of the firm's merchandise was carried by the railway and this traffic was forecast to rise to 300 tons annually. By January 1938 the waiting room was becoming too small to accommodate the firm's traffic, and the company attempted to double the area that it rented.[261] However, it was not until

March 1940 that adequate warehouse accommodation was provided in the body of a former Cambrian Railways 45ft brake third. By 1953 the firm's traffic had risen to 600 tons per annum and more storage space was required.[262] Following representations to the Commercial Superintendent at Paddington it was decided that the firm should have first refusal of any vacant accommodation.[263] In 1952 Messrs Silcock complained about damage caused to their stock while in transit to Llanfair and a deficiency in the stock held at the station, claiming £66 0s 6d in compensation for their losses. Following an investigation by Mr Sutton, the Chief Goods Clerk at Welshpool, the amount claimed was reduced to £61 3s 3d.[264] Late in 1954 consideration was given to handling Messrs Silcock's traffic from Welshpool and distributing it by road transport, but the matter does not appear to have been taken any further.

Lever Brothers

Lever Brothers also dealt in animal feeds which were stored at the station. Their products were delivered to farms within a ten mile radius of Llanfair.[265]

The station as it appeared from the landing, with two covered wagons waiting to be unloaded and returned to Welshpool. The enamelled sign on the station building drew attention to Messrs Silcock's presence at the station. The lorry on the platform was probably collecting feedstuffs for delivery to farms in the district. R.W. KIDNER

Here WD Peate and Son's lorry, CEP 103, is seen next to the warehouse road while coal was being bagged and loaded. Another lorry, which may have belonged to the Montgomeryshire Farmers Association, appears to have been loading from wagons in the back road. The canopies covered the entrances to the Long Shed.

R.W. KIDNER

THE LAST YEARS OF THE GOODS SERVICE

In the last years the station was manned by a porter. His duties included entering up delivery sheets, checking all 'smalls' traffic for delivery in the area, accepting goods for dispatch, collecting cash, looking after stores belonging to Messrs Bibby and Silcock, and dealing with all parcels traffic including deliveries. At one time the Welshpool spare porter had assisted at Llanfair by putting traffic in store and repairing broken sacks but the post had been abolished. The Llanfair porter's duties left insufficient time for him to attend to Messrs Silcock's stock sheets.[245]

Traffic in sheeted wagons at Llanfair was particularly susceptible to pilferage between 5.30pm and 8.00am when the station was unattended. The station was also unattended when the porter delivered parcels in the town. Many people in the Llanfair area were able make use of animal feeds and the station routine was well known. In 1952 fifteen sacks of feed were lost in three months while on 20th June twenty-three bags went missing.[246] The Divisional Traffic Superintendent, Mr Tom Sellars, arranged for additional staff to be provided when the animal feeds were received at Llanfair so that it could be put into store immediately. He also called for additional checks to be made on the stock in hand and made it clear that he would regard any future losses as being due to lax working which would not be tolerated.[247]

The entrance to the goods yard and weigh-bridge table.   MIKE LLOYD

The end of the line.   MIKE LLOYD

One of the locomotives attending to stock on the landing. The importance of coal traffic to the railway is apparent in this view. 1951.

Mike and Irene Lloyd travelled over the light railway while on honeymoon. Here Irene is seen in the yard at Llanfair.
MIKE LLOYD

The Long Shed and warehouse siding seen after the railway had closed. The canopy over the nearest doorway had been removed and a window had been provided in the gable end.
AUTHOR'S COLLECTION

No. 822 shunting at the neck of Llanfair yard. The hedge marked the boundary between the railway and the Welshpool to Dolgellau road. 12th October 1951.

F.W. SHUTTLEWORTH

Guard Cecil Thomas supervising shunting at the Welshpool end of the station.
AUTHOR'S COLLECTION

[1] Great Western Railway Central Wales Division Sectional Appendices January 1923 and March 1943

[2] MT6 1150 4 Second Board of Trade inspection

[3] Great Western Railway Central Wales Division Sectional Appendix January 1923

[4] Rail 92 76 Cambrian Board 2nd February 1905

[5] Speed Restrictions J. Williamson to G.C. McDonald 17th November 1911

[6] Great Western Railway Weekly Train Notice 11th August 1927

[7] The Welshpool and Llanfair Ralph I. Cartwright Rail Romances 2002 p. 118

[8] Great Western Railway Central Wales Division Sectional Appendices January 1923 and March 1943

[9] NLW W&L Archive GWR era papers

[10] *Birmingham Weekly Post and Midland Pictorial* May 16th 1958

[11] *Montgomeryshire Express and Radnor Times* November 3rd 1956 p. 9

[12] *Llanfair Railway Journal* No.118 January 1991 p.9

[13] Great Western Railway Central Wales Division Sectional Appendix March 1943

[14] Rail 1057 613 Welshpool & Llanfair history file 16th December 1897 and 18th February 1898

[15] Rail 722 2 W&L Board 20th February 1902

[16] Rail 722 2 W&L Board 24th April 1902

[17] Rail 722 2 W&L Board 11th July 1902

[18] Rail 722 2 W&L Board 28th August 1902

[19] Rail 722 2 Works Committee 11th August 1902

[20] Rail 722 2 Works Committee 2nd September 1902

[21] Rail 722 2 Works Committee 6th August 1902

[22] Cambrian Railways Register of water cranes, turntables, travelling and stationary cranes p.93

[23] Rail 1057 623 Plan of W&L terminus 28th November 1905

[24] Frederick Le Manquais Photograph tranship shed 16th April 1938

[25] Cambrian Railways Register of water cranes, turntables, travelling and stationary cranes p.93

[26] *The Montgomery County Times and Shropshire and Mid-Wales Advertiser* 11th October 1902

[27] NLW WL M 1 Welshpool station

[28] Rail 1057 620 Smithfield siding 1903–1906

[29] Rail 1057 620 Smithfield siding 1903–1906

[30] Rail 722 3 W&L Board 26th September 1908

[31] Rail 92 72 Cambrian Board Smithfield siding 26th October 1903

[32] Rail 92 78 Cambrian Board Smithfield siding 13th February 1906

[33] Rail 92 86 Cambrian Board 3rd January 1911

[34] Rail 1057 726 The Smithfield siding and the Cambrian Railways Act 1913

[35] Rail 82 80 Cambrian Board Castle Caereinion proposed crossing place 2nd January 1907

[36] NLW WL M 26 Proposed timber stacking ground for Mr Barker 7th February 1907

[37] Welshpool Borough Council minutes 9th May, 13th June 1907

[38] Rail 92 83 Cambrian Solicitor to Cambrian Board 5th January 1909

[39] Rail 1057 726 The Smithfield siding and the Cambrian Railways Act 1913 (S.24)

[40] Rail 722 3 W&L Board 11th May 1906

[41] Welshpool Borough Council minutes 9th May 1907, 13th August 1908

[42] Rail 92 88 S. Williamson and Cambrian Solicitor to Cambrian Board 7th July 1913

[43] Rail 1057 726 Cambrian Board 28th February 1913

[44] NLW WL C 14 General Manager and Traffic Manager 14th and 20th October 1913

[45] NLW WL M 308 Cambrian Railways 40ft plan of Welshpool

[46] NLW WL C 14 General Manager and Traffic Manager 14th and 20th October 1913

[47] NLW WL M GWR 40ft plan Welshpool 135a (1925) and 135b (1932)

[48] NLW WL C 14 General Manager and Traffic Manager 14th and 20th October 1913

[49] Rail 92 95 Cambrian Traffic and Works Committee 11th October and 3rd November 1920

[50] NLW WL M 107 Plan showing proposal to remove the carriage shed siding 16th November 1937

[51] Frederick le Manquais Mace Photograph of Smithfield siding and carriage shed 16th April 1938

[52] NLW WL M 132a GWR closure proposals 25th November 1947

[53] P. Whitehouse photograph 9th July 1949

[54] Great Western Railway Service Time Tables No.16 3rd July – 24th September 1939, 28th October 1940 u.f.n

[55] Rail 722 2 Board 8th July 1901

[56] A House and a Stipend Roger L. Brown in *Sayce Papers V.2 Eisteddfod Church and Community* Ed. Roger L. Brown, Welshpool Church Press, 1996

[57] Rail 92 72 A.J. Collin to Cambrian Board 7th May 1903

[58] Great Western Railway Central Wales Division Sectional Appendix March 1943 p.108

[59] Rail 92 73 Cambrian Board Appendix D Plan of surplus land at Church Street 27th October 1903

[60] Rail 722 3 Works Committee 11th December 1903

[61] *The Changing face of Welshpool* Powysland Club 1998 p.89

[62] Great Western Railway Central Wales Division Sectional Appendix March 1943 p.108

[63] Rail 92 72 A.J. Collin to Cambrian Board 7th May 1903

[64] *The Montgomery County Times and Shropshire and Mid-Wales Advertiser* 22nd March 1902

[65] MT6 1150 4 Plan showing route and crossings in Welshpool 1901

[66] Rail 722 2 Board 11th July 1902

[67] Rail 92 87 S. Williamson to Cambrian Board 29th February 1912

[68] Rail 722 4 Works Committee 6th May 1912

[69] Rail 722 4 Works Committee 9th August 1912

[70] Rail 722 4 Board 14th Oct 1912

[71] *Great Western Railway Magazine* September 1937 p.421

[72] *The Changing face of Welshpool* Powysland Club 1998 p.105

[73] *The Montgomery County Times and Shropshire and Mid-Wales Advertiser* 7th January 1905

[74] *The Changing face of Welshpool* Powysland Club 1998 p.107

[75] *Llanfair Railway Journal* No.152 1999 p.17

[76] Great Western Railway Sectional Appendix March 1943 p.108

[77] Rail 92 73 Cambrian Railways Board Appendix B 6th July 1904

[78] Great Western Railway Sectional Appendix Central Wales Division January 1923

[79] Rail 92 73 Cambrian Railways Board Appendix B 6th July 1904

[80] Great Western Railway Sectional Appendix March 1943 p.109

[81] Rail 92 74 Cambrian Railways Board 12th October 1904

[82] *The Montgomery County Times and Shropshire and Mid-Wales Advertiser* 10th and 17th September 1904

[83] Great Western Railway Central Wales Division Sectional Appendix March pp.108–9

[84] *The Montgomery County Times and Shropshire and Mid-Wales Advertiser* 25th January 1908

[85] Rail 722 6 Light Railway Order 1899 Clause 24

[86] Rail 722 2 Works Committee 5th December 1900

[87] Rail 92 72 A.J. Collin to Cambrian Board 7th May 1903

[88] Rail 722 2 W&L Board 31st January 1901

[89] MT6 1084 4 Light Railway Commissioners to Board of Trade Report re: Draft Amendment Order 1901

[90] Rail 722 2 W&L Board 8th July 1901

[91] Rail 722 2 W&L Board 4th Mar 1904, 12th April 1905

[92] AN 97 20 The Railway Executive Branch Line Committee Scheme W 17 17th October 1950

[93] *Birmingham Weekly Post & Midland Pictorial* May 16th 1958 Article by Vivian Bird

[94] SLS Journal v.32 1956 p.347–348

[95] Rail 92 72 Cambrian Board Golfa Derailment 11th December 1903

[96] Rail 923 40 Public and Service timetables

[97] Rail 722 3 Board 12th April 1905

[98] Rail 722 4 Board 27th April 1914

[99] Welshpool Borough Council minutes 21st August 1914

[100] Rail 722 4 Board 21st Jun 1915

[101] *The Welshpool & Llanfair Light Railway* Lewis Cozens 1951 p.18

[102] Rail 722 4 Works Committee 6th May 1912

[103] *Llanfair Railway Journal* No. 79 April 1981 p. 9

[104] *The Welshpool & Llanfair Light Railway* Lewis Cozens 1951

[105] *The Welshpool & Llanfair* Ralph I. Cartwright Rail Romances 2001 p.59

[106] NLW W&L archive Plan WL 345 Derailment at 4m 32c 11th October 1923

[107] Rail 722 3 Works Committee 11th Dec 1903

[108] Rail 722 3 Board 20th April 1904

[109] NLW W&L archive Plan WL 137 Reconstruction of accommodation overbridge at Castle Caereinion 4m 52½c 25th July 1932

[110] NLW W&L Archive Plan WL M 6 Castle Caereinion station (undated proposal)

[111] Rail 92 80 Cambrian Board 2nd January 1907

[112] Rail 722 3 Board 4th Mar 1904

[113] Rail 722 3 Board 20th April 1904

[114] Rail 1057 619 Correspondence re passing place and timber traffic 1909–1910

[115] Rail 722 3 Board 15th Feb 1907

[116] MT6 1632 2 Castle Caereinion passing place and siding Col. Druitt to the Board of Trade 15th June 1907

[117] MT6 1632 2 Castle Caereinion passing place and siding G.C. McDonald to Col. Druitt 18th September 1907

[118] MT6 1632 2 Castle Caereinion passing place and siding Col. Druitt to G.C. McDonald 4th October 1907

[119] Rail 1057 619 Correspondence re passing place and timber traffic 15th December 1909

[120] Rail 722 3 Board 26th September 1908

[121] Rail 1057 619 Correspondence re passing place and timber traffic 24th June 1909

[122] Rail 1057 619 Correspondence re passing place and timber traffic 16th Mar 1910

[123] Rail 92 85 Cambrian Board 2nd May 1910

[124] *Llanfair Railway Journal* No. 125 p. 22

[125] Mike Christensen personal communication

[126] NLW W&L Archive WL GWR 19 Agreement between GWR and C.H. Jones 24th June 1946

[127] *Birmingham Weekly Post & Midland Pictorial* May 16th 1958

[128] Last trip on the Welshpool & Llanfair W. A. Tulpin *Trains Illustrated* December 1956 pp.621–624

[129] Great Western Railway Central Wales Division Sectional Appendix 1943 p.108

[130] Rail 923 Cambrian working timetables

[131] Rail 937 GWR working timetables

[132] Great Western Railway Central Wales Division Sectional Appendix 1943 p.108

[133] *Llanfair Railway Journal* No. 188 p.9

[134] *Llanfair Railway Journal* No. 160 pp.10–11

[135] Rail 722 5 Directors Report 1901

[136] *Railway Observer* No.273 v.21 1951 p.265

[137] *Express and Times* 3rd November 1956 p.9 'The End of the Line'

[138] *The Montgomery County Times and Shropshire and Mid-Wales Advertiser* 16th May 1903

[139] Rail 722 4 W&L Board 14th October 1912

[140] *Express and Times* 3rd November 1956 p.9 'The End of the Line'

[141] Rail 250 718 GWR CWD Traffic Research Committee Minute 141 2nd November 1937

[142] Rail 92 89 H. Jones to S. Williamson 3rd July 1914

[143] Rail 1057 613 A.J. Collin to C.S. Denniss 15th Jul 1898

[144] Rail 722 2 W&L Board 29th August 1901

[145] Rail 722 2 W&L Board 26th September 1901

[146] Rail 722 2 W&L Board 20th February 1902

[147] Rail 92 73 Cambrian Chief Engineer's report to Board 10th August 1904

[148] Great Western Railway Record of Important Bridges and Viaducts

[149] Rail 923 40 Cambrian Railways Public and Service Timetables 1913

[150] NLW WL M 8 Heniarth Gate

[151] W.A. Camwell photograph 29th April 1941

[152] L&GRP 19462/3 6th August 1949

[153] *Railway Observer* v..26 1956 p.107

[154] The *Montgomery County Times and Shropshire and Mid-Wales Advertiser* 11th October 1902

[155] Rail 722 3 W&L Board 20th April 1904 Report on the Engineer's final certificate

[156] Rail 722 3 Works Committee 15th February 1907 W&L Board 23rd September 1907

[157] Rail 722 3 W&L Board 26th September 1908

[158] Rail 722 4 Works Committee 17th May 1909

[159] Rail 722 4 Works Committee 30th July 1909

[160] Rail 722 4 Works Committee 3rd June 1911

[161] *The Montgomery County Times and Shropshire and Mid-Wales Advertiser* 29th July 1911

[162] Rail 722 4 Works Committee 10th January 1916

[163] Great Western Railway Central Wales Division Sectional Appendix March 1943 p.108

[164] MT 54 85 Welshpool and Llanfair deposit plans

[165] Rail 722 2 Board 20th March and 18th April 1901

[166] Rail 92 72 A.J. Collin to Cambrian Board 7th May 1903

[167] MT6 1150 4 Second Board of Trade Inspection

[168] Rail 1057 622 Dolrhyd Mill 1903–1922

[169] Rail 1057 622 Dolrhyd Mill 1903–1922 James Burgess file note 16th June 1920

[170] NPR 2 26 Cambrian Staff Register 1870–1950 Folio 102 Cheshire and Chester Record Office

[171] Rail 722 3 Works Committee 7th December 1908

[172] Rail 1057 622 Dolrhyd Mill 1903–1922 General Manager to Cambrian Board 8th August 1912

[173] Rail 1057 622 Dolrhyd Mill 1903–1922 Cambrian Chief Engineer to General Manager 2nd August 1913

[174] Rail 1057 622 Dolrhyd Mil 1903–1922 Cambrian memoranda 12th –31st August 1912

[175] Rail 1057 622 Dolrhyd Mill Cambrian General Manager to R.C. Anwyl 22nd October 1920

[176] Rail 1057 622 Dolrhyd Mill 1903–1922 General Manager to Superintendent of the Line 4th January 1922

[177] Rail 1057 622 Dolrhyd Mill 1903–1922 D.O. Jones to S. Williamson 6th February 1922

[178] Rail 92 72 C.S. Denniss to Cambrian Board 29 June 1903

[179] Rail 92 72 Engineer's report to Cambrian Board 26th October 1903

[180] Rail 92 72 Engineer's report to Cambrian Board 9th December 1903

[181] *The Montgomeryshire Express and Radnor Times* 10th December 1912

[182] *The Montgomery County Times and Shropshire and Mid-Wales Advertiser* 14th December 1912

[183] Rail 722 2 Works Committee 6th August 1902; Board 25th September 1902

[184] Cambrian Railways: Turntables, water supply and cranes ledger

[185] Rail 1057 622 Dolrhyd Mill 1903–1922 Memoranda from Mr Pryce Welshpool 19th & 27th August 1912

[186] Cambrian Railways: Turntables, water supply and cranes ledger

[187] *The Montgomery County Times and Shropshire and Mid-Wales Advertiser* 13th January 1912

[188] Rail 92 87 Engineer to Cambrian Board 6th November 1912

[189] Rail 279 37 GWR CWD DTMO Notice No.281 Llanfair tank 20th October 1928

[190] Rail 92 76 C.S. Denniss to Cambrian Board 1904

[191] Rail 722 3 Board 20th April 1904

[192] Rail 92 76 C.S. Denniss to Cambrian Board 1904

[193] MT 6 1302 Llanfair (Tanllan siding) 1904

[194] Rail 1057 619 Castle Caereinion passing place and timber traffic J. Conacher & C.S. Dennis November 1909

[195] Rail 722 4 Works Committee 7th May 1909

[196] ML Peate *Lanfair Railway Journal* No. 170 Jan 2004 pp.8–10

[197] *The Montgomery County Times and Shropshire and Mid-Wales Advertiser* 25th October 1902

[198] NLW W&L archive Plan WL 9 Llanfair station (undated)

[199] Rail 722 2 Report of Works Committee to Board 22nd May 1902

[200] Rail 722 2 Works Committee 6th August 1902; Board 25th September 1902

[201] Rail 722 3 Board 20th April 1904

[202] NLW W&L archive Plan WL 80 Llanfair station (September 1903)

[203] Llanfair terminus looking east, Anderson photograph in *County Times Supplement* 4th April 1903

[204] *Official Handbook of Railway Stations etc* The Railway Clearing House 1912 Edition p.368

[205] NLW W&L archive Plan WL 9 Llanfair station (undated)

[206] NLW W&L archive Plan WL 9 Llanfair station (September 1903)

[207] *The Welshpool & Llanfair* by R.I. Cartwright Rail Romances 2002 p.34

[208] *The Welshpool & Llanfair* by R.I. Cartwright Rail Romances 2002 p.34

[209] H.C. Casserley negative 54972 dated 24th August 1948

[210] NLW W&L archive Plan WL 9 Llanfair station (undated)

[211] NLW W&L archive Plan WL 9 Llanfair station (undated)

[212] NLW W&L archive Plan WL 9 Llanfair station (undated)

[213] *Llanfair Railway Journal* No. 76 July 1980 p.7

[214] *The Welshpool & Llanfair* by R.I. Cartwright Rail Romances 2002 p.32

[215] *The Welshpool & Llanfair* by R.I. Cartwright Rail Romances 2002 p.32

[216] Photograph by FW Shuttleworth October 1951

[217] GWR Central Wales Division: New Works commencing January 1925 NLW FACS 687

[218] Rail 722 3 Works Committee 5th May 1903

[219] Rail 722 3 Works Committee 7th July 1903

[220] Rail 722 3 Board 1st September 1903

[221] Rail 722 3 Works Committee 11th Dec 1903

[222] Rail 722 3 Board 4th March 1904

[223] Rail 92 78 Mr Thomas' timber traffic 2nd January 1906

[224] Rail 92 89 Proposed Agricultural Association for the Llanfair, Llanerfyl and Llangadfan etc 6th January 1914

[225] Rail 92 89 Proposed Agricultural Association 13th February 1914

[226] Rail 722 4 Works Committee 19th February 1914

[227] Rail 722 4 Works Committee 15th April 1914

[228] Rail 722 4 Board 27th April 1914

[229] NLW W&L archive Plan WL 96 Llanfair station (undated)

[230] Rail 722 4 Board 21st June 1915

[231] Rail 722 4 Board 17th December 1915

[232] Central Wales Division: New Works commencing January 1925 NLW FACS 687

[233] Central Wales Division: New Works commencing January 1925 NLW FACS 687

[234] Divisional Traffic Manager Oswestry to Mr Watson Station Master Weslshpool 22nd January 1938

[235] Mr Watson Station Master Weshpool to Divisional Traffic Manager Oswestry 25th January 1938

[236] Mr Watson Station Master Weshpool to Divisional Traffic Manager Oswestry 28th July 1938

[237] CGMO Paddington (A. Maynard) to Divisional Traffic Manager Oswestry 25th July 1939

[238] Mr Watson Station Master Weshpool to Divisional Traffic Manager Oswestry 26 July 1939

[239] Divisional Traffic Manager Oswestry to Mr Watson Station Master Weslshpoo13th November 1939

[240] Mr Watson Station Master Weshpool to Divisional Traffic Manager Oswestry 5th March 1940.

[241] Rail 250 468 GWR General Manager's report to the Traffic Committee 29th Mach 1946

[242] *Saga by Rail: Great Britain and the Isle of Man* J.I.C. Boyd Oakwood Press 2007 p.32 (shows brake 3rd)

[243] H.C. Casserley negative 54973 24th August 1948 (shows clerestory carriage)

[244] L&GRP 19426 Llanfair yard 9th July 1949 (shows 40ft van body)

[245] Mr Parry, Station Master Weshpool, to Divisional Traffic Manager Oswestry 25 August 1952 NLW WL BR 12

[246] Mr Sutton, Chief Goods Clerk, to Mr Parry, Station Master Welshpool, December 1952 NLW WL BR 12

[247] T.C. Sellars to Mr Parry 9th December 1952

[248] Mervyn Peate cited in *The Welshpool & Lanfair Light Railway* Lewis Cozens 1951 p. 29

[249] NLW Welshpool and Llanfair Archive, W.D. Peate and Sons letterhead

[250] Welshpool and Llanfair Archives National Library of Wales WL BR 2

[251] Mr Parry, Station Master Weshpool, to Divisional Traffic Manager Oswestry 10th April 1955

[252] Rail 92 73 New ledger accounts 4th May 1904

[253] M.L. Peate in *Llanfair Railway Journal* No. 170 pp.8–10

[254] Fixed space and storage accommodation NLW WL/BR/2

[255] Mr Parry, Station Master Weshpool, to Divisional Traffic Manager Oswestry 3rd July 1953

[256] Mr Parry, Station Master Weshpool, to Divisional Traffic Manager Oswestry 10th April 1955

[257] Advertisement *The County Times* 14th July 1956

[258] T.C. Sellars to Mr Parry, Welshpool 9th December 1954

[259] Mr Sutton, Chief Goods Clerk Welshpool, to Mr Parry, Station Master Welshpool, December 1952

[260] Divisional Traffic Manager Oswestry to Mr Watson, Station Master Welshpool 12th November 1937

[261] A.E. Hoe, R. Silcock & Sons Ltd to A. Maynard, CGMO Paddington 18th January 1938

[262] Mr Parry, Station Master Weshpool, to Divisional Traffic Manager Oswestry 3rd July 1953

[263] Mr Parry, Station Master Weshpool, and Divisional Traffic Manager Oswestry July 1953

[264] Mr Sutton, Chief Goods Clerk, to Mr Parry, Station Master Welshpool December 1952

[265] Mr Parry, Station Master Weshpool, and Divisional Traffic Manager Oswestry July 1953

THE BIRMINGHAM LOCOMOTIVE CLUB VISITS THE RAILWAY IN 1949

Each year the Birmingham Locomotive Club includes in its outdoor programme a trip over a light railway or other line not normally available to passengers and Saturday July 2nd was the occasion of an even more ambitious venture. The party numbering sixty-nine left Birmingham Snow Hill by Western Region diesel railcar No.14 at 7.50am and proceeded by a scenic route to Welshpool via Stourbridge Junction, Kidderminster, Bewdley, and the beautiful line through the Wyre Forest. There was a stop at Woofferton to reverse; a similar stop was made, and a pilotman picked up, at Shrewsbury, and then the railcar set out via Hanwood junction to Welshpool.

Half the party was conveyed over the 2' 6" gauge Welshpool and Llanfair section of the Western Region, arousing the interest of the townspeople, as the passenger service ceased in 1931. While one section boarded the train the other went by special Crosville bus to inspect the engines of the Steetly Co. Limited at the Whitehaven quarries, Porthywaen.

The narrow gauge train consisted of 0-6-0 tank No. 823 *Countess*, four open coal wagons fitted with station seats and a brake van. The engine whistled, a shower of water fell on the travellers and the train set off watched by a crowd of local people. Soon the train crossed Church and Union Streets then passed through Bronybuckley where the travellers had an embarrassingly close view of some house interiors. The riding of the track was extremely smooth and the photographers had a field day in the glorious weather. Many were the salutations from farm workers en route to Llanfair Caereinion, where another group of people was waiting on the platform, including the vicar, who was obtaining notes for broadcast on the Welsh News service. The return to Welshpool was not without interest; a baker's delivery van stood on the metals for loading, and necessitated a bit of juggling as the unexpected train approached!

In the afternoon the two contingents changed over. The Porthywaen quarries after the narrow gauge trip provided something of an anti-climax. At Llanymynech, the Shropshire and Montgomeryshire connection was noted in the distance, as were the present Llanfyllin line and the course of the original one. Near Llynclys the remains of the earthworks of the long abandoned narrow gauge tramway from Porthywaen to the canal were seen. Finally the quarries were reached behind Porthywaen station. The sidings lie on three levels, the two lower being standard gauge worked by GWR No. 1331 (the Fox Walker tank from the Whitland and Cardigan Railway), while at the top level – the quarries proper – are served by the only 4ft gauge industrial system in the country. Locomotive power is provided by two four-coupled saddle tanks of conventional Bagnall design.

The return journey to Birmingham began at 5.30pm and was made via Shrewsbury and Wolverhampton. The diesel rail car made some fast running and the 19½miles from Wellington to Wolverhampton, for which 33minutes were allowed, were covered in 22min. The smooth running of the whole trip by the Western Region at a busy weekend deserves commendation. The attendant success shows, however, the possibilities underlying 'railfan' excursions such as those that have been exploited by USA railways.

Another special train ran on 9th July attended by forty-one enthusiasts, some coming from as far afield as Halifax and Lincoln. On this occasion the train crew were Driver George Jones (Belan), Fireman Fred Williams and Guard Cecil Thomas. The special left Welshpool at 12.30pm and with several pauses en route for inspection and photography, again in beautiful weather, reached Llanfair at 1.20pm. The return journey departed at 2.30pm and Welshpool was reached at 3.30pm, where an inspection of the locomotive shed was made and the other tank engine, No. 822 *The Earl* was brought out for the photographers.

Sources: *Modern Transport 1949*, SLS Journal v.25 1949 No.294 pp. 217–218, *The Birmingham Gazette* 4th July 1949, *The Railway Magazine* 1949 pp.409–10

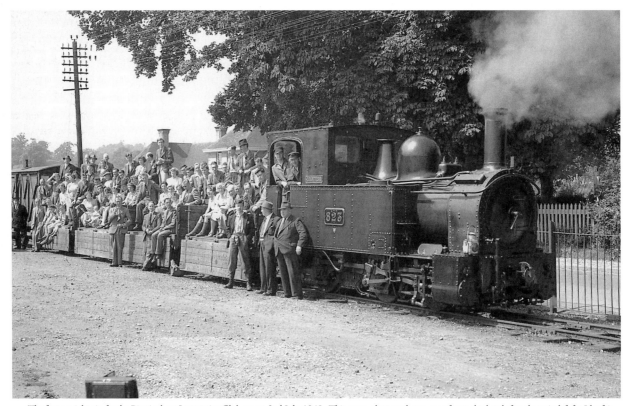

The first special train for the Birmingham Locomotive Club ran on 2nd July 1949. This group photograph was one of several taken before the train left for Llanfair.
A.N.M. GLOVER cty. KIDDERMINISTER RAILWAY MUSEUM

CHAPTER SEVEN

LIVING ON BORROWED TIME

No. 823 Countess *and crew waiting in the loop before working a train to Llanfair. The Smithfield and its standard gauge siding are seen to the left of the locomotive. The Cambrian goods warehouse and Long Mountain feature in the background. 11th May 1949.*
P.M. ALEXANDER

IN 1947 proposals were made to close the railway and in November plans were drawn showing the work required to put the permanent way in good order if the line was retained and the bridges and other structures that were to be removed if it was to be abandoned.[1] When the views of local traders were canvassed, they did not object to the closure of the line.[2] Despite the uncertainty about the line's future, in November 1947 *Countess* was sent to Swindon for a general repair and was followed by *The Earl* in March 1948.[3] When James Boyd visited the line in spring 1948 he was told that although closure had been considered, someone had decided otherwise. Local opinion was that it was intended to keep the locomotives running for as long as possible.[4]

On 1st January 1948 the Welshpool and Llanfair Light Railway passed into public ownership. The Transport Act 1947 required the British Transport Commission to ensure that its revenue was sufficient to fund expenditure taking one year with another. In a paper to the Transport Commission the Secretary of the Railway Executive argued that some branch lines were so poorly patronised that they did not provide any useful purpose to the communities that they purported to serve, because passenger traffic had largely disappeared and freight traffic only represented a fraction of the capacity of the line. The decline in the use of branch lines was attributed to the growth of bus services and the development of road services for goods. Over short distances many traders appeared to prefer road transport to rail.

Although expenditure on branch lines had been kept to a minimum, it was apparent that in many cases operating costs could not be recovered from revenue and there was little prospect of improving the position in the immediate future. The Railway Executive was not prepared to bear the heavy losses made by unremunerative lines and its members believed that its policy of closing branch lines was the continuation of one followed in the interwar years by the four grouped companies. In many cases communities were served by competing train and bus services so that the closure of branch lines resulted in the removal of duplicate services. In those cases where hardship would be incurred, alternative facilities could be provided by replacement bus services for passengers and

No. 822 The Earl climbing Sylfaen bank with a sheep special bound for Welshpool in 1947.

No.823 on the warehouse road at Welshpool narrow gauge yard with the stock of the SLS special that travelled over the line on 19th June 1954.

F.W. SHUTTLEWORTH

road deliveries for goods. However, the Executive was not prepared to offer replacement services that were equivalent to those provided by the railway.

Decisions to close branch lines were made after the Branch Line Committee had evaluated the value and volume of traffic and it had been compared with the cost of maintaining and operating the line. In coming to a decision on whether to close a branch line, the development potential of the area that it served was also considered. Before the final decision to close a line was taken, the local authorities, principal traders and the National Farmers Union were informed of the intention to close the line so that they could maker their representations. Bus operators and the Road Transport Executive were also consulted.[5]

In July 1950 Welshpool Borough Council received a letter from Mr Tom Sellars, the Oswestry District Traffic Superintendent, stating that the Railway Executive felt that the time had arrived when serious consideration should be given to closing the Llanfair Railway. If it was decided to close the line, alternative arrangements would be made to carry the traffic by road. When Members discussed Mr Sellars' letter, the Mayor, Mr W.C. Ainge, said that many people in the Llanfair district were against the line being closed and this view was supported by Mr C.S. Thomas, a goods guard who worked on the line. However, Mr R. Cowey felt the line had been a nuisance for a long time and that its closure would be a step in the right direction. After a short debate it was decided to inform the Railway Executive that they would deplore the closure of the branch and asked that no action should be taken until all the interested parties had been consulted.[6/7]

On 30th August a deputation consisting of Mr Ainge, Councillors H. Blockley and R.P. Turner and Mr J. Ben Davies, the Town Clerk, met Mr Sellars who explained that the line was completely uneconomic. A considerable amount of traffic was being lost because of the length of time taken to tranship goods at Welshpool. Although Mr Sellars could not commit the Railway Executive, in his opinion the replacement road service would be quicker than the railway and probably just as cheap. The deputation came to the conclusion that although no closure date had been decided upon, it seemed as if the Railway Executive would shut the line irrespective of any objections that were received, and that no useful purpose would be served by the Council pursuing the matter any further.[8] Montgomery County Council decided that if an adequate road service was provided, it would not oppose the closure.[9] The Editor of The County Times concluded that there was no need to regret the proposed closure because the replacement road service would be better than that provided by the railway and the cost to customers would not increase.[10]

When the Branch Line Committee met on 17th October 1950, a proposal to abandon the Welshpool and Llanfair Light Railway and replace it with a lorry service was discussed. In the year to 31st August 1949, the line carried 6,600 tons of goods traffic, 3,560 parcels and dealt with 275 wagon loads of livestock. Beasts were forwarded to Lancashire and wool was sent to Bradford and Newtown. Coal was received from the north Wales, north Staffordshire and south Yorkshire coalfields; basic slag came from Ebbw Vale, Scunthorpe and Hawarden Bridge; while animal feedstuffs originated from the Liverpool area. In addition to the single return trip made each weekday, two hundred and fifty-four extra trips had been made during the year conveying 954 loaded, and 814 empty, wagons. Although closure of the line would produce savings of £2,729, it was not considered to be unremunerative. However, there were frequent delays to traffic and standard gauge wagons were often detained at Welshpool until suffi-cient narrow gauge wagons became available. Road haulage was considered to be more economical than the railway because the Road Transport Executive's subcontractors were prepared to carry freight from Welshpool to Llanfair for 8s per ton inclusive of transhipment charges.

WELSHPOOL AND LLANFAIR LIGHT RAILWAY : CLOSURE CASE 13th NOVEMBER 1950

REVENUE FOR THE YEAR TO 31st AUGUST 1949

	Local to Branch	Through traffic Outwards	Inwards	Local to Branch	Through traffic Outwards	Inwards
	No.	No.	No.	£	£	£
Parcels		157	3,405		27	582
	Tons	Tons	Tons			
Freight						
General merchandise	5	62	812	6	109	1,607
Coal			3,155			1,659
Other minerals	−	—	2,647			2,283
Total	5	62	6,614			
Livestock	Wagons	Wagons	Wagons			
	109	148	18	92	837	30
Miscellaneous receipts						
Tenancies and tranship charges				572		
Total receipts for year to 31st August 1949				670	973	6,161

	£
Total receipts for year to 31st August 1949	7,804
Add : May 1950 increases	1,278
1949 receipts at 1950 rates	£9,082

ESTIMATED ANNUAL LOSS OF RECEIPTS

	Branch £
Freight train traffic	
Merchandise	6
Livestock	92
Other receipts	
Estate and Engineer's departments	22
Total annual receipts	120
Add : May 1950 increase	16
	136
Less : rental value of former engine shed at Welshpool	35
Estimated annual reduction in receipts if the branch is closed	£101

ESTIMATED ANNUAL REDUCTION IN EXPENDITURE

	£
Repair and renewal of way, works, and estate property	1,630
Repair and renewal of locomotives and wagons	631
Train working and station expenses including staff	1,926
Interest savings	1,483
Reduction in carting agent's commission on C&D traffic within cartage Boundary	60
	5,730
Less: net cost of alternative road services in lieu of existing rail	2,900
Estimated annual reduction in expenditure if the branch is closed	£2,830

ESTIMATED NET INCREASE IN NET REVENUE

	£
Estimated annual reduction in expenditure	2,830
Less : estimated annual loss of revenue	101
Estimated annual increase in net revenue if the branch is closed	£2,729

OTHER ITEMS OF IMPORTANCE

Resleepering required in 1950 and 1951 if the branch is kept open	£5,000

The British Transport Commission's Solicitor advised that clauses in the 1899 Light Railway Order requiring the line to be maintained at all times could be interpreted as meaning maintained at all times when the railway was in existence, while covenants over land conveyed to the railway requiring a halt to be provided at Golfa in perpetuity could not be enforced. In the Solicitor's view, Montgomery County Council would welcome the removal of the railway as it would facilitate road improvements and development schemes in Welshpool. Thus there were no legal objections to the closure of the line. Having considered all the facts, the Committee recommended that the railway should be closed, the materials recovered and the line abandoned. On 25th November 1950 the British Transport Commission approved the closure of the line.[11/12]

A visitor to the line in September 1951 was informed that it would be closed within the month. Closure seemed imminent because milepost 0 had been removed and lay by the side of the narrow gauge track in the main line goods yard. Standard gauge sleepers had been placed by the side of the narrow gauge rails and it appeared that once the line was closed the standard gauge tranship siding would be extended towards the site of the Llanfair Railway passenger terminus.[13]

The goods service

After the passenger service was withdrawn, a goods train ran over the branch four times a week. It left Welshpool at 11am to arrive at Llanfair an hour later, calling at the intermediate stations beyond Raven Square as required. Two hours were allowed to shunt Llanfair yard before the train returned to Welshpool where arrival was due at 3pm. In the following September the time spent at Llanfair was reduced to an hour. The service was not changed until September 1935 when a 7.30am goods service from Welshpool was introduced, which returned from Llanfair at 9am with a livestock train on Mondays only. An afternoon livestock train ran to Llanfair at 4pm, if required, returning as a goods that arrived back at Welshpool at 6.5pm. The 11.am service continued to run on Tuesdays, Thursdays and Fridays. In September 1938 the 11am service was retimed to leave Welshpool half an hour later and the time spent at Llanfair was reduced to half an hour. Although no further changes were shown in the Great

John Charles, the photographer's son, helps to load parcels into an open wagon at Welshpool watched by Station Master Sid Parry, Chief Inspector J. Jones, Driver Percy Evans and Guard Dick Morgan.
NLW, GEOFF CHARLES COLLECTION

No. 823 Countess taking the daily goods over the Lledan brook at Seven Stars, while school children watched from Brook Street.

The train beginning to round the mill curves on its way to Llanfair.

During a break in shunting at Llanfair, Ted Foulkes and M.L. Peate are seen here discussing the next move with Guard Dick Morgan, watched by Firemen Fred Williams and John Charles.

NLW, GEOFF CHARLES COLLECTION

Western service timetables,[14] reports in the railway press suggest that the goods train ran daily in 1945 and 1946, but that by 1947 the service had dwindled to two trains a week.[15/16/17] The service timetable remained unchanged until September 1948 when a daily goods service was provided. The Monday-only livestock trains seem to have been abolished and the time allowed for shunting Llanfair yard was increased to an hour. From Mondays to Fridays the train left Welshpool at 11.30am and was expected back at 2.30pm. On Saturdays the goods departed from Welshpool at 8.00am and arrived at Llanfair an hour later. It returned from Llanfair at 10am and was due back at Welshpool at 11am. Although the Saturday service was abolished in June 1953, it was reinstated in September 1954.[18]

UNDER THREAT OF CLOSURE AGAIN

The future of the line was examined again in April 1955 when new proposals to close it were made. Analysis of traffic for the year to 30th June 1954 showed that just over 5,900 tons of goods had been carried, the number of parcels handled had

No. 822 shunting Llanfair yard in the last months before the railway closed. Loaded wagons that had just arrived from Welshpool stand next to the former passenger platform while the locomotive removed empty wagons from the warehouse road.
A. W. V. MACE

Having dressed Llanfair yard, No. 822 was waiting for time before taking the 1.30pm train back to Welshpool. 12th October 1951.   F.W. SHUTTLEWORTH

fallen to 2,386 items, and only 45 wagons of livestock were dealt with. However, receipts had increased slightly. About $3\frac{1}{2}$ miles of track needed replacement sleepers, requiring expenditure of £5,000, while further work on the permanent way costing £2,100 would be required within three years. The locomotives needed repairs that were estimated to cost £1,600. If the line closed, savings of £9,348 could be made, but traffic valued at £3,110 per annum would be lost to road transport and receipts estimated to be worth £1,400 would be foregone because inbound goods could only be charged as

far as Welshpool. Additional cartage charges estimated at £1,066 would be incurred and the standard gauge tranship siding would have to be extended by 80 yards to facilitate the transfer of traffic from rail to road vehicles. No objections were expected from the local authorities so in July the Western Region Board approved the closure.[19]

The proposal to close the line was reported by *The County Times* on 26th November 1955 and was met with a mixed response from the farming community.[20] Although the Llanfair branch of the NFU wished to retain the line because the

WELSHPOOL AND LLANFAIR LIGHT RAILWAY : CLOSURE CASE APRIL 1955

REVENUE FOR THE YEAR TO 30th JUNE 1954	Outwards No.	Inwards No.	Total £
Parcels	106	2,280	712
Freight	Tons	Tons	
Freight	27	2,612	4,875
Coal and coke	—	3,263	3,535
Total	27	5,875	8,410
Livestock	Wagons	Wagons	
	45	—	95

	£
Total receipts for year to 30th June 1954	£9,217

ESTIMATED ANNUAL LOSS OF RECEIPTS	£
Parcels	5
Freight	522
Coal and coke	843
Livestock	30
Difference in rates charged from Welshpool and Llanfair	1,400
Estimated value of traffic lost to road haulage	3,110
Estimated annual reduction in receipts if the branch is closed	£4,510

ESTIMATED ANNUAL REDUCTION IN EXPENDITURE	£
Traffic staff	1,159
Permanent way staff	1,194
Train working staff	1,411
Staff total	3,764
Maintenance and renewal of rolling stock	1,619
Maintenance and renewal of the permanent way, bridges etc.	936
Train working expenses	540
Interest	2,489
	9, 348
Less : additional cartage costs	1,066
Estimated annual reduction in expenditure if the branch is closed	£8,282

ESTIMATED INCREASE IN NET REVENUE	£
Estimated annual reduction in expenditure	8,282
Less : estimated annual loss of revenue	4,510
Estimated annual increase in net revenue if the branch is closed	£3,772

OTHER ITEMS OF IMPORTANCE	£
Repairs to branch engines	1,600
Resleepering 1955	5,000
Resleepering in the next three years	2,100
Exceptional costs incurred if the branch is kept open	£8,700

Cost of extending the standard gauge tranship siding if the branch is closed	£500

cost of transporting coal and fertilisers to Llanfair by road would be more expensive, some farmers maintained that the service provided at intermediate stations on the line was inconvenient and that a country lorry service would be a great improvement. Concern was expressed that if the line closed, fences would no longer be maintained and that the undergrowth would not be cleared, allowing vermin to breed there.[21/22]

At a meeting called by Llanfair Parish Council, concern was expressed that the loss of the branch would lead to increases in haulage charges for parcels and freight traffic. It was decided to oppose the proposal to close the line on the grounds that six thousand tons were carried over the line at a cost of 4s. per ton. If carried by road, the rate would rise to 16s. per ton and the extra cost would fall on the local community. The increased cost of road transport was estimated to be £3,600 rather than the £1,600 reported in the closure case. The carriage of freight by road would require additional wharfage and storage space at Llanfair. This could only be achieved by the erection of warehouses that were estimated to cost £2,500. The estimated savings on repairs to the track would be offset by the provision of four additional lorries that would be needed to carry goods from Welshpool to Llanfair. The Commission would have to bear the annual cost of maintaining fences and clearing undergrowth once the line closed. Llanfair councillors considered that the Commission's estimate of the savings arising from the closure of the line were based on incomplete and unrealistic estimates. They were also concerned that once the line had closed, material increases in charges for road haulage would be made which would greatly encourage migration from the countryside into urban areas. A subcommittee consisting of Messrs D.H. Peate, T.O. Roberts and E.C. Jones was appointed to draft a memorandum setting out the Council's objections to the closure of the line. Copies of the memorandum were sent to Mr Clement Davies M.P., Llanfyllin Rural District Council and the local branch of the NFU with a request that they should join the Parish Council in opposing the closure of the line.[23/24]

When Llanfair Parish Council met on 9th January 1956 Mr Peate produced figures showing that closure of the line would result in higher charges for coal, fertilisers and animal feedstuffs. Mr J.E. Hughes believed that closure of the railway would result in a staggering increase in the cost of living in the area and that the Council should move immediately to stop the closure of the line. Mr B.A. Williams expressed surprise at the apathy of the farming community who would be more affected by increased prices than householders. At the suggestion of Mr J.H. Lewis, it was decided to call a public meeting on Wednesday 18th January to discuss the implications for the district if the line was lost. Representatives of neighbouring parish councils, the Llanfair branch of the NFU and any other interested parties were invited to attend the meeting. Mr Peate, who had been in communication with the British Transport Commission, was asked to collate the information to be presented at the meeting.[25/26]

BY BRAKE VAN TO LLANFAIR

The sky was rather overcast as we left Shrewsbury on the 10.25am for Welshpool in April 1956. We saw a War Department Austerity 0–6–0 tank shunting at the GW and L&NW Joint Line / Shropshire and Montgomeryshire exchange sidings and by the time we crossed the Welsh border it was raining. When we arrived at Welshpool we signed indemnity forms in the Station Master's office and crossed the forecourt to the narrow gauge yard.

There we found No. 822 shunting and when it had completed its task it propelled its train out of the yard towards Llanfair, onto the incline leading to the canal bridge, then retired to the engine shed to replenish its water supply while the train rolled onto the loop. The locomotive then propelled the train onto the former passenger siding where the brake van was loaded with a large and varied array of parcels traffic which included such items as tins of paint, boxes of chickens, large quantities of pork pies and a huge pram which Mr Cecil Thomas the guard had considerable difficulty in getting through the van door.

When the loading was complete we set off on our journey, climbing the steep gradient over the canal bridge towards the Church Street level crossing. Here the fireman dropped off to open the gates, the guard shutting it after we had passed through. We now curved our way through the narrow alley between the Welshpool houses and after passing Seven Stars climbed through the housing estate to Raven Square where the line has a level crossing in the middle of a cross roads. Here begins the long climb to Golfa; the scenery on this particular stretch is very fine as the line clings high above the Welshpool reservoirs and the woods of the Powis Estate are across the valley to the south.

As we passed through Golfa we noticed the disused loop, shelter and cattle loading ramp. It was not long before we passed through Sylfaen Halt which has its loop truncated into a siding. From here it was a short run to Castle Caereinion where we had to stop to open the level crossing gates. This station boasts its long disused signal box, passing loop, shelter, cattle loading ramp and a forlorn traction engine slowly rusting away.

We stopped near Dolarddyn to unload concrete troughs for a gang who were repairing a culvert. The petrol platelayers' trolley stood at the side of the line covered with a tarpaulin to protect it from the rain which was falling heavily as Welsh rain can. By now the Guard had lit the stove and the van was very cosy indeed. Before starting off we picked up a mother and her two children and gave them a lift as far as Cyfronydd.

On leaving this station, where sheep wagons were stabled, the train crossed the stone Brynelin viaduct and came to an exceptionally pretty stretch in the woods alongside the River Banwy.

After crossing the Banwy bridge we entered the last intermediate station, Heniarth. Travelling on, among the trees on the northern bank of the Banwy we curved past the pretty Dolrhyd water mill. After passing the railway's water tank we came upon the first signs of Llanfair, the remains of the timber siding and soon we were rounding the final curve to enter Llanfair Caereinion station.

We ate our sandwich lunch in the old waiting room as it was still raining. In a little time, however, the weather cleared and we were able to explore the station yard.

After about an hour the train started on its return journey. Stopping only for water at the tank alongside the Banwy, we made a much faster run as the gradients were mostly in our favour. We were, however, held up near Church Street level crossing due to a car and a van being parked on the line. After they had been removed, we continued over the crossing and arrived back at Welshpool station in time to catch the 3.10pm back to Shrewsbury.

Source: J.E. Tennant and P.D. Wigley *Welshpool & Llanfair Society Journal No. 3, reprinted in the Llanfair Railway Journal* No.155
April 2000

On 18th January Mr Peate presented the costs set out in the BTC closure case and showed that rates charged for road haulage would be more expensive than the through rates charged for carriage of freight by rail. He remarked that the increased cost would be carried by local people and that the limited storage space at Llanfair would prevent people from ordering large quantities of coal to obtain discounts. Mr Peate suggested if the railway closed, road haulage charges should be made at the existing through rates. When the railway to Dinas Mawddwy closed, deliveries to the area were made by road at no extra cost to local traders. Mr R.P. Turner, Sylfaen, explained that he was a member of Welshpool Borough Council and the Transport Users Consultative Committee. Welshpool would not oppose the closure of the line because the route through the town could be used for road improvements and other purposes. Although he viewed the proposed closure with alarm, he believed that it would be difficult to make a case to retain the line because it was Government policy to close branch lines that were uneconomic when they ran through districts which were unlikely to be developed in the foreseeable future. As the TUCC was due to consider the case for closing the line two days later, Mr Turner agreed to ask the Committee to defer consideration of the proposal and to receive a delegation of representatives from the areas affected by it. Mr I. Trant, Maesmawr, thought that the TUCC was unlikely to help them and suggested that the Railway Development Association should be invited to investigate the BTC case for closure. When the Association investigated the proposed closure of a branch line on the Isle of Wight, they found that many of the Commission's figures were unsound. Mr R.G. Millward, Llangyniew, suggested that the cost of replacement sleepers should be spread over several years instead

---

PROFESSOR TULPIN'S LAST TRIP ON THE WELSHPOOL & LLANFAIR

On 15th September 1956 there was a certain amount of normal locomotive smoke to be seen near Welshpool station as one approached it from the town but in front of the buildings drifted a smoke cloud of a lighter shade that seems to be peculiar to small engines when they have been fired just before the first run of the day. So there was early confirmation of the rumour that a train was to be run to Llanfair Cereinion that afternoon.

Four dropsided mineral wagons as "open seconds" (to use that description far more appropriately than in normal official practice) were found coupled between two brake vans, and the train was headed by outside framed 0–6–0 tank engine No. 822. No formal statement of ownership was obvious on the locomotive and it was too clean to suggest immediately that it belonged to British Railways, but so it did. Its long chimney and the bunching of mountings on its short boiler called to mind the motive power on the lines described by the Rev. W Awdry and his imitators, but it was clear that wherever the engine had started life, it had passed through Great Western hands.

Station staff and trainmen were placing platform seats from the main station on the wagons and a platform truck was used as a stepping stone to ease the climb into the vehicles. The sides of the wagons were lifted into position and locked by cotters, the station master collected from the passengers signed statements that they would not claim damages from British Railways even if harm should befall them, the officials exchanged signals that all seemed well, and off we went.

With hissing cylinder-cocks and very soft beats from the chimney, the engine took the train at a walking pace up over the canal bridge and to a stop just short of the main north-south highway through Welshpool. The fireman went ahead with a red flag to stop the traffic until the locomotive more effectively blocked the road, when he returned to the footplate.

Perhaps the best known action photograph of the Welshpool to Llanfair line is that of a train passing between houses with fully occupied lines of washing and on this day the scene was reproduced as we went by some of the older properties in Welshpool. Further on, the newer houses have gardens stretching down to the line and there the surroundings were more colourful; but everywhere doors were open and the householders stood waving to one of the few parties of the public to travel on the Llanfair line since 1931. A bright day would have made the trip idyllic, but at least it did not rain, nor were the passenger incommoded by even the heaviest emissions from the chimney as a light east wind carried them ahead of the engine when it was toiling up the 1 in 30.

For much of the distance from MP 1 to MP 3 (GW standard quarter posts are used) the route is like a winding country lane with steep grassy banks and bushes close to the vehicles on both sides. The extra resistance of one sharp curve obviously slowed things down until the engine was given another notch and then confidently coped. Her beats were uniformly strong, clean cut and equally spaced; "sweet and true at the front end" primly sums it up.

On a light 2ft 6in gauge railway used only for freight traffic for the last 25 years the riding of the four-wheelers was extraordinarily good and one ceased to worry about that signed indemnity, at least on the up grades. And even down 1 in 30, surely an engine and the two brake vans would hold back four wagons on dry rails? Certainly they did on this occasion and no one had any qualms.

The countryside in this district has beauty typical of the Welsh border, and the line brings one into intimate acquaintance with it. As a pleasure trip on a fine summer's day, a journey on the Welshpool and Llanfair Railway must surely be unsurpassed in Great Britain, but one thought regretfully of the times when passenger trains ran over it and how much more thoroughly it must have been appreciated for utilitarian transport on stormy days of wind and rain. But Crosville buses do the work now and British Railways take their cut of the profit.

On September 15th the journey to Llanfair was completed in 55 minutes, which was the time allowed for regular passenger trains. There had been a stop to precede a cautious crossing of a public road with a "blind" intersection at the site of Castle Caereinion station, where the signal box still stands. On the other side of the track at this point was a traction engine with the mechanism above the boiler apparently well preserved, but with the chimney corroded to a colander and ready to fall off.

The train and its passengers were thoroughly photographed at Llanfair. Here quantities of coal in the open and cattle food under cover showed the character of the freight traffic that has kept the line going for a quarter century after the passenger trains were discontinued.

On the return journey from Llanfair, the locomotive took water from an overhead tank near the site of Dolrhyd Mill, again a stop was made at Castle Caereinion, and Welshpool was reached without incident.

The seats were soon removed from the wagons and most of the passengers stood by to see the train shunted back into the sidings. Just when the driver must have been opening the regulator, a juvenile passenger decided that the quickest way to get to the other side of the train was to climb over the combined centre buffer and coupling between two of the wagons, put the scheme into immediate operation and, getting clear as the train started to move, avoided a possibly fatal accident by a split-second. Few people witnessed this incident and no voice was raised in criticism, but it emphasised the belief that on occasions of this kind every child should be handcuffed to a sturdy adult.

Source: Trains Illustrated December 1956 pp.621–24

of being presented as a single capital sum. Other speakers believed that the closure of the line would encourage further depopulation of the district.[27/28]

When Llanfair Parish Council met on 6th February, a long discussion took place about the position that it should adopt with regard to the proposed closure. The options were to oppose the closure of the railway under any circumstances or to ensure that the through freight charges continued if the railway closed.[29] At a public meeting held three days later, representatives of the Parish Councils and NFU decided to send a resolution to the General Manager of the Western Region in the following terms:

> 'Unless a clear undertaking is forthcoming from the Western Region of British Railways that delivery costs by any alternative form of transport shall be equivalent to the through rates levied by the British Transport Commission when the Welshpool and Llanfair Light Railway was in existence, this conference is unanimously opposed to the closure of that railway and will be prepared to see officials to discuss this decision and matters arising from them.'

When Mr Turner enquired if those present had any intention to make more use of the line if it was kept open, Mr J.E. Hughes replied that goods ordered by his firm delivered by rail to Welshpool were brought to Llanfair by road, so it seemed as if British Railways did not try to make full use of the line. When he proposed a resolution stating that the absence of a railway to Llanfair would prejudice the town's development, it was opposed by Mr J.E. Moon, Chairman of the Llanfair branch of the NFU, on the grounds that industrial development would make it even harder to recruit farm workers.[30/31]

While the debate about the future of the line continued, services were suspended on 1st February because both engines were no longer serviceable. On 18th February No.822 was taken to Oswestry works where it received a heavy intermediate overhaul. The engine was set to work again on 15th March and No. 823 was taken into Oswestry Works and stored.[32/33]

On 4th April representatives of the Railway Executive held a private meeting in Llanfair with the local railway cartage agents, W.D. Peate & Sons Ltd and Messrs Morgan Brothers, when a proposition was put to them which they agreed to consider. Following this meeting the BTC officials met representatives of the Parish Council and the NFU. Mr Stanley Harvey, the Chairman of the Branch Line Committee, intimated that there was a possibility that fertilisers could be carried without increased prices, and that increases in charges for the carriage of coal could be no more than 3d per hundredweight. In his view the Commission had gone as far as it could to reduce the impact of price increases and a bulk scheme had been devised for parcels. Mr Harvey made it clear that there was no hope of keeping the line open and said that No.822 had only been patched up for a few weeks extra service. A BTC spokesman told *The County Times* that every effort had been made to alleviate any possible inconvenience caused by the closure of the line. Mr Oliver Velton, the District Traffic Superintendent, told *The Express* that there was no alternative

to the closure of the line and that the Commission would make a submission to this effect to the TUCC at its next meeting. Mr Turner was reported as saying that when the railway closed, the position would not be as bad as they had feared. In light of the assurances received at the meeting with the representatives of the Railway Executive, Llanfair Parish Council withdrew its objection to the closure of the line.[34/35/36]

When the TUCC met on 20th April its members decided that in view of the understanding reached between the Commission and local road haulage contractors, there was insufficient reason to keep the line open. When the decision was discussed by members of Llanfair Parish Council, Messrs J.H. Lewis, J.E. Hughes and E.C. Jones expressed disappointment about the loss of the railway which they believed would be a heavy blow to the area as it would increase the cost of living. Since the BTC had still not made any firm commitments with regard to the rates for the carriage of coal and fertilisers after the railway closed, the Clerk was instructed to obtain a schedule of freight charges incorporating the favourable terms that had been proposed at the meeting with the representatives of the Railway Executive.[37/38]

On 13th October 1956 a notice appeared in *The County Times* announcing that the freight train service between

BRITISH TRANSPORT COMMISSION
BRITISH RAILWAYS
(Western Region)

NOTICE

CLOSING OF WELSHPOOL AND LLANFAIR LIGHT RAILWAY

The British Transport Commission hereby give notice that on and from Monday, 5th November, 1956, the freight train service between Welshpool and Llanfair Caereinion will be withdrawn and the line closed for all purposes.

The collection and delivery services for freight traffic in less than truck loads and parcels traffic in the area will be maintained.

Facilities for dealing with merchandise in full truck loads are available at Welshpool and the collection and delivery of such traffic will be undertaken when desired.

Information in respect of arrangements for dealing with traffic and any other matters arising out of the closing of the line will be supplied on application to:—

MR. O. VELTON,
District Traffic Superintendent,
OSWESTRY
(Telephone No. Oswestry 189,
Extn. 232).

or

Station Master,
WELSHPOOL
(Telephone No. 2231).

K. W. C. GRAND,
General Manager.

Paddington Station,
September, 1956.

THE SLS 'LAST TRAIN' 3rd November 1956

The Newtown Silver Band entertain the crowd in the standard gauge goods yard.

Railway enthusiasts gather in the Llanfair Railway yard.

Waiting for time.

Approaching New Drive level crossing.

On Golfa bank.

At Castle Caereinion.

Ted Williams watering the engine.

Welshpool and Llanfair would be withdrawn on and from Monday 5th November and that the line would be closed to all traffic. However, the delivery and collection of parcels and goods in less than wagon loads would continue in the area once served by the railway.[39]

THE LAST TRAINS

During the last week of the goods service, townspeople, local railwaymen and railway enthusiasts from Birmingham, London and Manchester made a final journey over the line. On Friday, 2nd November the guard's van of the last goods train to Llanfair was crowded with passengers who had paid 2s 3d for a second class return ticket and signed an indemnity endorsed with a sixpenny stamp. Guard Dick Trow, who started with the Cambrian in 1918 and had spent much of his railway career working from Welshpool, was in charge of the train. In contrast, the enginemen were relative newcomers. Driver Alf Swannick, Gobowen, had recently transferred to Welshpool while his mate, 16 year old Ted Williams, Llan-fyllin, had fired No. 822 for the first time on the previous Monday.

Shortly after 11.30am the train passed through the narrow gauge yard where cattle trucks could be seen, a reminder of the traffic in livestock that once kept the line busy on market days. Parked beside them was their successor, one of British Railways' new cattle lorries resplendent in maroon and cream paintwork. Passing Cyfronydd, sheep trucks stabled in the loop were a reminder of the heavy traffic that the line carried during the Second World War. Once Heniarth had been reached, the permanent way gang's motorised trolley was seen at the side of the line, while Jack Williams, Les Dunning and Ivor Broxton dismantled the waiting shed that had been erected more than fifty years previously.

The train was met at Llanfair by the Porter in Charge, Mr Harold Evans, who collected the parcels from the Guard. Mr Evans had worked at the station for about four years, booking inwards and outwards goods and delivering parcels around the town. While the crew attended to their duties, some of the travellers left the train to travel back to Welshpool by bus on the first stage of their journey home.

Once shunting had been concluded and the yard had been properly dressed for the last time, the crew refreshed them-selves before working the last goods train back to Welshpool. Shortly after leaving Llanfair they stopped at the water tower to fill No. 822's tanks. At Heniarth and Cyfronydd the train stopped to load the remains of the waiting sheds that had once protected passengers and their parcels from the elements. Arriving at Seven Stars, the train stopped to let two elderly ladies and a very small boy alight, a reminder of the days when passengers from Llanfair and the surrounding countryside travelled to Welshpool to shop or sell their produce at the markets in the town.[40]

On Saturday 3rd November, the Stephenson Locomotive Society organised a special 'last train' from Welshpool to Llanfair and back. Special tickets were printed for the occasion and No. 822 was fitted with one of its nameplates. Although a great many people wished to travel on the train, the nine open wagons and two brake vans could only accommodate 120 passengers. The special was worked by the same crew that had taken the last goods train to Llanfair on the previous day. Mr G. W. Holland, Swindon, Headquarters Locomotive Inspector, Mr Oliver Velton, District Traffic Superintendent Oswestry, and Mr Sidney Parry, Welshpool's station master, were also present. Many townsfolk and visitors gathered on the Smithfield Road to reminisce and watch the train depart.

Shortly after 2.30pm the train pulled out of the station yard to the sounds of martial music provided by the Newtown Silver Band. Church Street was thronged with people and the train climbed away from Seven Stars smartly. Houses near the line at Bronybuckley were decorated with bunting, flags and streamers and the train was cheered on its way. Along Brook Street from Standard Quarry to Raven Square all traffic was at a standstill. The band was standing in the centre of the road playing *Pomp and Circumstance* and *The Dead March* from *Saul*, while cars had been abandoned as their owners stood to photograph the train. Just beyond Raven Square the train came to standstill and old employees stood on the footplate or climbed into the van.

Eventually the train drew forward and began the ascent of the Golfa accompanied by a procession of motor vehicles on the nearby road. Seen from the train, every hedge, field, gate and copse contained a photographer and leaves were dislodged from trees as the engine climbed the incline. There was a large knot of photographers at the summit of the line and the regulator was closed for the descent towards Sylfaen where a small group of people greeted the train. People from the farm brought their children with them to see the train pass.

After crossing Coppice Lane the usual cautious descent to Castle Caereinion was made where the band greeted the train. Mr Pat Garland, the SLS Midland Area Chairman, added a *last train* headboard below the *SLS special* board. Mr Garland, Mr R Cowey, Mayor of Welshpool, M.L. Peate, Chairman of Llanfyllin District Council, and Mr E.C. Jones, Clerk to Llanfair Parish Council, were then photographed with the engine before the train continued on its way to Llanfair.

Llanfair station was entered with both whistles blowing and further tributes from the band. The engine ran round its train and left at about 4pm in failing light. *The Earl's* tanks were replenished at the water tower and it became difficult to keep warm in the open wagons. There were now about 150 people on board, local people having joined at Llanfair. The gates at Castle were open and the train passed through the station without pausing. There were more spectators at Sylfaen and all the way to Welshpool.

Approaching Welshpool the train drew to a stand at the Stop Board in a haze of blue smoke from hot brake blocks. As the special train ran over the level crossing at Raven Square, the band stood on the roundabout, the bandsmen blowing as hard as they could. The train was cheered along Brook Street, through Bronybuckley, past Seven Stars and over Church Street. The engine's whistles shrieked on the descent from the canal bridge to Smithfield Road. As the train passed the engine shed, a shower of rockets went up so that it passed under an arch of coloured flares and exploding crackers. The climax was reached as the special crossed Smithfield Road. A 2251 class 0–6–0 and a 'Manor' class 4–6–0 standing in the station joined in with gusto on their whistles until the train drew to a halt. It was late and soon most of the passengers had disappeared into the night. Then stillness descended and only the band playing Handel's *Dead March* could be heard.[41/42/43]

On Thursday morning, 8th November 1956, No. 822 returned to Llanfair to collect the stock that had been worked to the station six days previously. On returning to Welshpool they were left with the rest of the wagon fleet in the narrow gauge yard where they remained until disposed of in March 1960. After the engine's fire had been dropped, it entered the shed to await its fate.[44] A visitor to the line on 3rd August 1957 found that No. 822 was still at Welshpool shorn of its name and number plates.[45] It was not until 7th May 1958 that the locomotive was taken to Oswestry to join No. 823 in store at the Works.[46]

Narrow gauge rolling stock awaiting disposal in Welshpool yard on 31st March 1959.   ALAN WYCHERLEY, KIDDERMINSTER RAILWAY MUSEUM

Countess *and* The Earl *stored at Oswestry Works on 16th September 1958.*

[1] NLW WL/M/ 132A GWR Proposal to close the line 25th November 1947
[2] AN 97 20 Branch Line Committee W&L closure papers 17th October 1950
[3] Rail 272 250/1 Engine Nos. 822 and 823 history cards
[4] *SLS Journal* v.25 1949 No.285 pp.6–7
[5] AN 97 20 The Secretary, Railway Executive to the Chief Secretary British Transport Commission: Passenger and Freight transport services in rural areas 4th January 1951
[6] Welshpool Borough Council minutes 18th July 1950
[7] *The Montgomery County Times and Shropshire and Mid-Wales Advertiser* 20th July 1950
[8] Welshpool Borough Council minutes 27th September 1950
[9] *The Montgomery County Times and Shropshire and Mid-Wales Advertiser* 16th September 1950
[10] *The Montgomery County Times and Shropshire and Mid-Wales Advertiser* 30th September 1950
[11] AN 97 20 Branch Line Committee W&L closure papers 17th October 1950
[12] AN 13 1722 W&L closure papers 25th November 1950
[13] *SLS Journal* v.27 1951 No.317 p.272
[14] Rail 937 GWR service timetables 1931–1947
[15] *Railway Observer* v.15 1944/5 No.196 p.214
[16] *SLS Journal* v.22 1946 No.257 p.125
[17] *Railway Observer* v.17 1947 p.177
[18] Rail 921 BR service timetables 1948–1955
[19] AN 174 112 W&L closure papers April 1955
[20] *The County Times* 26th November 1955
[21] *The Express and County Times* 10th December 1955
[22] *The Express and County Times* 19th December 1955

[23] *The County Times* 3rd December 1955
[24] *The County Times* 17th December 1955
[25] Llanfair Parish Council minutes 9th January 1956
[26] *The County Times* 14th January 1956
[27] *The County Times* 21st January 1956
[28] *The Express and County Times* 21st January 1956
[29] Llanfair Parish Council minutes 6th February 1956
[30] *The County Times* 11th February 1956
[31] *The Express and County Times* 11th February 1956
[32] Rail 254 250/1 Engine Nos. 822 & 823 history cards
[33] *The Express and County Times* 25th February 1956
[34] *The County Times* 7th April 1956
[35] *The Express and County Times* 7th April 1956
[36] Llanfair Parish Council minutes 9th April 1956
[37] Llanfair Parish Council minutes 4th June 1956
[38] *The Express and County Times* 9th June 1956
[39] *The County Times* 13th October 1956
[40] *The Express and Times* November 3rd 1956
[45] *Railway Observer* v.27 1957 No.342 p.237
[46] *The Welshpool & Llanfair Light Railway* Ralph Cartwright and R.T. Russell, David and Charles 1972
[41] *SLS Journal* v.32 1956 No. 378 *Only Yesterday* J.I.C. Boyd p.349–353
[42] *The County Times* 10th November 1956
[43] *The Railway Magazine* v.103 1957 pp.52–3
[44] *The County Times* 10th November 1956

No. 822 The Earl at the Welshpool end of Llanfair platform in 1925. Although painted in Great Western livery and fitted with steam heating, there was no safety valve cover.
A.W. CROUGHTON, Cty. MICHAEL WHITEHOUSE

CHAPTER EIGHT
ROLLING STOCK

No. 822 The Earl with a mixed train standing next to Smithfield Road in the 1920s. At this time one carriage was sufficient to accommodate intending passengers on all but market and show days.
COLLECTION ROGER CARPENTER

THE first proposals for rolling stock were made in 1897 by Everard Calthrop who recommended that a small quantity of rolling stock should be acquired for the opening of the line and that further purchases could be deferred until experience of the type of traffic offering had been gained. It was intended to order two six-coupled tank locomotives capable of taking 40 tons up a gradient of 1 in 30. If the traffic justified it, a locomotive of the type used on the Bársi Light Railway would be acquired. This engine would be capable of taking a maximum load of 60 tons up the ruling gradient of 1 in 30 and would be used on market days or when the traffic was heavier than usual. All rolling stock was to be fitted with automatic vacuum brakes.

Mr Calthrop's proposals for carriages and wagons were strongly influenced by his work on the Bársi Light Railway. He recommended that two carriages should be purchased for the opening of the railway. The first would be 40ft long and 7ft 6in wide and capable of seating sixty passengers. It would have a central gangway with tramway type seating along its sides. The second carriage would be similar but of shorter length. Two low-sided wagons 24ft long and 7ft wide with removable bolsters and ends were to be provided for goods and timber traffic. For cattle traffic, two special wagons, 30ft long and 7ft wide with end doors, would be acquired. Each wagon would be able to carry up to 16 beasts. Two transportation cars 22ft long and 7ft wide would be required to carry standard gauge wagons. Four high-sided, four-wheeled goods wagons and a 5 ton travelling crane were also required. The estimated cost of the rolling stock was about four thousand pounds.[1]

The nature and quantity of rolling stock required for the railway was not considered again until October 1900 when the costs of building and equipping the line were re-estimated before an application was made to the Treasury for an increase in the Free Grant. Mr Calthrop's proposals were sent to Mr Denniss so that he would be able to provide an estimate of the cost of rolling stock when he met the Llanfair Railway's Works Committee on 31st October.[2] At the meeting, a schedule outlining the stock required to operate the line was agreed.[3] For reasons that were not recorded, Mr Denniss refused to countenance the use of transporter wagons[4/5] while the possibility of using electric power was dismissed as being too expensive.[6]

PROPOSALS FOR ROLLING STOCK

Quantity and description of stock	£
3 engines	4,500
2 large bogie passenger coaches	900
2 small third class coaches	400
40 goods wagons	1,000
4 covered goods wagons	150
12 covered cattle trucks	1,000
1 travelling crane	150
Total	£ 8,100

211

After the meeting with the Works Committee, Mr Jones, the Cambrian Railways' Locomotive, Carriage and Wagon Superintendent, gave the matter further consideration. In a memorandum to Mr Denniss he suggested that if one set of coaches was sufficient to work the trains, two locomotives would suffice, but if two sets of coaches were required, another locomotive would be needed. His preference was for six-coupled tank engines. A bogie composite carriage 35 feet long, capable of holding about 45 passengers, would suffice for most services. If two sets of coaches were required, two composites would be needed. Two third class carriages would be required to strengthen trains on fair and show days. Mr Jones advised against buying cattle wagons because they could only carry three beasts in each wagon. He believed that two covered goods wagons would be sufficient at the outset. Forty open goods wagons, some with drop sides, would be required for the line. Ten timber trucks would also be needed, while a travelling crane would be an advantage.[7]

MR HERBERT JONES' REVISED PROPOSALS FOR ROLLING STOCK

Quantity and description of stock	£
3 engines @ £1,500 each	4,500
2 large bogie passenger coaches @ £450 each	900
2 small third class coaches @ £150 each	300
40 goods wagons @ £25 each	1,000
10 timber trucks @ £25 each	250
2 covered goods wagons @ £60 each	120
1 travelling crane	150
Total	£ 7,220

In December 1900 a further meeting was held between the Works Committee and Cambrian officials. Mr Denniss advised that three locomotives should be provided from the outset because, if two were in constant use, there would be no contingency in the event of a breakdown, so traffic could be seriously impeded. However, Mr Addie stated that only two could be afforded and eventually agreement was reached about the rolling stock to be ordered. Mr Jones was instructed to obtain suitable designs for the rolling stock authorised by Mr Addie.[8]

ROLLING STOCK AUTHORISED BY MR ADDIE

Quantity and description of stock	£
2 engines @ £1,600 each	3,200
2 large bogie passenger coaches @ £450 each	900
1 third class coach	200
40 goods wagons @ £25 each	1,000
4 covered goods wagons @ £60 each	240
2 cattle trucks @ £85 each	170
10 timber trucks @ £25 each	250
1 travelling crane	150
2 brake vans @ £ £120 each	240
Total	£ 6,350

When the Llanfair Directors met on 31st January 1901, Mr Jones submitted the plans and estimates for the initial rolling stock. For reasons that were not recorded, he advised against the purchase of a travelling crane at the outset. While he thought that there was no immediate need to place an order for the locomotives, he stated that it could take up to a year

and a half between placing an order and receiving the engines at Welshpool. Mr Jones was empowered to interview firms with a view to obtaining tenders to equip the railway with rolling stock, and to report the outcome of his enquiries to a future meeting. His remuneration was set at 150 guineas plus expenses.[9]

On 22nd June Mr Jones met the Llanfair Directors to discuss the tenders that had been received for the locomotives. The Board decided to accept Beyer Peacock's tender for two engines at a price of £1,630 per engine, the price to be reduced to £1,570 per engine if a third was ordered within six months.[10] The Llanfair Directors asked the Cambrian Board to confirm their decision before any expense was incurred and the issue of the number of engines to be ordered was reopened.[11] Although Mr Denniss persuaded his Directors to insist that three locomotives should be acquired,[12] the Llanfair Board maintained that their company was unable to afford a third engine and there the matter eventually rested.[13/14] On 24th October 1901 Beyer Peacock confirmed receipt of an order for two locomotives at a price of £1,630 per engine. A set of working drawings costing £25 was also ordered.[15]

At the October meeting of the Llanfair Board Messrs R.Y. Pickering's tender for passenger and goods stock was accepted. Mr Jones was given the authority to order three bogie carriages with automatic vacuum brakes and forty eight unfitted goods vehicles. The carriages and wagons were to be delivered during 1902 or at such time arranged by Mr Jones. An order for timber wagons was deferred.[16]

ROLLING STOCK ORDERED FROM MESSRS R.Y. PICKERING

Quantity and description of stock	£
2 composite carriages @ £345each	690
1 third class carriage	235
40 open goods wagons @ £25 10s each	1,020
4 covered goods vans @ £65 each	260
2 cattle wagons @ £52 each	104
2 goods brake vans @ £84 each	168
Total	£ 2,477

In February 1902 it seemed likely that the railway would be ready for inspection by the Board of Trade in late July or early August, so Mr Collin advised the Directors to press for the delivery of the rolling stock in time for the inspection.[17] The following month the Works Committee were astonished to find that the plans for the locomotives were incomplete and that work on building them had not commenced. Mr Jones was invited to attend the next Board to explain the situation.[18] The Beyer Peacock engines index book records that on 22nd March, the day after the Works Committee met, a preliminary order was placed for the materials required for the Llanfair Railway locomotives.[19]

When Mr Jones met the Directors on 26th March, he stated that he saw no difficulty in obtaining the rolling stock in time for the line's opening. However, the locomotives had to be specially designed and the drawings had not been completed. He thought that the engines would not be ready for another eight or nine months and possibly longer. On 9th April the Earl of Powis wrote to Messrs Beyer Peacock seeking assurances that the engines would be completed and delivered to Welshpool in time for the Board of Trade inspection.[20] At the beginning of May the company replied that it would make its best endeavours to complete the locomotives in time for the inspection,[21] and the drawings were finalised on 7th May 1902.[22] In the interim the Llanfair Secretary, John Evans, wrote to W.G. Bagnall Ltd to see if they would be prepared to hire locomotives to the railway and, if so, on what terms.[23] On 5th June Mr Jones wrote to Mr Evans providing assurances that good progress was being made on the construction of the locomotives.[24]

No. 1 *The Earl* was delivered to Welshpool on 2nd September 1902 [25] and had to be stored under a tarpaulin on a temporary siding because the engine shed had not been completed. Mr Jones was instructed to write to Beyer Peacock to ensure that the other locomotive was not dispatched until the Llanfair railway was in a position to store it.[26] Despite his best endeavours, the locomotive arrived at Welshpool on 27th September.[27] The first eleven goods wagons were received at Welshpool on 10th October and were followed by another ten on the 19th.[28] Delivery of the rest of the stock continued until 2nd February 1903 when the two cattle wagons were received.[29]

THE LOCOMOTIVES

Mr Jones followed Mr Calthrop's advice and ordered two six-coupled locomotives for the line.[30] Although he is known to have visited five narrow gauge lines in North Wales[31], the extent to which he was involved in the design of the Llanfair engines is not clear. The only surviving specification for the locomotives is one made by Beyer Peacock.[32] Notes made by H. Guthrie, one of the company's draughtsmen, indicate that they were to be similar to the Glyn Valley 0–4–2 tank engines, but with six-coupled wheels and no condensing gear.[33] Beyer Peacock did not supply many narrow gauge locomotives to mainland Britain and some authorities believe that a builder who specialised in locomotives for light railways would have favoured an 0–6–2 tank engine.[34]

The locomotives were allocated progressive numbers 4418 and 4419 but subsequently these numbers were taken by two Argentine Great Western Railway 2–6–0 goods engines.[36] The progressive numbers carried by the Llanfair Railway locomotives were first allocated to an order received from the Buenos Aires Great Southern Railway in November 1891 for four compound 4–4–2 tanks which were not built.[37]

Beyer Peacock supplied two compact six-coupled locomotives with outside frames, outside cylinders, Walschaerts valve gear and a short firebox that occupied the full width of the frames. The connecting rod drove the middle wheel set. They were fitted with steam sanding gear, the sand pipes being placed on either side of the middle wheel set. After the

---

BEYER PEACOCK & Co. LTD SPECIFICATION FOR ORDER 8868[35]

PROGRESSIVE NUMBERS 3496, 3497

WELSHPOOL AND LLANFAIR LIGHT RAILWAY 2ft 6in GAUGE

SPECIFICATION

Maximum speed 25mph
Minimum curves at sidings 3 chains (198ft)
Maximum load per axle 7 tons
Specified load behind engines 40 tons up an incline of 1 in 30 at 10mph
Length of incline 4 miles of 1 in 30
Weight of rails 41¼ lbs per yard
Brakes automatic vacuum, hand screw
Motion Walschaerts

DIMENSIONS

Cylinders	diameter	11½ in	Buffer height from rail		2 ft 2 in
	stroke	16 in	Water capacity		350 gallons
Wheel diameter		2 ft 9 in	Heating surfaces	tubes	396.3 sq ft
Boiler	length	7 ft 0 in		firebox	37.0 sq ft
	outside diameter	3 ft 5⅛ in		total	433.3 sq ft
Tubes	number	119	Fire grate area		7½ sq ft
	diameter	1¾ in	Fuel capacity		22 cu ft
	length	7 ft 3¼ in	Boiler pressure		150 lbs
Total wheelbase		10 ft 0 in	Weight	empty	16-7-2
Front to middle axle		4 ft 2 in		full	19-18-0
Middle to rear axle		5 ft 10 in	Tractive effort	85%	8,175 lbs

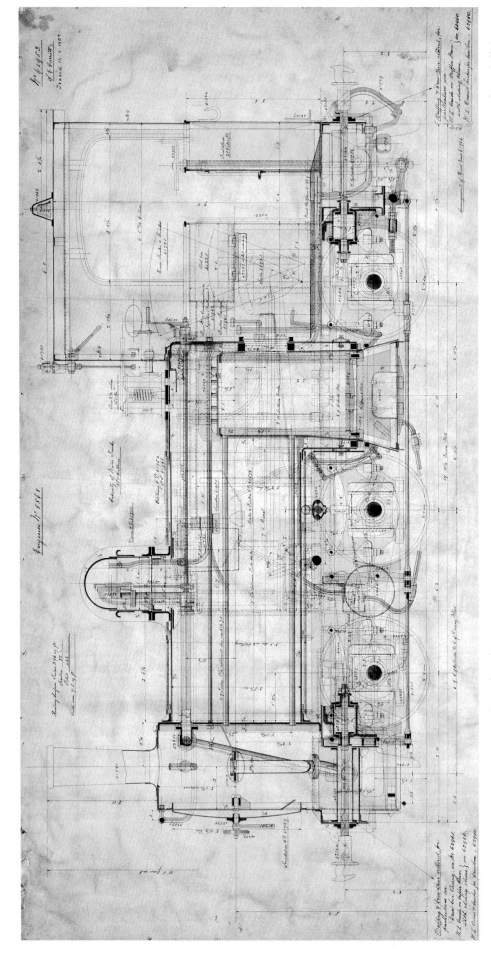

Beyer Peacock & Co. Ltd. General Arrangement drawing for Order 8868: Section.

Beyer Peacock & Co. Ltd. General Arrangement drawing for Order 8868: Plan.

No. 2 The Countess *in photographic grey at Gorton.*   BEYER PEACOCK

Welshampton derailment of 1897, all Cambrian locomotives carried a re-railing jack. On the Llanfair Railway engines, they were usually carried above the cylinder on the left-hand side. A stovepipe chimney surmounted the smokebox whose door was secured by a locking wheel and handle. The un-superheated boiler was quite short to minimise the risk of uncovering the firebox crown on the severe gradients. A dome of moderate size was carried on the centre of the boiler, while Ramsbottom safety valves were mounted over the firebox. The single whistle was mounted in front of the spacious cab that had large square windows in the weatherboard and also accommodated the bunker. A small bell mounted in the cab roof was rung on the approach to level crossings in Welsh-pool.[38] At Mr Jones' request, the locomotives were fitted with Norwegian chopper couplings that had so impressed him when he visited the North Wales Narrow Gauge Railway.[39]

EARLY MODIFICATIONS

In October 1902 *The Earl* and twenty wagons were hired to the contractor while the line was being completed but neither the locomotive nor the wagons proved entirely satisfactory in service. The locomotive spread the track when it passed over curves of up to ten chains radius, while the wagons often derailed when they were placed next to the engine.[40] When wagons broke away from the ballast trains in which they were working on 6th and 10th November, confidence in the design and safety of the rolling stock was badly shaken. Mr Jones found that the first breakaway occurred because the wagons had not been coupled correctly, and on the second occasion a chain had been used to couple the first wagon to the engine. Although Mr Jones defended the design of the couplings robustly, he recommended that the wagon stock should be fitted with side chains as an additional safeguard. The other difficulties were attributed to the severe gradients, sharp

curves, and incomplete state of the permanent way which raised doubts about whether the formation was fit for purpose.[41]

When Mr Collin's views were canvassed, he reported that since *The Earl* had been put to work, it had been impossible to keep the track from spreading on curves of up to ten chains radius. The locomotive's rigid wheelbase was the longest of any on the Welsh narrow gauge, although the curves on the Llanfair Railway were comparable to those of the other lines. The Engineer maintained that it was the long wheelbase that caused the track to spread. The permanent way on curves of up to six chains radius was being strengthened with tie bars, while additional spikes had been driven in on curves of six to ten chains radius. Mr Collin noted that the Contractor believed that the couplings were too stiff and had implied that they were the cause of the derailments.[42]

At the end of January 1903 tests on the couplings were carried out in the presence of Beyer Peacocks' representatives. On the first trip, the coupling hooks rose when the engine passed over badly packed sleepers in Welshpool yard and they eventually disengaged, uncoupling the train. The trials were then abandoned for the rest of the day to allow the hooks to be modified. On the following day, a trip over the line was attempted, but after passing through Welshpool, the engine became derailed on a curve and the front bogie of the leading carriage dropped between the rails. Once both vehicles had been re-railed, the journey to Llanfair continued without incident.[43]

The issue was settled by Major Druitt when he inspected the line on behalf of the Board of Trade. The Inspector found that the central buffer couplings had insufficient lateral and vertical movement. He concluded that they would cause derailments on the numerous sharp curves and refused to sanction the opening of the line until they had been modified.[44] The couplings were redesigned to allow $2\frac{1}{2}$in side play each way and 1in lift and the drawgear fitted to the rolling stock was modified accordingly.[45]

A special meeting of the Cambrian Board was held on 8th May 1903 to consider proposals for easing the sharp curves on the railway and modifying the locomotives to reduce the damage that they caused to the permanent way. When Mr Collin outlined proposals to improve the formation, it became clear that even minor alterations would be prohibitively expensive because more land and property would have to be acquired. Mr Jones reported that he had met Beyer Peacock's Chief Engineers and had evaluated five proposals to modify the locomotives to enable them to take the curves more easily.

The first proposal was to rebuild the locomotives as 4–4–0 tank engines by replacing the leading pair of wheels with a bogie. However, the position of the cylinders and frames meant that it would not be possible to get a satisfactory type of bogie and the extensive structural alterations would be expensive. The second option was to convert the locomotives into 2–4–0 tanks. The leading coupling rods would be removed and the existing axleboxes on the leading axle would be replaced with ones that allowed the axle one inch lateral play in each direction. Both these proposals gave the engines a fixed wheelbase equivalent to 5ft 10in, resulting in locomotives that would be less stable in traffic. As four-coupled engines, they would probably be over-cylindered so that the

PROPOSED MODIFICATIONS TO THE LLANFAIR RAILWAY ENGINES				
TYPE	MODIFICATION	TIMESCALE	COST	WORK LOCATION
4-4-0T	Fit bogie	14 weeks	£195	Welshpool
2-4-0T	Fit sliding axleboxes	7 weeks	£80	Welshpool
0-6-0T	Shorten wheelbase	16 weeks	£225	Manchester
0-6-0T	Flangeless centre wheels	1 week	Nominal	Welshpool
0-6-0T	Provide more side play	3 weeks	£10	Welshpool

No. 1 The Earl in lined livery at Llanfair on 1st July 1909.

LCGB, KEN NUNN

B/L.

Cambrian Railways Company.

Locomotive Superintendent's Office.

Oswestry. December 8th, 1902.

Dear Sir:-

Welshpool & Llanfair Light Railway.

Permanent Way and Rolling Stock.

In reply to your letter of the 1st inst. I send attached a diagram shewing clearly that an Engine with a ten feet rigid wheel base would easily pass round a curve of 3 chains radius, but as a matter of fact the Engines supplied have of course a certain amount of side play allowed, and that side play will continually increase up to a certain point as the Engines work. The Engines were specially designed to work on curves of this radius, but at the same time they were also built to meet the requirement of taking a heavy load up a gradient of 1 in 30.

The fact that the Engines have been working for a period of about a month over the section of line which it was deemed sufficiently completed to permit of them running, and that they have not been off the road on any one occasion, although some of the curves are considerably sharper than 3 chains radius (in one case the curve is about 2 chains radius) clearly shews that the Engines are capable of doing what they were designed for.

If the conditions laid down are strictly complied with, namely that the curves are kept to a radius of 3 chains, and that the gradients are not to exceed 1 in 30, I feel sure that both Engines are Rolling Stock will work satisfactorily.

Yours truly,

Herbert Jones

C.S. Denniss Esqr.,

General Manager.

Source: Rail 1057 6B

No. 823 Countess fitted with steam heating in Great Western unlined livery. The plate carrying the train heating and vacuum pipes, centre buffer coupling, and safety chains was larger than the one fitted when the locomotive was built. W.H. WHITWORTH

boiler pressure would have to be reduced. The resultant reduction in tractive effort would cause additional train miles to be run because the number of carriages that could be taken over the line would have to be reduced from three to two, and the maximum number of wagons that could be taken up the gradients of 1 in 30 would be reduced from nine to six. Messrs Beyer Peacock estimated that the brake power would be reduced by between 38 and 48 percent, which was inadvisable on a line with long, steep gradients.

In Mr Jones' opinion, the locomotives rode exceedingly well as 0-6-0 tanks. Since this arrangement was steadier and more powerful than a four-coupled design, three further proposals for a six-coupled type had been devised. A scheme to reduce the fixed wheelbase by 10 inches had been considered. Nine inches would be removed between leading and middle axles and the distance between the middle and trailing axles would be reduced by 1in. However, the cost of the proposal was out of proportion to its benefits, the work would take sixteen weeks and the engines would have to be sent to Manchester. The next proposal was to remove the flanges on the wheels of the middle axle at nominal cost. The alteration would not change the rigid wheel base, would only provide very limited relief to the road, and would increase the wear on the leading and trailing tyres. Mr Jones dismissed this proposal as being unsafe.

The final proposal appeared to provide the most practical solution. By giving additional side play of $\frac{1}{8}$in each way in the leading axleboxes and side play of $\frac{1}{4}$in each way in the trailing axleboxes, total side play of $\frac{3}{8}$in each way would be achieved which was the equivalent of reducing the fixed wheelbase to 8ft 6in. There would be no loss of power but the wear and tear on the locomotives would be increased. The work could be carried out in about three weeks at Welshpool at an

estimated cost of £10 per engine.[46] Mr Jones recommended that the alterations should be given a trial and the work was completed on 15th May.[47] Once modified, the locomotives gave little trouble in service.[48]

On 28th September 1903 two spring hangers broke while *The Earl* was working a service between Castle Caereinion and Cyfronydd. The driver packed the spring and the engine worked the branch services for the rest of the day. The spring hangers were renewed with thicker material to increase their strength. Mr Jones attributed the cause of the fractures to a defect in the permanent way, but Mr Collin was able to repudiate the allegation.[49]

By 1908 the locomotives had run over 73,000 miles in service and the axles supplied by Beyer Peacock were renewed using carriage axles that were turned down to the original dimensions. In 1911 *The Earl's* leading and driving axles failed as did the leading and trailing axles on *The Countess* and again they were replaced with carriage axles. On 25th May 1914 services were suspended when *The Countess* fractured an axle after working the first train of the day. The spare engine could not work the branch because it had broken its trailing axle three weeks earlier. *The Earl's* wheel set was returned from Oswestry and work continued through the night to repair *The Countess* so that the engine was available for work by 6 a.m. on the following day. Subsequently, axles made from nickel chrome steel were used on both locomotives.[50]

INTO THE GREAT WESTERN

The locomotives were taken into Great Western stock in August 1922.[51] No.1 was taken to Oswestry during the four weeks ended 31st December 1922[52] and returned to Welshpool as No. 822 on 13th March 1923. The following day No. 2 was sent to Oswestry works returning to Welshpool as

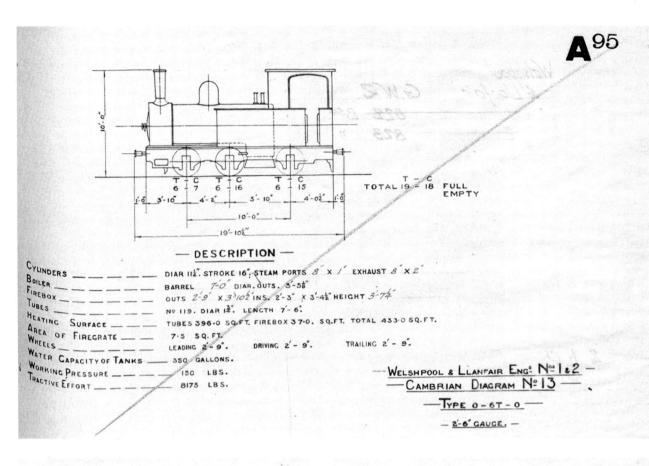

T - C   T - C   T - C
6 - 7   6 - 16 6 - 15   T - C
                                TOTAL 19 - 18 FULL
                                               EMPTY

1'-0"   3'-10"   4'-2"   5'-10"   4'-0½"   1'-0"

10'-0"

19'-10½"

— DESCRIPTION —

CYLINDERS _____ DIAR 11½". STROKE 16". STEAM PORTS 8" X 1" EXHAUST 8" X 2"
BOILER _____ BARREL 7'-0" DIAR. OUTS. 3'-5⅝"
FIREBOX _____ OUTS 2'-9" X 3⁵-10½" INS. 2'-3" X 3'-4½" HEIGHT 3'-7¼"
TUBES _____ Nº 119. DIAR 1¾". LENGTH 7'-6".
HEATING SURFACE _____ TUBES 396·0 SQ.FT. FIREBOX 37·0. SQ.FT. TOTAL 433·0 SQ.FT.
AREA OF FIREGRATE _____ 7·5 SQ.FT.
WHEELS _____ LEADING 2'-9".   DRIVING 2'-9".   TRAILING 2'-9".
WATER CAPACITY OF TANKS _____ 350 GALLONS.
WORKING PRESSURE _____ 150 LBS.
TRACTIVE EFFORT _____ 8175 LBS.

— WELSHPOOL & LLANFAIR ENGˢ Nº¹ 1 & 2 —
— CAMBRIAN DIAGRAM Nº 13 —

TYPE O - 6T - O

— 2'-6" GAUGE. —

Built 1902.

T - C   T - C   T - C   T - C
6 - 7   6 - 16 6 - 15   TOTAL 19-18 FULL
5 - 9   5 - 16 5 - 15   17 - 0 EMPTY

10'-0"

1'-0½"   3'-10"   4'-2"   5'-10"   4'-0½"   1'-0½"

10'-0"

19'-11⅝"

DESCRIPTION.

CYLINDERS _____ DIAM. 11½". STROKE 16".
BOILER _____ BARREL 7'-0". DIAM. OUTS. 3'-5⅛".
FIREBOX _____ OUTS. 2'-9" X 3'-10½" INS. 2'-3" X 3'-4½" HEIGHT 3'-7¼".
TUBES _____ Nº 136. DIAM. 1⅝" LENGTH 7'-3¼".
HEATING SURFACE _____ TUBES 420·5 SQ. FT. FIREBOX 36·5 SQ. FT. TOTAL 457 SQ. FT.
AREA OF FIREGRATE _____ 7·5 SQ. FT.
WHEELS _____ COUPLED 2'-9".
WATER CAPACITY OF TANKS _____ 350 GALLONS
WORKING PRESSURE _____ 150 LBS.
TRACTIVE EFFORT _____ 8175 LBS.

LATE WELSHPOOL & LLANFAIR Nº 1 & 2.

ENGINE Nºˢ 822 & 823.

TYPE O - 6 - O
          T

2'-6" GAUGE

Source: Rail 254 109

No. 822 The Earl *modified by the Great Western Railway.*
AUTHOR'S
COLLECTION

No. 823 on 5th July 1923.[53] It is probable that they were repainted in Great Western livery while at Oswestry. The new number plates were set in the centre of the side tanks, necessitating the removal of the nameplates to the cab sides. No. 823's nameplates were too long to fit on the cab sides in their original form, so they were shortened to *Countess*. Brass safety valve covers were not fitted until some time after the Grouping, *Countess* being recorded running without one in April 1926.[54]

Both locomotives were overhauled at Welshpool during the winter of 1924–25 when No. 822 was given a heavy general repair and No. 823 received a heavy repair. By the end of the decade the Beyer Peacock boilers needed to be replaced and a scheme to modify the locomotives was devised. On 11th November 1929 No. 822 was stopped and taken to Oswestry for a heavy intermediate repair.[55] A new boiler with a large dome and topfeed was designed and built at Swindon then dispatched to Oswestry where it was fitted to No. 822 on 30th December 1929.[56] *The Earl* was set to work again on 3rd April 1930 allowing *Countess* to be stopped on 12th April so that it could be dealt with. The new boiler for No. 823 was sent to Oswestry on 8th April, fitted on 7th August[57] and the locomotive was set to work again on 10th October 1930.[58]

Although the replacement boilers did not have Belpaire fireboxes, in many other respects Swindon standards were applied remorselessly. The stovepipe chimney was replaced with one of Swindon design complete with a copper cap; the regulator in the dome was lubricated from on top in the old Dean manner; topfeed was applied through fittings of a standard Great Western pattern, but which was much smaller

than those on most Great Western domed boilers; and the safety valves were encased in a standard Swindon cover that was almost as tall as the dome. The cab sides were extended by $8\frac{1}{4}$ inches and the whistles were relocated to the cab roof.

The engines were vacuum-braked, with a small ejector instead of a pump for maintaining vacuum. The large ejector and the brake-application valve were of the standard type used on vacuum-fitted, steam-braked Swindon engines, but the steam-brake setter was omitted. The valves and pistons were oiled by a sight-feed lubricator of a non-standard type. The pipes entered the smokebox on the right-hand side under cover of a rectangular casing reminiscent of those that were seen on Swindon 4–6–0s that received large superheaters in later years.

In accordance with Great Western practice, the driver stood on the right of the footplate, where the regulator and brake-handle could be reached with ease, but the reversing lever was on the left, suggesting that the engine originally had left-hand drive but had been incompletely converted. It would be interesting to know whether this unusual circumstance agreed with the drawing office records at Swindon, or, on the other hand, was just a case where the shops used their discretion to do (or not to do) an awkward job in their own way and said nothing about it.

The firedoor was in the usual Swindon style and the 1in tubes appeared to be large for such a short boiler-barrel. The firebox ends of the tubes could be seen easily as there was no brick arch. A standard injector was carried on the frame behind each cab-step and the coal watering hose dangled out of the left-hand side of the cab as jauntily as from a 'King'.[59]

Countess's boiler and smoke box under repair at Oswestry Works.

SUMMARY DIMENSIONS WHEN NEW BOILERS FITTED[60]					
Cylinders	diameter	11½ in	Buffer height from rail		2 ft 2 in
	stroke	16 in	Water capacity		350 gallons
Wheel diameter		2 ft 9 in	Heating surfaces	tubes	420½ sq ft
Boiler	length	7 ft 0 in		firebox	36½ sq ft
	outside diameter	3 ft 5⅛ in		total	457 sq ft
Tubes	number	136	Fire grate area		7½ sq ft
	diameter	1⅝ in	Fuel capacity		22 cu ft
	length	7 ft 3¼ in	Boiler pressure		150 lbs
Total wheelbase		10 ft 0 in	Weight	empty	17-0-0
Front to middle axle		4 ft 2 in		full	19-18-0
Middle to rear axle		5 ft 10 in	Tractive effort	85%	8,175 lbs

The locomotives did not require further attention until 23rd October 1941 when No. 822 was stopped and sent to Swindon factory for an intermediate repair, arriving there on 16th December 1941. The work was completed on 18th February 1942 and No. 822 was set to work on 14th March. However, all cannot have been well as the engine paid a brief visit to Oswestry from 30th April to 19th May 1942. No. 823 continued to work until stopped on 12th November 1946 but then languished at the back of Welshpool engine shed while the line's future prospects were considered. In September 1947 it was transferred to Oswestry but again no work was carried out there. On 7th November No. 823 was seen at Birmingham in a goods train hauled by War Department class 2–8–0 No. 79224 en route to Swindon.[61] The engine entered the factory on 3rd December for a general repair and was set to work again on 13th February 1948.[62]

Although in poor condition, No. 822 worked the railway by itself for over a year. On 30th November 1947 it failed and services over the line were suspended until 11th December while repairs were carried out. No. 822 continued to work until stopped on 1st March 1948. Three days later it entered Swindon factory for a general repair which was completed on 24th June. The locomotive returned to Welshpool on 5th July 1948.

WESTERN REGION ENGINES

When the locomotives returned from Swindon there was little to indicate that they now belonged to the state. By March 1951 they had been fitted with 89A shed plates on the smokebox door and their nameplates had been removed.[63] Both engines continued to work the line until 27th May 1953 when No. 823 was stopped, taken to Oswestry, and given an unclassified repair. The engine was set to work again in July and No. 822 was stored in Welshpool engine shed. No. 823 required further attention at the end of August 1953 but then worked the branch until it was stopped on 1st February 1956. Although the intention to close the branch had been announced, No. 822 was given a heavy intermediate repair

No.822 standing over the pit at the back of the narrow gauge engine shed at Welshpool with a 'Not to be moved' board above the Norwegian buffer/coupling. 19th June 1954.
F.W. SHUTTLEWORTH

and subsequently received an outsized whistle plate whose purpose seemed to be to direct steam from the safety valves over the cab. In the interim, services over the branch had to be suspended for want of an engine. On 15th March 1956 No. 822 returned to Welshpool and No. 823 was taken into store at Oswestry. No. 822 worked the line until it closed and remained in the engine shed at Welshpool until 7th May 1958 when it too was removed to Oswestry Works. Subsequently both locomotives were acquired by the preservation company.[64]

LOCOMOTIVE SUMMARY HISTORIES					
W& L No.	PROGRESSIVE No.	RECEIVED	GWR No.	NEW BOILER	CONDEMNED
1	3496	2 Sep 1902	822	30 Dec 1929	17 Aug 1961
2	3497	27 Sep 1902	823	7 Aug 1930	27 Jul 1962

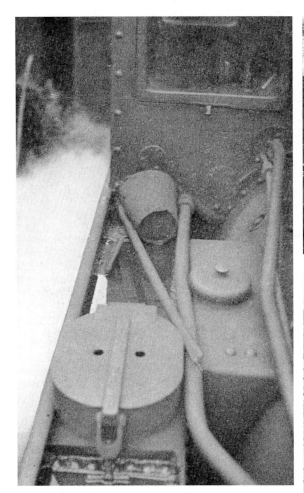

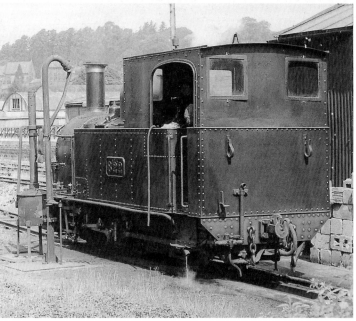

A95

Gauge 2' 6"

G.W.R.
ENGINE HISTORY.

No. 822 Engine.

WLL No 1 * Earl
* Beddows

BUILT	1902	AT Beyer Peacock LOT
Type	0 6 0 T 29	Cost £ 1630 (Including £ for Boiler.) Tank Capacity 350
Weight { Empty 17 0 / W.O. 19 18	Tractive Effort 8175	Cylinders 11½ X 16

REPAIRS.

89

Tender Attached	Date Stopped			Date set to work			No. of days stopped	Station	Date Report received			Classification of Repair and Miles	Boiler Change or Renewal
												W.O.L.	1
	17	10	24	10	7	25	85	Welshpool	24	1	25	HC 28.313	
	11	11	29	3	4	30	125	Oswestry Shed	2	4	30	HI 85.486	R 77
	23	10	41	14	3	42	142	Welshpool				I 145.725	
	30	4	42	19	5	42	19	Oswestry Shed	13	6	42	R	
	30	11	47	11	12	47	11	Welshpool 7/12				I	
	1	3	48	24	6	48	115	Swindon Pool Jan 3/3				G 184.876	
	20	4	53	15	3	56	977	Oswestry Shed 20/4/6				HI 209.221	—
								Awaiting Decision per Loco Office 19/2/52				4.666	
								Still awaiting decision 16/7/52 pending loco Superintendents confirmation of branch line closing				213.887	
	24	11	56					To Store @ Oswestry.					

$ See Corr. Ref No 99020 dated 9/4/56.
Application to purchase a chimney from either Engine No 822 or 823 when
withdrawn from service. WS Bayes

◇ See Corr. Ref No 63962 dated 29th March '51.
Application for one nameplate:-
WS Baxter.

See Corr Ref 99455/16/6. 22/8/51
application for one nameplate
from either 822 or 823
& providing a bell.
Mr Ogden.

* See Corr. Ref No 95095 dated 6th Dec '49.
Application for one nameplate:-
WS. R.S. Watkins
43. Burghley Road,
St Andrews,
Bristol. 6.

◇ $ Sold to the Welshpool & Llanfair Light Railway Co.
* Condemned Taken out of Stock 14/8/61

Age 59 years. Ref. L 03409 - 14/8/61.

Total Miles

Residual Value

4,500—10-28—Ext. 180 (26).

Source: Rail 254 250

G.W.R.
ENGINE HISTORY.

Gauge 2'6"   No. 823 Engine.

BUILT _1902_   AT _Beyer Peacock_   LOT _See below_   W.L. No. 2 & Countess

Type _0-6-0 T_   Cost £ _1630_ (Including £ for Boiler.)   Tank Capacity _350_

Weight { Empty _17 . 0_   W.O. _19 . 18_ }   Tractive Effort _8175_   Cylinders _11½ × 16_

REPAIRS.

Tender Attached	Date Stopped	Date set to work	No. of days stopped	Station	Date Report received	Classification of Repair and Miles	Boiler Change or Renewal
	16 1 25	20 3 25	53	Welshpool	21 3 25	H 36,773	
	18 8 28	23 8 28	5	Heniarth	- - -	L See corres 75268	
	12 8 30	10 10 30	131	Welshpool	25 10 30	H(I) 99.954	R 75.800
	12 11 46	13 2 48	458	Oswestry Shed		G. 176.959	
	27 5 53	3 7 53	37	" "		U 16 203	
	29 8 53	31 8 53	2	" "		LC 223 162	
	15 3 56			To Store at Oswestry		223.135	
	1 2 56			Oswestry			

$ See Corr Ref No. 99020 dated 9/4/56.
Application to purchase a chimney from either Engine No. 822 or 823
when withdrawn from service :- Mr Bayes.

* See Corr Ref No. 95095 dated 6th Dec '49.
Application for one nameplate :-
Mr R.E. Wilkins,
123. Burghley Road,
St Andrews, Bristol. 6.

See Corr Ref 99455/16/-
22/8/51
application for one number
and one bell from either
822 or 823
Mr Ogden.

X See Corr Ref No. 90154 dated 9/11/49
Application to purchase one nameplate :-
Mr A.R. Brown,
Isleworth, Middlesex.

Condemned _24/7/62_

Age _60_ years.   Ref. _L 03011/1_

Sold to Welshpool & Llanfair Railway Socy. 28/9/62.

Total Miles _223162_

Residual Value

4,500—10-28—Est. 789 [26].

Here No.822 The Earl had paused at Seven Stars before crossing Union Street. The shed to the right of the locomotive was once the waiting room but after the line closed to passengers, it saw use as a coffin maker's workshop. The house in the background is Seven Stars Cottage. H.B. TOURS

LOCOMOTIVE LIVERIES

1902–1915

When the locomotives arrived on the line, they were painted in Cambrian Railways black. In photographs the paintwork on the smokebox often appears to be quite noticeably lighter than that on the rest of the engine.[65] The metal plates that carried the chopper couplings, safety chains and vacuum pipes were painted red. The cylinders, tanks and bunker were lined with an orange band $\frac{3}{4}$in wide, edged on both sides with $\frac{1}{8}$in red lines. In the early years boiler bands received the same treatment. The front, sides and back of the cab were lined in red.

Elliptical brass number plates with raised edges, numbers and letters were carried on the cabsides. The plates carried the words WELSHPOOL & LLANFAIR above the number and LIGHT RAILWAY below it. The lettering followed the longer axis of the ellipse. Rectangular brass nameplates, with raised edges and letters were carried in the centre of the tank sides, while the builder's plate was attached to the side of the smokebox.[66] The background to these plates was probably painted red.

1915–1922

During the latter part of the Great War, at least one of the locomotives is believed to have been painted grey without any lining.[67] By the Grouping both locomotives are thought to have been painted black and, if lined, French grey panels would have been applied.[68] A photograph of No. 2 at Llanfair

circa 1922 shows the locomotive without any discernible lining.[69]

1923–1947

The Great Western painted the boiler barrel, tank sides and ends, firebox casing, safety valve cover, weatherboard, cab sides, handrails and boiler handrails green. Black was used for the chimney, smokebox wrapper, door fittings, the tops of the tanks and their fittings, the handrail on the smokebox and everything below the footplate. The valvegear, motion bars, crosshead, connecting and coupling rods were bright steel, while the metal plates that carried the couplings, safety chains and vacuum pipes were vermillion. The cast-iron number plate was placed in the centre of the tank sides with the initials G and W in yellow, shaded black, set on either side. The edges of, and numerals on, the number plate were painted yellow. The locomotives were not lined.[70/71/72]

1948–1956

When the locomotives returned from Swindon in 1948 they were painted in Great Western colours but the company's initials were omitted. No. 823 had the letter 'W' painted in a creamy white underneath the centre of the number plates.[73] The locomotive was still in this livery when taken into store in 1956. When No. 822 returned to work the branch in March 1956 it was painted unlined black with the sides of the number plates and figures thereon painted a creamy white.[74]

Brake composite No. 2 as supplied by R.Y. Pickering with the monogram and running number in a circlet.
R.Y. PICKERING

PASSENGER STOCK

Third class saloon No. 3 and one of the brake composites at Llanfair. The monogram had been dispensed with but the running number retained the circlet.

The three carriages appear to be based on Mr Calthrop's proposals and owed little to contemporary Cambrian practice. At either end of the carriages there was an open balcony which gave access to a saloon with a central gangway. The oak-framed bodies, clad with mahogany panels, sat on steel underframes that were carried on bogies with American type equalising bars. Two steps gave access to the balconies whose ends and sides were fitted with 'lazytongs' gates. The gates at the end of the balconies allowed the guard to pass between the carriages. The saloons were entered through half-glazed sliding doors. The seating was placed lengthways along the sides of the carriages and luggage racks were fitted above the seats. The large windows gave the carriages an airy feeling, alternate windows being given quarter lights that opened inwards. Lighting was provided by oil lamps. The carriages were unheated, so in winter foot warmers were provided.

The brake composite carriages seated thirty-six passengers in three saloons that were separated by half-glazed sliding doors. The guard's compartment was situated between the first class and third class smoking saloons, and provided very limited accommodation for 'smalls' traffic. There was seating for ten passengers in the first class saloon, four in the third class smoking saloon and twenty-two in the third class non-smoking saloon. The seats in the first class saloon were covered by cloth and the floor was carpeted. The seats in the third class saloons were made of alternating slats of pitch pine and Kauri and the floor was fitted with oak battens. The third class carriage seated forty-six passengers: sixteen in the smoking saloon and thirty in the non-smoking saloon. The seating and flooring were of the same type as in the third class saloons of the brake composites.[75]

On market days before the Great War, the railway was heavily used and there were occasions when passengers had to travel in the brake vans.[76] In 1913 Mr W.A. Jehu complained that there were insufficient carriages to accommodate intending passengers on Welshpool fair days.[77] After investigating the matter, Mr Williamson asked the Llanfair Directors to provide an additional carriage but his request was refused because there were no funds to pay for a new one.[78] When the Cambrian General Manager pressed the Directors to reconsider the matter, they asked him to provide a statement showing the extra revenue that the proposed carriage would generate, and there the matter ended.[79]

Relatively few changes were made to the carriages over the years. In April 1911 advertising space in the carriages was let to a Mr J. Abrahams of Forest Gate for 10s 0d per space per annum.[80] How many spaces were taken was not recorded. Complaints were made about the dim light provided by the oil lamps so in April 1913 Mr Williamson suggested that they should be replaced with acetylene lamps at an estimated cost of £32 16s 0d. However, the Directors decided the work was beyond their company's means.[81] In October 1923 the Great Western fitted the carriages with incandescent lighting and they received steam heating apparatus during the following month.[82] By 1926 panels had replaced the lattice work on the ends of the balconies.[83] After the passenger service was withdrawn, the carriages were taken to Swindon where they are believed to have been stored in the paint shop before they were scrapped.

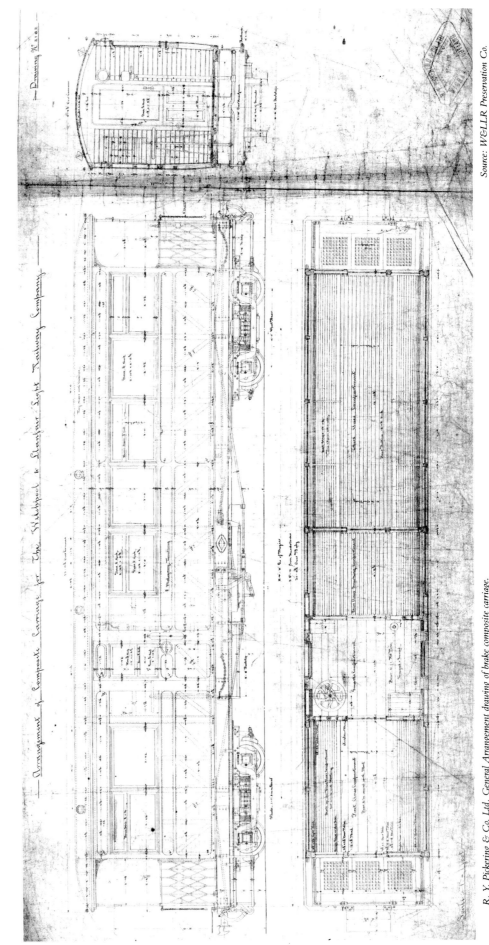

Arrangement of Composite Carriage for The Welshpool & Llanfair Light Railway Company

— Drawing No 2102 —

Source: W&LLR Preservation Co.

R. Y. Pickering & Co. Ltd. General Arrangement drawing of brake composite carriage.

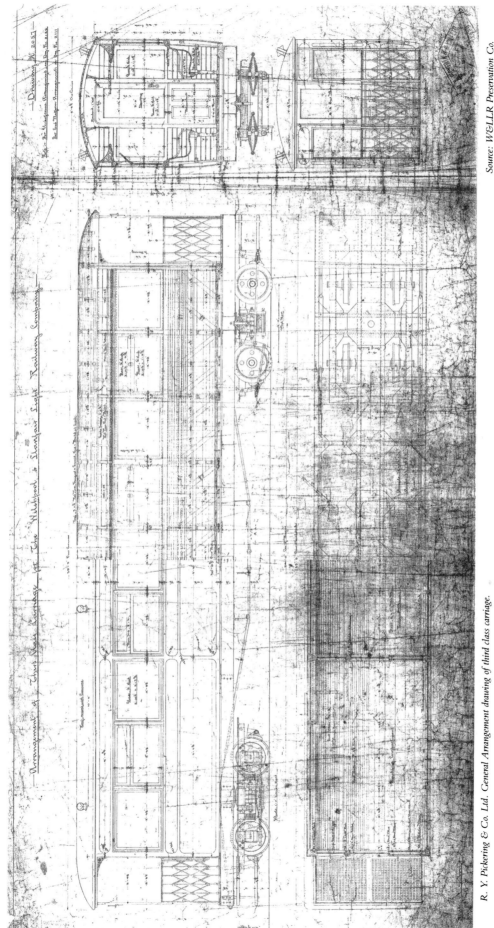

R. Y. Pickering & Co. Ltd. General Arrangement drawing of third class carriage.

Brake composite No.1 in green livery in 1922.
GREAT WESTERN RAILWAY

Third class saloon No. 3 as GWR No. 4154 at Llanfair in 1930 after the lattice work on the balconies had been replaced with panels and steam heating apparatus had been fitted. Here the carriage was carrying the simplified livery of 1927–1931.
LGRP

The GWR coat-of-arms carried after the livery was simplified in 1929. The mouldings follow the colouring of the panels that they encompass.

PASSENGER STOCK LIVERIES

1903–1909

When the carriages were delivered from Messrs Pickering the upper and waist panels on the sides and ends were painted white and the lower panels bronze green. The mouldings were bronze green with a broad black band along their edges. A gold line was superimposed along the centre of the black band, and a fine red line was painted along the centre of the gold line. The underframes were black and edged with a fine red line. Roofs were white but soon became discoloured in service.[86]

The class designation was placed in the waist panels on the carriage sides in gold letters of uniform height that were shaded blue. On the brake composites the class designation was placed in the centre of the end panels, but on the third it was in the centre panel. The class designation was also set in the waist panels on the balcony ends. The waist panel on the guard's compartment door was not lettered. The carriage number, placed within a garter, was set in the middle of the central lower panel. The number and garter were painted in gold, the whole being about 5½in high. The company monogram was placed at the same level in the centre of the outer panels. The monogram is only apparent in early photographs of the period.[87]

1909–1922

By 1911 the eaves and upper panels were also painted bronze-green.[88] The eaves panels now carried the characters W.&.L.R. (with four full stops) in 3½in gold characters that were shaded red. The moulding on the waist panel of the guard's compartment door was plated over and lettered GUARD, the positioning of the class designation was unchanged

but the garter encircling the running number was dispensed with.[89]

1923–28

The Great Western painted the carriages in the then recently reintroduced chocolate and cream livery. The lower and waist panels were Windsor brown, while the upper body and eaves panels were cream. It is not certain whether the frames of the windows and quarter lights were painted in Windsor brown or mahogany. The mouldings were painted black edged with 7/16in gold lines. This painting scheme was applied to the side and ends of the carriage bodies. The roofs, rain strips and ventilators were white. All ironwork on the balconies, the footsteps, the underframe and the bogies was painted black.

The running numbers were carried at both ends of the waist panels on the body sides. The class designation was set in the waist panels of the sides and ends. Ownership was indicated by a central garter crest flanked by the crests of Bristol and London in the lower panels, and the letters GWR above the garter crest in the waist panel. All letters and numerals were gold shaded black.[90]

1929–1931

By 1930 a simpler painting scheme had been applied to the carriages. The lower and waist panels were painted Windsor brown while the upper and eaves panels were cream. Mouldings were no longer painted black, but followed the colouring of the panels that they encompassed. A new coat of arms set in the centre of the lower panel replaced the garter crest.[91] The panels that replaced the iron gates in the balcony ends were painted brown or black.[92]

PASSENGER STOCK

SUMMARY DATA [83]

Builder		R.Y. Pickering & Cᵒ·	Width	over body	6 ft 6 in
Year built		1902		over footboards	6 ft 6 in
Number	brake composites	2		over balcony	5 ft 10 in
	third	1		over underframe	5 ft 10 in
Price	brake composites	£345 0s 0d		internal	5 ft 11¼ in
	third	£235 0s 0d	Height	rail to roof	10 ft 0 in
Seating	brake composites	1ˢᵗ x 10, 3ʳᵈ x 26		floor to roof	7ft 0¹/₁₆ in
	third	46 x 3ʳᵈ		floor to cantrail	6 ft 5¼ in
Length	over buffers	37 ft 0 in	Wheel diameter		1 ft 11 in
	over cornices	35 ft 4¾ in	Body		Wood
	over headstocks	35 ft 0 in	Underframe		Steel
	over body	30 ft 0¾ in	Axleboxes		Oil
	bogie centres	24 ft 0 in	Buffers		Centre
	bogie wheelbase	4 ft 0 in	Drawgear		Drop catch
Width	over cornices	6 ft 8¾ in	Brake		Automatic vacuum

SUMMARY HISTORIES [84]

W&LLR Nᵒ	GWR Nᵒ	DELIVERED	TYPE	RENUMBERED	CONDEMNED
1	6338	22 Jan 1903	Brake composite	28 Jul 1923	9 May 1931
2	6466	22 Jan 1903	Brake composite	21 Jul 1923	9 May 1931
3	4154	22 Jan 1903	Third	21 Jul 1923	11 Apl 1931

H.C. CASSERLEY

The stock of the 12 noon train from Welshpool standing in the platform road at Llanfair on 24th August 1948.

GOODS STOCK

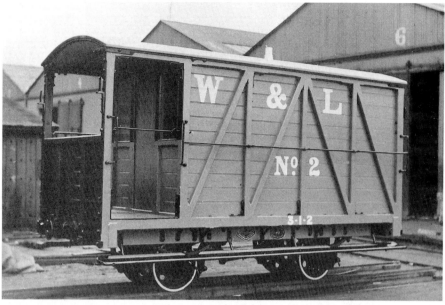

Brake van No. 2 as supplied by R.Y. Pickering. The end of the verandah appears to be painted red.
R.Y. PICKERING

Mr Jones seems to have drawn heavily on contemporary Cambrian practice when designing the goods stock and Mr Calthrop's proposals seem to have been largely disregarded. All the stock had wooden bodies and underframes, were of limited carrying capacity and ran on four wheels. The brake vans, covered vans and cattle wagons had bodies with external timber framing.

BRAKE VANS

The two brake vans appear to have been based on a Cambrian design dating from the 1890s that had outside frames and a single veranda. While the standard gauge vans were given doors on the sides of the veranda, all that was provided for the narrow gauge vans was a simple drop bar.[93] From the veranda a boarded doorway led into the van that was heated by a cast iron stove. A brake standard, that operated brakes on all the wheels, was placed inside the van near the entrance. Two lockers also served as seats.[94]

Shortly after the line opened to passenger traffic, the vans were modified by letting a door into the sides.[95] This made it necessary to move the stove which was placed on the opposite side of the van to the brake standard. Sliding doors were provided on the outside of the vans in place of the central panel. The vans were also provided with vacuum pipes but

---

BRAKE VANS

SUMMARY DATA[100]

Builder	R.Y. Pickering & Co.	Height	rail to roof	9 ft 0 in
Year built	1902		floor to roof	6 ft 2⅞ in
Number built	2		floor to cantrail	5 ft 4 in
Price per van	£84 0s 0d	Springs		2 ft 6 in
Length	over buffers	16 ft 0 in	Wheel diameter	1 ft 11 in
	over headstocks	14 ft 0 in	Body	Wood
	wheelbase	7 ft 0 in	Underframe	Wood
Width	overall	6 ft 4 in	Axleboxes	Oil
	over cornices	6 ft 1½ in	Buffers	Centre
	over headstocks	5 ft 10 in	Drawgear	Drop catch
	internal	5 ft 4 in	Brake	Screw inside

SUMMARY HISTORIES[101]

W&LLR Nº	GWR Nº	DELIVERED	TARE	RENUMBERED	CONDEMNED
1	8755	11 Nov 1902	3-3-0	22 Dec 1923	12 Mar 1960
2	8759	11 Nov 1902	3-7-1	9 Feb 1924	12 Mar 1960

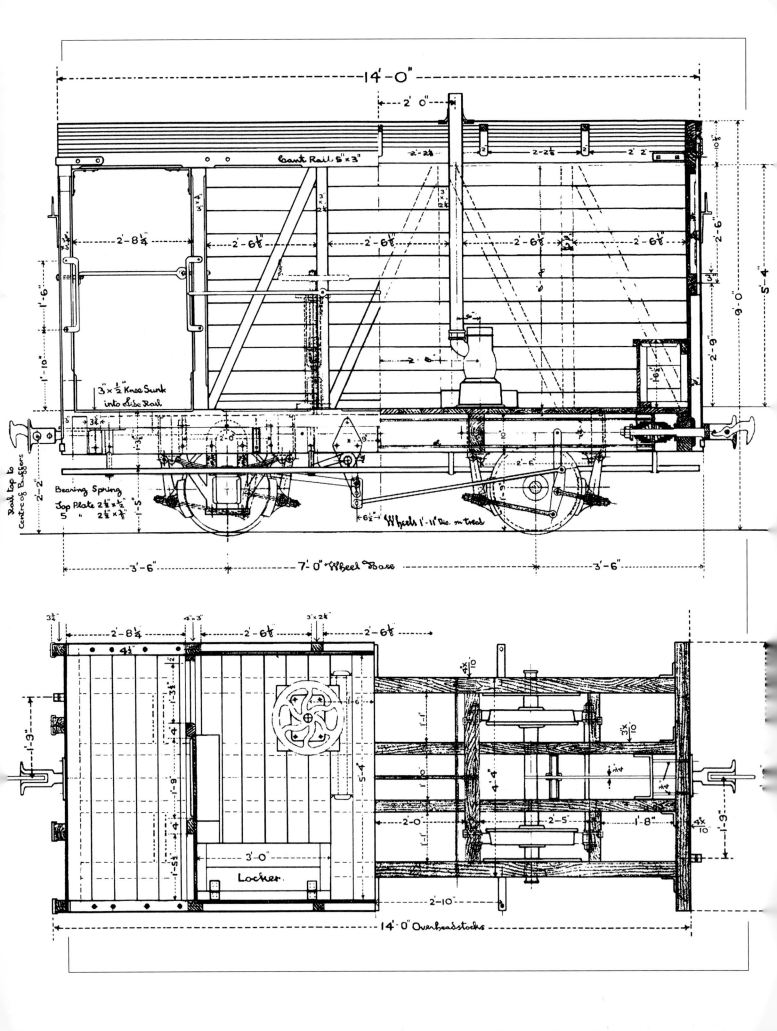

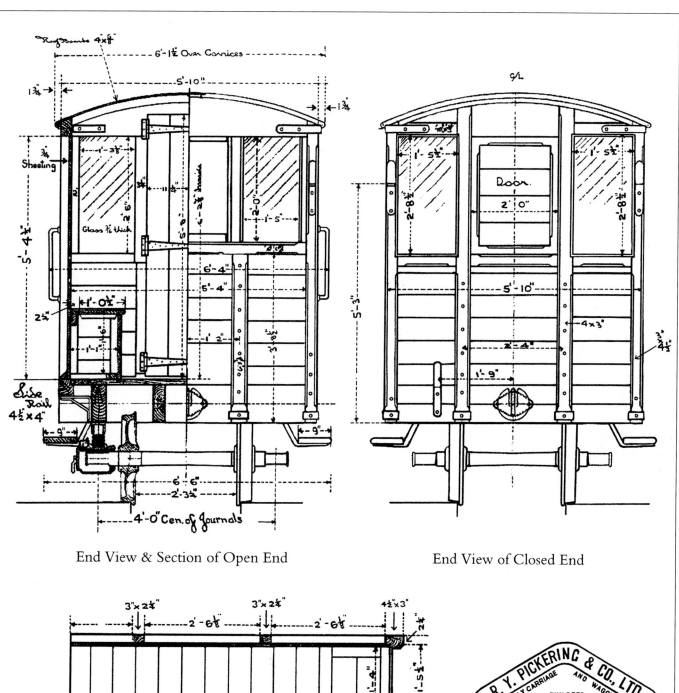

End View & Section of Open End

End View of Closed End

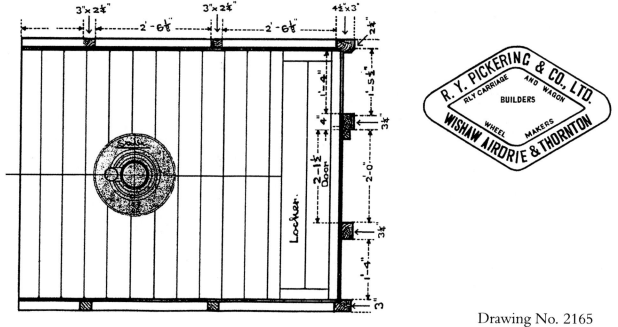

R. Y. PICKERING & CO., LTD.
RLY CARRIAGE AND WAGON
BUILDERS
WHEEL MAKERS
WISHAW AIRDRIE & THORNTON

Drawing No. 2165

Brake van No. 8759 at Welshpool carrying the Great Western goods stock livery of 1937–1947.

did not receive vacuum brakes. Further modifications were made at some time between 1909[96] and 1922 when the external frames on the body sides were renewed with three cross-braced panels, the central door was boarded over and the sliding doors were moved to the sides of the veranda which was enclosed at its end.[97] At the same time, the brake standard was moved to occupy a position between the two doors.[98] The lamp irons at the veranda end were removed from the pillars to be replaced by a single iron on the buffer plank, while those at the other end were moved to the sides

of the pillars and a third lamp iron was added on the buffer plank.[99]

Minor alterations were made by the Great Western who fitted sanding pipes. A bevelled rain strip was added above the upper surface of the side rail to prevent the accumulation of water. In later years a piece of roofing material was extended over the sliding door to prevent rainwater running between the door and body side.[100] Both brake vans were acquired by the preservation company.

No. 2 as GWR No. 8759 at Welshpool in 1951 still carrying the Great Western livery of 1937–1947.
PHOTOMATIC

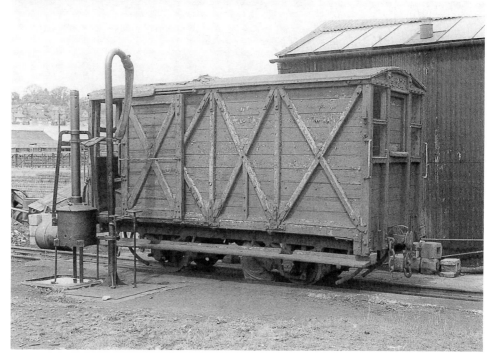

One of the brake vans receiving attention at the pit outside the engine shed. The 'G' and 'W' carried between 1923 and 1936 were beginning to emerge from underneath the flaking paintwork, but the lettering and running number that were once carried on the door had disappeared completely Much of the chimney had rotted away.
R.W. KIDNER

Covered van No. 4 at Wishaw before dispatch to Welshpool.
R.Y. PICKERING

COVERED VANS

The covered vans were similar to the Cambrian Railways' six ton covered vans. They differed from the standard gauge vans in having external sliding doors, sides that were braced with vertical pillars and ends that had oblique pillars.[103] Relatively few modifications were made to them over the years. When in Great Western ownership, the vans received the same modifications to the side rail and the roof that were made to

the brake vans. The linkage between the brake lever and shoe was modified to the form seen on the Swindon-built cattle wagons. No. 100665 had a wagon label clip that was carried on the fourth and fifth rails of one side.[104] After the railway closed, Nos. 4 and 6 were acquired by the preservation company.

COVERED VANS

SUMMARY DATA[104]

Builder		R.Y. Pickering & Co.	Height	rail to roof	9 ft 0 in
Year built		1902		floor to roof	6 ft 2⅞ in
Number built		4		floor to cantrail	5 ft 4½ in
Price per van		£65 0s 0d	Springs		2 ft 6 in
Length	over buffers	16 ft 0 in	Wheel diameter		1 ft 11 in
	over headstocks	14 ft 0 in	Load		4 tons
	internal	13 ft 10¾ in	Body		Wood
	wheelbase	7 ft 0 in	Underframe		Wood
Width	overall	6 ft 6 in	Axleboxes		Oil
	over cornices	6 ft 1½ in	Buffers		Centre
	over headstocks	5 ft 10 in	Drawgear		Drop catch
	internal	5 ft 4 in	Brake		Single

SUMMARY HISTORIES[105]

W&LLR N°	GWR N°	DELIVERED	TARE	RENUMBERED	CONDEMNED
3	100663	24 Nov 1902	2-10-0	12 Sep 1923	6 Oct 1956
4	100664	24 Nov 1902	2-10-0	23 Sep 1923	12 Mar 1960
5	100665	19 Nov 1902	2-10-0	Jun 1923	12 Mar 1960
6	100666	19 Nov 1902	2-10-0	23 Sep 1923	12 Mar 1960

Covered van No. 100665 carrying the Great Western livery of 1937–1947.

Van No. W100666 in British Railways livery. 8th September 1951.
F. W. SHUTTLEWORTH

F. A. WYCHERLEY

General Arrangement of Covered Goods Van for Welshpool & Llanfair Rly. Co.

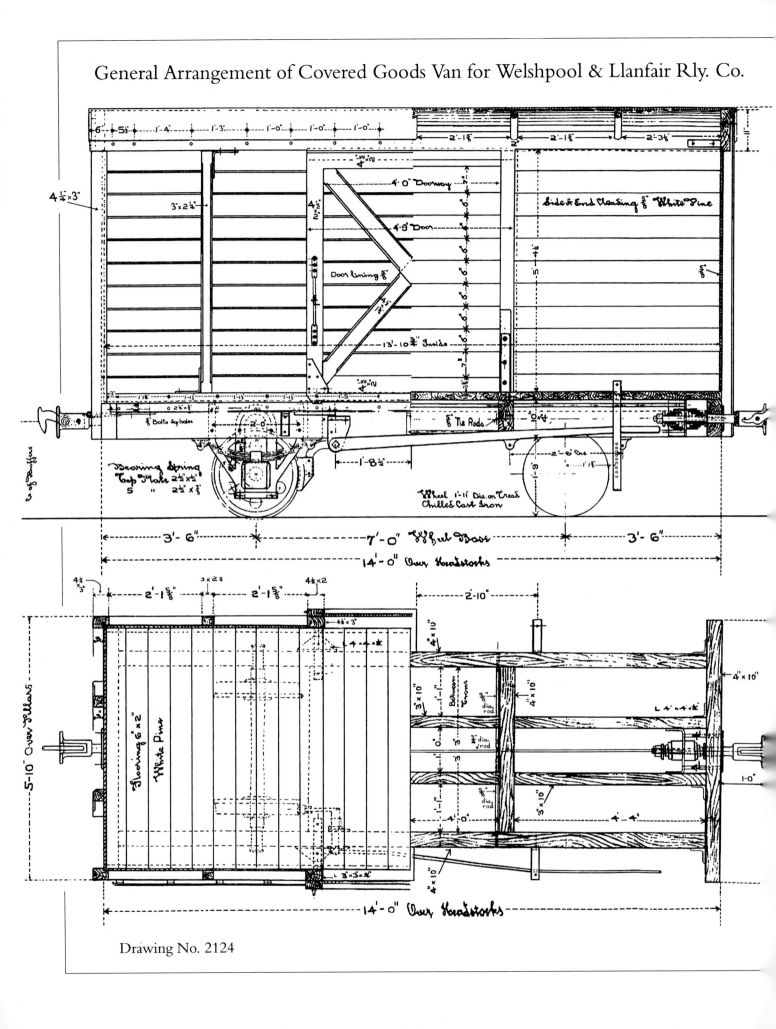

Drawing No. 2124

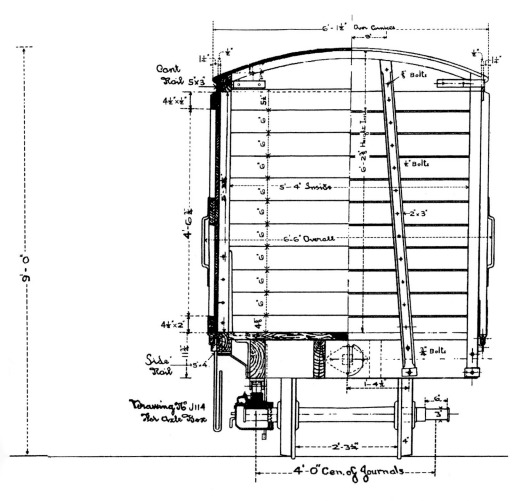

Original Drawing by R. Y. Pickering & Co. Ltd.
This version from BR (WR) Swindon Drawing Office.
Electronically cleaned and restored by Peter Ellis.

F. A. WYCHERLEY

CATTLE WAGONS

The cattle wagons were the last items of rolling stock to be delivered to the railway before it opened and were fitted with side chains when received from the makers.[107] When built, the lower five rails were separated by a 2in gap but in Great Western ownership they were replaced by seven rails set next to each other. Rectangular slots were made between the first three rails, while the seventh rail was much narrower than the others. The linkage between the brake lever and shoe was altered to the form found on the Great Western cattle wagons.[108] Despite Mr Jones' reservations about the carrying capacity of narrow gauge cattle wagons, they were able to carry a maximum of seven cows or thirty-two sheep.[109] Both Pickering-built cattle wagons were scrapped.

No. 8 as supplied by Messrs R. Y. Pickering. The cattle wagons were fitted with side chains before they left the builders premises.
R.Y. PICKERING

CATTLE WAGONS

SUMMARY DATA[109]

Builder	R.Y. Pickering & Co.	Height	rail to roof	9 ft 0 in
Year built	1902		floor to roof	6 ft 2⅜ in
Number built	2		floor to cantrail	5 ft 4½ in
Price per wagon	£52 0s 0d	Springs		2 ft 6 in
Length over buffers	16 ft 0 in	Wheel diameter		1 ft 11 in
over headstocks	14 ft 0 in	Load		4 tons
internal	13 ft 10 in	Body		Wood
wheelbase	7 ft 0 in	Underframe		Wood
Width overall	6 ft 1½ in	Axleboxes		Oil
over cornices	6 ft 1½ in	Buffers		Centre
over headstocks	5 ft 10 in	Drawgear		Drop catch
internal	5 ft 4 in	Brake		Single

SUMMARY HISTORIES[110]

W&LLR No	GWR No	Delivered	Tare	Renumbered	Condemned
7	13623	19 Feb 1903	2-12-2	23 Feb 1924	3 Nov 1956
8	13626	19 Feb 1903	2-12-2	8 Feb 1924	5 Oct 1956

In February 1924 No. 8 became No. 13626 in Great Western stock and received the livery shown here.   J.P. RICHARDS

Cattle wagon W13623, once W&L No. 7, seen at Llanfair in 1951 in the company of a sheep wagon with six rails.   PHOTOMATIC

General Arrangement of Cattle Wagon for Welshpool & Llanfair Light Rly. Co.

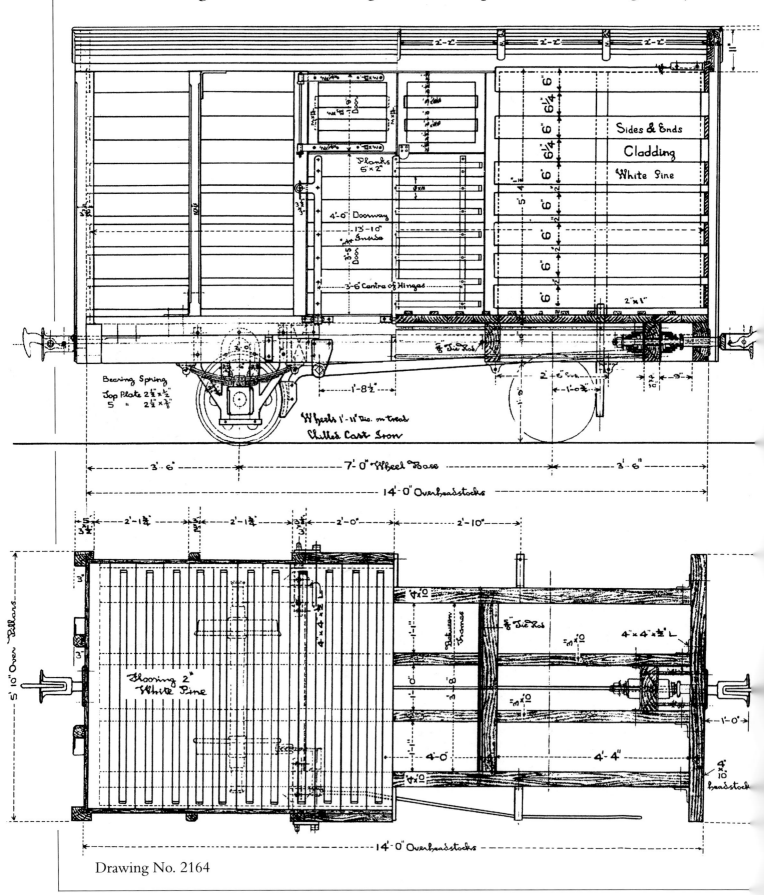

Drawing No. 2164

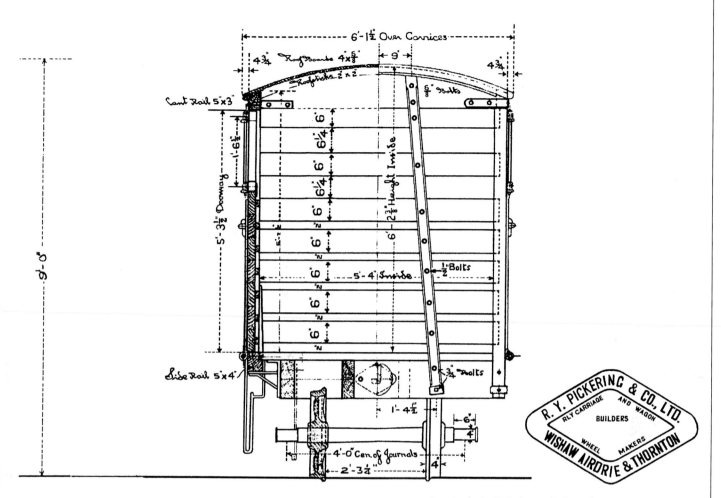

Drawing by R. Y. Pickering & Co. Ltd.
Electronically cleaned and restored by Peter Ellis.

Pickering cattle wagon No. 13623, once Welshpool & Llanfair No. 7, at Welshpool in October 1955. Note the revised spacing and number of rails.

MIKE LLOYD

OPEN GOODS WAGONS

In 1901 the Cambrian Railways had a large fleet of two-plank dropside wagons that were rated to carry up to eight tons. Mr Jones may have used these as the basis for the design of the forty open goods wagons that were ordered for the light railway. The narrow gauge wagons also had dropsides but had four rails, the upper rail being wider than the other three. There were three straps on each side, those at each end being shaped like an inverted J. The ends were reinforced with an L section stanchion that was shaped into an inverted V.[112] Mr Jones intended that the wagons should have had a central dumb buffer but at Messrs Pickering's insistence they were fitted with automatic couplings.[113] When the wagons were built, their axleboxes were not sprung, so in February 1904 plans were drawn at Oswestry to fit them with six leaf springs retrospectively.[114]

In about 1906 two open wagons were converted into flat wagons, for use as match trucks when round timber was being carried, by removing their sides and ends.[115] In 1911 six wagons were converted to carry livestock. The subsequent history of these vehicles is dealt with under the heading *Sheep wagons*.

The Great Western replaced the original sides and ends with bodies that had four rails of equal width and fitted two door bangers on each side. Five straps, three extending from the hinges and two aligned with the door bangers, replaced the three fitted by Pickering. On the ends, two T section stanchions replaced the inverted V that was fitted when the wagons were built.[116] After the railway closed, Nos. 11, 14, 34, 42 and 46 were acquired by the preservation company.

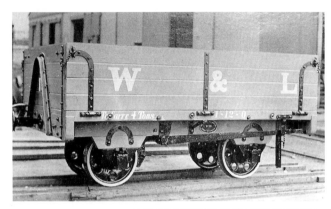

RALPH CARTWRIGHT COLLECTION

Pickering-built wagons in the first Great Western livery to be carried by the light railway's open wagons. No. 71680 was once Welshpool and Llanfair No. 31.

J.P. RICHARDS

OPEN WAGONS

SUMMARY DATA[116]

Builder		R.Y. Pickering & Co.	Height	rail to top of side	4 ft 9¾ in
Year built		1902		internal	2 ft 1in
Number built		40	Springs		2 ft 6 in
Price per wagon		£25 10s 0d	Wheel diameter		1 ft 11 in
Length	over buffers	12 ft 0 in	Load		4 tons
	over headstocks	10 ft 0 in	Body		Wood
	internal	9 ft 8 in	Underframe		Wood
	wheelbase	5 ft 6 in	Axleboxes		Oil
Width	overall	6 ft 4 in	Buffers		Centre
	over headstocks	6 ft 4 in	Drawgear		Drop catch
	internal	6 ft 0 in	Brake		Single

SUMMARY HISTORIES[117]

W&LLR N°	GWR N°	DELIVERED	TARE	RENUMBERED	CONDEMNED
9	34143	10 Oct 1902	1-19-0	22 Sep 1923	12 Mar 1960
10	34144	10 Oct 1902	1-14-2	23 Aug 1924	12 Mar 1960
11	34154	10 Oct 1902	1-16-0	9 Feb 1924	12 Mar 1960
12	34156	10 Oct 1902	1-19-1	8 Mar 1924	12 Mar 1960
13	34157	10 Oct 1902	2-0-0	20 Sep 1924	12 Mar 1960
14	34159	10 Oct 1902	1-15-0	22 Sep 1923	12 Mar 1960
15	34161	10 Oct 1902	1-17-0	22 Nov 1924	12 Mar 1960
16	34163	10 Oct 1902	1-16-0	10 May 1924	12 Mar 1960
17	34168	10 Oct 1902	1-14-2	22 Dec 1923	12 Mar 1960
18	34170	10 Oct 1902	1-17-3	05 Apl 1924	12 Mar 1960
19	34172	10 Oct 1902	1-16-0	22 Sep 1923	12 Mar 1960
20	34176	28 Oct 1902	1-16-0	05 Apl 1924	12 Mar 1960
21	71550	28 Oct 1902	1-17-0	23 Aug 1924	12 Mar 1960
22	71551	28 Oct 1902	1-17-0	22 Sep1923	12 Mar 1960
23	71584	28 Oct 1902	1-19-0	22 Nov1924	12 Mar 1960
24	71588	28 Oct 1902	1-15-1	29 Sep 1923	12 Mar 1960
25	71594	28 Oct 1902	1-16-0	9 Feb 1924	12 Mar 1960
26	71610	28 Oct 1902	1-17-2	9 Aug 1924	12 Mar 1960
27	71619	28 Oct 1902	1-14-2	30 Jun 1923	12 Mar 1960
28	71635	28 Oct 1902	2-0-0	18 Nov 1924	12 Mar 1960
29	71648	28 Oct 1902	1-14-0	21 Aug 1923	12 Mar 1960
30	71668	19 Oct 1902	1-16-0	8 Mar 1924	12 Mar 1960
31	71680	19 Oct 1902	1-12-0	1 Aug 1923	12 Mar 1960
32	71687	19 Oct 1902	2-2-0	21 Jun 1924	12 Mar 1960
33	71690	19 Oct 1902	1-15-0	12 Sep 1923	29 May 1954
34	71692	19 Oct 1902	1-18-0	20 Sep 1924	12 Mar 1960
35	71697	19 Oct 1902	1-16-0	18 Oct 1924	12 Mar 1960
36	71699	19 Oct 1902	1-16-0	22 Dec 1923	12 Mar 1960
37	71701	19 Oct 1902	1-15-1	20 Sep 1924	12 Mar 1960
38	71702	19 Oct 1902	1-16-0	30 Jun 1923	12 Mar 1960
39	71704	19 Oct 1902	1-17-1	08 Mar 1924	21 May 1955
40	71728	10 Nov 1902	1-17-0	17 Nov 1923	12 Mar 1960
41	71736	10 Nov 1902	1-17-0	05 Apl 1924	12 Mar 1960
42	71738	10 Nov 1902	1-15-2	10 May 1924	12 Mar 1960
43	71743	10 Nov 1902	1-16-1	10 May 1924	12 Mar 1960
44	71758	10 Nov 1902	1-18-0	17 Nov 1923	12 Mar 1960
45	71776	24 Nov 1902	1-16-0	23 Aug 1924	12 Mar 1960
46	71794	24 Nov 1902	1-14-0	30 Jun 1923	12 Mar 1960
47	71818	2 Dec 1902	2-1-1	02 Feb 1924	12 Mar 1960
48	71821	24 Nov 1902	1-15-0	18 Oct 1924	21 May 1955

Arrangement of Four-Ton Open Wagon for Welshpool & Llanfair Light Rly. Co.

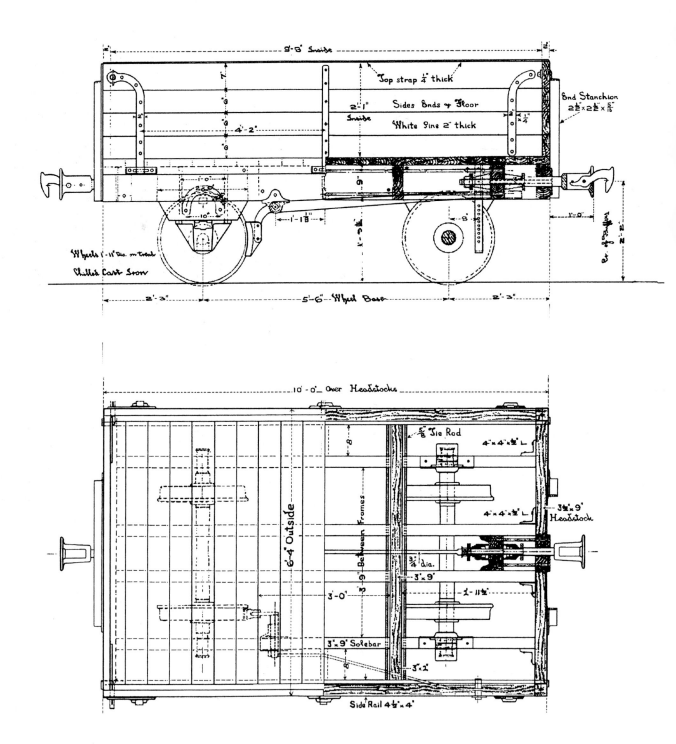

Original drawing by Cambrian Railways, Oswestry.
Electronically cleaned and restored by Peter Ellis.

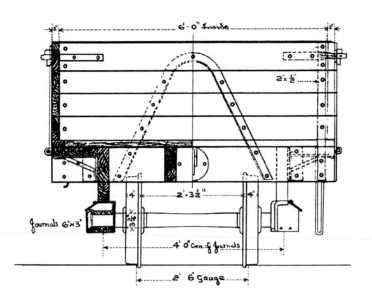

6'-0" Inside

2" x ½"

2'-3¼"

4" 4"

Journals 6"x3"

4' 0" Cen. ℄ Journals

2' 6" Gauge

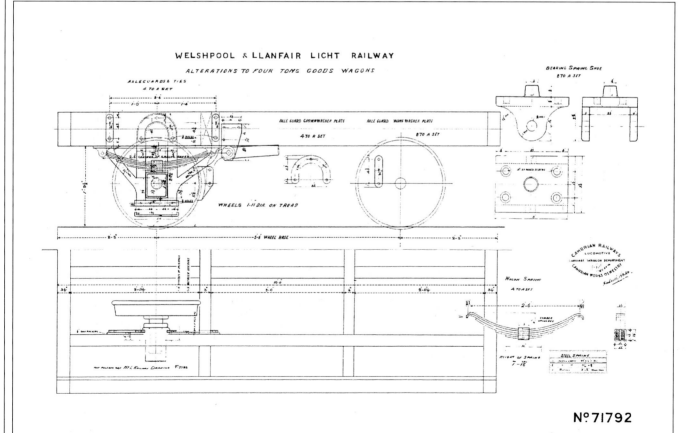

WELSHPOOL & LLANFAIR LICHT RAILWAY

ALTERATIONS TO FOUR TONS GOODS WAGONS

AXLEGUARDS & TIES
4 TO A SET

BEARING SPRING SHOE
8 TO A SET

AXLE GUARD CROWN WASHER PLATE   AXLE GUARD WING WASHER PLATE

4 TO A SET   8 TO A SET

WHEELS 1·11 DIA. ON TREAD

5-6 WHEEL BASE

CAMBRIAN RAILWAYS
LOCOMOTIVE
CARRIAGE WAGON DEPARTMENT
CAMBRIAN WORKS OSWESTRY

WAGON SPRING
4 TO A SET

2-6

STEEL SPRING

HEIGHT OF SPRING
7·18

No 71792

TIMBER WAGONS

Shortly after the railway opened, Mr Denniss asked the Llanfair Directors to provide ten or twelve timber trucks so that long timber could be carried over the line.[119] They were designed by Mr Jones who asked for an additional payment for the work. The Llanfair Directors considered that the design of timber trucks was covered by the agreement made with Mr Jones in 1901 so they refused to pay him.[120] In September 1903 Messrs Pickering quoted a price of £44 for each wagon, this being considerably more than the £25 estimated by Mr Jones. When Mr Addie made enquiries into the apparent discrepancy, Messrs Pickering's representatives explained that while they could produce a timber wagon without bearing springs or centre couplings for about £25, they believed that such wagons would be dangerous. The company offered to send two wagons on approval at a cash price of £44 per wagon or a credit price of £52 4s 2d per wagon to be settled by the payment of five annual instalments of £10 8s 10d. The Works Committee decided to place an order for ten wagons, subject to approval by the Cambrian, and asked Messrs Pickering to send three wagons on approval before completing the order.[121] In March 1904 six wagons were delivered to Welshpool[122] which were paid for in ten instalments made over five years.[123] The order for the four remaining trucks eventually lapsed.[124] In service the bolster could be removed so that the wagon could be used as a match truck.[125]

In the interwar period, timber traffic was increasingly lost to road haulage, particularly where the distance between a plantation and sawmill was relatively short. By the end of the 1939–1945 war, the timber trucks saw very little use, so in March 1946 the Traffic Committee authorised their conversion to open wagons.[126] By 5th September they had been rebuilt as dropsided wagons at Oswestry Works. Like the open wagons of 1902, they had four rails but the sides were only given three lengths of strapping that extended from the hinges. Circular door banger plates were carried on the third rail.[127] Two straight T-section stanchions were provided at the ends. The rebuilt wagons were shown on diagram O48. None of these wagons were preserved.

No. 49 newly built at Wishaw.   R.Y. PICKERING

Pickering-built timber wagons painted in the Great Western livery of 1923–1936 awaiting traffic. The three wagons nearest to the camera were numbers 8516, 8514 and 8523 once numbers 51, 49 and 54 respectively in Welshpool and Llanfair stock.

TIMBER WAGONS

SUMMARY DATA[127]

Builder	R.Y. Pickering & Co.	Height	rail to top of pins	5 ft 4¼ in
Year built	1904		floor to top of pins	2 ft 7¾ in
Number built	6	Springs		2 ft 6 in
Price per wagon	£44 0s 0d	Wheel diameter		1ft 11in
Length over buffers	10 ft 6 in	Load		4 tons
over headstocks	8 ft 6 in	Body		Wood
internal	8 ft 4 ins	Underframe		Wood
wheelbase	4 ft 0 in	Axleboxes		Oil
Width headstocks	6 ft 4 in	Buffers		Centre
over bolster	6 ft 0 in	Drawgear		Drop catch
over pins	5 ft 6 in	Brake		Single

SUMMARY HISTORIES[128]

W&LLR Nº	GWR Nº	DELIVERED	TARE	RENUMBERED	REBUILT	CONDEMNED
49	8514	7 Mar 1904	1-14-2	9 Aug 1924	5 Sep 1946	12 Mar 1960
50	8515	7 Mar 1904	1-14-0	9 Aug 1924	5 Sep 1946	12 Mar 1960
51	8516	7 Mar 1904	1-14-1	9 Aug 1924	5 Sep 1946	12 Mar 1960
52	8518	7 Mar 1904	1-14-2	21 Aug 1923	5 Sep 1946	12 Mar 1960
53	8521	7 Mar 1904	1-14-2	21 Jun 1924	5 Sep 1946	12 Mar 1960
54	8523	7 Mar 1904	1-14-1	9 Aug 1924	5 Sep 1946	12 Mar 1960

Proposed Arrangement of Timber Truck for Welshpool & Llanfair Light Rly. Co.

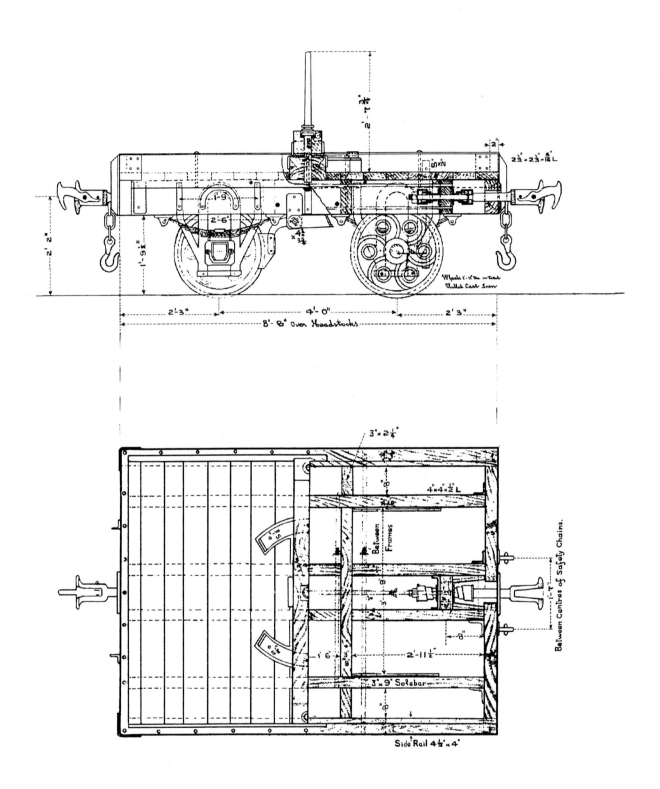

Drawing No. 2697

Drawing by R. Y. Pickering & Co. Ltd.
Electronically cleaned and restored by Peter Ellis.

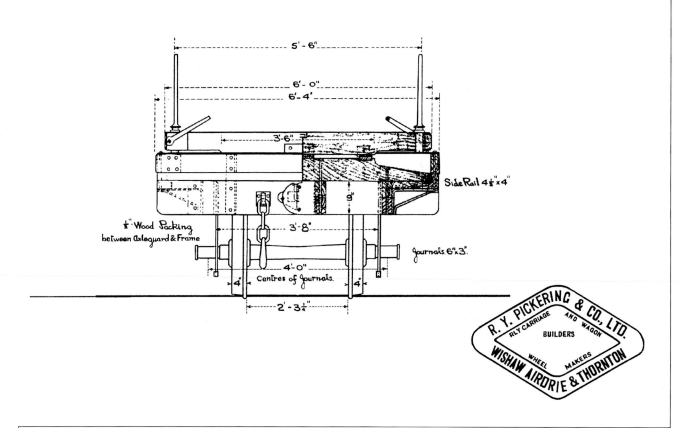

5' - 6"
6' - 0"
6'- 4'
3'- 6"
Side Rail 4½" x 4"
9"
½" Wood Packing
between Axleguard & Frame
3'- 8"
Journals. 6" x 3".
4'- 0"
Centres of Journals.
4"
4"
2'- 3¼"

R. Y. PICKERING & CO., LTD.
RLY. CARRIAGE AND WAGON
BUILDERS
WISHAW AIRDRIE & THORNTON
WHEEL MAKERS

Welshpool and Llanfair timber wagon No. 52 was rebuilt as a dropsided wagon No. 8518 in September 1946. It was recorded in a train at Welshpool on 14th September 1956 still in Great Western livery.

R.M. CASSERLEY

'2961' class 0–6–0 No. 2362 outside Oswestry works with a train carrying open wagons rebuilt from Welshpool & Lanfair timber trucks.   MILEPOST 92½

Swindon-built timber truck No. 17350 was rebuilt as an open wagon at Oswestry Works in September 1946. Here it had been loaded onto a container wagon to transport it back to Welshpool.
MILEPOST 92½

Sheep wagon No. 71701, once open goods wagon No.37, in the first Great Western livery carried by the railway's goods stock.   J.P. RICHARDS

SHEEP WAGONS

In 1911 Mr Charles Conacher, the Cambrian Traffic Manager, met several sheep dealers to find out why so many animals were driven to market.[130] It appeared that the line had insufficient wagons to handle the traffic, so Mr Conacher suggested that six open wagons should be converted to carry livestock.[131] Mr W.H. Gough, the Cambrian Goods Manager, met the Llanfair Railway's Works Committee on 20th February when he submitted a sketch showing what was proposed. The work was approved by the Committee at an estimated cost of £18 10s 10d.[132] The numbers of the wagons so treated were not recorded in the Cambrian Railways rolling stock register nor were they identified in the Great Western wagon registers. A photograph of Llanfair station in June 1925 shows a distant view of one of these wagons which has five rails and is similar in appearance to those in existence when the railway closed.[133]

In March 1930 six wagons were made flat and fitted with ripple sides to carry cattle, while in September 1937 a seventh open wagon was also converted.[134] The sides and ends of these open wagons were removed, battens were placed across the floors, and sockets were mounted on the side rails and buffer planks. The framework forming the sides and ends was then slotted into the sockets to create a wagon that could carry cattle or other livestock. At a later date a door that dropped to form a ramp giving access to the wagon was fitted.[135] Corrugated iron sheets were placed inside the sides, creating the ripple effect, but these were soon dispensed with. The sides and ends could be removed when required to create a flat wagon.

GWR SHEEP WAGON CONVERSIONS[136]

W&LLR No.	GWR No	Converted
9	34143	4 Mar 1930
16	34163	4 Mar 1930
19	34172	4 Mar 1930
23	71584	4 Mar 1930
27	71619	4 Mar 1930
32	71687	4 Mar 1930
36	71699	24 Sep 1937

When J.P. Richards visited the line, he photographed sheep wagon No. 71701 carrying the Great Western goods stock livery of 1923–1936, although its conversion from an open wagon is not recorded in the wagon registers.

Lewis Cozens found eight sheep wagons on the branch in April 1951 but only three of them carried the same numbers as the wagons recorded as being converted by the Great Western. The company's wagon registers do not show that more wagons were converted into sheep wagons or that any sheep wagons were rebuilt as open wagons.

SHEEP WAGONS AS AT 1st APRIL 1951.[137]

W&LLR No.	GWR No	Rails
9	34143	6
10	34144	5
16	34163	5
17	34168	5
19	34172	6
24	71588	5
36	71699	5
37	71701	5

Sheep wagon No. 71699 at Welshpool on 22nd November 1947. This example has five rails.
JOHN ALSOP COLLECTION

A sheep wagon with six rails painted in the Great Western livery applied from 1937. Entry to the wagon was provided by the ramp at the right-hand side.
JOHN ALSOP COLLECTION

Two sheep wagons with five rails at Welshpool.

The cattle wagons built by the Great Western for the Vale of Rheidol branch are seen here by the Llanfair Railway warehouse at Welshpool. 3rd November 1956.

F. W. SHUTTLEWORTH

THE GREAT WESTERN CATTLE WAGONS

Two cattle wagons were ordered on Lot 914 in June 1923 for use on the 1ft 11½in gauge Vale of Rheidol branch.[138] The design was based on the Pickering-built cattle wagons of 1903, but the new wagons had steel underframes, steel frames and L-section stanchions made of iron. They had brake levers on each side of the wagons that acted independently of each other. The order was completed on 2nd December 1923[139] and the wagons were shown on diagram W9.[140]

Although sheep had been carried in open wagons before the grouping, this traffic was soon lost to road transport and the cattle wagons saw very little use on the Vale of Rheidol.[141] Both wagons were converted to 2ft 6in gauge under order 3529 of 1937 and were set to work on the Welshpool and Llanfair branch.[142] Both survived the closure of the line, No. 38088 being acquired by the preservation company, whilst No. 38089 went to the Festiniog Railway.

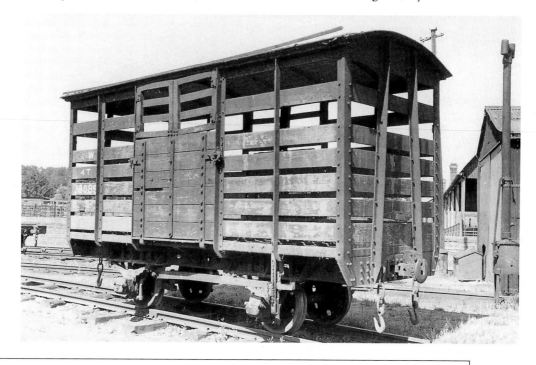

Cattle wagon W38089 at Welshpool in 1949.
D. M. LEE

CATTLE WAGONS

SUMMARY DATA[142]

Builder		Great Western Railway.	Height	rail to roof	8 ft 7 in
Year built		1923		floor to roof	6 ft 1in
Lot		914		floor to cantrail	5 ft 4⅛ in
Number built		2	Springs		2 ft 6 in
Diagram		W9	Wheel diameter		1 ft 6 in
Length	over buffers	16 ft 8⅛ in	Load		4 tons
	over headstocks	14 ft 0 in	Body		Wood
	internal	13 ft 10 in	Underframe		Wood
	wheelbase	7 ft 0 in	Axleboxes		Oil
Width	overall	6 ft 0 in	Buffers		Centre
	over headstocks	5 ft 6 in	Drawgear		Drop catch
	internal	5 ft 4 in	Brake		Either side

SUMMARY HISTORIES[143]

GWR No.	BUILT	TARE	CONDEMNED
38088	2 Dec 1923	3-2-0	12 Mar 1960
38089	2 Dec 1923	3-2-0	12 Mar 1960

Swindon-built cattle wagon W38089 at Llanfair in 1951.   PHOTOMATIC

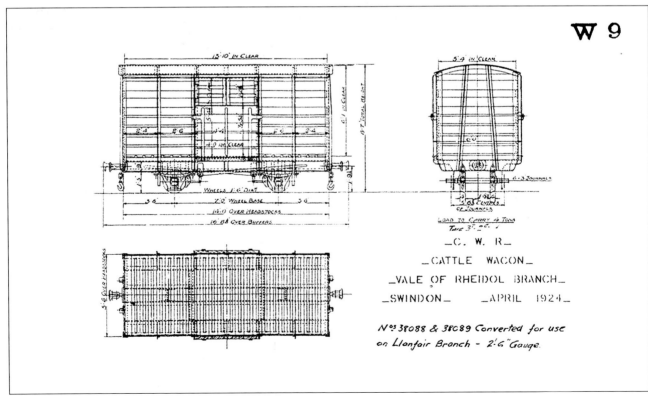

THE GREAT WESTERN TIMBER TRUCKS

Six single timber trucks were ordered on Lot 928 in December 1923.[145] As with the Swindon-built cattle wagons, they were an updated version of the Pickering design having steel under-frames and brake levers on either side of the wagon. The order was completed on 23rd August 1924[146] and the wagons were shown on diagram J6.[147]

In 1946 four of the timber trucks were taken to Oswestry works where they were rebuilt as dropside wagons. The upper three rails were the same width but the lowest one was about half the width of the others.[148] Nos. 17349 and 17353 were never rebuilt and from September 1946 they were the only timber trucks on the railway.[149] None of these wagons were preserved.

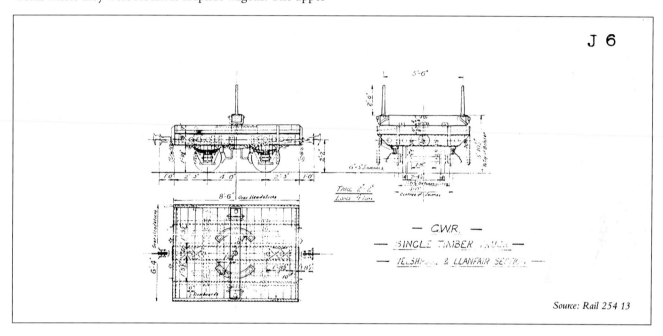

J 6

— G.W.R. —

— SINGLE TIMBER TRUCK —

— WELSHPOOL & LLANFAIR SECTION —

Source: Rail 254 13

Timber truck No. 17349 after completion at Swindon.   GREAT WESTERN RAILWAY, Cty. DAVID HYDE

No. 17350 was built as a timber truck at Swindon in June 1924 and converted to a dropside wagon in September 1946. This 1948 view enables a comparison to be made with the open wagons built by Messrs Pickering. No. 71776 was built in 1902 as W&L No. 45. Its sides and ends were renewed by the Great Western in the 1920s when the straps, stanchions and door bangers seen here were fitted. Here both wagons were carrying the Great Western livery of 1937–1947.
                                                                                                                H.C. CASSERLEY

TIMBER TRUCKS

Summary data[149]

Builder		Great Western Railway	Height	floor to top of pins	2 ft 7¾ in
Year built		1924		bolster to top of pins	2 ft 0 in
Lot		928	Springs		2 ft 6 in
Number built		6	Wheel diameter		1 ft 11 in
Diagram		J6	Load		4 tons
Length	over buffers	10 ft 6 in	Body		Wood
	over headstocks	8 ft 6 in	Underframe		Steel
	wheelbase	4 ft 0 in	Axleboxes		Oil
Width	over headstocks	6 ft 4 in	Buffers		Centre
	over bolster pins	5 ft 6 in	Drawgear		Drop catch
Height	rail to top of pins	5 ft 10½ in	Brake		Either side

Summary histories[150]

GWR No.	Built	Tare	Rebuilt	Condemned
17349	25 Jun 1924	2-2-0	-	12 Mar 1960
17350	25 Jun 1924	2-2-0	5 Sep 1946	12 Mar 1960
17351	23 Aug 1924	2-2-0	5 Sep 1946	12 Mar 1960
17352	23 Aug 1924	2-2-0	5 Sep 1946	12 Mar 1960
17353	23 Aug 1924	2-3-0	-	12 Mar 1960
17354	23 Aug 1924	2-3-0	5 Sep 1946	12 Mar 1960

J.LL. PEATE AND SONS' OPEN WAGONS

In August 1903 R.Y. Pickering & Co. designed an open wagon for Messrs J. Ll. Peate and Sons, coal and lime merchants of Llanfair. Although the principal dimensions were the same as the Llanfair Railway's open goods wagons, Peate's wagons had fixed sides with three feet wide doors set in their centres. The wagons were fitted with Wood's patent axleboxes and leaf springs. The straps on the body sides were straight.

Peate's five narrow gauge wagons were numbered 2, 5, 6, 7 and 8 and painted maroon with white lettering. Their ironwork may have been black. They were registered with the Cambrian and fitted with that company's registration plates. The wagons were scrapped at Llanfair in 1935.[193/194/195/196]

Wagon No. 2 at the makers in 1903.

R. Y. PICKERING

J. LL. PEATE & SONS' OPEN WAGONS

SUMMARY DATA[196]

Builder	R.Y. Pickering & Co.	Height	rail to top of side	4 ft 9¾ in
Year built	1903		internal	2 ft 1in
Number built	5	Springs		2 ft 6 in
Price per wagon	Not known	Wheel diameter		1 ft 11 in
Length	over buffers	12 ft 0 in	Load	4 tons
	over headstocks	10 ft 0 in	Body	Wood
	internal	9 ft 8 in	Underframe	Wood
	wheelbase	5 ft 6 in	Axleboxes	Not known
Width	overall	6 ft 4 in	Buffers	Centre
	over headstocks	6 ft 4 in	Drawgear	Drop catch
	internal	6 ft 0 in	Brake	Single

General Arrangement of a Wagon for J. Lloyd Peate & Son, Llanfair.

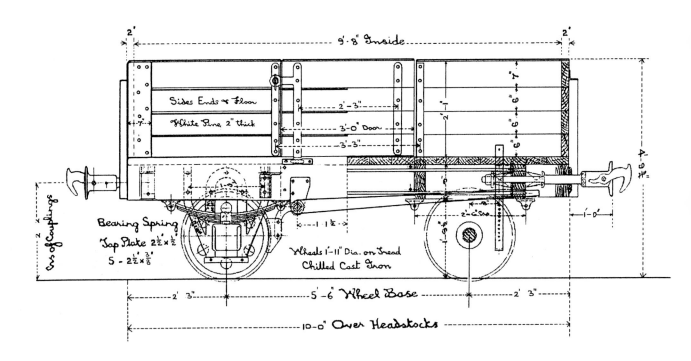

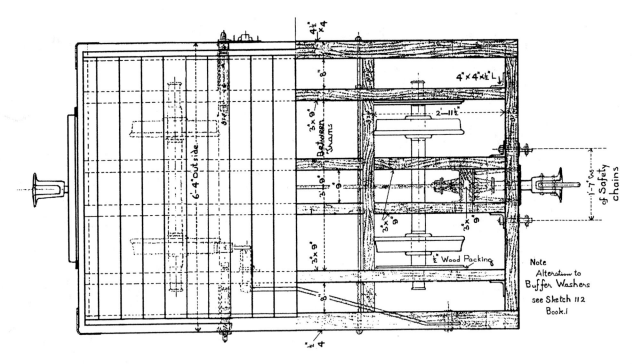

Drawing No. 2613

Drawing by R. Y. Pickering & Co. Ltd.
Electronically cleaned and restored by Peter Ellis.

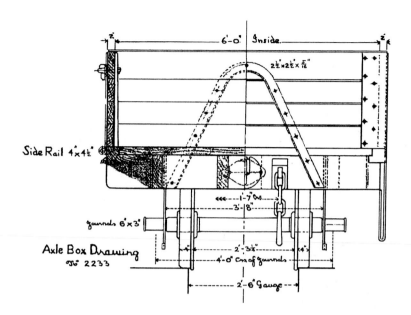

6'-0" Inside.

$2\frac{1}{2}"\times2\frac{1}{2}"\times\frac{5}{16}"$

Side Rail 4"x4½"

Journals 6"x3"

Axle Box Drawing
N° 2233

1-7"Crs
3'-8"
2'-3¾"
4"
4'-0" Crs of Journals
2'-6" Gauge

R. Y. PICKERING & CO., LTD.
RLY CARRIAGE AND WAGON
BUILDERS
WHEEL MAKERS
WISHAW AIRDRIE & THORNTON

One of the Pickering open wagons modified by the Great Western and seen here on the tranship siding.

GOODS STOCK LIVERIES

1903–1922

Freight stock was painted light grey with black ironwork.[152] When stock was modified or repainted, the strapping on the solebars was painted grey. When the covered vans, cattle wagons and brake vans were repainted, it is probable that the outer surface of their external wooden frames were painted black and that this practice continued until the Great War.[153] A photograph of Llanfair circa 1915 shows two covered wagons with black frames, while the other two have grey frames.[154] When delivered from Messrs Pickering, the brake vans had red ends[155] but by the Grouping the ends were painted grey.[156] The roofs of covered vans, cattle wagons and brake vans were painted white but soon assumed a grey appearance in service.

The characters W&L were applied to the sides of goods stock. At first, letters 8in tall with serifs were used on all stock except for covered vans and brake vans, to which 11in letters were applied. Brake vans and covered vans were lettered on the upper body sides. The company initials were painted on the doors of cattle wagons.[157] When goods vehicles were repainted, 8in letters became standard except on flat wagons which had no lettering.[158]

When new, the running numbers of brake vans, covered vans and cattle wagons were painted on the sides but when they were repainted, the running number was carried on the ends.[159] Open wagons and timber trucks carried the running number in the centre of the ends, while timber trucks also had the number painted on their bolster. On vans, cattle wagons and the bolsters of timber trucks, the running number was prefixed NO., the N having serifs on all but cattle wagons. On vans the numbers were 6in high while those on cattle wagons were 4in tall.[160]

With the exception of brake vans, the maximum load that could be carried was painted on the left-hand side of the bottom rail, taking the form *To Carry 4 Tons*. The tare weight expressed in tons, hundredweights and quarters was carried on the right-hand side. Brake vans had the tare weight painted centrally on the lower horizontal member of the outside frame.[161] When repainted, the style was reversed to follow Cambrian practice, with the tare weight on the left and LOAD 4 TONS painted on the right. All lettering was executed in block capitals.[162]

Elliptical cast-iron plates with the words WELSHPOOL & LLANFAIR above the number, and LIGHT RAILWAY below it were attached to the solebars of all goods stock except timber trucks which carried their number plates on the end of the side rails. The numbers on the plates were prefixed 'No.'. Builder's plates were carried on the solebars of the covered vans, cattle wagons, and brake vans. Number and maker's plates were painted black with white letters, numerals and edges.[163]

1923–1936

Wagons and vans were painted Great Western wagon stock grey with white letters and figures.[164] On the open wagons the letters G and W were placed on the second and third rails, towards the end of the vehicle between the hinge and door banger straps.[165/166] On covered vans the letters were carried on the upper body sides,[167] while on the cattle wagons they were placed on either side of the door pillars on the fifth and sixth rails.[168] Guards vans were lettered on the middle and end panels above the centre of the cross bracing.[169] On timber trucks the letters were squeezed onto the sides.[170] On the sheep trucks the G and W were painted on the side rail on either side on the central socket in very small letters.[171] On all goods stock except the sheep wagons the letters were about 8in tall.

Running numbers were usually painted on the lower left-hand side of goods stock in figures that were 5in tall.[172] On cattle wagons the numbers were placed on the same rail as the company initials,[173] while on sheep wagons they were painted on the side rail as well as the lowest rail of the detachable sides and ends.[174] On the brake vans the running number was painted on the bottom of the sliding door.[175] Tare weights were painted on the lower right-hand side of most goods stock and took the form *Tare 1–16–2* in characters that were 2½in tall with 3½in capital letters. The capacity of the wagon was placed to the left of the word 'tare', taking the form *4 Tons*.[176] On cattle wagons the capacity and tare was carried at the same level as the running number.[177] The capacity was omitted from brake vans.[178]

1937–1947

Goods rolling stock continued to be painted grey with white lettering. One authority states that the goods stock was painted bauxite brown in the late 1930s[179] but the accounts of other visitors to the line do not confirm this assertion. A colour photograph of withdrawn stock at Welshpool in September 1959 shows two covered vans with peeling grey paintwork beneath which a coat of brown paint can be seen.[180]

The letters GW were usually painted on the lower left-hand side of the body.[181] The maximum load that the wagon could carry was painted on the rail below the one carrying the letters in the form '4T', while the running number was usually placed on the lowest rail.[182] Again vehicles with roofs were an exception; on cattle wagons the lettering, capacity and running numbers were painted on the upper rails, while this information was painted on the lower sides of the sliding doors of covered and guards vans,[183] although the capacity was not recorded on the brake vans.[184] The tare weight was carried on the lower right-hand side taking the form '1–16'. On cattle wagons the tare weight was probably painted on the upper rails. Lettering and running numbers were painted in characters that were 5in tall but from about 1942 they were reduced to 3in. The carrying capacity was painted in characters 2in tall.[185]

Many wagons and the brake vans continued to carry Great Western livery into the early 1950s. In 1951 a visitor to the line found that with three exceptions, all the open wagons were painted grey with Great Western lettering.[186] Some wagons still carried the last Great Western livery when the line closed.[187]

1948–1956

In 1951 the four covered vans and three open wagons were reported as having been painted light grey and received numbers with a W prefix.[188] The tare weight was carried on the lower right-hand side and took the form '1.16'.[189] Some cattle wagons also received the W prefix.[190] The style and positioning of the running numbers and load followed latter day Great Western practice. The condition of the paintwork on some vehicles was very poor in the last years with exposed woodwork and peeling paint. The cattle and sheep wagons appear to have been particularly badly affected in this respect.[191]

The poor condition of the goods stock led to complaints about damage and delay to traffic. Wagon sheets were sent to Worcester to be redressed many times over the years and by the end they were incapable of preventing damage to goods during heavy rain.[192] Ted Lewis recalled that it was Harold Reeves' skills in repairing the goods stock that helped keep the line going. After the closure of the railway the surviving vans and wagons were concentrated in the narrow gauge yard at Welshpool from where they were sold on 12th March 1960.

No. 822 The Earl *and one of the brake vans in the narrow gauge yard at Welshpool. The brake van is seen with the large initials that were carried between 1923 and 1936. The standpipe water column was supplied by the Isca Foundry, Newport.*   H. B. TOURS

[1] Rail 1057 613 Harrison & Winnall to C.S. Denniss re rolling stock schedule and estimate 2nd October 1900

[2] Rail 1057 613 Harrison & Winnall to C.S. Denniss re rolling stock schedule and estimate 2nd October 1900

[3] Rail 1057 613 C.S. Denniss to Harrison & Winnall re estimated cost of rolling stock 1st November 1900

[4] Rail 1057 613 C.S. Denniss to Harrison & Winnall re estimated cost of rolling stock 1st November 1900

[5] Rail 1057 613 A.J. Collin to C.S. Denniss re Rolling stock and transport wagons 5th October 1900

[6] Rail 1057 613 C.S. Denniss to Harrison & Winnall re estimated cost of rolling stock 1st November 1900

[7] Rail 1057 613 H.E. Jones to C.S. Denniss re W&L rolling stock 5th November 1900

[8] Rail 1057 613 Rail 1057 Memorandum of meeting re W&L rolling stock 19th December 1900

[9] Rail 722 2 W&L Board 31st January 1901

[10] Rail 722 2 W&L Board 22nd June 1901

[11] Rail 1057 613 H.E. Jones to C.S. Denniss re Engines for the W&L 1st July 1901

[12] Rail 1057 613 Cambrian Board resolution re Number of W&L locomotives 3rd July 1901

[13] Rail 1057 613 W&L Secretary to C.S. Denniss re Third engine 27th September 1901

[14] Rail 92 70 C.S. Denniss to Cambrian Board re Third engine 2nd October 1901

[15] Rail 722 2 W&L Board re Order for locomotives 31st October 1901

[16] Rail 722 2 W&L Board re Carriage and wagons ordered 31st October 1901

[17] Rail 722 2 W&L Board 20th February 1902

[18] Rail 722 2 W&L Works Committee re progress on locomotives 21st March 1902

[19] NWMSI Beyer Peacock Engines index book Order 8868 W&L locomotives 22nd March 1902

[20] Rail 722 2 W&L Board re progress on locomotives 26th March 1902

[21] Rail 722 2 W&L Board re progress on locomotives 22nd May 1902

[22] NWMSI Beyer Peacock Engines index book Order 8868 W&L locomotives 7th May 1902

[23] Rail 722 2 W&L Board re Enquiry to W.G. Bagnall 24th April 1902

[24] Rail 722 2 W&L Board re progress on locomotives 11th July 1902

[25] Cambrian Railways Rolling stock register p.6–7

[26] Rail 722 2 W&L Works Committee 2nd September 1902

[27] Cambrian Railways Rolling stock register p.6–7

[28] Cambrian Railways Rolling stock register pp.70–72

[29] Cambrian Railways Rolling stock register pp.70–72

[30] Rail 1057 613 Rolling stock specification

[31] Rail 92 71 H.E. Jones and C.S. Denniss 11th November 1902

[32] Beyer Peacock Order 8868 Museum of Science and Industry Manchester

[33] H. Guthrie notebook v. 3 p. 61 Beyer Peacock Archive MSI Manchester

[34] Ralph Russell cited in *Llanfair Railway Journal* No. 169 p. 21

[35] Beyer Peacock General Dimensions of Engines and Tenders Order 8868 MSI Manchester

[36] Beyer Peacock Engines Index Book No.49 MSI Manchester

[37] Beyer Peacock General Dimensions of Engines and Tenders Order 7552 MSI Manchester

[38] Beyer Peacock photograph of No. 3497 W&LLR No. 2 *The Countess*

[39] Rail 92 71 H.E. Jones and C.S. Denniss 11th November 1902

[40] Rail 722 2 W&L Board 23rd October 1902

[41] Rail 92 71 H.E. Jones and C.S. Denniss 20th November 1902

[42] Rail 92 71 A.J. Collin and C.S. Denniss 29th November 1902

[43] Draft report in Beyer Peacock Archive MSI Manchester

[44] MT 6 1150 4 Board of Trade Inspector's report 6th February 1903

[45] Beyer Peacock Engines Index Book 49 MSI Manchester

[46] Rail 92 72 Cambrian Railways Special Board 6th May 1903

[47] Rail 92 72 Cambrian Railways Board 10th June 1903

[48] Rail 92 89 H.E. Jones to C.S. Denniss 3rd July 1904

[49] Rail 92 72 Cambrian Board 11th December 1903

[50] Rail 92 89 H.E. Jones to C.S. Denniss 3rd July 1914

[51] Rail 254 250/1 Engine Nos. 822 & 823 history cards

[52] Rail 254 80 GWR Engines 1922

[53] Rail 254 81 GWR Engines 1923

[54] LCGB Kenn Nunn Collection negative 4760 *Countess* at Welshpool 6th April 1926

[55] Rail 254 250/1 Engine Nos. 822 & 823 history cards

[56] David Hyde cited in *Llanfair Railway Journal* No. 157 October 2000 pp. 12, 13, 16

[57] David Hyde cited in *Llanfair Railway Journal* No. 157 October 2000 pp. 12, 13, 16

[58] Rail 254 250/1 Engine Nos. 822 & 823 history cards

[59] Last trip on the Welshpool and Llanfair *Trains illustrated December 1956* pp.621–24

[60] Rail 254 109 GWR weight diagram B54 Rail

[61] *Railway Observer* v. 18 1948 No. 227 p. 11

[62] Rail 254 250/1 Engine Nos. 822 & 823 history cards

[63] Rail 254 250/1 Engine Nos. 822 & 823 history cards

[64] Rail 254 250/1 Engine Nos. 822 & 823 history cards

[65] L&GRP 57800–2 Photographs No.1 *The Earl* in service at Welshpool and Llanfair pre 1910

[66] L&GRP 57800–2 Photographs No.1 *The Earl* in service at Welshpool and Llanfair pre 1910

[67] Ralph Cartwright *The Welshpool & Llanfair Light Railway* Rail Romances 2002 ISBN 1900622068 p. 142

[68] J.N. Slinn *Great Western Way* p. 212

[69] J.H. Russell *A pictorial record of Great Western Absorbed Engines* Oxford Publishing Company 1978 ISBN 902888749 p. 240 Fig. 584

[70] J.N. Slinn *Great Western Way* HMRS 1978 p. 31–33

[71] Real Photographs T7509 No. 823 The Countess

[72] J.H.L. Adams No. 822 *The Earl* April 1935

[73] Colour-Rail No. 823 at Welshpool in green livery 2nd March 1955

[74] Colour-Rail No. 822 at Castle Caereinion in black livery 9th June 1956

[75] Pickering drawing No. 2162 (brake composites) and No. 2057 (third)

[76] *The Montgomery County Times and Shropshire and Mid-Wales Advertiser* 9th May 1903

[77] Rail 92 88 S. Williamson to Cambrian Board 7th October 1910

[78] Rail 722 4 W&L Board 2nd May 1913

[79] Rail 722 4 W&L Board 12th September 1913

[80] Rail 722 3 Works Committee 20th February 1911

[81] Rail 722 4 W&L Board 2nd May 1913

[82] GWR carriage registers 4001–5000, 6001–7000

[83] L&GRP 12845 No. 4154 at Llanfair 1930

[84] Pickering drawing No. 2162 (brake composites) and No. 2057 (third)

[85] Cambrian Railways rolling stock register pp.70–71; GWR carriage registers 4001–5000, 6001–7000

[86] R.Y. Pickering photographs of passenger stock when new; L&GRP 57800/1 in service

[87] Lettering etc: R.Y. Pickering photographs; LCGB Ken Nunn collection H2212 stock without monogram 1st July 1909

[88] Levi Jones postcard showing all carriages in green at Dolrhyd franked 2nd Oct 1911

[89] Great Western Railway photograph of brake composite No. 1

[90] Real Photographs Negative W2104

[91] J.N. Slinn *Great Western Way* HMRS 1978 p. 63–65

[92] L&GRP 12845 3rd class saloon No. 4154 at Llanfair 1930

[93] R.Y. Pickering works photograph of goods brake van 1902

[94] R.Y. Pickering general arrangement drawing No. 2165 goods brake van 1902

[95] Cambrian Railways drawing April 1903

[96] Levi Jones postcard train passing Dolrhyd weir (post 1908 with all green coaches)

[97] GWR official photograph goods brake van No.2 c.1923 in LRJ No.76

[98] *Saga by rail: Great Britain and the Isle of Man* J.I.C. Boyd, Oakwood 2007 p. 39 lower

[99] GWR official photograph goods brake van No.2 c.1923 in LRJ No.76

[100] H.C. Casserley negative 54974 24th August 1948

[101] Cambrian Railways rolling stock register; Pickering general arrangement drawing No. 2165

[102] Cambrian Railways rolling stock register; GWR wagon register 8001–9000

[103] R.Y. Pickering works photograph of covered van 1902

[104] Photomatic N149 No. 100665 c.1951

[105] Cambrian Railways rolling stock register; Pickering general arrangement drawing No. 2144

[106] Cambrian Railways rolling stock register; GWR wagon register 100001–110000

[107] R.Y. Pickering works photograph of cattle wagon 1903

[108] J.P. Richards photograph of No.13626 in GWR livery of 1923–1936, Photomatic negative N150

[109] *The Welshpool and Llanfair*, R.I. Cartwright, Rail Romances 2002

[110] Cambrian Railways rolling stock register; Pickering general arrangement drawing No. 2164

[111] Cambrian Railways rolling stock register; GWR wagon register 13001–14000

[112] R.Y. Pickering works photograph of open goods wagon 1902

[113] Rail 92 71 H.E. Jones to C.S. Denniss 11th November 1902

[114] Oswestry Works drawing No. 71792 5th February 1904

[115] Cambrian Railways photograph of timber train at the Smithfield, Real Photographs negative 2574

[116] J.P. Richards W&L No. 31 as GWR No. 71680 photographed at Welshpool

[117] Cambrian Railways rolling stock register; Pickering general arrangement drawing No. 2087

[118] Cambrian Railways rolling stock register; GWR wagon registers 34001–35000, 71001–72000

[119] Rail 722 3 Works Committee 7th July 1903

[120] Rail 722 3 Works Committee 9th November 1903

[121] Rail 722 3 W&L Works Committee 16th November 1903
[122] Cambrian Railways rolling stock register p.71
[123] Rail 722 3 W&L Directors 13th September 1904
[124] Rail 722 3 W&L Works Committee 20th June 1906
[125] Cambrian Railways photograph: timber train at the Smithfield October 1906
[126] Rail 250 468 GWR General Manager's report to the Traffic Committee 29th March 1946
[127] R.M. Casserley negative 85338K No. 8518 as an open wagon 14th September 1956
[128] Cambrian Railways rolling stock register; Pickering general arrangement drawing No. 2697
[129] Cambrian Railways rolling stock register; GWR wagon register 8001–9000
[130] *The Montgomery County Times and Shropshire and Mid-Wales Advertiser* 29th July 1912
[131] Rail 722 4 Works Committee 12th February 1911
[132] Rail 722 4 W&L Works Committee 20th February 1911
[133] *Narrow Gauge Railways of the British Isles* P.B. Whitehouse and J.B. Snell, Bracken Books 1989 p. 87
[134] GWR wagon registers 3001–4000, 7001–8000
[135] J.P. Richards photograph of No. 71701 undated
[136] GWR wagon registers 34001–35000, 71001–72000
[137] *The Welshpool & Llanfair Light Railway* Lewis Cozens 1951 pp. 26 & 27
[138] *Great Western Railway Goods Wagons* A.G. Atkins, W. Beard, R. Tourret, Tourret Publishing 1998 p. 36
[139] John Lewis personal communication based on extract from GWR lot book at York
[140] Rail 254 13 GWR diagram book
[141] *The Vale of Rheidol Light Railway* C.C. Green, Wild Swan 1986 p. 220
[142] *Great Western Railway Goods Wagons* A.G. Atkins, W. Beard, R. Tourret, Tourret Publishing 1998 p. 422
[143] GWR diagram W9 and wagon register 38001–39000
[144] GWR wagon register 38001–39000
[145] *Great Western Railway Goods Wagons* A.G. Atkins, W. Beard, R. Tourret Tourret Publishing 1998 p. 422
[146] John Lewis personal communication based on extract from GWR lot book at York
[147] Rail 254 13 GWR diagram book
[148] Photograph of No. 17350 as a dropsided wagon in author's collection
[149] R. W. Kidner photograph at Welshpool in 1950s
[150] GWR diagram J6 and wagon register 17001–18000
[151] GWR wagon register 17001–18000
[152] R.Y. Pickering photographs of rolling stock as built
[153] Levi Jones postcard train passing Dolrhyd weir brake van with black body frames
[154] *Llanfair Railway Journal* No. 167 April 2003 p. 21
[155] R.Y. Pickering photographs of brake van No. 2
[156] GWR official photograph of brake van No.2

[157] R.Y. Pickering photographs of rolling stock showing form and positioning of lettering
[158] J.N. Slinn *Great Western Way* HMRS 1978 p. 212
[159] J.N. Slinn *Great Western Way* HMRS 1978 p. 212
[160] R.Y. Pickering photographs of rolling stock showing position of numbering
[161] R.Y. Pickering photographs of rolling stock showing position of tare weight and maximum load
[162] J.N. Slinn *Great Western Way* HMRS 1978 p. 212
[163] R.Y. Pickering photographs of rolling stock showing number plates
[164] *Great Western Way* J.N. Slinn HMRS 1978 p. 107–110
[165] J.P. Richards Open wagons Nos. 71680, 71794 in author's collection
[166] L&GRP 57907 Open wagon 71687 in livery of 1923–1937
[167] L&GRP 57705 Covered van in livery of 1923–1937
[168] J.P. Richards Cattle wagon No. 13626
[169] R.K. Cope Brake vans photographed at Welshpool 8th October 1931
[170] L&GRP 57809 Timber trucks in livery of 1923–1937
[171] J.P. Richards Sheep wagon No. 71701
[172] L&GRP 57907 Open wagon No. 71687 in livery of 1923–1937
[173] J.P. Richards Cattle wagon No. 13626
[174] J.P. Richards Sheep wagon No. 71701 in author's collection
[175] R.K. Cope Brake vans photographed at Welshpool 8th October 1931
[176] L&GRP 57907 Open wagon No. 71687 in livery of 1923–1937
[177] J.P. Richards Cattle wagon No. 13626
[178] R.K. Cope Brake vans photographed at Welshpool 8th October 1931
[179] *Narrow Gauge Railways in Mid Wales (1850–1970)* James I.C. Boyd Oakwood Press 1986 p. 257
[180] *Llanfair Railway Journal* No. 183 April 2007 p. 34
[181] Frederick le Manquais Brake van No. 8759 photographed 16th April 1938
[182] H.C. Casserley Negative No. 54963 Open wagon No. 17350
[183] H.C. Casserley Negative No. 54973 Covered van No. 100663
[184] H.C. Casserley Negative No. 54974 Brake van No. 8759
[185] *Great Western Way* J.N. Slinn HMRS 1978 p. 116–7
[186] *Railway Observer* v.21 1951 No. 273 p. 265
[187] H.C. Casserley Negative No.85338 Open wagon No. 8518 and another in GWR livery 14th September 1956
[188] *Railway Observer* v.21 1951 No. 273 p. 265
[189] Photomatic Negative N151 covered van No. 100665
[190] Photomatic Negative N151 Cattle wagon No. 38089
[191] Photomatic Negative N150 Cattle wagon 13623, sheep wagon 34172
[192] Chief Goods Clerk Welshpool to T.C. Sellars 17 November 1954
[193] M.L. Peate cited in *The Welshpool and Llanfair Light Railway*, Lewis Cozens 1951 p. 29
[194] *Private Owners on the Cambrian*, Mike Lloyd WRRC 1998
[195] *The Welshpool and Llanfair*, R.I. Cartwright, Rail Romances 2002
[196] Pickering general arrangement drawing No. 2613

The permanent way gang's trolley photographed at Welshpool on 22nd November 1947. By this date it had been replaced by a motorised trolley.

JOHN ALSOP COLLECTION

F. A. WYCHERLEY and H. C. CASSERLEY

ACKNOWLEDGEMENTS

My grateful thanks are due to the following for the assistance they gave in the preparation of this book: John Alsop, Andrew Bannister, Alan Ballard, Peter Bennett, Michael Bentley, Harry Boden, Roger Carpenter, Ralph Cartwright, R. M. Casserley, John Copsey, Mike Christensen, Edward Dorricott, Michael Dunn, Emyr Evans, Dilys Griffiths, Dean Hammond, Peter Jacques, J. R. Jones, John Lewis, Ted and Len Lewis, Irene Lloyd, Brian Poole, Dr. Reece Pryce, Richard Newcombe, David Southern, Ted Talbot, Chris Turner, Terry Turner, Tudor Watkins and Michael Whitehouse.

Particular thanks are due to Peter Ellis for his painstaking work in restoring the drawings of the goods vehicles built by R. Y. Pickering; David Postle for providing access to the collections at Kidderminster Railway Museum; and to Tim Shuttleworth for access to his superb collection of photographs that capture the essence of the railway in the later years of the goods service.

Without the help and guidance of the staff of the following institutions it would not have been possible to attempt this work: Birmingham Central Library, The Kithead Trust, The Museum of Science and Industry, Manchester, The National Archive, The National Library of Wales, National Museums and Galleries of Wales Department of Industry, The National Railway Museum, Newtown Public Library, Powys County Archive Office, The Powysland Museum and Montgomery Canal Centre.

Finally, I should like to thank Paul Karau for suggesting that a new history of the Welshpool and Llanfair Light Railway should be written, and for his help and enthusiasm in seeing it come to fruition, and to June Judge for her considerable help with the manuscript.

Glyn Williams

APPENDICES

APPENDIX I
STRACHAN'S LOCOMOTIVES

J. Strachan No.3

Hunslet Engine Company standard gauge 0–4–0 saddle tank No. 365 was built in 1885 for Messrs Holme and King. It is known to have been used on the Rotherham Main Colliery branch extension in 1897–98. It was subsequently used on Mr Strachan's Welshpool and Llanfair and Tanat Valley contracts. The Contractor made extensive use of the Smithfield siding at Welshpool during the construction of the Llanfair Railway both to unload plant and materials and to remove spoil from the light railway. The spoil from the railway may have been used to widen the formation of the Cambrian main line between Welshpool and Forden in preparation for the doubling of the line, and it is possible that No.3 was used in connection with this work.

J. Strachan No.8

Little is known about this small 2ft 6in gauge 0–4–0 tank engine that had outside frames, side or pannier tanks and no cab. It may have been built at the Falcon Engine Works, Loughborough or by Black Hawthorn & Co. of Gateshead. Nothing appears to be known about the locomotive's history before its use on the Welshpool and Llanfair contract. It was offered for sale by auction on 15th May 1903.

J. Strachan No.9

Margaret class 0–4–0 saddle tank No. 1655 was built by W.G. Bagnall of Stafford in 1901 for use on the Welshpool and Llanfair contract. The 2ft 6in gauge locomotive arrived at Welshpool in September 1901 and may have still been on the line in June 1903. By September of that year it had been transferred to Welham, near Market Harborough, where it was used on the construction of a marshalling yard for the L&NWR. It remained in Strachan's stock until May 1913 when it was sold to Jees Hartshill Granite and Brick Company of Hartshill, near Nuneaton, where it carried the name *Butcher*. No. 1655 was scrapped in 1945.

J. Strachan number unknown

Hunslet 0–4–0 saddle tank No. 307 of 1883 was delivered new to the Twywell Iron Ore Company Limited and employed at the Woodford mines Twywell, Northamptonshire until transferred to E.P. Davis' Gretton Quarry circa 1890. It worked there until about 1900. By autumn 1902 the locomotive was working on the Welshpool and Llanfair contract.

Locomotives owned by Mr J. Strachan used on the Welshpool and Llanfair Light Railway contract

Locomotive	Make & number	Built	Type	Gauge	Cylinders	Wheel diameter	Wheelbase
J. Strachan No. 3	Hunslet No. 365	18 Sept 1885	0–4–0 Saddle tank	Standard	Outside 10in × 15in	2ft 8in	Not known
J. Strachan No. 8	Not known	Not known	0–4–0 tank engine	2ft 6in	Outside	Not known	Not known
J. Strachan No. 9	Bagnall No. 1655	17 Sept 1901	0–4–0 Saddle tank	2ft 6in	Outside 7in × 12in	1ft 9in	3ft 6in
No. unknown	Hunslet No. 307	12 March 1883	0–4–0 Saddle tank	2ft 6in	Outside 7in × 10in	1ft 8in	Not known

APPENDIX II   GWR MODIFICATIONS DRAWING

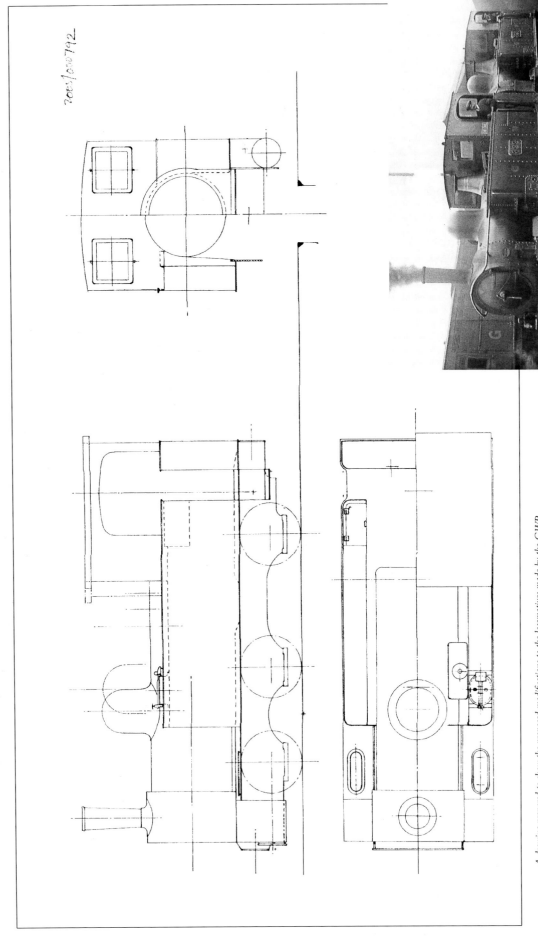

A drawing prepared to show the proposed modifications to the locomotives made by the GWR.
Cty. KIDDERMINSTER RAILWAY MUSEUM

Although not shown on the drawing, the stovepipe chimney was replaced with one of Swindon design fitted with a copper cap. In addition to a new boiler fitted with topfeed and a larger dome, the cab was extended at the front and a second whistle was provided. The whistles were now carried on the roof. The pipes entered the smokebox on the right-hand side under a rectangular casing.

WELSHPOOL & LLANFAIR LIGHT RAILWAY

ENGINE SHED & CARRIAGE SHED AT WELSHPOOL

SCALE 4 FEET TO AN INCH.

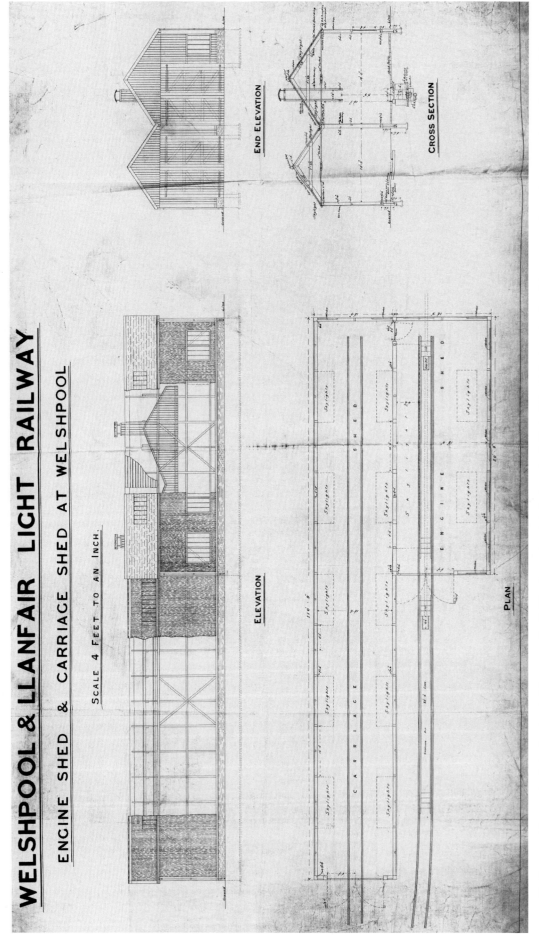

ELEVATION

END ELEVATION

CROSS SECTION

PLAN

The first proposal for an engine shed and carriage shed that was capable of holding three coaches. As built, the engine shed had additional lights let in the side and there was no smoke trough, a semi-circular vent being provided on the roof. The carriage shed could hold two coaches.

Source: NLW W&L Archive

APPENDIX IV SEVEN STARS STATION

During the afternoon of Sunday 14th June 1931 thunderstorms caused severe flooding in Welshpool. This view of Seven Stars cottage and station was one of a series of photographs made by J. R. Bunnage to record the event and provides a partial view of the waiting shelter five months after the railway closed to passengers.
COLLECTION RALPH CARTWRIGHT

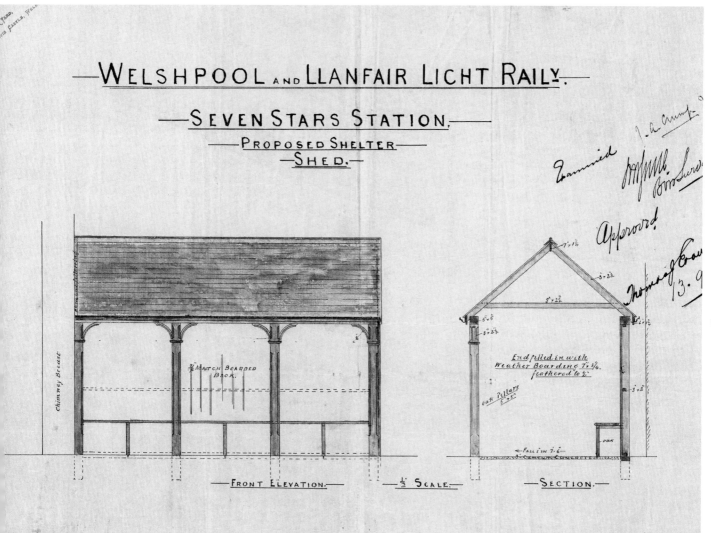

APPENDIX V

PROPOSED SHELTER AT SYLFAEN.

SCALE:- 2 FEET TO AN INCH.

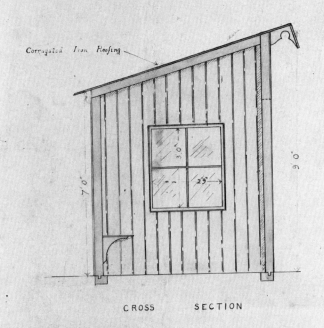

Corrugated Iron Roofing

CROSS SECTION

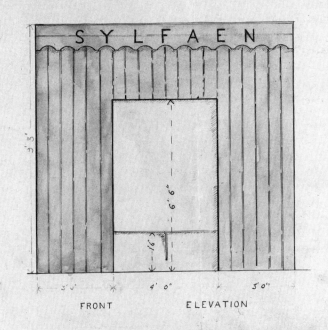

SYLFAEN

FRONT ELEVATION

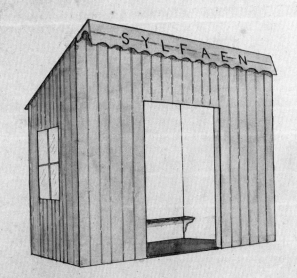

SYLFAEN

PERSPECTIVE VIEW

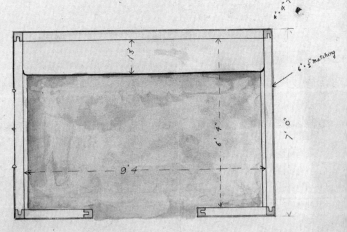

PLAN

Source: NLW W&L Archive

APPENDIX VI BRIDGE MAINTENANCE

Bridges on the Llanfair Railway were maintained by members of the Bridge Department who were based in the Van Railway yard at Caersws. Every bridge on the line was inspected each year and a detailed inspection was made at five-yearly intervals to plan future work. In later years staff from the Bridge Department travelled over the line on the Wickham trolley which was driven by the ganger in charge of the branch. Material required for repairs and maintenance was either carried to the site by the goods train or delivered by the Bridge Department's Thornycroft lorry.

To inspect the bridge over the Lledan Brook between Church Street and Union Street it was necessary to walk along the watercourse. Access was gained through the arch of the bridge that carried the brook under the main road. The masonry walls and steel girders were inspected with the aid of a paraffin floodlight which was used for tunnel inspections, whilst shafts of light came through the gaps in the decking.

Source: Memories of members of the Bridge Department recounted to Brian Poole.

The Wickham trolley at Sylfaen on 17th May 1956.
HUGH DAVIES

The railway was carried along the course of the Lledan Brook on steel joists that supported longitudinal rail bearers. The viaduct was boarded over as a safety measure.

APPENDIX VII GROUND FRAME AND POINT LOCK

F. A. WYCHERLEY

Facing point lock.

Welshpool Yard No. 3 ground frame.

EPILOGUE

THE first attempt to preserve the Llanfair Railway was made in September 1952 when officers of the Narrow Gauge Railway Society held an informal meeting with representatives of British Railways. The tentative asking price for the infrastructure was put at between five and six thousand pounds; the two locomotives were valued at £300, while the wagons were priced at £5 each. The estimated annual cost of running the line was £3,460. If the railway was acquired by the society, the carriage of parcels and goods would be prohibited and the County Council was thought to be unwilling to let its trains cross public roads. The membership took the view that preservation of the whole line was beyond the society's capacity but decided to preserve the two locomotives if they were offered for sale.[1/2]

In 1956 with closure imminent, two groups expressed interest in acquiring the line. The first in the field was the Branch Line Society's Welshpool and Llanfair section which ultimately gave its support to the Welshpool and Llanfair Light Railway Preservation Society. An informal meeting held in the narrow gauge yard at Welshpool on 15th September 1956 was addressed by William Morris and many of those present agreed to join the preservation society.[3/4] The society's first formal meeting was held in London on 23rd November 1956[5] and negotiations were opened with the British Transport Commission with the objective of purchasing the land, track and rolling stock.[6] While attempts to reopen the railway were welcomed in Llanfair, at Welshpool the Borough Council refused to countenance the re-introduction of a train service between Smithfield Road and Raven Square.[7]

From February 1957 until March 1963 the Town Clerk, Mr J. Ben Davies, was in regular contact with the Western Region's Estates Department, and later its London Midland equivalent, with a view to purchasing the course of the light railway through Welshpool. The Council intended to use the track bed for parking at the Smithfield, road improvements between the canal bridge and Bronhaul, and housing development from Bronhaul to a point near Standard Quarry.[8] Negotiations were protracted because of the ongoing discussions with the preservation society, the presence of redundant rolling stock in the narrow gauge yard,[9] and difficulties encountered in defining the boundaries at certain locations along the line.[10] In an attempt to bring the purchase to a successful conclusion, the assistance of the local Member of Parliament, Mr Clement Davies, was sought. Although a price was agreed in 1960, further delay occurred while the Shrewsbury Division was transferred to London Midland Region, so the purchase of the town section by the Council was not completed until 25th March 1963.[11]

Between November 1956 and June 1958 the preservation society struggled to win members, raise funds and convince the various authorities that its plans were feasible.[12] Even then it was still unable to purchase the line outright, so in 1959 provisional agreement was reached to lease the line from the British Transport Commission.[13] In July 1959 working parties began to clear the line from the Smithfield towards Golfa and by September nine of the line's goods vehicles had been acquired. When the price asked to move them to Golfa siding was deemed to be unreasonable, certain members took matters into their own hands and horses were used to draw the vans and wagons to the western side of Llanfair & Guilsfield Road level crossing.[14] The following year they were joined by an open wagon that had been stranded in the standard gauge yard.[15]

On 4th January 1960 the Welshpool & Llanfair Light Railway Preservation Company was incorporated but a further year was spent negotiating the terms of the lease. With the loss of the town section looming, it became apparent that Llanfair would become the centre of the railway's operations although for a time there were hopes that the Welshpool terminus might be established on the eastern side of the Llanfair & Guilsfield Road level crossing. The company's first locomotive, a four-wheeled diesel built by Ruston and Hornsby Ltd., arrived on the line on 28th March 1961. In July 1961 No. 1 *The Earl* returned to Welshpool and by the end of the year five bogie carriages, seven bogie wagons and two vans had been acquired from the Admiralty's Lodge Hill & Upnor Railway. In February 1962 a four-wheel Planet diesel arrived from the same line. The following October saw the welcome return of No.2 *The Countess* from Oswestry Works.[16]

On 3rd October 1962 the British Transport Commission (Welshpool and Llanfair) Light Railway Leasing Order was issued for the railway from a point on the south western side of Llanfair & Guilsfield Road level crossing to the terminus at Llanfair Caereinion and became effective on the 12th of the month.[17] The first public passenger trains ran between Llanfair and Castle Caereinion on 1st December 1962 in connection with the Llanfair fair.[18] The official reopening of the line took place on 6th April 1963, sixty years to the day after the line had opened to passenger traffic. While the inaugural train ran from Welshpool to Llanfair and back, the public service for the first season operated between Llanfair and Castle Caereinion. Services between Welshpool and Llanfair were re-established on 18th July 1981 when a new terminus at Raven Square was opened.[19]

[1] *Llanfair Railway Journal* No. 181 October 2006 p.11
[2] *The Welshpool & Llanfair Light Railway* Ralph Cartwright and R.T. Russell, David and Charles 1972
[3] *Llanfair Railway Journal* No. 67 April 1978 pp.8–9
[4] *Llanfair Railway Journal* No. 141 October 1996 p.25
[5] *The Welshpool & Llanfair Light Railway* Ralph Cartwright and R.T. Russell, David and Charles 1972
[6] Western Region Estate and Rating Surveyor to J. Ben Davies 12th September 1957
[7] Welshpool Borough Council Summary of proposed acquisition of the light railway 14th January 1958
[8] District Valuer to Welshpool Borough Council 7th February 1962
[9] Western Region Estates Division to Welshpool Borough Council 6th July 1959
[10] Welshpool Borough Council briefing paper prepared for Clement Davies 9th August 1960
[11] Harrison's to Welshpool Borough Council 27th March 1963
[12] *Llanfair Railway Journal* No. 67 April 1978 pp.8–9
[13] *The Welshpool & Llanfair Light Railway* Ralph Cartwright and R.T. Russell, David and Charles 1972
[14] *Llanfair Railway Journal* No. 167 April 2003 pp.14–15
[15] *Llanfair Railway Journal* No. 187 April 2008 pp.9–10
[16] *The Welshpool & Llanfair Light Railway* Ralph Cartwright and R.T. Russell, David and Charles 1972
[17] *Llanfair Railway Journal* No. 185 October 2007 p.19
[18] *Llanfair Railway Journal* No. 168 July 2003 p.25
[19] *The Welshpool & Llanfair*, Ralph I. Cartwright, Rail Romances 2002

The tranship siding with the wagon weighbridge and office to the left of the tranship shed.

ROGER HOLMES

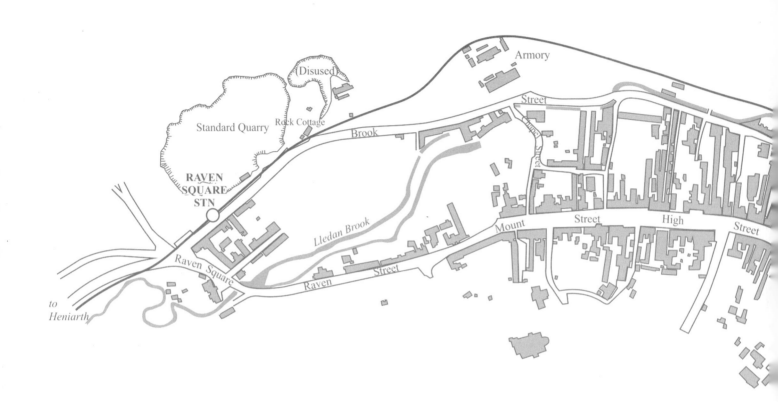

Disused

Armory

Street

Standard Quarry   Rock Cottage   Brook

**RAVEN
SQUARE
STN**

Lledan Brook

Street   High   Street

Mount

*to
Heniarth*   Raven Square   Raven   Street

WELSHPOOL c.1903
Showing the route of the
W & L Light Railway
through the town